D1219946

THE POLITICAL ECONOMY OF COMMUNISM

The
Political Economy
of Communism

P. J. D. WILES
Professor of Economics, Brandeis University

WITHDRAWN

HARVARD LIBRARY

WITHDRAWN

HARVARD UNIVERSITY PRESS
CAMBRIDGE, MASSACHUSETTS
1962

© *Basil Blackwell & Mott, Ltd., 1962*

Soc 830.62.85
B
Cellar
~~Government~~
X7722

HARVARD
UNIVERSITY
LIBRARY
OCT 2 1963

HX
A4
W5
C.3

PRINTED IN GREAT BRITAIN

95*141

TO CAROLYN

Nec me animi fallit Graiorum obscura reperta
difficile inlustrare Latinis versibus esse,
multa novis verbis praesertim cum sit agendum,
propter egestatem linguae et rerum novitatem.

—LUCRETIUS, *De Rerum Natura*, I,136.

PREFACE

THIS book is supposed to introduce the graduate student, who has majored in 'mainstream' economics, to the critical study of Communist economic theory and practice. It assumes that he knows already very much: Western welfare and growth economics, a little statistics, Marxism, the economic organization of Communist countries and the outlines of their recent history. It says to him, 'Here you are, having absorbed all this disparate matter; now you will need to organize it, to relate one part to another, to translate one language into the other, to tell one kind of Communist from another, to empathize with their internal discussions. Above all you must see where Communist theory and practice merely confirm "mainstream" theory, where they add to it, where they correct it, and where they demand totally new development.'

The book is therefore unsuitable for undergraduates, except here and there, since it assumes too much. It is also less suitable for its professed purpose than it should be for four reasons. The writer has not sufficiently kept up with the immense, and increasingly interesting, volume of Communist economic books even in the languages he reads easily: English, French, German, Russian, Spanish. Secondly, he has almost wholly omitted the East European satellites, even Poland. And although at every point he has inserted the due notice that Yugoslavia or China is different the references are based on altogether too little reading. Even so he may plead in mitigation a genuine attempt to cover the ground, and a general determination to break the Soviet monopoly of what must still be called 'Sovietology'. Then again certain subjects have been omitted to shorten the book and preserve some continuity of thought: international trade, banking, inflation, income distribution, forced labour, perspective planning, and above all, agriculture. The present tense normally indicates 1960. Where it does not, I have said so.

Fourthly I have been far too deeply involved in all the controversies and discussions that have attended the birth of 'Sovietological' economics to be anything like impartial. Should the book be reviewed, the unwary neophyte is strongly recommended to read the reviews. In particular Chs. 5 and 16 represent extreme personal views, which of course should, but perhaps will not, command the assent of expert colleagues. Nearly every chapter adduces what I hope is a new contribution. Evidently, then, the subject has not yet settled down if it is so easy to innovate, and the time is not ripe for an undergraduate textbook.

Another indication of the unripeness of time is the proliferation of new classifications and concepts. Although personally responsible for most of it, I look forward to the stern and original critic who will one day wield Occam's Razor in this undergrowth. If the use of ordinary speech is pre-scientific, and the onset of jargon stands at the beginning of systematic study, further progress is almost identical with simplification. In the meantime all the jargon is explained in the glossary.

If it is not pompous to dedicate a bad book to a good principle, this book is dedicated, not to the unity of human knowledge, for that is still a goal of the far future, and if we reach for it too soon we trip up; but at least to the compatibility of all true statements. There may well not be any truth in economics, but it is more certain that there are not two truths. It is high time to remove the intellectual barriers, even if only from the minds of the learned and powerless.

———

I am indebted to the publishers of the following journals for permission to re-use certain passages:

Oxford Economic Papers (Sept. 1953),

Soviet Survey, latterly *Survey* (Oct. 1961),

Ost-Europa (2-3/1960),

Ost-Europa/Wirtschaft (Dec. 1958),

Soviet Studies (Oct. 1955),

Economic Journal (June 1956).

The passages on Yugoslavia owe much to a trip thither financed by the International Institute of Education.

'Op. cit.,' 'loc. cit.' and 'ibidem' refer only to works mentioned in the footnotes of the same chapter.

CONTENTS

PART IV—ESCHATOLOGY

GLOSSARY OF TERMS AND ABBREVIATIONS

AER. American Economic Review.

ALLOCATION MODELS. See Models, and Ch. 4. For convenience I set out here briefly the list of models considered:
(1) CC: central physical allocation throughout, including consumers and workers;
(2) the same, with passive money superimposed;
(3) CM: the central authority behaves like an ideal public monopoly on a market, using money to give such instructions as will most satisfy consumers and workers, who are independent;
(4) ICM, the inversion of (3): the state uses the price mechanism to reconcile consumers and workers to its arbitrary output decisions;
(5) CWE: as in a capitalist war economy, where final outputs only are settled by the planners, much as in (3) or (4), and the intermediate factors of production are bid for in the open market, acquiring the scarcity values that the planned final output pattern imposes;
(6) FM: full market, pure laissez-faire;
(7) RM: regulated market, many controls but all indirect. The centre inihbits but gives no direct commands, profit remains the sole indicator;
(8) CM/RM: the central authority decides investment projects, which are then currently operated according to the market, by decentralized management.

'BODY.' My generic name for intermediate planning authorities of all kinds. E.g. it includes both Ministries and Sovnarkhozy.

CB. Current Background, same origin as ECMM.

CC. Centralized command. See Allocation models.

CDSP. *Current Digest of the Soviet Press*, New York.

COMMUNIST COUNTRIES OR ECONOMIES. 'Soviet-type', q.v., plus Yugoslavia.

CWE. Capitalist war economy. See Allocation models.

DC. Decentralized command. See Allocation models.

DDR. German Democratic Republic.

DISTRIBUTION. See Raznaryadka.

ECMM. Extracts from Chinese Mainland Magazines, American Consulate-general in Hong Kong (roneoed; can be found only in the best libraries).

ELECTRONIC MARKET. See 'Perfect Computation'.

ENTERPRISE. Generic, neutral term for a producing unit; both 'Firm' and 'Establishment', qq.v.

ENTERPRISE FUND. The erstwhile 'director's fund', a fund freely available to the director, or to the director and the trade union in consultation. Fed by specified deductions from enterprise profits.

ESTABLISHMENT. A firm deprived by central planning of most of its independence. See 'Enterprise'.

FIRM. A fairly small independent decision-making unit, e.g. a peasant, a kolkhoz, a capitalist factory or group of factories. See 'Enterprise'.

FM. Full market. See Allocation models.

FULL COMMUNISM. The anarchic utopia produced long after the proletarian revolution by the further rise in productivity. See Chs. 17, 18.

FYP. Five Year Plan.

GOELRO. Lenin's electrification commission, the first Soviet planning body.

GOSPLAN. The government's co-ordinating organ that is technically (not politically) responsible for the plan. Also at Republic level in U.S.S.R.

INDICATORS. Operation orders centrally laid down, to be followed by enterprises in making detailed decisions, notably on the Sortament, q.v.

KOLKHOZ. Collective farm, a kind of producer's co-operative.

KOLKHOZ MARKET. The official free market in a Soviet-type economy, where are exchanged the food surpluses of all producers, craft products and many second-hand or stolen articles.

KOLKHOZNIK. A member of a kolkhoz, q.v.

KOMMUNA. Russian for a community in which consumption and production are both socialized.

KOMMUNIST. Authoritative Soviet party journal.

KOMUNA. Basic unit of local government in Yugoslavia.

KOMUNIST. Authoritative Yugoslav party journal.

KONTRAKTATSIA. The making of detailed contracts, in accordance with the plan, by subordinate bodies.

MEGA. *Marx-Engels Gesamtausgabe*, Berlin 1930.

MODEL means in this book not a system of macro-economic equations but an institutional set-up. We distinguish:
    Ownership models, q.v.;
    Allocation models, q.v.;
    Distribution models (see Ch. 9).

MR. Managerial Revolution.

MTS. Machine Tractor Station, the nationalized machinery centres for kolkhozy. Abolished in 1958.

MUNICH BULLETIN. Strictly *Bulletin of the Institute for the Study of the U.S.S.R.*, Mannhardtstrasse 6, Munich.

NEP. Lenin's New Economic Policy, 1921-8, a kind of market socialism with many capitalist elements. See Ch. 2.

N.KH.: *Narodnoye Khozyaistvo*, the Soviet statistical abstract.

O-P. *Ost-Probleme*, digest of the Communist press published in Bonn.

OWNERSHIP MODELS. See Models, and Ch. 1. For convenience I set out here briefly the list of owners considered:
    (i) private individuals;
    (ii) shareholders in large companies;
    (iii) public boards as in Western nationalization;
    (iv) the state directly;

OWNERSHIP MODELS (cont.)

    (v) the consumers co-operatively;

    (vi) ex-capitalist producers co-operatively;

    (vii) the workers in a nationalized establishment, syndically;

    (viii) local authorities;

    (ix) the people as consumers and producers at once;

    (x) the whole economy as one (ix), without money.

P.KH.: *Planovoye Khozyaistvo*, a Soviet economic journal.

PERFECT COMPUTATION. The centralized solution of the allocation problem, making correct allowance for the scarcities of all factors and the utilities of all products, in an 'electronic market'.

PLANNER'S TENSION. The obligation to produce more than one easily can, embodied in the enterprise's plan by the central planners.

PRODUCTION PRINCIPLE. The administration of the economy through intermediate authorities (Ministries) which specialize in particular products, wherever the enterprises are located. See 'Territorial', and Ch. 8.

RM. Regulated market. See Allocation models.

RAZNARYADKA. The list of customers to whom in a command economy a product must be 'distributed', and of the quantities each must get. See Ch. 9.

SOCH., or SOCHINENIA. Russian for opera omnia.

SORTAMENT. The detailed qualitative breakdown of a class of output; often left free to enterprise decision in accordance with Indicators, q.v.

SOVIET-TYPE COUNTRIES or ECONOMIES. U.S.S.R., China, Poland, D.D.R., Czechoslovakia, Rumania, Hungary, Bulgaria, Albania, North Korea, North Vietnam, Mongolia.

SOVKHOZ. State farm, a nationalized farm like a nationalized factory.

SOVNARKHOZ. See Territorial.

TENSION. See Planner's Tension.

TERRITORIAL PRINCIPLE. The administration of the economy through intermediate authorities (Sovnarkhozy) which cover particular areas, whatever products the enterprises therein may produce. See 'Production', and Ch. 8.

TOZ. *Tovarishchestvo obrabativayushchee zemlyu*, association for cultivating the soil. See p. 9.

TR. Translated.

V.E.: *Voprosy Ekonomiki*, a Soviet economic journal.

WAR COMMUNISM. The period summer 1918 to spring 1921, of a moneyless command economy.

WEST. The advanced capitalist nations.

WESTERN ECONOMICS. The non-Marxist economics evolved in the 'West', q.v., to whatever area or social system it refers.

WHOLESALE PRICES. Means in this book the prices of producers' goods.

ZAGOTOVKA. Obligatory deliveries of produce, at low prices, by kolkhozy or peasants to a Soviet-type government.

ZAKUPKA. The nominally voluntary purchases of a Soviet-type government from kolkhozy or private peasants, at something approaching kolkhoz market prices.

THE POLITICAL ECONOMY OF COMMUNISM

PART I

INSTITUTIONS AND IDEOLOGY

CHAPTER I

POSSIBLE SOCIALISMS (OWNERSHIP MODELS)

1. THIS book is informed by the belief that there is such a thing as the logic of institutions: that an economic model will function in the way that it does, and have the political effects it has, *partly* for internal, purely economic reasons inaccessible to the sociologist or historian. It is claimed, therefore, that a new institutionalism is possible, neither purely descriptive nor purely bogus like the old, so justly discredited among economists, and independent up to a certain point of other disciplines, yet drawing upon them and flowing back into them, and in its own right rigorous and respectable.

No field of study is an 'island entire unto itself'; this field overlaps with many others, but curiously enough perhaps least with Keynesian macro-economics. Fluctuations in employment are simply a facet of all market economies alike, having hardly any institutional effects or results. But our institutional analysis is intimately concerned with the economics of growth and 'welfare' (i.e. resource allocation and income distribution), and with various non-economic disciplines. Most conclusions drawn from a model are of course economic, but with due hesitation a few political ones are also drawn, in the hope all the same of not falling prey to over-simplification or Marxism. Certainly no very high claims are here put forward for 'modelology'. It is, for instance, the writer's strong opinion that model (iv) is incompatible with political freedom; but he would not be surprised to see in certain times and places complete freedom under an attenuated version of the model, or moderate freedom under a moderate version. Further, the social sciences are full of unspoken, because unperceived, premises. For instance the connexion between model (iv) and totalitarianism might be altogether broken by Extreme Affluence (Ch. 20), or by better computers and activity analysis (Ch. 10).

In this chapter we analyse the economy by the various types of ownership to which it may be subjected. The ownership models are known throughout the book by small roman numerals. Ch. 4 gives the various systems of resource allocation; the allocation models have arabic figures throughout, and, since they are the most often referred to, they also have abbreviations (see list of abbreviations). Ch. 9 lists systems of distributing goods once produced; distribution models have large roman numerals throughout. All these three systems of models are summarized in the glossary.

This use of the word 'model' is perfectly different from that found in Western econometrics, where it means a set of algebraical formulae in which each symbol stands for some purely statistical magnitude or purely economic propensity; and the interaction of the symbols is supposed to explain how in real life the trade cycle works or the economy grows. Our 'models' are institutional; they represent possible politico-economic set-ups. This use of the word is Polish, since Poland is—or was—the country in the world where the choice of set-up is most seriously and freely discussed. Such discussion also goes on in India and—behind closed doors—in Yugoslavia and China; it was a favoured activity of the Utopian socialists; and it was common in Lenin's Russia. The Utopian socialists also experimented on a small scale: unsuccessfully, because they could never put the tax- and police-power of a state behind their chosen model. In Israeli agriculture many models have been tried out in a more permanent and practical way. But Communism provides the most heroic examples of such model-building in practice: when we contemplate the headlong dogmatism of Mao, Stalin and Tito in this matter we may justly call them Utopian socialists, imposing their Icarias not on a few volunteer migrants but on many captive millions. The economist is lucky indeed to be the contemporary of these men (provided he is not their compatriot), since they set him questions of greater interest and importance than, possibly, any men have ever set. Almost no corner of economic science is irrelevant to the answering of these questions, from the theory of value to the sociology of economic growth.

What follows is very far from exhausting all the logical possibilities. Not all imaginable or even existing[1] models would fit the scheme without further elaborating it, even after allowing for mixed forms. Mixed, indeed, all actual forms are, and the schema much more presents the ideal models than describes the untidy picture of life; I do not indicate minor divergences except where they are of interest. Nor is any theory of history or economic development implied; models succeed each other in various orders and for various reasons.

Our definitions of socialism and capitalism are exceedingly simple: public and private ownership respectively of the means of production. No apology is made for this: it is quite certainly the only logical and useful distinction. All others seem to be designed so as to prejudice the reader against one or other concept, besides being unusable. Thus to say that 'really Stalin was a capitalist because he liked to accumulate capital' is just an idiotic play on words. At one time, to be sure, it was reasonable to include an equal income distribution, not directly connected with the value of labour performed, in the definition of socialism. But that would then leave the whole field of publicly owned systems paying wages on ordinary principles without a name, and confine the word socialism to the Chinese People's Communes. True, our own simple dichotomy leaves something to be desired in the context of income distribution: the Anglo-Scandinavian model of private ownership plus generous social services has to be called capitalism. But I am deeply convinced that if the words capitalism and socialism are to be scientifically usable at all, and operative definitions substituted for those emotionally loaded, my distinction does the least violence to common speech.

By Communism I mean of course any model imposed by a Communist Party, including the League of Yugoslav Communists.[2] Stress is laid throughout on the similarity of the technical problems faced by Communist, other socialist, and capitalist models. Communism does not greatly alter these problems, though it very greatly affects the choice of model. Communist totalitarianism is essentially a political and psychological phenomenon, as Yugoslavia, a state

[1] Thus I have consciously omitted all tribal and feudal models; slavery; Karl Wittfogel's 'Asian Mode of Production'; and the 'people's capitalism' advocated by Dr. Erhard in West Germany or by the British Liberal Party.

[2] The various other aliases—Polish United Workers' Party, Hungarian Socialist Workers' Party, Vietnam Workers' Party, etc.—have only historical significance and no Communist pretends there is today any distinction.

much more totalitarian than, say, Poland but possessing a market economy, demonstrates beyond a peradventure. A Communist command economy is called 'Soviet-type' in order to distinguish it from the Yugoslav model.

2. First there will accompany each model, creating it or being created by it, a *theoretical or* de jure *owner*, who is the 'ultimate boss' of the means of production, in whose 'name' or under whose 'auspices' production is carried on. An economic ideology grows up in favour of the owner, who tries to show that his predominance in the economy is necessary, or at least rightful. Stigmata of being the theoretical owner in any model are the receipt of the lion's share of the profit, and the capacity to sue and be sued. But often the *de jure* owner loses most of these powers to a new *de facto* owner; we then say that the ideology is out of step with the working model. Of the infinitely many possible theoretical owners and models the following concern us:

(i) *the private individual*, owning by inheritance or personal accumulation, and managing what he owns. He corresponds to the model we shall call *primitive capitalism*, and his ideology is the sacrosanctity of private property. This model includes a purely peasant economy.

(ii) the *anonymous shareholders* in a large limited liability company. Model: *managerial capitalism*. In this state of affairs the manager is by sheer necessity someone other than the body of the shareholders, and there is an inevitable conflict between ideology and model. E.g. a company can sue its own shareholders (who may, for instance, include the managing director of its main competitor) for trespass on 'its' property. And often the company's profit is not taxed simply as if it were the shareholders' income any more, but is subjected to a special tax regime. The *de facto* owner is of course the manager, but while he may dispose of the profit in many ways he cannot legally, as a salaried man, appropriate it to himself. Indeed he is under an obligation of varying force to give some of it to the shareholders. Sometimes this model is a mere cover for (i)—a large primitive capitalist having raised a little outside equity capital. Sometimes it is a prelude to

(iii) the *public board* of a *nationalized* industry or firm, operating on a free market independently of the state. Model: *managerial socialism*. This has come about quite naturally in the nationalized sectors of free countries, and strong elements of it are also present in Yugoslavia and perhaps Poland (where experts have high claims and Party loyalists low claims to managerial power). But managers are unpopular people, and even under socialism lack a supporting ideology. In Britain there were at least the beginnings of such an ideology before the war: the boards were trustees, holding the firm or industry independently of the state on behalf of the nation. One could imagine them appointing subordinate managers by way of examination, thus forming a sort of 'socialist mandarinate'; a class of free managers conceived of as public servants whose ideological *raison d'être* was their professional qualification.[1] But the Labour Party was hostile to the trustee idea, and after the war reorganized and extended the nationalized sector on a watered-down model (iv). The Conservatives have on the whole maintained the new tradition of weak central control; certainly there is no longer any talk of trusteeship. In France and—much more so—Yugoslavia the ideology of nationalization is that of model (vii), while the working model is in fact largely (iii).

(iv) the *state machine*, operating the economy through regular organs of state. Model: *state socialism*. Here the industries are not managed by independent public boards but by ministries or local authorities. That is, management is part of the state machine, and the concept of an independent, albeit public, corporation is held to be too decentralized. It is as if a single capitalist corporation were responsible for all production; operating at one end on a free labour market as monopsonist of all labour and at the other end through the shops as a monopolist of all consumer goods; and *transferring*, rather than selling or buying, intermediate and investment goods among its branches. Property is 'socialist state property, which is a monolith serving as a base for the state production sector, which in turn forms one big factory with thousands of intraorganization cells which we know under the name of "establishments" '.[2] Establishments are only independent in so far as they must be for convenience and efficiency.

Thus in U.S.S.R. their profits *essentially* flow into the state budget, under regulations not called a 'profits tax' but 'deductions from profit', and the establishment's right to retain part of its profits is viewed as a concession. The separate accountability of establishments (khozraschet) was evolved only after the heroic period of 'War Communism', in deference to empirical necessities; it is still subject to all sorts of exceptions (e.g. machine tractor stations

---

[1] Cf. R. H. Tawney, *Equality*, London 1931.
[2] J. Popkiewicz, 'Bureaucracy or Market?', *Zycie Gospodarcze* (Warsaw), June 30, 1957.

until their abolition). The capacity to sue and be sued—a sort of legal khozraschet—is very restricted, and does not apply at all between establishments coming under one ministry or Sovnarkhoz. The state is constantly referred to as the 'single boss' (odin khozyain). The ideology of this system is of course state worship and the command economy. *It is, with (x), the only model that tries to govern the relations between firms, i.e. abolishes the free market.*

Soviet industry is the paradigm of this system, but there are many elements of it in British post-war nationalization: where a specified Minister is responsible before Parliament for the acts of the public board, has almost unlimited legal powers of interference with the board, and often such legal duties as to appoint the members of regional boards subordinate to the national board. Moreover, competition between boards is frowned on by British Socialists, who are constantly demand ng the 'co-ordination' of the gas and electricity boards, or the road and rail executives in the transport board.[1]

But if in subordinating the board to the Minister and in their incipient attack on the market mechanism as a link between boards the Labour Party approached the Communist model (iv) it certainly did not arrive at it. A British public board under close Ministerial control is at once too governmental and too decentralized for Communism. For except under Stalin the Communist ideal has been a non-state, purely 'social', i.e. persuasive not coercive, authority that will administer the economy even after the state has withered away (Ch. 17, Sec. 2). But it must also be a single authority, administering the whole economy from one centre.[2] The public corporation on the other hand is the device of a reformist Socialism, which gradually nationalizes one industry after another and mistrusts the state machine enough to set up bodies that are still almost as independent as a capitalist firm, differing mainly in the unimportant fact that they make no profits for private shareholders. This is not revolution. The Communist idea is to take over as much as possible at once, and in practice to subject it directly to the state machine. The totalitarian state, which substitutes the unity of powers for

---

[1] They have not hitherto had their way: competition is particularly fierce between the gas and electricity boards, certainly more fierce than had they been left in the hands of (British) capitalists.

[2] Under Stalin the pretence was abandoned that this administrative chore was not part of the coercive, political state. But it is now being strongly revived in connexion with the drive towards Full Communism. Yet whether the planning organ is 'political' or 'social' it is still supposed to be completely centralized.

the division of powers, must clearly administer everything itself. There is no fundamental distinction between a Glavk and a Soviet Ministry, as there is between a public corporation and a British Ministry; or between a Soviet civil servant and a Soviet manager. There is no economic civil service, in any way distinct from the body of managers and engineers. Such decentralization as there is has come about through administrative necessity, as conscious modifications of the ideal unity.

Marxists who do not like this system call it state capitalism, and lump it together with (ii) or even (iii).[1] Their point is that the ruling bureaucracy is as good as a private owner of the nationalized means of production, and uses them to exploit the rest of the people. This is true, but not inevitably true, and it is muddling to call any system of public ownership capitalism. The name of state capitalism is best reserved (as it was by Lenin) to the war economy of a capitalist state, in which the government manages, as in model (iv), but the capitalists own. Here the ideological contradiction is so evident that the system could hardly survive in peacetime.

There follow the three co-operative models. A co-operative is, by definition, an enterprise with 'members', not 'employees', or at least members as well as employees. However, the difference between 'member' and 'employee' is not always clear, nor indeed that between 'member' and 'shareholder'.

The loosest co-operative is (v), in which the owners are *the consumers of the enterprise's product*. Model: principles of Rochdale, *or consumers' co-operation*. Most people, from both ends of the political spectrum, refuse to regard this as socialism at all. Indeed some of its main supporters hold it to be a third way between capitalism and socialism. Retail trade is its main field, but farmers also practise it when they co-operatively own and manage, say, a rural electricity network, an artificial insemination business, or a seed and fertilizer purchasing agency—all things that would other-wise have been supplied by independent capitalist or socialist enter-prise outside the farm. Co-operation in respect of things that would otherwise be done *on* the farm comes under (vi) below. What makes this system less important is that it only works where it really is

---

[1] E.g. Zinoviev, *Speech to XIV Party Congress*, Dec. 1925; Dedijer, *Speech to Institute of International Affairs*, Stockholm, May 6, 1957; Ch. Rakovsky, *Byulleten' Oppositsii*, 25–6 (quoted by L. Schapiro, *The Communist Party of the Soviet Union*, London 1960, p. 382).

possible for the consumers to run an enterprise, so that outside the fields mentioned it is excessively rare.[1]

Note that the direct assumption of command by the consumer in this model is quite different from his indirect influence over the enterprise via what is called consumer's sovereignty. Any market economy where there is competition makes the consumer 'sovereign' in this way, but to call him on the strength of that the boss or owner would be empty rhetoric. If a consumer's co-op. is in competition with normal shops the consumer is 'sovereign' over them all equally, whether he owns them or not. If the co-op. is a monopoly, or at least rejects profit as a criterion, the consumer is using his institutional command to deprive himself of economic sovereignty.

We turn to (vi) *the producer in a co-operative enterprise.* This man owns in a semi-capitalist manner, possesses 'shares' in, the capital of the enterprise in which he himself works. The model will here be called *producer's co-operation.* Though it looks so like (vii) as a working model, it is in ideology at the opposite pole of socialism. For there has been no initial expropriation, on the contrary the producer is a small capitalist who has brought in his own capital voluntarily, and may well still be getting interest on it. Even his voting strength at meetings may be based on his capital contribution as well as his labour, and he probably keeps a small private business on the side. This, then, is a right-wing, gradualist sort of socialism, making some allowance for the unregeneracy of human beings. In the old Russian artel[2] (of craftsmen), in the collective ejido[3] of the Laguna region in Mexico (a collective farm rather like the Soviet) and in many places in Israel[4] and Spain[5] this kind of thing has happened quite spontaneously and worked at least as well as native capitalism. Note, however, that the technique of production is in each case simple, and the co-operators are the social and

---

[1] The Port of London is run mainly by the shipping companies that use it. Another amusing instance is, formally, the U.S. Federal Reserve System, which is the property of its member banks. Just as a Communist government herds peasants into a Kolkhoz, so the U.S. government has set up this bankers' co-operative and tries to use it against the member banks. Mutual insurance companies also provide the shadow without the substance of the model.

[2] C. B. Hoover, *Economic Life of Soviet Russia,* New York 1932, pp. 233–241.

[3] Clarence Senior, 'Reforma Agraria y Democracia en la Comarca Lagunera', in *Problemas Agrícolas e Industriales de Mexico,* vol. VIII No. 2 (includes long bibliography).

[4] The moshav ovdim or workers' village. Cf. H. Halperin, *Changing Patterns in Israel: Agriculture* (London 1957).

[5] Joaquín Costa, *Colectivismo Agrario en Espana* (Madrid 1915), Chs 11, 15, 16, 17; Gerald Brenan, *The Spanish Labyrinth* (Cambridge 1943), Appendix I; Franz Borkenau, *The Spanish Cockpit* (London 1937) passim.

economical equals of each other. The system is hardly compatible with great inequalities of education and reward.

Moreover it is after all intended for small capitalists, who if they do not think of it by themselves may well feel it as an expropriation. And small capitalists are not as polite as large ones. Again and again enterprises on model (ii) have been peacefully nationalized, while the attempt to do the same to model (i) has led to bloodshed. For the peasant or small capitalist, uniting so many functions in himself, stands to lose so much more by nationalization or co-operatization: not merely his right to an unearned income, but his managerial control and the fruits of his own manual labour. With or without compensation, he is a much tougher nut to crack than the 'alienated' and already semi-socialized managers and shareholders of model (ii). So resistance to the imposition of (vi) from without can be very sanguinary indeed. Hence the principal case of (vi), the Communist kolkhoz, is attended by a continuing daily conquest of the peasant.

Voluntary or no, there are many degrees of socialism in these co-operative establishments. Thus the collective ejido has grown looser since it began,[1] the kolkhoz has been steadily tightened. And in many Soviet-type countries there are looser forms than the kolkhoz, which are used to lead up to it. Thus in U.S.S.R. the TOZ[2] (cultivating association, in which livestock was individually held and crops were still individually harvested) was liquidated in 1930. These TOZes had been formed voluntarily and were quite successful. Not so their Chinese equivalent, the 'mutual aid groups'. Similar to the TOZ, they yielded first to Agricultural Producers' Co-operatives, which were a low-grade form of kolkhoz, and then to the People's Communes (Ch. 17). Rumania in 1957, alone of the Stalinist countries, showed the reverse trend: the new kolkhozy of 1957 were of a low-grade kind that pay rent on the land the members contribute. In all these models the democracy will probably be more genuine than in (vii), if the establishment was set up voluntarily; and it will certainly be a façade for model (iii) in the contrary case. The Soviet kolkhoz chairmen are indeed a specially skilled, separate class, a freely transferable 'mandarinate' of socialist managers.

The method of income distribution in this model resembles that in (i) from which it grows. It is a dividend depending on the

---

[1] In most cases the crop is now harvested and sold by small groups within the ejido, which continues to work as a unit for sowing and cultivation (Senior, op. cit., p. 74).
[2] Cf. N. Jasny, *The Socialized Agriculture of the U.S.S.R* (Stanford 1949), pp. 299–304.

profits of the enterprise and awarded (in default of any payment for capital brought into the co-operative) on the basis of work performed. In the extreme case of the kolkhoz there was until recently no stability of earnings at all: everything was dividend and there were no contractual wages. In the collective ejido on the other hand (despite the language of Senior, op. cit., p. 74), there are both wages and dividends. Wages differ according to skill and there are also piece-rates. They are the same in the whole Laguna region. Dividends are equal for members of a particular ejido.[1]

(vii) The most extreme left form of co-operation is where the theoretical owners are the *workers in a nationalized establishment*. Model: *Syndicalism*. Here the capitalist (or in Yugoslavia in 1950 the state) was expropriated and the factory integrally handed over to its workers, who did not previously own it at all. Since it begins with an expropriation, this model is never unpopular with the workers—they never object to the removal of capitalists or state officials from the factory, even if they have not asked for it. At most they remain sceptical. This is obviously more socialist than (vi), at least in its origins, but its relation to (iv) is also interesting. Both are completely socialist, but for the single, central boss in (iv) we now have many peripheral bosses, and the danger of tyranny yields to the danger of anarchy. In socialist circles (vii) is also in a sense more 'left-wing' than (iv); i.e. more optimistic, more reliant on the unaided 'socialist consciousness' of the masses. In practice, however, your industrial worker has neither the interest nor the capacity for management, and the director mostly has things his own way—unless the Party cell dominates. So in Yugoslavia while this is the *de jure* model the *de facto* model is (iii). In West Germany the Mitbestimmungsrecht[2] has not been developed so far as the Yugoslav workers' councils, but the same tendencies are evident; this, then, is (ii) or even (i) masquerading as (vii).

In (vii) the typical income is a regular, predictable wage; profits are reckoned after deducting it, and some of these in turn are distributed to the workers as a bonus. Thus in practice the methods of payment in (vi) and (vii) may grow to resemble each other,

---

[1] H. Infield, *Co-operative Communities at Work*, London 1947, p. 83.
[2] Cf. Royal Institute of International Affairs, 'A West German Managerial Revolution', in *World Today*, June 1951; H. Wachenheim, 'German Labour Asks Co-Management', in *Foreign Affairs*, Jan. 1953; H. J. Spiro, *The Politics of German Co-Determination*, Harvard, 1958. For similar tendencies in France compare A. Sturmthal, *Journal of Political Economy*, 1953.

though they begin from very different ideological starting-points. For in (vi) the 'ideological owner' is a co-operatized small capitalist making something akin to profit, while in (vii) he is a worker earning wages. The recent (1958 onwards) transition of kolkhoz payments to a more contractual and regular basis is hailed as part of the transition of the kolkhoznik to the status of a worker, and of the kolkhoz itself to a socialist enterprise. In Yugoslavia the movement is in the opposite direction, with the wage being steadily assimilated to the profit.

Characteristically in all these co-operative models the permanent workers are not 'employees' but 'members'. In the kolkhoz the head is not even a 'manager' or 'director' but a 'chairman'. However in the collective ejido and the Yugoslav factory the manager is separate, and exercises direct technical control like a civil servant under a parliamentary minister. And in Yugoslavia the worker betrays his origin by still being called an employee.

(viii) *The people organized in a local authority.* We shall call this model *municipal socialism.* It is derived from the Communes of the Utopian socialists. In their ancestral form these Communes were to be nearly autarkic (e.g. Robert Owen's 'parallelograms of paupers', Fourier's 'Phalansteries'), and are thus quite unsuited to a modern industrial society. But the system has been an established fact in one such society (Yugoslavia) since 1954, and here the Yugoslavs (who call their local unit the Komuna) seem to have genuinely broken through a sort of 'thought barrier': the municipality need not merely provide *services* for *local* people, it can set up factories or farms which supply goods to the whole world. Thus (viii) has been freed from autarky and parochialism, and enters the lists as a potential all-round champion. Western municipal socialism is a non-ideological version of this same model. But Western socialists are still confined by the 'thought barrier', and would find it very queer for a municipality to trade outside its boundaries.[1] Note the conflict, muted, inside the British Labour Party,[2] strident and public between U.S.S.R. and Yugoslavia, between (viii) and (iv); and the perfect compatibility of (viii) with (vi) and (vii). But (iv)

---

[1] Some do, however, notably in human manure from their sewage works. One thinks inevitably in this context of Kingston, Surrey.

[2] Certain local councils objected strongly to the nationalization of their gas works. The objectors were not only Conservatives, but party loyalty has on the whole restrained the Labour councillors. There has also been a conflict between (v) and (iv) in Britain, as it has been proposed to nationalize insurance, much of which is co-operative.

can be rearranged so as at least to bear a strong superficial resemblance to (viii). This it now does in Rumania, and to a lesser extent in U.S.S.R., by means of the territorial principal of organization (see Ch. 8).

(ix) *The people as both consumers and producers at once.* This we shall christen *community socialism.* These are the Utopian Communes put into modern practice. Examples: the early Soviet agricultural Kommuna,[1] the Israeli kibbutz and kvutza, the Hutterite communities.[2] Consumption as well as production is in common (crèches, dining-halls);[3] management is democratic, production tends to be autarkic, income is distributed equally or in accordance with need, not on the basis of work done. Money is not used inside the system, only in its external relations. This is plainly the most 'left-wing', 'advanced' or 'socialist' of all models. Its demands on 'socialist consciousness' are very high indeed. The Chinese People's Communes (Ch. 17, Sec. 4) bear strong traces of this tradition.

(x) Indeed, this tradition impregnates all Communist ideas of the end-stage of human society, or *Full Communism,* our last ownership model. We may say that in all these alike the whole nation is turned into a single Commune, in which planning embraces all activities from consumption to the choice of a job.

These, then, are the main models that concern us. We turn to their several connexions with *laissez faire* and the price-mechanism.

3. *Laissez faire* is normally understood as freedom of production and location decisions: a purely market concept concerned only with business details. But before we come to that there is *institutional laissez faire*: is government, law and public opinion indifferent between the models? Are enterprises of each model permitted to develop freely under the judgment of the market and the willingness of people to work in them? Is there institutional competition or institutional monopoly? Are taxation and licensing indifferent between models?

Astonishingly little attention has been paid to these questions. Yet they seem to the writer absolutely crucial. For, first, obviously institutional *laissez faire* is a good thing in itself: it enables that model to win that workers prefer or come to prefer, i.e. it subjects

---

[1] Jasny, loc. cit.

[2] H. Infield, op. cit., Ch. 2. The Hutterites are descendants of the Anabaptists who migrated to U.S.A. On U.S. communities generally cf. A. E. Bestor, *Backwoods Utopias,* U.S.A. 1950.

[3] In the early heroic period of Kibbutzim even clothes; but this is a thing of the past.

dogma to the test of experience. Nor is it only a market test to which the competing models submit: an inefficient (by profit standards) model which people like to work in for lower reward may beat a more profitable but less happy model. Thus small shops survive, paying their owners profits lower than the average wage of an assistant in a supermarket; Hutterite communities survive, despite a tremendous renunciation of modern ways and living standards, etc., etc. And of course not all people like the same thing, so that if the test of competition shows that most small shops succumb to supermarkets the fact of *laissez faire* nevertheless permits the eccentric to open another small shop—if he really likes that life let him have it. Thus at least some square pegs find square holes, or at the very least the boring of square holes is not forbidden. On the other hand where the model is compulsory we may be working neither in the most efficient nor in the happiest way, unless by some chance we all resemble each other *and* the chosen model is the 'best' one for us. Moreover, since men and techniques change, the best model of to-day may be tomorrow's second best, and that is yet another argument for institutional *laissez faire*.

Secondly, freedom does not mean that the State must never intervene to protect a particular model; for every kind of circumstance may militate against fair and equal opportunity, and a sort of Federal Trade Commission may be necessary here too to protect true *laissez faire*. The 'peaceful coexistence' of various models may require some kind of police action; for instance in many countries capitalist traders have conspired to strangle consumers' co-operation. Even model (iv) *can* coexist. For a part only of the economy can be submitted to central planning, while a free market subsists in the rest. Indeed this is what always happens, and technically it is a very great advantage to the planners, since it provides a cushion for all their miscalculations. If their plans cause the demand for any product or factor of production to exceed or fall short of supply, there is the free market to absorb or disgorge the differences. True, there are political difficulties: the free enterprises may work either too well or not at all. For instance, they are told to keep off certain raw materials or markets required in the planned sector, so they cease to make profits. They must then somehow be included in the plan, perhaps even subsidized; then why not nationalize them and be done? Or at the other extreme they successfully exploit the bottlenecks and the black markets that central planning invariably creates, and become irrationally profitable.[1] Then either the plan is changed so as to put them out of business or again they are nationalized. But none of that lies in the technical necessities of model (iv); rather in the likely political reaction of the sort of state that establishes it. All other models are, so far as their mere machinery goes, as compatible with true democracy as with totalitarianism.

Political totalitarianism, moreover, (if not Marxist) may well permit institutional *laissez faire*. This was more or less the case with the Jacobins and the Nazis. Or if its theology is basically economic it may enforce a model other than (iv), as in Yugoslavia (vii and viii, and woe betide you if you express doubts about them), or in many capitalist countries (where at certain periods it has been dangerous to support iii, iv or vii). In Yugoslavia the slogan 'our own road to socialism' has meant not institutional *laissez faire* at all, but the right of the local Communist Party to settle its own model: *cujus regio ejus religio*. In Poland the slogan does or did mean at least some *laissez faire*, a defined region for social experiment, so that groups of citizens may find their own road to socialism; but Poland was for some time in 1957 hardly a totalitarian country.

To *enforce* a model other than (iv), then, is even more totalitarian than freely to choose (iv). It implies that the ruling group knows what people 'really' want, and is going to give it them at any cost. The classic case of this is the Communist refusal to let collective farms freely and fairly compete with peasant farms. But one cannot exempt many British socialists from the same condemnation, since unlike the socialists of Western Europe they evidently intended[3] (iii) to be a universal pattern, not subject to empirical tests. The electoral pendulum, however, brought about a coexistence of (iii) and (ii) before (ii) could be altogether destroyed. To all scholarly attempts to see which is better these socialists turned a deaf ear. A universal (iii), imposed at one blow, would have saved them this forcible confrontation with a social experiment.

Finally it is not sufficiently realized that institutional *laissez faire* has already given rise to countless experiments. In free countries

---

[1] Thus the PAX enterprises in Stalinist Poland were more profitable and probably more efficient than the centrally planned state enterprises (G. Pisarski, 'PAX', in *Zycie Gospodarcze*, July 7, 1957); and I once met a Western capitalist who sold, in Moscow, the non-ferrous metals of one Communist country to another, at a handsome profit.

[3] I use the past tense because the Party Congress of Oct. 1957 makes it probable that this tendency has been finally defeated.

every one of our first nine models has very often been tried out. Even in free countries where advocates of (i) and (ii) have a disproportionate influence on law, opinion and government, other models are seldom interfered with. Indeed they often obtain subsidies and legislative favours. We are, then, entirely justified in pointing to the empirical results in free countries as an indication of the relative efficiency of the models; keeping always the big qualification that different people have different traditions—it is not a question of 'own ways to socialism' but of 'own ways to economic organization of any kind'. Economic experiments are the common property of all mankind. The more experimental, polycentric Communism of today has as much to learn from as to teach the rest of the world.

4. There is not space here to be more than very brief and dogmatic as to the results of experience. The models do *not* on the whole follow each other in any kind of historical sequence, whatever Marxists may suppose, except perhaps for the first three.

(i) works well still in trade and agriculture all over the world, but is gradually giving way to (ii) as techniques and the educational level of managers progress. (ii) is the natural successor to (i) under institutional *laissez faire*, and (iii) the natural successor to (ii), somewhat as Marx said it was; though the difference is much less marked than between (i) and (ii), and the necessity of the change is much less obvious (unless the shareholders are expropriated). There are political arguments on either side, but economics gives no clear indication. Thus while Britain has nationalized even long distance road haulage West Germany is keeping even atomic power out of state hands.

(iv) produces higher rates of growth than any other system, and most countries have to resort to it in war—proof indeed of its formidable efficiency. But the model is ill suited to providing the minor satisfactions of a consumer: e.g. it produces excellent guns and quite good TV sets, but bad clothes. It is intolerably arbitrary, having no profit criterion, and thus creates great intellectual malaise among the economic intelligentsia. It also leaves far too little initiative to managers; and the targets set can always be so ambitious as to impose an intolerable strain on all involved. Then, too, no central plan is in fact so perfect but that a little black marketing, a little peripheral illegality, a discreet neglect of the plan's minor provisions, is indispensable to the fulfilment of the major targets; so the political problem arises, what *are* the major targets in my plan?, and the moral problem, what laws *ought* I to violate? This also is an intolerable situation, and it is not surprising that model (iv) has a bad press all over the world today. The free world is un-attracted by its ugly face, Yugoslavia has thrown it over altogether, China, Poland and Hungary have abandoned very much of it, Soviet, Czech and East German economists are thinking revisionist thoughts about it, and Khrushchev is making curious experiments with it, which remind one of an ignorant surgeon desperately operating on the wrong part of a dying patient. Nevertheless, in all its Stalinist grandeur it caused the Soviet economy to grow faster than any major economy has ever grown, and formed the material base for the greatest empire the world has ever seen.

(v), (vi) and (vii) have already been sufficiently discussed when they were introduced. To recapitulate the main conclusions: (v) only applies in trade and in agricultural services, (vi) does well in handicrafts if voluntary, (vii) is intended for large-scale industry and has almost always failed. The performance of (vi) in agriculture is a large special subject for which we have no space.

(viii) has only been tried fully in Yugoslavia, though in a mild way there has been successful municipal enterprise all the world over. The relations between a large factory and the Yugoslav komuna in which it happens to be located are not easy, and it is early yet to call the system a success or a failure. The main trouble in Yugoslavia is that the komuna, finding this splendid new field of investment in industry open to it, has neglected its primary duty to provide the drains. An outsider would suppose this was merely growing pains, but the Yugoslav authorities are in fact cutting down the investment powers of the komuna again (1958–59).

(ix) is of course clean out of this world. Clearly no ordinary person will accept socialized consumption; and if work is to be quite unrelated to income the 'Main Street' moral pressure on the indi-vidual to work properly must be of an intensity one can only call totalitarian. Moreover, the community cannot well exceed a certain size, and cannot exist in a town;[1] or psychological difficulties will bring it down. In fact the socialist community may be said to be a monastery where breeding is allowed: it is only for the dedicated. The parallels with monasticism are many and striking.

---

[1] To every generalization its exception: G. A. Tokaev (*Betrayal of an Ideal*, London 1954, Ch. 17) describes just such a community of Moscow university students in 1930. It was fairly successful, but liquidated as an ultra-left deviation; as had been all the rural communities during collectivization (Jasny, loc. cit.). Klaus Mehnert describes another urban commune in *Jugend in Sowjetrussland* (Berlin 1932), pp. 175–193.

There is a religion or at least a strong, explicit common Welt-anschauung; a period of novitiate (with the difference that children of members need not undergo it); a Rule, which differs according to the Order to which the community belongs (thus the Hutterite communities pay allegiance to the *Schmieden Leut'*, the *Darius Leut'* and the *Lehrer Leut'*, and only the latter order permits the use of buttons; the kibbutzim belong to the three left-wing parties, Mapam, Achdut Avoda and Mapai, and only in the Mapai kibbutzim can consumers' durables be privately owned on any scale). There are dangers of corruption and enticement faced by those members whose duties take them out into the towns. Spiritual pride, too, has its parallel in the selfishness of the member who works excessively hard, out of mere devotion. And finally economic success brings wealth, and that brings violations of the Rule, eventually destroying the whole spirit of the thing—a deep internal contradiction for the Marxist kibbutz, which exacts no vow of poverty and is fundamentally materialist.[1]

The march towards (x) Full Communism is, in terms of our models, the extension of (iv) to include the consumer's acquisition of products and the worker's choice of jobs; or the imposition of (ix) over the whole economy, its conversion into one single commune. We discuss this at length in Chs. 17-20.

The fact of institutional *laissez faire* in free countries makes nonsense of most Marxist prophecies of doom. So long as the laws permit the internal structure of an enterprise to develop and adapt itself (and capitalist law is not perfect in this respect), there is no chance that 'capitalist monopoly' should 'become a fetter upon the method of production which has flourished with it and under it. The centralization of the means of production and the socialization of labour reach a point where they prove incompatible with their capitalist husk. This bursts asunder. The knell of capitalist private property sounds. The expropriators are expropriated.'[2] On the contrary capitalism is a thing of very many forms, which are constantly changing so as to remain compatible with the 'centralization of the means of production'. It must not therefore be described as a husk, but as a constantly rejuvenated skin. The best example of this is the invention of limited liability, which made possible

---

[1] On reflection I have left this as it was written in early 1958. The Chinese People's Communes (Ch. 18) contradict it at many points, including the alleged impossibility of an urban commune. Let the passage stand as a warning against generalization, proof of the depth of Chinese totalitarianism, and a correct prediction of the subsequent (1960) decline of the urban commune in China.   [2] K. Marx, *Das Kapital*, Book I, Ch. 24/7.

the Managerial Revolution, unforeseen by Marx. It is in countries of *any* type which show no capacity for institutional change that there are revolutions: France in 1798, Russia in 1917, Hungary in 1956. Of Hungary we may well write, parodying Marx: 'The decentralization of the means of production and the liberation of labour become so urgent a necessity that they prove incompatible with their Stalinist husk. This bursts asunder. The knell of Stalinist public property sounds. The expropriators are expropriated.'

5. We turn to *laissez faire* as ordinarily meant: not the freedom of the enterprise to organize itself but its freedom to produce, set prices, hire, fire, situate itself and choose techniques. To answer these questions is to describe how resources are allocated. We shall distinguish three degrees of *laissez faire*, and by the same token three main categories of allocation model (the list in Ch. 4 is more complete):

FM, the Free Market or the *laissez faire* economy. The enterprise may do everything not forbidden by civil law. There is no state intervention on any grounds, and a neutral tax policy designed solely to raise revenue.

RM, *the Regulated Market or the controlled economy*. All initiative still rests with the enterprise, which however is now hemmed in not only by ordinary civil law but also by current state economic regulations. These might be mainly fiscal (taxes and subsidies), or banking (differential interest rates, discriminatory credit control), or physical (rationing, licensing). Here, too, would come the injunctions of the Anti-Trust Division or the Federal Trade Commission, the operations of public purchasing bodies in security and crop markets, and most of such orders as a British minister usually gives to a nationalized industry.

CC, standing for Central Command or the *command economy*. The state takes over all main initiative, and the enterprise's freedom of action is limited to fulfilling state orders better and quicker. These orders might be in monetary or physical terms, and are of infinite variety. Their study is central to the political economy of Communism, and occupies Chs. 4 to 10. Here, however, we need consider only the three broad categories.

It may help the reader to think of certain commonly used words in connection with these three systems: FM—Marktwirtschaft; RM—Soziale Marktwirtschaft, gelenkte Wirtschaft, dirigisme; CC—Befehlswirtschaft, Zwangswirtschaft, central planning. But the definitions will become clearer as we proceed. We shall often require to lump FM and RM together—as *market* economies; and RM and CC together—as *planned* economies.

Capitalism, socialism and co-operation have no logical connexion at all with the choice between FM, RM and CC; except that model (iv), which is identical with CC, is a form of socialism. But the historical and psychological connexion is long and intimate. Outside Yugoslavia, and now also Poland and Hungary, there can be few economically uneducated people who do not equate capitalism with FM and socialism with CC; whereas, in fact, there has never been such a thing as capitalist pure FM, and Yugoslav socialism might at one time have approached FM more nearly than, say, French capitalism. The vast majority of all non-Communist economies in the world are and are meant to be RM, but the left-wing economies (including the Yugoslav) do as a matter of fact cluster about the CC end of RM. And the dogmatic capitalists cluster at the FM end of RM: e.g. West Germany, Switzerland.

6. *All* models then, except (iv) and (x), can be RM or FM, which is only to say that the state can leave the enterprise perfectly free, or not. *All models except (iv) and (x) necessitate a market relationship between enterprises: if there are no central orders, things must be freely bought and sold. The free market is a sort of neutral fluid in which all these models can coexist competitively.* In (iv) and (x), which are identical with CC, enterprises are not firms, but only branch establishments. This is by definition socialist and by definition non-market.

This 'logical necessity of a market' is highly important. Those who wish to de-Stalinize their economies *must* create a free market, as the Yugoslavs discovered; those who dislike the laws of supply and demand *must* Stalinize their economies. There is no third way. The main function of the vast Stalinist economic bureaucracy is to do administratively the things the free market does automatically; *either* the consumer and the profit motive tell the producer what to do (with or without the aid of competition among producers) *or* the central planner tells him. Resource allocation is either circumferential or central, either market or non-market. Indeed these last four words demonstrate that the dichotomy, command economy or market, is logically exhaustive. Either the enterprise receives orders from above as to where to obtain materials and transmit products, or it does not. If it does not it must agree with those who deliver to it or to whom it delivers. But such a process of agreement is by definition a market, however imperfect.

Where there is a market the choice between capitalism, socialism and co-operation is still open, indeed every variant of all three can coexist peacefully in one small country. Where there is not, only the Stalin model or Full Communism (= (iv) or (x) = CC) are in the long run possible, though there may be 'state capitalism' for a while. The difference between FM and RM is trivial compared with the gulf between RM and CC. For under RM the whole choice of model is still open, nay the choice of socialism itself; and in any case resource allocation is still made by the consumer at the circumference, and initiative rests with the enterprise not the government, which merely prevents certain things.

7. Such is the essence of the ten models. But they cannot be fully understood until we have examined their relation to various other things: profit, social services, trade unions, full employment, regionalism, economic growth. We begin with profit.

In all market models, *profit* is the main motive of the enterprise. It may well not wish, as in Western economic textbooks, to maximize profit, but it will certainly be keen to avoid loss. For the basis of the market economy is that loss-makers cease to exist. The allocation of resources and the proportions of the various products are therefore more or less determined by private profit; private in the sense that it is the enterprise's, not the state's. In RM the state is continually intervening to ensure a better coincidence of private with social profit than can be the case under pure *laissez faire* (incidentally social profit is also not the state's; it simply means the good of the community). Whether it succeeds or not we cannot decide here; the point for us is that it continues to rely absolutely on private profit as the motive force, only rigging the market so as to make different things privately profitable.

All this is well understood in Yugoslavia, where the enterprise seeks quite openly, as it is officially meant to, its private profit. But it is much less well understood in the British nationalized sector, which we are again forced to diagnose as a piece of muddled and moderate Stalinism. 'Production for use, not profit' (what is the difference?); 'taking account of social need' (why not make social need profitable to satisfy, by redistributing incomes?);—all the old Marxist misunderstandings of the function of a market are very much alive in the ideology of British nationalization. It lacks entirely that Twentieth Century, streamlined Titoist look. Thus it often seems in model (iii) that no one takes the profit, but rather the 'trustees' fix price and output so as not to make it. The state takes its normal tax as from a capitalist firm, and for the rest the 'trustees' are legally debarred from helping themselves. So prices are often too low, and if ever profit is made it is ploughed back.

In model (iv) the object is plan-fulfilment, and the motivating force must therefore be a plan-fulfilment bonus. Ideally this would be directly paid out of the central treasury, but—whether because it has not been thought of, or simply for administrative reasons— the bonus is in fact paid, according to some central regulation of course, out of the enterprise's gross revenue. This is merely a corollary of khozraschet (see Ch. 2). Therefore some interest in profit remains: not for its own sake, but as a *sine qua non* for the all-important plan-fulfilment bonus. Profit is naturally less impor- tant than the fulfilment of the priority parts of the plan. Even when it is itself one of the rubrics in the plan it still ranks junior to the physical output targets. And profit arises now as a difference between centrally planned, not freely fixed, costs and prices. It is, therefore, much more likely to be arbitrary and irrational, and, we may even perhaps be thankful it has less influence on output than the physical targets in the plan; which will have certainly been more carefully thought out by the authorities. If profit does became a major target within this model, and if incomes are made to depend on it, enterprises will put in compensation claims when their physical targets are altered in a manner unfavourable to profits. This leads to appalling complications; e.g. in the war economy of a capitalist state.

Model (iv), then, is distinguished by the variety of objectives it can set before the enterprise: gross output, net output, cost of production, a batch of detailed physical targets, etc., etc. Profit is only one of these. But profit will arise wherever money is used, no matter how irrationally, and must be disposed of. Here the 'theoretical owner' comes in, as explained in Sec. 2. And in model (iv) alone profit is not private: it belongs to the state. But state profit too may diverge from social.

As to model (ix), in so far as it is autarkic it operates without money or profit; if it has market relations the socialist community behaves like any other enterprise; and if it operates within a com- mand economy it obeys, disobeys and misinterprets the central plan as would any other enterprise.

For the individuals inside model (ix), and the enterprises in (x), there is no profit nor indeed any money. Their objective is, as in (iv), plan-fulfilment; but their stimulus is social regard or a social conscience.

8. In all the preceding we have absolutely neglected *welfare* issues, concentrating only on the position of the enterprise. The protection of the poor, however defined, is compatible with any of the first eight models, and it may also be wholly neglected by any of them; except that in models (vi), (vii) and (viii) the *working* poor at least are put in a position of command, and so are likely to protect themselves by the very nature of the model. In (ix) and (x) however, and to some extent in (vi), the young, the old and sick are inside the model. It would deny its nature if it did not protect them fully. There is no other logical connection between the Welfare State and Socialism.

In Stalin's version of model (iv) the race was to the swift and the security police took the hindmost; the down-and-out's last resource was literally to get himself arrested as a vagrant. It was 'To Each According To His Labour'. But in the satellite models (iv) much more care is taken of the poor: pre-1956 Hungary had unemployment pay (unknown in U.S.S.R.) and pre-1948 Yugoslavia opened her social services to all workers, not merely trade unionists (as in U.S.S.R.). All sorts of Western countries, from California to Spain, have very complete social services. To all these cases we can apply the slogan 'To Each According To His Need'—a slogan the Communists quite falsely restrict to their own side of the Iron Curtain, and to the far future. However, there is undoubtedly a strong traditional connexion between Socialism and the Welfare State in the minds of the economically uneducated; and those who believe in the former are, if not Stalinists, the strongest supporters of the latter.

9. The position of *trade unions* differs in a more interesting and systematic manner. The climate of primitive capitalism is hostile to them, but perhaps not as hostile as that of state socialism. For a trade union is essentially a market phenomenon, a bargaining device, and has no logical place in a non-market economy. But trade unions are 'labour' and therefore in some sense 'socialist'— like the Welfare State the connexion is psychological and traditional, not logical. So model (iv) has to include pseudo-trade unions; as we know Stalin's unions did duty for a Ministry of Labour (abolished), for social insurance funds (absorbed by them), and for productivity teams. Nor has any post-Stalin development essentially altered this. It is in models (ii) and (iii) that the trade union is most at home,

bargaining against its large, civilized employer, private or public.

It should be the same in model (v), but in British experience at least not so: the mass of consumers who run the enterprise resent very much the suggestion they are not perfect employers.[1] *Vox populi vox dei*; but if the employers also are poor and numerous which is the populus? Besides, model (v) makes large ideological claims: if everyone is a consumer and consumer is the ideological owner it is enough for the particular worker that he too is a consumer, and trade unions are selfish particularism. Time, however, has heavily eroded the Rochdale ideology, and the British co-ops are now almost as heavily managerialized as the Swedish co-ops, which have not had such difficult relations with their trade unions.

Models (vii) and (viii) make still greater difficulties, for in them the producer is sovereign (since the Yugoslav komuna is not autarkic its members think of its enterprises essentially from the producers' point of view; they are selling to all the world). How can the sovereign producer strike against himself?—the question is laughable Stalinist hypocrisy with reference to (iv), but serious and burning in (vii) and (viii). Very briefly, two answers seem possible. One is that the worker's council is no doubt an elected body, but after all it is elected to manage and must take a manager's point of view; and this being necessarily more hardheaded and long-term than the workers' point of view, we still need trade unions. The second is that the enterprise is a unitary polity with a unitary government competent to represent all interests. The first view prevails in Yugoslav industry, while the second has had minority support in both Poland and Yugoslavia; it corresponds to no actual model (viii) known to the writer.

In (ix) and (x) genuine trade unions are inconceivable. In (x) the state must even direct labour, all wages being equal (Ch. 17).

Finally, trade unions are ideologically incompatible with model (vi). What would a group of very small capitalists, who never employed any labour and have now agreed to co-operate with each other, want a trade union for? In practice, however, the usual conflict must arise between manager and managed; especially where force was used to constitute the co-operative in the first place. In no organization in the world would a trade union be in practice more desirable than in a Soviet kolkhoz. But not even Stalinism could entirely emasculate the local units of so dispersed

---

[1] Ed. A. M. Carr-Saunders, *Consumers' Co-operation in Great Britain* (London 1938), pp. 350–7; G. D. H. Cole, *A Century of Co-operation* (London 1944), Ch. 20.

and variegated a union; so the ideology has prevailed, and none has ever been formed. However in that very similar system, the Mexican collective ejido, the ordinary members do have a trade union.

10. We end with two more imponderable questions. First, which model most promotes economic growth? Growth is the most important part of economics, but it involves very many non-economic factors. Growth is largely a question of how you use the model, not what it is; largely, then, a matter of the particular society's ideals and capacity for self-discipline. Some few things can be said, however. The co-operative models (v), (vi), (vii), which give so much power directly to the majority of poor people, will normally favour consumption over investment, stability of employment over technical progress, and equality over incentives, thus diminishing growth. A free market will not attain such rates of growth as a controlled one in which growth is favoured (e.g. the Yugoslav or West German controls). But controls may have quite other ends in view, as in Britain, and indeed they may fail to achieve their ends whatever they are. In this case more freedom might mean more growth. This was the correct opinion of Adam Smith, in the very different circumstances of his day. Finally the sort of government that is disagreeable enough and dogmatic enough to instal model (iv) will certainly opt for forced investment, unequal incomes, and all the other unpleasant necessities for growth. Moreover, the model itself facilitates such a course, since it permits the indefinite expansion of the capital goods industry without reference to consumption at all; it absolutely ensures maximal employment of all factors of production available; and it makes possible every conceivable incentive scheme, not merely those that the market makes profitable.

We are not, then, bound to expect, but we should in practice fear, the greatest rate of economic growth in a command economy; and the smallest in a co-operative one. This is merely because the former is the least and the latter the most democratic model.[1]

11. Secondly there is the Managerial Revolution. In a work that tries desperately to stick to economics it would be inappropriate to say very much about this essentially socio-political phenomenon.

---

[1] It would be very dangerous to generalize about the communities—model (ix)—in this context. Kibbutzim, with their quasi-Marxist views and hostility to private wealth, are also prepared to make great sacrifices for economic growth. Many of the other Utopian communities have been of a very opposite temper.

Nevertheless, it is the obvious duty of the economist to contribute that which only he can.

I understand by this term the divorce of theoretical ownership or 'ultimate boss-ship' from practical control *in any institutional model*; or the actual transfer of theoretical ownership and ideological primacy to such new practical controllers. In every case—and this is still part of the definition—the practical controller wins because he works full time on the job and is technically better educated. So there is no need for a Managerial Revolution in primitive economies. But a large modern kolkhoz, a Yugoslav industrial enterprise, a kibbutz, a Swedish consumer's co-op., or a Stalinist planning bureaucracy are quite as likely to suffer from this sort of ideological de-naturing as a capitalist corporation. The peasants, the workers' council or the Communist Party find themselves taking a back seat to experts with a very neutral attitude to ideology, just as do capitalist shareholders.

This, then, is not the original, more romantic notion of the MR as an actual revolution by a self-conscious class seeking power. For this there seems to me to be no evidence. Nor has it much to do with the mistrust of bourgeois experts shown by Communists immediately after they take over power—a fear of a Managerial Counter-Revolution. It is merely the grey notion that things are very complicated, and the experts will take over the world, reducing all systems to uniformity.

By enumerating models (ii) and (iii) as being among the more serious institutional possibilities we have already allowed for some model changes brought about by the MR. The more serious case, however, is that of continuing discrepancy between the theoretical and the *de facto* model. Thus notoriously in U.S.A. we have primitive capitalism in theory and (mostly) managerial capitalism in fact; and in Yugoslavia syndicalism and managerial socialism respectively. Does this sort of thing matter? Is such a situation deeply unstable? Does theory adapt itself to fact or vice versa? These questions take us outside the comfortable realm of the technically necessary consequences of the models, and plunge us into politics and psychology; i.e. they cannot be answered in a general way at all. For instance, we might say that U.S.A. is a free country governed by men of empirical temper, so that the theories people hold are not very important and a discrepancy of the kind mentioned can last a long time without doing anyone any harm; indeed, theoretical owners and economic ideologies might be dispensed with altogether. Or we might point to the Harvard School of Business, and say that its cachet is coming to confer ideological respectability on the new *de facto* owners, so that a business degree will become a *sine qua non* for a business career, and a 'capitalist mandarinate' will arise like the 'socialist mandarinate' alluded to in Sec. 2 (iii); in which case managerial capitalism would become a very stable model.

In Yugoslavia, on the other hand, the governing class is not of an empirical temper, and takes the nonsense it thinks very seriously indeed. This situation then is explosive. For instance, a heresy might arise inside the Party that managerial socialism was more consonant with the facts and ought to be sanctified. The opposite heresy, that syndicalism be given *de facto* power, is of course Djilasism and unacceptable. Here at any rate is an interesting tension, though it is beyond the writer's powers to resolve it.

The same tension exists in the Stalinist model: who shall plan, the Central Committee of the Party or the state bureaucracy? Who shall manage, the Party cell secretary or the director? As a new generation of proletarian experts has grown up this question has become not less but more acute.[1] Now, having no strong views about economics, a Fascist party will not care. But what a Communist party has to fear, it seems, is doing itself out of a job, and letting the civil servants take over. It thrives when there is strain, irrationality, popular discontent, discrepancy between what is natural and what is ideologically right. It languishes when the model works smoothly and the people accept it. Thus in all Communist countries the Party is indispensable in agriculture[2] (an essentially capitalist occupation), and agricultural civil servants are the merest bottle-washers. But in industry socialist models are quite acceptable, and the technocrats tend to take them over. And the passage of time, which makes the worst systems more tolerable, also helps the technocrats; so that the technocrats versus party issue is more actual in U.S.S.R. than elsewhere.

Thus as it overcomes resistance and wins acceptance for its model the party saws off the branch on which it sits. State, law, civil servants and regularity take over in a gradual Thermidor. What can it do against this? Answer; change the model, re-stir the ant-heap, re-create the discrepancy between ideology and fact. In

---

[1] Cf. Wiles in ed. G. Grossman, *Value and Plan*, University of California Press, 1960; Wiles in *Soviet Survey*, London, April-June 1959.

[2] Cf. Zhdanov, *Speech to XVIII Party Congress*, 1939; Djilas, 'Savez ili Partija?' (League or Party?), *Borba*, Jan. 4, 1956.

particular, it can switch to a model with fewer technocrats in it, or at least fewer very important technocrats. Notoriously this is what Khrushchev has done: as we show in Ch. 2, Sec. 8, and Ch. 8. The product-wise model (iv) with a few central Ministries yields to the place-wise model (iv) with many Sovnarkhozy—the latter carefully kept apart from the local authorities. Thus there is a big and inconvenient change, which is *per se* a good thing for a Communist party, and such a change moreover that the regional party boss is now bigger than any man in the state machine.

Rule by a Communist party is thus not at all the same thing as the Managerial Revolution. On the contrary, the latter means, as here defined, rule by technocrats. The Soviet party has resisted it by a minor model change within the Stalinist pattern: the territorial principle, referred to above. The Yugoslav party was much more radical. Proceeding from an ideological, not merely an empirical, appreciation of the threat, it scrapped the planning bureaucracy altogether and went over to the market. Thus there may be a Managerial Revolution within each plant, but since mergers are prohibited the thing is almost impossible at national level. The Yugoslav party is safe at least from this. The Chinese party seems to be experimenting with a third solution: the permanent conversion, without model change, of the individual state bureaucrat into a really dedicated, not merely nominal, Communist ('Red and Expert'). The poor man must do a month's manual labour a year, and is subject to constant brainwashing. The danger here is one that Zhdanov (op. cit.) more or less foresaw: if there is no proper distinction between Party and State the former will lose its dynamism with its separateness. As well merge priesthood and laity.

It may possibly be that Chinese dynamism is indestructible. This, however, is not the place for prophecies of this kind. I only cannot help remarking that those who hold a Managerial Revolution inevitable under Communism, and look forward with optimism to this for the future, show in their writing singularly little detailed knowledge of the Communist system in any country. They never consider Yugoslavia or China, and they invariably contrive to write about U.S.S.R. as if the Party had no influence, and the territorial principle had been introduced for economic reasons.[1]

---

[1] Such views often rely on selective quotation from D. Granick, *The Red Executive*, Doubleday, New York 1960. Mr. Granick is not blameless here, as he does lean towards these errors, but in very qualified form. A healthy corrective, showing the strong influence of the Party even in U.S.S.R., is G. Hough's *The Role of Local Party Organs in Soviet Industrial Decision-Making*, Harvard doctoral thesis, 1961.

CHAPTER 2

THE HISTORICAL SEQUENCE OF MODELS UNDER COMMUNISM

THERE are thus very many possible ways of organizing a socialist or semi-socialist, and indeed a capitalist, economy. In this chapter we list all the main models used by any Communist country. No pretence is made at deep analysis, although the reader is in every case referred forward to such analysis should it later be made. Our object here is to sketch briefly for reference the chronological order and the political context.

1. From November 1917 to summer 1918 in Russia was the period of *workers' control and land reform*. Banks, railways, foreign trade and a few large works were nationalized, the remainder of industry, trade, transport and construction was left in private ownership. But all establishments were alike subjected to supervision (kontrol') by the workers in them, who elected councils independently of the trade unions. Normal market relationships were supposed to obtain between the firms, which continued to be managed, whether by capitalist owners, or, in the case of large nationalized establishments, by their former salaried managers. Foreign capital was sought, the foreign debt of private firms was not repudiated, new concessions were offered to foreigners. On the land the few large estates that remained were divided up locally among the peasants, including kulaks, and all land was formally nationalized. Here, too, of course normal market relationships prevailed. The land reform was presented as a step from 'feudal' to 'capitalist' relations. This to some extent it was, but mainly it meant a regression to primitive peasant agriculture. A very few exemplary large farms were kept intact, as state farms.

This model was Lenin's own, which he had elaborated just before the Revolution. It was meant to be transitory—to serve the purposes of the Party until the proletarian revolution had occurred in Germany and its own hold at home had been consolidated. The model was not thought of as socialist, being indeed a mixture of what we have previously called models (i), (ii) and (iii)—and Lenin did not hold (iii) or any market system to be socialist. It was born in chaos—the chaos of the Revolution itself—and it lived in the chaos it itself generated. For the land 'reform' was in fact carried out by decentralized violence, without legal process or proper survey or registration of title, without even Party control; and the new workers' councils were unanswerable to any sensible or central control, and proceeded to piece-meal nationalization although this was not in the programme.

2. The second model (1918–21) was that of the *naïf doctrinaire Communists* Larin and Kritsmann, to whom Lenin devolved control of the economy when the civil war broke out, and diverted his attention. Capitalists could no longer be left in control, especially as some of them did in fact engage in sabotage; and new foreign capital was out of the question since foreign firms were also confiscated. So virtually everything was nationalized bar agriculture, in which no formal change occurred, except that compulsory procurement took the place of voluntary sale. Secondly the workers' councils, which had been causing absolute chaos, were brought under control of the trade unions.

So far the changes were merely a commonsense response to necessity. But what follows is not. A tight planning bureaucracy issued from the centre production orders in physical terms to every enterprise. There was no market at all except a black market, and money was supposed to be withering away. The very wages were paid, where possible, mainly in kind. In other words this was the previous chapter's model (x).

It is a great mistake to suppose that this second model was at the time conceived as a war economy. True, the war forced universal nationalization, but nationalization can take many forms. True, there is usually inflation in wartime, but governments do not normally boast of their intention further to debauch the currency. True, there is often rationing in wartime, but rations are normally paid for, and it is a far step from ordinary rationing to the actual abolition of money and the delivery of goods in lieu of wages; nor can it be held to help the war effort if the post office and the tramways cease to charge money. True, central physical planning is common in belligerent countries, but not to anything like the detailed extent here used. Moreover there was peace in 1919, between the civil and Polish wars, and the Party then explicitly reaffirmed this second model as its peacetime model, at the 9th Congress.

Later, after the model had failed, it came to be called *War*

Communism, in order to suggest a temporary necessity. But at the time there was no such talk, although there was indeed the most complete chaos. For the central planners did not dovetail their orders to make sure they were technically compatible with each other (method of balances: Sec. 4 below); the refusal to use money in wholesale and inter-enterprise transactions led to a fantastic proliferation of physical detail, quite beyond the planners' capacity, and to the most absurdly irrational particular decisions; the payment of wages in kind left consumers hopelessly dissatisfied with the particular things they received, yet forbidden to exchange them. More serious still, the model entailed the direction of labour: for if all real wages are equal how else can labour be got to move where the planners want it? Nay, more, if wages were differentiated so as to *attract* labour hither and thither then the centre would be sharing the initiative with the workers, and this would diminish the purity of the model. But the direction of labour is unpopular and 'un-Socialist'. Only a few brave logicians like Trotsky had the courage of their convictions. But more than from these technically inherent defects the model suffered from the intractability of the human material and the disturbances of war. Citizens went on to the black market because with production so low they needed it to live; and anyway they lacked the social discipline such a system requires. Moreover, no economy can work well if the area it includes is daily altered by a fluid battle line.

However, there War Communism stands, an embodiment of the economic dreams of a certain kind of Communist. Money, the root of all evil, and the market, in which nothing is seen but capitalist anarchy, are destroyed, and every operation of the economy is centrally planned by physical orders, from the workers' choice of his job through all inter-enterprise transactions to the consumer's choice in the shops. Indeed there are no longer any such choices: all choices are made by the centre. The whole economy is one single big enterprise, and the management of the economy is identical with the government of the country; there are no quasi-independent public boards, regarded as the non-political trustees of particular industries or enterprises. On the contrary central power must participate and penetrate everywhere. Indeed, the whole country is one single big Commune, since the consumer and the worker are fully included in the plan; and the model can only be understood as a futuristic attempt to establish full Communism on the spot.

3. This system was recognized as intolerable in early 1921, after the Polish War, the Kronstadt revolt, and the constant refusal of the peasants to deliver produce for nothing (this latter caused a continuous smouldering civil war between the government and more than half the population). In its place Lenin, turning again to the economy, substituted the third model, the *New Economic Policy*. He needed all his prestige to do so, as this was market socialism in large enterprises only, there being petty capitalism everywhere else. The NEP thus bore a strong resemblance to Lenin's own first model, which we have seen was valid until the summer of 1918.

Petty capitalism requires no explanation: normal market relationships, perfect and imperfect, reigned. Two things only need to be noted. First, the system normalized relations with the peasants, who were no longer forced to deliver anything but simply bargained for what prices they could get, and were subjected to an ordinary tax. Hence their happy memories of the NEP, and 'Lenin myth' that still lives in the countryside. Agriculture recovered rapidly, until towards the end of the 'twenties knowledge of anti-Kulak sentiments in Moscow damped down peasant investment. Obviously petty capitalism will work well under a Communist government as far as current production goes; but it will not invest, and so the economy will not grow, unless the government exercises a quite special restraint in its ideological pronouncements. This was not possible in NEP Russia, as it has been in Gomulka's Poland, since there was always an influential left wing, too strong to discipline, actively opposed to the NEP. Secondly the Communist trade unions were now faced with private capitalists in industry and construction. From being controllers of the economy they reverted to the ordinary 'bourgeois' role of protecting the workers, a role they had some difficulty in forgetting under Stalin. They bargained with and struck against private employers in a normal Western manner, and by extension occasionally did the same in the nationalized sector.

Market socialism, the new regime for nationalized industry, was never accepted ideologically, and found no defenders in principle. 'I was not trained to trade', a Party worker complained to Lenin when the NEP began, and even the most right-wing Communists seem to have thought of market socialism as only a passing phase. Characteristically, great stress was laid throughout the NEP period, not on the market and on rational prices, but on decentralization as a counter to inefficiency, waste and bureaucracy; and it was hardly

appreciated that the market and the profit motive are an almost inevitable consequence of decentralization. Market socialism came
about almost in a fit of absence of mind, and the vision of a non-
bureaucratic but centrally planned economy continued to blind the
Communists to the significance of what they were actually doing.
What they *were* actually doing was to permit groups of factories
known as trusts to maximize their profits on free markets, adapting
price and output to this end. Nevertheless between one state enterprise and another strong elements of barter remained, and detailed
interference from the centre, always possible in principle, often
occurred in fact. Access to the market was seen as a privilege.
The trusts' profits belonged automatically to the State, and could not
be spent without central permission. This is of course a key point,
since as we saw in Ch. 1 the essence of an economic model is
the ownership and disposal of profits; i.e. the state remained the
'ideological owner'.

A great deal of paper work was done on the problems of central
planning, and although almost none of it resulted in effective and
coherent orders being given to the economy the NEP was intellectually the peak period of Soviet economic thinking. Almost any
view of central planning and of the problems of growth discussed
today in the West, or in the newly liberalized atmosphere of
Moscow, finds its rudimentary forbear in a suggestion made by a
Soviet economist during the NEP.

During this period, then, the Soviet economy had much the
structure of modern social-democratic Britain. It was a mixed
economy, capitalist in the countryside, retail trade and small
industry, nationalized as to the 'commanding heights': railways,
banks, foreign trade, large industry. Only the nationalized sector
was planned, and this planning was principally of the 'investment'
or 'development' sort common to backward non-communist
countries today. For all that a government can really control and
order in such an economy is specified investment projects, like
electrification, very popular at the time with Bolsheviks. Even
the current output of nationalized industries cannot be planned,
since they sell in large part to the unplanned sector. For all but
these development projects the central plan consisted in mere
forecasting, and was no more a plan than the British Economic
Surveys.[1] Indeed the Russian word for annual plan in this period

---

[1] Cf. Ch. 4, Sec. 3.

was Kontrol'niye Tsifry—not 'control figures' but 'check figures'. The current outputs in the annual plan were pious hopes or good predictions, not orders. The second plan era began precisely when the annual 'Check figures' were rechristened the annual plan and became the law of the land (Oct. 1, 1928). From this month almost the whole Soviet economy was theoretically under orders.

4. With 1928 and the first *Five-year Plan* intellectual night re-descended. In the prevailing atmosphere of Stalinism all rational thought was discouraged, and energy concentrated on the sheer blind increase in the physical production of arbitrarily chosen commodities. The chosen model of the economy was now number (iv) of the previous chapter: industry, transport, construction, trade, and about one-tenth of agriculture (the sovkhozy) were national-ized,[1] and subject to the above-mentioned direct physical planning. Until today there has been no radical change in U.S.S.R. since 1928. The rest of agriculture was co-operative (the kolkhozy) and subject to a most bewildering *ad hoc* mixture of the market and central command. Stalin's kolkhozy were so much the product of special circumstance that they fit most ill into any theoretical schema. Lacking space to describe them in great detail, we almost wholly omit them. In addition there was a surprisingly large private sector, subject solely to the market and controlled as any state might control economic activity: by taxation and licence. This sector included the private plots of collective farmers, the allotments of workers (especially state farm workers), second-hand consumer goods of all sorts, domestic service, a certain amount of private tuition and medicine, and the construction of small private dwelling-houses.[2]

How did this differ from War Communism? Briefly, as model (iv) does from (x), and first in the persistence of *money*. Money had been restored to an important role at the beginning of the NEP, under the slogan of *Khozraschet* ('economic accounting'). At that time this simply meant that responsibility was decentralized to trusts (and indeed later to enterprises), who must seek to avoid waste (the curse of War Communism, where no one was respon-sible) and cover their costs. They were consequently compelled to pay each other in money for goods and services rendered, and

---

[1] A great deal of retail trade (eventually, all rural but no urban trade) and some un-mechanized craft manufacture was formally not nationalized but co-operative. In practice, however, this made little difference. The village co-operative shop and the craftsmen's artel had by no means the special status of the kolkhoz.

[2] Very many houses were private: about one-third of the urban population, and all members of collective (not state) farms, lived in private houses.

D

to account to the government for their use of funds. Their profits remained Treasury property through all changes. The Soviet idea was and remains that the whole state sector is one big trust, not a series of independent public corporations (Ch. 1, Sec. 2/iv). This inconvenient theory had actually been put into practice under War Communism, with the result that there was no distinction between the state budget and the revenues and outlays of nationalized enterprises, nor did these pay money to each other for transactions within the state sector.[1] Thus to 'put an enterprise on Khozraschet' means to separate its account from the budget.

But since at the beginning of the NEP all this was to be in terms of prices settled in a market, Khozraschet came very close to being an order to maximize profits, i.e. an order to adapt outputs to the market. It thus began as an indirect injunction to the producer to satisfy the consumer. Khozraschet is clearly essential for market socialism and presents no theoretical difficulty or interest inside such a system.

However, when central planning was reinstated, money was retained and remained influential for certain decentralized decisions, and to a certain extent in the minds of the central planners (Chs. 4 to 10). Administrators at all levels were meant to be highly cost-conscious, so that khozraschet was retained simultaneously with central planning, although it is improbable that anyone in authority knew exactly why or exactly what the consequences would be. Perhaps the most important consequence of this kind of khozraschet is its fixing of *responsibility* upon the manager of the enterprise or other unit subjected to separate accounting. In the modern Soviet system, the establishment is indeed a separate unit and feels itself to be such, even though it has very few powers of independent decision. This is largely because, although deprived of such freedoms, it has had responsibility squarely thrust upon it.[2]

But there is no real reason why decentralized responsibility for waste should be imposed in monetary terms: a physical audit, a

[1] This principle is not unknown under capitalism: British government departments do not pay the Post Office, which is also a government department, anything for their mail. In Tsarist Russia this also applied to the railways, whose receipts and expenditures figured in the budget. The very word 'Khozraschet' began its career with the extra-budgetary funds of the Tsarist government.

[2] Along with monetary khozraschet, there had to be created at the beginning of the NEP a sort of legal khozraschet, in that each firm acquired the right to sue and be sued in civil actions, such as breach of contract by another firm (although not as between two firms under one ministry, in which case the dispute was subject to arbitration by the minister). This too survived the end of the NEP.

sort of combined stock-taking and efficiency inspection, would do just as well. Money is not in fact necessary for central *physical* planning (which is what Stalin reintroduced). But its existence certainly makes possible a great deal of decentralized *initiative*, which the central planners may or may not welcome; especially in settling details, the 'sortament' (Ch. 4, Secs. 9, 10). Moreover at each end of the nationalized sector, money has important effects on consumers and workers.

For, secondly, *the consumer was free to buy or not to buy*. He had money (chiefly an earned income, but there were also social services, the interest on state loans, and inherited wealth) and he could spend it how he liked. There was then consumer's choice but not consumer's sovereignty—the planner at the centre was sovereign: i.e. the consumer could react but not influence.

Thirdly, there continued to be a *free labour market*. The direction of labour was model (x), or Trotskyism, so the appearance of freedom here had to be maintained. In consequence the planners did in fact differentiate wages so as to attract labour where it was most wanted. Incidentally, there was a further and very much greater differentiation designed to increase the productivity of labour once it had been got into the desired occupation, and it is with this latter that Stalin's name is most publicly and indelibly associated (piece-work and Stakhanovism). Differentiation between trades and areas was however also practised, and it is only this kind that is a technical necessity of the model chosen.[1]

Fourthly, order and consistency, though certainly not rationality in the technical economic sense, were brought into the central plans. For a start, *plans were drawn up covering a period of time ahead*, whereas under War Communism a stream of orders was issued currently and *ad hoc*. An outline was given for five years, from which annual and even quarterly plans were deduced; more detail was put into these latter, and the centre then passed them down to subordinate authorities, typically the industrial ministries, which added still more detail and subdivided them among their trusts. The trusts further elaborated the annual plan and subdivided it among their enterprises, where the director's orders to the workers (especially his setting of the 'norm') may be regarded as the outermost

---

[1] In fact labour was secretly directed in a very large number of ways, as well as being subjected to the pull of the market (Ch. 7). The differentiation of wages by Stalin was politically, socially and ideologically a much greater event than our cursory treatment implies.

concentric ripple of Moscow's economic commands. *Timetables* were worked out for the passage of the annual and quarterly plans down to the enterprise, with allowance at every state for counter-suggestion and even initiative from below. But these were scarcely ever adhered to, the plan always arriving after the period it covered had already begun. In the interval, managers, knowing roughly what was wanted, would carry on under an improvised extrapolation from their last quarterly plan.

In addition to receiving an orderly hierarchical procedure, planning acquired at least a rudimentary consistency of content. This was the '*Method of balances*', which began to be applied towards the end of the first FYP. Before that, and under War Communism, physical orders might be given to produce, say, so much steel without the requisite quantity of coke production being also ordered. The 'method of balances' consists in making a budget of, say, coke production, stocks at the beginning of the period, and imports: and seeing that it coincides with consumption (ascertained by applying technical input/output ratios to the outputs ordered for coke-using industries), exports and stocks at the end of the period. It differs *toto coelo* from rational choice in a command economy, as we show in Ch. 10.

5. Outside the Soviet Union there have been a number of other institutional models. The first and most deviant of these was produced in *Yugoslavia* in the years 1950–52. Since this book is essentially concerned with the command economy not much will be said about this model. Essentially it is market socialism, but the motives of the Yugoslav Communists for introducing it have often been misinterpreted (not least by the writer), and these things are best described here at some length.

When Tito split from Stalin in 1948, the Yugoslav Communists faced the question, 'What went wrong?' It is as much as to say, Stalin died in Yugoslavia not in 1953 but in 1948.

The first advocate of economic reforms was Boris Kidrič (1912–53). At the time of the break with Stalin he was president of the Economic Council and of the Federal Planning Commission. As late as April 1948 he had, it would appear, no special quarrel with the system.[1] A year later in his speech to the second plenum of the

---

[1] Speech on the budget, *Borba*, April 24, 1948. There is a longish passage on the standard of living where the question of 'administration versus law of value' would have fitted in very appropriately, had he wished to raise it.

Central Committee,[1] he was half way over to market socialism. In a long passage he wrestles with what we may call 'administration versus law of value', and concludes emphatically that in all small questions of consumer goods supply and demand is better than any kind of central planning. There is not one word or hint about workers' councils. The same omission is still more glaring in Kidrić's much later and more definitive piece on the new economy.[2] Not to mention them at this date was surely to imply disapproval. Indeed in the great discussion on the introduction of the workers' councils in the Skupština (June 1950) Kidrić also spoke, but characteristically avoided the councils themselves, concentrating on the reorganization of the state machine.[3]

Thus, contrary to what I have said elsewhere,[4] it was indeed practical questions of choice and planning, and not the larger ideological questions, that first roused Yugoslavia from her dogmatic slumbers. With his doctrine of 'socialist commodity production' (Ch. 3, Sec. 2) Kidrić did try to provide an ideological underpinning for his views on a freer market. But that is dry stuff, far less exciting than the ideological innovations served up by Tito himself. These were two in number: the doctrine of the withering away of the state, with its un-Marxist assertion that the planning bureaucracy forms part of the state *proprement dit*,[5] and so may be asked to 'wither away'; and the doctrine and practice of workers' councils.

The workers' councils came in quite suddenly, and without the longer gestation period to which the free market itself was subjected. By the end of 1949 the first experimental councils had arisen in the larger factories, with an advisory role alone, and in the latter half of 1950 all enterprises, including state shops and farms, were handed over to councils with much the powers they have today. Also in 1950 price and output decisions were devolved to enterprises, in accordance with Kidrić's original preoccupation.

The intellectual origin of the workers' councils was perhaps with Tito himself. Certainly it was he who introduced them to the

---

[1] *Komunist*, March 1949.
[2] 'Theses on the Economics of the Transition Period in Our Country,' *Komunist*, Nov. 1950.
[3] *Komunist*, July–Sept. 1950.   [4] *Encounter*, London 1957.
[5] See Ch. 17.

Skupština on June 26, 1950.[1] As we show in Ch. 18, he could quote no Marxist source for them, but derived them directly from the 'withering away of the state', which he misunderstood. Tito's new doctrine on this latter point was the third great Yugoslav innovation. It was purely ideological, and we return to it in Ch. 17.

It is striking, and very typical of Communism, that not only is it impossible to infer workers' councils from the withering away of the state, either in general or by quotations from Marx, but also this immense upheaval was introduced without any discussion. From fairly extensive bibliographies I can trace just two publications on the subject before Tito's speech of June 26th,[2] which committed the country to this course of action. Moreover, as we have seen, Tito and Kidrič seemed to run on parallel lines, never really meeting. Neither in his speeches refers to the reforms of the other, or seems to have been inspired by them. At least, however, it is plain that in practice without Kidrič's advocacy of a freer market there could have been no workers' councils, for they would have had nothing to administer—as later transpired in Poland (Sec. 7). Without Tito, Kidrič would have seemed ideologically unattractive, without Kidrič, Tito would have had no substance with which to back his dream.

On the technical, model-building side the command economy was largely abolished and enterprises were permitted to seek their private profit. The central control mechanisms which necessarily remained were not, however, such as come naturally to a western welfare state. That is to say the principal control mechanism is neither interest, turnover tax nor material licensing, but qualitative banking controls and regulations as to the disposal of profit. Starting from the Stalinist organization which had been imposed upon them, the Yugoslavs scrapped nearly all of it except its financial provisions, and turned these into the main weapons of control. Thus not only were there no physical targets any more,[3] there were no monetary targets for current production or cost either. Only the wage-fund maximum and the regulations for disposing of profits remained. These latter were the *pièce de résistance* of the whole reform. The

---

[1] *Komunist*, July–Sept. 1950. Djilas made no identifiable contribution at this point. His real originality, while he was still a Marxist, lay in his doctrine that the Party must wither away simultaneously with the State. But this came after the economic reforms, and did not affect them.

[2] Drago Gizdić, *et al.*, *O Radnickim Savjetima*, Zagreb, June 1950, 39 pages, print of a speech at a conference of Aug. 1, 1949; M. Nikolć, 'O Radnickim Savjetima', in *Vesnik Rada*, Belgrade, 4–5, 1950. The bibliographies used are *Bibliografija Jugoslavije* (books and pamphlets only) and that in the back of each issue of *Ekonomski Pregled* (includes articles as well).

[3] Except for a very few basic commodities like steel.

new regulations left the disposal of profit largely to the workers' councils, and the significance of this is best described in the thickest Marxist prose:[1]

So, first, in distinction from the present system, where the whole surplus value, apart from the wage fund which supplies the necessary labour, goes to the state treasury where it is united and again redistributed, where, as a result, enterprises cannot take part in the distribution of the surplus value, in distinction from that in the new planning and financial system only one small part of the surplus value goes to the state treasury, or in other words, the majority of the surplus value is administered by the enterprise or workers' council as the case may be.

It is, then, to the regulations for distributing profit that most attention was and is directed. New regulations are constantly coming out, and it would be tedious to list them. Three things are important, however. First, the 'one small part' flowing into the treasury proved disappointingly large, and has remained so. Secondly, strict arrangements ensure that more profit is reinvested than paid out in bonuses to the workers. Partly these arrangements are the taxes levied by authorities other than the federal government: every political authority has its own investment fund, especially the Komuna, the lowest of them all (cf. Sec. 9 below). Partly the League of Communists and the enterprise director bring pressure to bear on the workers' council to reinvest even what remains after these taxes, on behalf of the enterprise itself; and Yugoslavia is entirely totalitarian enough for such pressure to be effective.

Then, thirdly, the body, be it a political authority, an enterprise or a bank, that has funds to invest may do so more or less where it pleases. An enterprise is not absolutely bound to expand itself, nor is a local authority bound to support local projects; though in fact parochial spirit ensures that this is so. But projects refused local funds can always apply for capital from banks or from higher political authorities, and investment consortia are very common. Thus there is a socialist capital market, admittedly of a highly imperfect kind,[2] which gives the lie direct to the unimaginative assertion that investment funds can only be allocated administratively if they are not privately owned. On the contrary, in Yugoslavia much investment money is simply auctioned.

[1] B. Kidrić, Speech to Belgrade trade union *aktiv*, *O Novom Finansiskom i Planskom Sistemu*, printed by 'Rad', Belgrade 1951.
[2] Described by E. Neuberger in *Public Policy*, Harvard, 1958; and in *Quarterly Journal of Economics*, Feb. 1959.

Thus *investment decisions are decentralized but the overall volume is not*, even though investment funds are never centrally pooled. To the author of this brilliant conception, Boris Kidrić, must go great credit for successful ingenuity.[1] It follows that the bonus to wages which a workers' council may distribute out of profits has remained very small.

Thus the Yugoslav RM operates with different weapons, derived from its experience of central physical planning, but the end result is not very different from any other RM. In two other respects, however, there is a more considerable difference from western democratic market socialism. The first is that this whole decentralization was carried out partly in the name of workers' control, and workers' councils were made the 'theoretical or *de jure* owner' of the system in the sense of Ch. 1. This book does not discuss the efficiency and genuineness of Yugoslav workers' control, though it is essential to remember its ideologically causative role. As far as this book is concerned, a workers' council is not different from an independent socialist manager. The distinctions belong to the sociology of the enterprise, not 'modelology'. Secondly, in stark contrast to western nationalization, no central monopolies were set up—clearly that would have been in direct conflict with the basic idea—but individual enterprises which, within each branch of industry, competed amongst themselves. Thus the British National Coal Board—a socialist monopoly in a naturally competitive industry—is anathema to a Titoist. Doubtless this has led to a far more rational price mechanism and allocation of resources than would have been the case, *ceteris paribus*, with a series of centralized public boards of the western type. But the actual rationality of Yugoslav prices and outputs must by no means be exaggerated. The turnover tax remains extremely high and irregular in its incidence, the differential profits tax referred to above has much the same effects, the railway system has hardly yet been touched by reform, and foreign trade only began to be rationalized in December 1960.

[1] Other changes must be dismissed, in a book on this large scale, in a footnote. The wage-fund maximum, mentioned above, proved to be a transitory anti-inflationary device. The self-interest of the workers' councils ensures that no unnecessary labour is employed, much as under capitalism existing shareholders resist new issues. Another transitory device was a tax on under-capacity use of plant; experience has shown that it is enough for the general atmosphere of the economy to be dynamic and aggregate demand sufficient. Again a system of this kind makes incomes unequal between one enterprise and another; so basic wages are regulated by normal collective bargaining and state action, while excessive profit distributions in particular enterprises are restrained by a differential profits tax.

In agriculture, Tito at first undertook a violent collectivization campaign (1949), to demonstrate his orthodoxy. But production fell, and after 1950 more and more things were questioned. So in 1953 agriculture was decollectivized—an obvious concession to the rural population in Yugoslavia's strained international position. While it is true that Yugoslav agriculture has grown and prospered since this measure the ideological justification is still awaited. All that the Yugoslav Communist Party can offer is that along with decollectivization they established an upper limit of ten hectares on land holdings,[1] and that machinery, irrigation works, etc., are held by voluntary co-operatives. It is hoped to socialize agriculture gradually and voluntarily, by the increase in the new types of capital good, held thus co-operatively, vis-à-vis the land itself, held privately. Latterly there has also been a great efflorescence of small private craftsmen in town and country. They may hire a very few employees, and they make considerable incomes. All in all, only a distinct minority of the labour force is employed by socialist enterprises in Yugoslavia.

There remains in existence a considerable central planning apparatus, engaged partly in 'persuasive' and partly in 'epiphenomenal' planning, as described in Ch. 4.

6. The next big model change—prior indeed in time to the decollectivization of Yugoslav agriculture—comes from the Soviet Union. This was the amalgamation of the collective farms in 1951: a measure associated with the rising young agricultural politician, Khrushchev. The average ratio of amalgamation was two and a half to one, but since 1951 the number of kolkhozy has continued steadily to shrink. At the time the amalgamation brought no serious changes in the MTS or in the planning procedure, though it undoubtedly made later changes possible. In these fields Khrushchev's proposal simultaneously to set up 'agro-towns' was defeated.[2]

7. The Polish *coup d'état* of October 1956 brought, in the long run, surprisingly little change. Indeed, after Communist order had been re-established, the ill-disciplined and factious Polish Communist Party was so little able to agree on changes that in practice

---

[1] Curiously enough a legal upper limit on peasant holdings is very unusual in a Communist country. Since the whole peasant system is scheduled for liquidation all attempts to regulate it are an admission of defeat, of its permanence, Large peasants are persecuted as kulaks, but are not forced to subdivide their land. There is also, of course, good economic sense in this, since large peasants have a much greater marketable surplus.

[2] Ch. 16, Sec. 7.

a kind of *immobilisme* set in similar to that of the French Fourth
Republic. Despite the merely intellectual ferment and innovation
in Poland, the Russians have introduced quite as many organizational changes since 1956, simply because they agreed on what should
be done. Immediately after October Yugoslavia was the
preferred model. The workers wrung from the Communists
workers' councils, which differed from the Yugoslav model in
that, first, they had indeed been wrung from, not imposed by,
the authorities, and secondly central physical planning remained.
The Party gradually re-established its power, the central planners
never relinquished theirs, and by 1958 the Polish workers' council
had been reduced to a mere formality. In the long run probably
more important changes within the nationalized sector were, first,
that Poland was the first bloc country radically to reform its wholesale prices (1959). Resisted by Stalinist elements, this reform both
made possible greater decentralization of decision[1] and improved the
rationality of central decisions. The principle of the reform was that
wholesale prices should have internally the same proportions as on
the world market. This was clearly right since the world market
represents the opportunity cost of any material to a country, whether
it be centrally planned or not. Secondly, new and independent units
were instituted between the planning ministries and the enterprises
(1958). These were the 'unions' (zjednoczenia). In principle and
origin the union is a voluntary co-operative body founded by the
enterprises in a given branch of industry, and is another imitation of
the Yugoslav model.[2] But like the workers' council it has been per-
verted by the resurgence of central Communist power into a mere
transmission belt of planning orders. It thus happened that at the
moment when the Russians were changing their intermediate planning organ from a branch to a territorial one the Poles were strengthening the branch principle. It appears to be purely a coincidence
that the Polish zjednoczenia and the Soviet Sovnarkhozy were being
founded at the same time. The zjednoczenia were the product
of two years' previous discussion and date from the period of
maximum Yugoslav influence, while the Sovnarkhozy in U.S.S.R.

[1] Ch. 6, Sec. 6.
[2] The Yugoslav 'chambers of commerce' are genuinely voluntary bodies which represent
a branch of industry before the government, circulate technical information and inform
members of each others' investment plans. One of their principal functions indeed is, by
circulating this latter information, to prevent the duplication of investments to which local
patriotism in Yugoslavia is prone. Soviet enterprises formed very similar units during the
NEP; they were, however, more frankly monopolistic than in Yugoslavia, and acted to raise
prices in a very straightforward capitalist way.

sprang fully armed from the head of Khrushchev—their period of gestation was about three months.

In agriculture the Polish October led to decollectivization, but, typically, an incomplete one. As in all communist countries in which a peasant agriculture is suffered to remain until collectivization, there had been in pre-October Poland no upper limit to a peasant's holding, nor was any introduced in the more liberal atmosphere after October. In consequence, the Polish decollectivization was ideologically even less well grounded than the Yugoslav. Subsequently (1959) the so-called Peasant Agricultural Circles were founded: government-sponsored but voluntary co-operatives for holding machinery, encouraging improvements, etc. These have their roots in pre-war Poland, and are probably in no way an imitation of Yugoslavia, although the resemblances must greatly complicate Poland's defence of her agricultural deviations in Moscow. Typically, few peasants have, as this is written, joined them.

8. The next major event in chronological order is again Soviet: the substitution of the *territorial* for the *production* principle, i.e. of the Sovnarkhoz for the ministry as an intermediate planning unit in industry and construction (*not* agriculture, transport or local services). The approximately 25 ministries dealt each with a group of related products, and enterprises ancillary to their production, wherever located. The approximately 100 Sovnarkhozy deal each with all enterprises in a given territory, whatever they produce (Ch. 8). It suffices here to say that this is no basic change in the model; the reform was of almost exclusively political inspiration and had the aim of moving the non-party state bureaucracy away from Moscow, so that the senior civil servants should not be more powerful than the local communist party bosses, by reason either of their presence in the capital or of the great size of the units they controlled. For the party was, as all political parties, organized territorially: there was, and is, a Communist Party of Azerbaijan, but there has never been a Communist party of the oil industry. So when the political or ideological need arose to subordinate the state even more fully to the party, it was a good move to reconstruct the state on the territorial principle and make sure that the intermediate planning organ was as small as and subordinate to the intermediate party organ. The Sovnarkhoz arose indeed from the post-Stalinist discussion of decentralization, but there is no necessary connexion between a *re-location* of intermediate authorities or a *redistribution*

of their competences and an increase in their independence. Such decentralization as has undoubtedly occurred in U.S.S.R. has quite other causes, or is at most due to side effects of the Sovnarkhozy: the fact that they are much more numerous than the old ministries, the increase in power that they bring to local party bosses, the great geographical distance between them and Moscow, etc. It would have been perfectly possible to combine decentralization with the old ministries,[1] and most of the decentralization has been due to a direct increase of the powers of the enterprise and a rationalization of prices.

9. In *China* the Stalinist model remained more or less intact, subject to the exceptions discussed in Ch. 9, until May 1958. In May of that year, in conjunction with increased Sino-Soviet tension and a swing to the political left in Peking, the Chinese *People's Communes* were founded. Formally the People's Communes are the Chinese substitute for kolkhoz amalgamation. Where the Russians had combined two and a half of the old collective farms into one, the Chinese amalgamated approximately forty, simultaneously making this very large body into the local authority of the state, responsible for civil registration, the local militia, small industrial enterprises within its boundaries, etc. The responsibility for small industry as well makes the People's Commune an *ersatz* Sovnarkhoz, while its coincidence with the organ of local government makes it unique. The People's Commune is thus not a collective farm at all, but a sort of all-embracing concentration camp. Its constitutional position has no parallel in the Soviet Union or Poland, where the economic administration— at least in industry and construction—is separate at every stage from the ordinary functions of state.[2] But it has—though no Chinese Communist would admit it—a parallel in Yugoslavia, where the local authority is also called Komuna, and has had since 1953 considerable nominal powers over the agricultural and other enterprises within its geographical boundaries, especially in the field of investment. Indeed, as explained in Ch. 1, Sec. 2, the Komuna is an alternative *de jure* owner to the workers' council in the Yugoslav system. Leaving such constitutional and ideological niceties aside, the Chinese People's Commune is further discussed in Ch. 17, Sec. 4.

[1] As was indeed decided at the Central Committee meeting in Dec. 1956, when Khrushchev temporarily lost his majority.
[2] For the view that the Sovnarkhozy will survive the withering away of the state proper see Ch. 17, Sec. 2.

10. While the Chinese were getting out of line the non-Polish satellites of U.S.S.R. were getting back into line, by switching from the production to the territorial principle. They did this, however, with a difference: using the ordinary organs of local government instead of setting up a parallel hierarchy à la Sovnarkhoz. Partly this was under Chinese influence—Chinese extremism appealed with especial force in Bulgaria; and partly it was a commonsense saving of administrative effort. It should be borne in mind that before these reforms, local government had rather the same economic responsibilities in every Communist country. These resembled those in other countries: domestic construction, local roads, drainage, water, 'buses, etc. It was thus far more logical to hand over large industry and construction to local government than to new units. Moreover, there were Soviet precedents for it, in Stalin's 'union-republican' and 'republican' ministries.[1]

Thus the question is rather why Khrushchev poured the territorial principle into the particular mould that he chose. The answer is, as already indicated, political and accidental: his suspicion of his technocratic colleagues at ministerial level, Pervukhin and Saburov, and his hatred of the rival Party leaders who openly bid for their support, Malenkov and Kaganovich. Above all, his defeat by this combination at the Central Committee meeting of Christmas 1956 must have rankled. So his prime determination was to destroy the technocratic ministries, and he chose the simplest possible reform: to hand over just their functions and no others to smaller *ersatz* ministries not located in Moscow. Moreover, there was a precedent for so doing, in the old Sovnarkhozy of War Communism and the early NEP. These had had, at least in light industry, surprisingly similar functions and status to the new Sovnarkhozy.

In the satellites, Poland and China, the old Sovnarkhozy were not even a memory. Nor was there any parallel to the quarrelsome, grass-roots-loving peasant Khrushchev, with his hostility to city slickers and technocrats. Nor was there any threat from the technocrats, or of a 'Managerial Revolution', since in all these countries Communism was too recent for there to be any technocrats of good Party standing. So in Poland and China the territorial principle took no root at all, in the satellites only by imitation and in much improved form.

[1] A 'republican' Ministry was under command of the republican Gosplan. In a 'union-republican' Ministry planning was a central function but the operation of certain (not all) plants was decentralized to the republican level. On 'planning' versus 'operation' cf. Ch. 7, Sec. 8.

In its own way Yugoslavia too has a territorial principle. Since 1953 the organ of local government (Komuna) has been the principal authority for investment decision over all economic enterprises in its area.[1] So great, indeed, are the powers of the Komuna, and so metaphysical the language in which it is praised, that it rivals the workers' council itself for the position of 'ideological owner'. The Komuna acquired this status not from an economic but from a political event: the new Constitution (strictly constitutional law) of 1951. This paid much lip-service to the purest Rousseauian direct democracy, especially at grass-roots levels. In Yugoslav political theory the Komuna is the basic organ of power, enjoying all the residual rights not specifically reserved for higher bodies. The 1953 reforms were merely the implementation of this in the economic field.

Very likely, too, Khrushchev got the whole idea of a territorial principle from Yugoslavia, during his 1955 visit. The Sovnarkhoz, or even better, the satellite organ of local government, is a Komuna without a market, responsible for current operation as well as investment.

In his own way Tito has also forestalled the Managerial Revolution. His free market, local authorities and workers' councils also leave no great central ministries, no place for top technocratic brass; and the party has a wonderful lever in the party fraction on each workers' council. Thus seeking simply reform, 'democracy' and general de-Stalinization, Tito made impossible a technocratic conspiracy of the kind that nearly unseated Khrushchev in December 1956. And no doubt this largely explains Khrushchev's interest in him; he cannot but have observed that there are no Saburovs and Pervukhins in Yugoslavia. The new Khrushchev model is a sort of Stalinized, non-market Titoism.

[1] For the purely economic tension between the production and territorial principles in Yugoslavia, cf. Ch. 8, Sec. 11.

CHAPTER 3

THE PECULIARITIES OF MARXIST ECONOMIC THOUGHT

Ah love could thou and I with fate conspire
To grasp this sorry scheme of things entire;
Would we not shatter it to bits, and then
Remould it closer to the heart's desire.
                    Fitzgerald, after Omar Khayyam.

Our task is not to study economics, but to change it. We are bound by no laws. There are no fortresses the Bolsheviks cannot storm. The question of tempo is subject to decision by human beings.—S. G. Strumilin, *Planovoe Khozyaistvo* 7/1927.

1. This chapter assumes a basic knowledge in the reader of Marxist economics and general ideology. It is certainly no substitute for such knowledge, but builds upon it in order to point some contrasts between Marxist and 'Mainstream' economics. As few elementary expositions of Marxism are written by economists these points are normally neglected. We begin with the major differences of basic presupposition, linger on the absence of 'welfare' economics, and then proceed to minor, specific points.

Marxism has no interest in economic choice, or the distribution of scarce resources between competing ends, i.e. in what many Western economists believe to be the chief concern of economic science. Marxists do not (until very recently) bother their heads about such questions as the correct price relations between different commodities, or the desirable extent of the international division of labour. They are interested instead in the liquidation of capitalist classes, in the industrialization of the country, the building up of a new intelligentsia, the raising of living standards or defensive potential. 'Welfare economics' is thus an intrusion into their system. We describe in Sec. 2 the general contours of an economics without a scarcity concept.

By origin, Communist economics is what the Germans call a *Stufenlehre*. In nineteenth-century Germany economics was dominated by the historical school, whose main objective was to discover through what institutional stages (Stufen) the world economy is passing century by century. They were not interested

47

in such minor matters as economic choice or the detailed analysis of the behaviour of the entrepreneur; indeed not in influencing government policy or in making small adjustments of any kind; but in predicting how things would go. In the early years of this school Marx was himself a student, and he was himself one of its greatest innovators and exponents. His debt to British economics is very great in detailed matters, for instance in the precise form of his theory of value. But the spirit of his economics is essentially German, not British: neither descriptive (how do entrepreneurs behave?) nor analytic (why is free trade a good thing?), but historicist (why is socialism inevitable?).

To German historicism the Communists, beginning with Marx himself, have added an interest in *making* things go in the direction desired or predicted: for a determinist to desire is to predict and to predict is to desire, yet it is still one's duty to further by all means in one's power that which is in any case inevitable. They added, then, to the German historicist's scientific prediction the politician's urge to influence events. As Marx himself said, 'the philosophers have only *interpreted* the world, in various ways; the point, however, is to change it'.[1]

Then, thirdly, Communist economics is not descriptive. For one of its functions is to be the theology of the ruling group, and like all theologies that have arisen within, or in revolt against, the Judaeo-Christian tradition it contains a large number of supposedly factual dogmas. Other religions rely on self-confessed myth, which is not to be understood as fact in any ordinary sense; or confine themselves to normative propositions. But Marxism is a secularized religion of a Western kind, and therefore demands that its myth be taken quite literally. It must thus close to itself whole areas of fruitful scientific enquiry. We find, for instance, until very recently in Poland, nothing about entrepreneurial behaviour, not even about the behaviour of socialist entrepreneurs. We do not find in the works of Soviet economists a study of how the socialist manager actually does conduct his socialist factory under the planning system, because of course that would be bourgeois objectivism. The study of Western living standards, deproletarization under capitalism and the Managerial Revolution is similarly theologized; and we meet very often that typical

[1] Theses on Feuerbach, XI.

phenomenon of the religion that includes a lot of factual dogma, the fundamentalist.

The fourth difference between Marxist and Western economists is very similar: it is the general attitude of messianism. Marxists believe that they are moving towards heaven on earth. Economic heaven on earth is precisely the last stage or Stufe. This of course is a legacy from nineteenth-century socialism. All socialists, probably even today, and certainly then, believe that we can and should move towards an economic millenium. Now of course if we are moving towards this economic heaven on earth, called 'Communism', obviously any sacrifice of the prosperity of present generations, any sacrifice of morality—which in any case we have learnt to call bourgeois morality—is justified. Nothing—absolutely nothing—may stand in our way since we are moving towards what is, quite literally, paradise. The essence of Lenin and his successors is simply this, that they are the executors of the prophet Marx. People who apply a totalitarian doctrine in practice must naturally subordinate all means to the end.

The recognized scheme of stages is as follows: the primitive economy, slavery, feudalism, a bourgeois revolution followed by capitalism, a proletarian revolution followed by socialism, and then communism. *All* of these stages are inevitable, owing to the dialectic of the changing 'relations of production'—the immanent causal logic of the economic process itself.[1] 'Socialism' here means that phase after the proletarian revolution when productivity has not risen sufficiently for everybody to have as much as he wants. In Marx's words: 'from each according to his capacity, to each according to his labour'. One has still to pay people by results because there is not enough to go round. Productivity, which incidentally has been rising during the whole period of capitalism, continues to rise under socialism even more swiftly than before, until in the end we enter an age of plenty called communism, in which the slogan becomes 'From each according to his capacity, to each according to his need.' To this basic concept, which colours everything that Communists do, we return in Ch. 17.

[1] Nevertheless no satisfactory account exists of what exactly the 'bourgeois revolution' was or is. For once it is recognized that the post-medieval European kings were on the whole opposed to feudalism such events as the English Civil War, the Glorious Revolution of 1688 and even the French Revolution became very difficult to fit into the Marxist scheme. Moreover, Marx himself toyed with a separate chain of development in Asia, which included the 'Asian mode of production' (K. Wittfogel, *Oriental Despotism*, Yale 1955, Ch. 9). This presented Stalin with obvious propaganda difficulties, so he suppressed it.

E

Fifthly, Communist economics is basically a study of power. The 'relations of production' generate 'classes', distinguished from each other by their 'ownership' or non-ownership of the means of production, and history is the tale of the war of these classes. Ownership thus connotes political power, and is all-important. No facts are more threatening and heretical than the divorce of ownership from control by limited liability companies under capitalism, and the Managerial Revolution. Even after the take-over of power differences in the form of ownership retain an obsessive fascination: e.g. kolkhozy are inferior *because* they represent merely co-operative, not state ownership; it is *risqué* to sell off the (nationalized) MTS equipment to them *because* it is a step away from 'socialist' ownership, however beneficial to production; Full Communism will entail a new kind of ownership, etc.[1]

History is thus the product of economic and specifically of ownership change, and it might be thought to follow that Marxists looked at all human affairs from an economic point of view. But the reverse is the case: being specialists in taking political power and creating Utopias they treat all economic thought as a means to this end. Their basic intellectual stance is thus utilitarian: however much politics is the 'superstructure' and economics the 'base' it is on the superstructure that they stand, viewing the base not as an object of unbiassed study in itself, but solely as the foundation of their political position. This is perhaps especially clear in their agricultural policy, and in their attitude to the scarcity problem, which we must now describe in more detail.

2. 'Scarcity' arose out of the marginal utility theory of value. Although the Menger-Jevons revolution occurred more than ten years before his death (1883), Marx seems never to have written one word on marginal utility itself: striking proof of his self-confidence and self-isolation. *A fortiori*, then, he neglected scarcity. In Engels's letters I have been able to trace five references to marginal utility and none to scarcity.[2] Though he is extremely sure the theory is

---

[1] These points are developed at greater length in Ch. 17.

[2] Jan. 5, 1888 to Danielson; Oct. 15, 1888 to Danielson; Feb. 8, 1890 to Sorge; Sept. 12, 1892 to Conrad Schmidt; Sept. 29, 1892 to Kautsky. These letters appear only to be available in Russian translation: *Marx-Engels Sochineniya* (Marx-Engels Institute, Moscow), vols. xviii and xix. This edition, the most complete we have, is notoriously incomplete owing to political vicissitudes. Mr. Vsevolod Holybnychy (*Studies on the Soviet Union*, I/1, Institute for the Study of the U.S.S.R., Munich, 1961) argues vigorously against my position. But he quotes no criticism by Marx of *marginal* utility, only of the pre-1871 subjectivist theories of value. In other words Marx attacked the wrong theories of his youth but neglected the correct theory of his old age. On this compare also Meek and Wiles, *Oxford Economic Papers*, Oct. 1955, Feb. 1956.

wrong, and disparages it with his usual vulgarity, he refers to it only very briefly in passing. Engels seems never to have seriously discussed the truth of the theory: it was obviously untrue since it contradicted Marx. His hostile interest was due to the growth of Jevonian socialists—the Fabians, who were thus heretics to be opposed. This, no doubt, is why the first reference is only in 1888, nearly two decades after the theory began.

As to 'scarcity' itself, the origin of the idea is best described by Professor L. Robbins. He gives as sources for his ideas solely writers who wrote after 1870: Menger, Mises, Fetter, Strigl and Mayer.[1] Even then the idea did not come in with a bang, as had the subjective theory of value itself, and anyone might be excused for not noticing it. Nevertheless the connexion between 'scarcity' and the subjective theory is extremely intimate. For the latter theory, being the first to emphasize demand, was the first to raise the question of the ends of economic activity in any detail. But once we start seriously considering economic ends, whether of the consumer or of the State, we see at once that they compete, and 'scarcity' economics begins.[2]

Now Marxist economics had already crystallized by this time. But, what is more important, all 'objective' theories of value, which base value on cost alone, be it labour-time or money cost, must hold average cost to be constant with changing output; otherwise output determines value and we are bound to ask, what determines output? Such theories are peculiarly ill adapted to any form of scarcity concept. The introduction of such a modification would have required the thorough recasting of the whole structure. For if output has no influence upon cost (since cost is constant) nor upon utility (since utility is neglected), the attention of the economist is not likely to be directed towards quantities of production at all. All the more then will he neglect the question of relative quantities, i.e. the allocation of scarce resources. Decisions as to relative quantities of output are the essence of welfare economics and the welfare pricing rules are merely tools whereby the correct quantities may be obtained. But in Marxist economics the pricing rules are the essence, for it is through the settlement of prices that exploitation, surplus value, capitalist breakdowns, etc., arise. A system of

[1] *An Essay on the Nature and Significance of Economic Science*, 2nd ed., p. 16. He quotes, however, an earlier reference in H. H. Gossen, *Entwicklung der Gesetze des menschlichen Verkehrs* (Brunswick 1854), p. 231.
[2] French economists have actually used 'rareté' as an alternative for 'utilité limite'.

Political Economy, in other words, which analyses the distribution of the national income between classes, and is used as a basis for historical predictions as to the course of *political* events, stands in sharp contrast to a system of *Economic* Economy which is by definition interested in the relative priorities of various kinds of output. To put it another way, Marx did not design his economics to assist in the planning of a socialist society—indeed, he vehemently eschewed all such aims, as he considered them Utopian. His economics set out to prove the inevitability of a proletarian revolution. Hence the very word 'economic' has an entirely different meaning in Marxism—it refers to the 'relations of production', the social or class relations between producers determined by the technique of production used.

It follows that when Marxists speak of the 'law of value', as they very often do, they are not usually thinking of scarcity or social utility. The 'law of value under capitalism' means for them exploitation and the class struggle. When they speak of the 'law of value under socialism' I am bound to confess that I do not see what many of them—until recently—have in mind at all. In fact they simply talk nonsense, since on the one hand the law of value cannot refer to exploitation, which has been abolished, and on the other the problem of choice is not recognized. Indeed many of them find a rather feeble content for the law of value by referring it to mere accountancy, which does, of course, persist under 'socialism' (khozraschet, Ch. 2 above). This is very clearly brought out by the anonymous (and therefore authoritative) article, 'The Teaching of Economics in the Soviet Union',[1] which created such a stir in U.S.A. during the Soviet-American honeymoon. There was a passage (pp. 519–27 in the translation) insisting on the importance of the law of value under socialism, which other Soviet economists had denied. Mr. Carl Landauer[2] was led by this to head his comment 'From Marx to Menger', but inspection of the passage shows that the anonymous author has no notion whatsoever of choice or consumer's sovereignty in mind—indeed has nothing very clear in mind at all. The same must frankly be said of P. M. Sweezy, who in his section 'Law of Value versus Planning Principle'[3] commits the crass error of maintaining that the one can *replace* the other—

[1] '*Pod Znamenem Marxisma*,' 7–8, 1943, translated in full in *American Economic Review*, Sept. 1944.

[2] *A.E.R.*, June 1944.

[3] *Theory of Capitalist Development*, London, 1952, p. 52.

as if a rational planning principle could be other than a law of value.

In their criticism of capitalism, again, Marxists point—as well they may—to fluctuations in the demand for goods due to speculation or avoidable changes in producers' incomes. But they do not recognize buried among these the fluctuations due to the rational play of consumers' sovereignty. They speak, too, of the 'disproportions' that may arise in an economy—between agriculture and industry in a backward country, between investment and consumption in a stagnant country, or as manifested even under 'socialism' in physical bottlenecks. They seem to think that all is done when these broad disproportions are abolished, not perceiving that the problem of choice exists apart from all such disproportions. The trouble is that *there is no Marxist micro-economics*, and therefore no grasp whatsoever of detail. There is only a nineteenth-century macro-economics of the *Stufenlehre* type. Surplus value itself is a macro-economical idea: Marx himself allows that its rate is an average for the whole economy, and that individual prices are settled on quite different principles,[1] and Sweezy abandons all pretence that a Marxist micro-economics so much as exists.[2]

The sole mention of scarcity in Marxist economics is in a somewhat different context, the distinction between 'socialism' and 'communism' described above. Under socialism there is still 'scarcity', while under communism there is 'plenty'. But the emphasis on the distinction is typically political, not economic. Scarcity raises problems of distribution, class enmity, and administration: 'here is this basket of goods, who shall have how much of it?'; not 'ought it to have been a different basket of goods?' or 'could it have been produced more cheaply?' The *economic* problem of scarcity is still not recognized. The approach to all subjects is with Lenin's classic question 'Who whom?' In contrast, modern economics starts by asking, 'How much of what?'

After Engels (died 1895) this gap in Marxist economic thinking has been extensively documented by marginalist economists[3] until the moment of the first Five-year Plan. Indeed some of these authors asserted that not only central planning but also public ownership was *theoretically* incompatible with rational choice. Incredible as it may now seem, this contention was for long accepted.

[1] *Capital*, iii, 12.   [2] Op. cit., pp. 128–30.
[3] F. A. Hayek (ed.), *Collectivist Economic Planning*, London, 1935; B. Brutzkus, *Economic Planning in Soviet Russia*, London, 1935; T. J. B. Hoff, *Economic Calculation in the Socialist Society*, London, 1949, Chs. 4 and 5.

Soviet economists, behind their iron curtain, stood aloof from the controversy and it was left to Mensheviks, Labourites, Social Democrats, and other unworthy characters to prove the contrary.[1] This historical sequence of events cannot have endeared the concept of 'scarcity' to Soviet economists.

Terminological difficulties also beset the Marxist who would think clearly about rational choice. He sometimes understands how this is achieved in a capitalist market, but he thinks of a socialist market as a contradiction in terms, so that the choice problem must be solved in some radically different way.[2] For his understanding here is beclouded by the irrelevant distinction between 'commodity turnover' (Warenumschlag, tovarooborot) and 'product exchange' (Produktenaustausch, produktoobmen). A 'commodity' is privately owned, and its 'turnover' enables surplus value to be realized; a 'product' is publicly owned, and it is 'exchanged' merely for the convenience of society, by administrative means. Thus the usual Marxist obsession with ownership brings to the fore an irrelevant distinction, and obscures the fundamental identity of exchange in all societies, so far as it concerns resource allocation.[3]

Indeed the theory of choice is extremely disruptive of all thorough-going collectivism. It shows that choices centrally made are more likely to be wrong even than the choices of complete *laissez faire*, let alone of a *laissez faire* suitably modified and controlled. Why, for instance, expand or subsidize a nationalized industry when other sorts of commodity are required? It takes us away from the most rational allocation of resources. We shift from Lenin's 'capture of the commanding heights', a purely political argument for nationalization, to—what? It has never been satisfactorily explained, and if choice is our only concern trustbusting would appear equally satisfactory. Again, all talk of society's common economic goals, of production for use not profit, loses its sting. For it is primarily by profit that we know in any detail what the goals are. We may

---

[1] The proof reached its climax in A. P. Lerner's *Economics of Control*, New York 1944.

[2] Thus Messrs. I. Lapidus and K. Ostrovityanov in their *Outline of Political Economy*, Martin Lawrence 1929, describe fairly adequately resource allocation under capitalism (Secs 1–3), but their passage on this problem under socialism makes no sense (Secs 38–40).

[3] Not surprisingly the Yugoslavs have been forced to break through this thought-block. 'Product exchange' will only prevail under Full Communism; in the present stage of socialism there should be 'Socialist commodity turnover' (Kidrić, 'Theses on the Economics of the Transition Period in Our Country', *Komunist*, Nov. 1950; Hadzi-Vasilev, 'Collective and Individual Interests', *Komunist*, Belgrade, Dec. 1957). In a cryptic passage the same orthodox Soviet Academician K. V. Ostrovityanov says that Soviet state products under 'Socialism' are commodities (ed. Y. A. Kronrod, *Zakon Stoimosti*, Moscow, 1959, p. 18).

correct and modify, but we cannot scrap this basis without a vast statistical mechanism for the central decision of outputs in accordance with peripheral preferences such as Gosplan has never dreamed of.

As late as 1917 Lenin demonstrated his total ignorance of the problem:

> With such *economic* prerequisites it is quite possible, immediately, overnight, after the overthrow of the capitalists and bureaucrats, to supersede them in the *control* of production and distribution, in the work of *keeping account* of labour and its products by the armed workers, by the whole of the armed population. (The question of control and accounting must not be confused with the question of the scientifically educated staff of engineers, agronomists and so on. These gentlemen are working today and obey the capitalists; they will work even better tomorrow and obey the armed workers.)
>
> Accounting and control—these are the *principal* things that are necessary for the 'setting up' and correct functioning of the *first phase* of communist society. *All* citizens are transformed into the salaried employees of the state, which consists of the armed workers. *All* citizens become employees and workers of a *single* national state 'syndicate'. All that is required is that they should work equally—do their proper share of work—and get paid equally. The accounting and control necessary for this have been so utterly *simplified* by capitalism that they have become the extraordinarily simple operations of checking, recording and issuing receipts, which anyone who can read and write and who knows the first four rules of arithmetic can perform.[1]

Note the emphasis on accounting and control. This is still what Communists really mean by economic planning. Much of Soviet economics, especially its monetary theory, places enormous weight on mere accounting. The very word *khozraschet*, which describes all the main rules for managers, means economic *accounting*, not economic *behaviour*; it corresponds more to the English 'economize' than to the German *bewirtschaften*. Yet accountancy—essentially the same under communism and capitalism—with its preference for the average over the margin and for *ex post* over *ex ante*, is peculiarly unsuited as a guide to entrepreneurial behaviour.[2] The principal tenets of khozraschet are: minimize costs on your own initiative, avoid loss, and fulfil the plan. When the plan includes the quantities and prices of all outputs and inputs and even the identities of most of the suppliers and customers, this is very

---

[1] *State and Revolution*, v/4; italics his. He sang a very different tune in 1922 (speech to 11th Congress). In fact this celebrated quotation is a little surprising, coming from the hand of Lenin. For in fact what he intended immediately after the revolution was mere workers' control over a still functioning capitalist market, and not a 'single national state syndicate'. Doubtless he was confused in his own mind.

[2] Cf. Wiles, *Price, Cost and Output*, 2nd ed., Oxford 1961, pp. 55-8.

different from Professor Lerner's Rule,[1] the instruction to managers appropriate in a scarcity-conscious economy. Soviet money, again, is not an allocating but an accounting and controlling (i.e. checking) mechanism. This is principally evident in the role of the banks, which is by no means to allocate credit to its most profitable use, but to check plan fulfilment: no cheque from one factory to another is cleared unless accompanied by an invoice for goods, which the bank checks against its own copy of the plan laid down for the firm.

It follows that the word 'accounting' is very often misused in the literature of rational choice under socialism. It is of course possible for there to be a 'rational system of economic accounting' in a centrally planned society. But this has no bearing on the questions of choice and resource allocation, which are entirely separate, and indeed can be solved without accountancy of any kind, as in the free competition of small peasants. We must not say 'accounting' when we mean 'allocation'.

A reliable and meaningful currency is on a different footing here from mere accountancy. But rational choice would be very difficult in a *Naturalwirtschaft* owing to the extreme difficulty of exchange, and therefore the crippling imperfection of the various barter markets. It follows that those who depreciate the usefulness of money are usually unaware of the problem of choice. And all Communists in fact depreciate money in one way or another (see Ch. 17).

3. From these essentials we turn to minor points. Marxism has bequeathed many specific legacies to Communist economic practice, some of them very important. Many experts would disagree, for it is commonly said that Marx provided no blueprint for the proletarian state, holding that to be Utopianism; he claimed to be a scientist and he refused to predict, much less to lay down, what should be done after the revolution. In this he was reacting against the excesses of his socialist contemporaries. For instance, Fourier had laid down that the socialist society should be a 'phalanstery' consisting of about 1,600 people living on about 5,000 acres in a self-supporting village. There were to be 5 meals a day, 3 different kinds of free love, and at 25 months the children were to learn to shell peas. Eventually 2,985,984 phalansteries were to include all humanity, and they were to be loosely federated under an Omniarch. That was the kind of socialism which

[1] Op. cit., p. 64.

Marx knew among his contemporaries. He despised phalanstery-mongering, and to that extent it is true that he avoided laying down a blueprint for a post-revolutionary procedure.

But this can be much exaggerated: he was, after all, a 'socialist' and the very word entails certain beliefs as to the ideal economic organization. He was also a politician: he published political programmes. In the Communist Manifesto he listed ten measures for the immediate aftermath of the seizure of power, including a heavily graduated income-tax, the nationalization of the banks and transport, etc. In the Critique of the Gotha Programme he defined 'socialism' and 'communism', or rather the stages to which those names were later given. In *Das Kapital* he banished money from the socialist economy (Ch. 17). The common Western view, that 'Marx said nothing about Socialism', is simply false. It is largely a product of our pre-occupation with scarcity economics and optimal resource allocation. Since, as we have seen, Marx had never heard of this problem, it is not surprising that he did not say how it should be solved under socialism. For the rest, and especially on institutional matters, he said a great deal. He only failed to lay down a blueprint in that, although he was extremely free of obiter dicta about post-revolutionary policy, he yet was careful not to be too dogmatic, and not to bring it together into a single work entitled *After the Revolution*. So from scattered passages in his works the Communists took what points of policy they could. It is convenient simply to list them, though, taken from the vast corpus of his writings, they form no co-ordinated whole.

(*a*) Nationalization. To Marx this was the definition of socialism, and he certainly did not regard insistence on nationalization as Utopian phalanstery-mongering. On the contrary it was the indispensable pre-requisite of planning. For Marx and all his successors attach, as we have seen, a very exaggerated importance to questions of formal ownership, and find it a logical contradiction that a proletarian state should plan production the instruments of which are owned by the bourgeoisie. Now in practice the sophisticated line taken by Western economists, that ownership is *quite* irrelevant, is also exaggerated. *Small* capitalists do resist planning, whether by a bourgeois, a proletarian, or any other state. Combining ownership with control, they reach for their rifles when threatened with the loss of either. To take control of large industry on the other hand—what Lenin called the 'capture of the commanding heights'—need seldom be formalized by a change of ownership. For if their new masters are reasonable the salaried managers accept them without a qualm, and the previous owners, being mere owners, are powerless. Such nationalization has seldom been a very significant event, and planning can easily be introduced without it; but the extension of socialism to agriculture, when it came, shook the Soviet system to its foundations. Yet without the collectivization of agricultural ownership there could have been no agricultural planning. The issue of public boards versus direct governmental ownership has already been covered (Ch. 1, Sec. 2 iv).

(b) Agricultural Co-operation. This is the doctrine of the *voluntary* kolkhoz, a huge subject for which this book has no space.

(c) Equal Pay. This does not mean equal pay between men and women only, though that is included. It means also equality between commissars and fitters. The historical fate of this demand has been discussed in Ch. 2, Sec. 4, but its ideological background is best taken here. It is not clear whether Marx saw that his definition of 'socialism' (to each according to his labour) was in contradiction to his constant recommendation of equal pay. Certainly when Stalin eventually abolished equal pay he quoted Marx's definition of 'socialism' with every justification. The extreme egalitarianism that reigned until Stalin may be explained as follows. There are many passages in Marx that recommend equal pay, and there is only one passage—that in the Critique of the Gotha Programme—upon which inequality could be based. This work was not among those most commonly studied. Moreover, almost all other socialists had demanded equal pay, and for all their professed contempt Communists have never shaken themselves quite free from non-Marxist socialist influences, where the canonical works do not specifically condemn them. Above all the Paris Commune (1871) had been much honoured by Marx—'that was the Dictatorship of the Proletariat'[1]—and it had instituted equal pay. So it was a good socialist thing to believe in, and immediately after the Revolution the Bolsheviks did in fact most painfully introduce it. In consequence, when it was abolished by Stalin in 1931–34 he did seem to be deviating from the true doctrine. It is no accident that Khrushchev is gradually reverting to equality, or that the Stalinist extremes of inequality have not been known in other Communist countries.

---

[1] F. Engels, Introduction (1891) to K. Marx, *The Civil War in France* (1871), sub fin.

(*d*) Planning. The capitalist economic system was condemned because, amongst other reasons, it was not planned. It was seen by Marx as a mere chaos, the 'anarchy of the market'. In other words he had not the slightest conception of consumers' sovereignty, the functions of a free price mechanism or the problem of allocating scarce resources between competing ends. *No more had any of his capitalist contemporaries.* No one was then in a position to show why *laissez faire* is not anarchy. The whole explanation of how *laissez faire* establishes consumers' sovereignty was evolved after Marx had written *Das Kapital*, that is to say after the great economic revolution of the 1870's, when Jevons and Menger invented marginal utility and the subjective theory of value. So for Marx capitalism was chaos and to abolish this chaos there had to be central planning.[1] He did not, of course, say how to plan, since he did not in the least understand the subject. On this single omission seems to rest the whole myth that he said nothing about the socialist future.

(*e*) Increased production and productivity. Marx, in fact, was interested in economic progress, which is a great deal more than can be said for most Western economists until the 1950's. They were interested in the problem of choice, in why *laissez faire* is, or is not, an ideal means of establishing consumer sovereignty. This problem is important, but has very little to do with economic progress (see Ch. 11). Marx wanted and approved of 'capitalist accumulation'— what we call investment—and advances in technique. He liked to think that inventions were constantly being made whereby products were becoming cheaper. He liked to think that there was a large group of disgustingly rich men amassing huge fortunes and ploughing them back into industry, because all this is economic progress. Admittedly he stated—quite falsely—that under the capitalist system the fruits of this were absolutely reserved for the capitalist class. But he did not therefore disapprove of it because he saw and stated that these fruits could be seized and enjoyed by the proletariat in due course; and naturally he predicted even more rapid economic progress after the revolution. His very definition of Communism was a stage in which there is much more productivity than under socialism.

(*f*) Worship of capital. Capital, then, is for Marx the great dialectical demiurge. His theory of value was a labour theory, but

[1] On the Yugoslav heresies as to this cf. Chs. 17 and 18.

the hero of the plot and the title of the book is Capital. He had a capital theory of history. It is capital that destroys the independent peasant and artisan, that creates the propertyless proletariat, that virtually socializes itself by its own concentration in the hands of a few monopolists, that causes the ever more damaging swings of the trade cycle until the final crash and revolution—a revolution that consists in a transfer of the owership of capital. And thereafter, as we saw in (e), from a malign tumour capital becomes a beneficent yeast; it is capital that raises productivity and the accumulation of capital that brings us from socialism to communism, where the dialectic ceases from troubling and human history glides to its eternal rest.

The post-revolutionary role of capital is hardly more than implicit in Marx himself. But in Lenin and still more in Stalin it is developed with almost idolatrous excess. Capital must be borrowed from abroad (Lenin); capital must be wrung out of the peasants by 'socialist exploitation' (Preobrazhensky); capital must be allocated interest free (almost everyone); no, interest must be charged, and this interest is necessarily and obviously the fund for further accumulation, so that capital reproduces and accumulates itself (Gorev, etc.).[1] The most capital-intensive method of production is *eo ipso* the most technically advanced.[2] To the whole plan era in particular we may well apply Marx's sarcastic description of the 'high' capitalism he himself knew:

'Accumulate, accumulate: that is Moses and all the Prophets.'

(g) Yet there is much mysticism about labour too. How not, if Marxism is a doctrine for the labour movement and rests on a labour theory of value? Marxist economists do not allocate scarce resources between competing ends; on the rare occasions when they consider this problem they 'distribute labour among the branches of production'. Neither land nor natural resources nor abstinence nor initiative, it is implied, are original factors of production at all; they are not, then—or so it would appear from many writings—scarce and their correct allocation is of no theoretical interest. Or again, Full Communism is presented as a shortening of the hours of labour much more than as an increase in the standard of living (which is not quite the same thing). When in 1928 Stalin and Bukharin

---

[1] An ancient Marxist idea about pre-revolutionary society, but only occasionally applied inside the Soviet Union, Cf. Grossman, *Quarterly Journal of Economics*, August 1953, p. 323.
[2] Cf. Grossman, op. cit., p. 337, and our Ch. 14-16.

wanted to do down Trotsky and Zinoviev, who thought the industrialization plans too ambitious, they promised pie in the sky to the people; and the precise kind of pie was the 7-hour day, shortly to be introduced.[1] Or, thirdly, when plans are not being fulfilled and production lags, what more natural than that the working class should perform in its own interest—though on the indispensable initiative of the workers' state—overtime at normal rates or Sunday shifts without pay?[2] The number of days in the week has several times been altered in order to increase or diminish the number of workdays in a year. Thus there have been 5-, 6- and 10-day weeks, sometimes concurrently in different factories.

At the moment (1959) the 7-day week is universal, with about 48 hours' work. But there is in U.S.S.R. a whole programme for reducing the work-week to 40 hours in a few years; a figure far lower than the free Western worker chose to work when he was down at the Soviet standard of living. Moreover, so low a figure is plainly undesirable in conditions of cold war, yet the reduction programme proceeds relentlessly. So curious a decision, flouting both popular taste and strategic necessity, can only be attributed to ideology. The Draft Party Programme[3] associates this reduction of hours with the march towards Full Communism (Ch. 17). Thus a prime characteristic of Utopia is a work-week of specific length.

Last and not least, work is a well-known Communist patent medicine. It is seriously thought to cure bourgeois heritages, criminal proclivities and deviations from the Party line. This is by old tradition the foundation-stone of Communist penology, and has resulted in 'corrective' labour being almost the only possible type of sentence.

4. No rent must be charged on land or interest on capital. This merits, by reason not of its importance but of its interest to Western economists, a section to itself. As far as the rent of land is concerned there are no exceptions to this rule, nor can it be seriously maintained

---

[1] And so, incidentally, it was: in the form of a three shift system in textile factories! This vast increase in night-work was actually passed off as a fulfilment of the promise of the 7-hour day. Today, however, shift-work is not much more common than in free countries, having been found very unpopular and inconvenient but not particularly profitable. Cf. S. Schwarz, *Labor in the Soviet Union*, London, 1953, Ch. 6.

[2] Called in U.S.S.R. Communist Sundays—a phenomenon of War Communism. Similarly after the *coup d'état* of February 1948 the Czechoslovak workers were made to do 'victory shifts' on Sundays. Latterly China has been the main scene of unpaid overtime; appropriately since her Party is the most extreme.

[3] *Pravda*, July 30, 1961.

that compulsory agricultural deliveries are a substitute at least for agricultural rents. There is no charge whatsoever for urban ground-sites.[1]

There are, however, several exceptions with regard to interest, although it is most specifically condemned by Marx (*Das Kapital*, I/22/3). In a command economy—as opposed to the Yugoslav economy—the rate of interest has no monetary or macro-economic function in any case, but it could have an allocative or micro-economic function, and much controversy has raged about this within and without Communist countries. It is possible to exaggerate the topic's importance since interest is such a very small charge in a rational pricing system, and there are so many far greater elements of distortion such as the extreme variability of the turnover tax.[2] It is interesting to list, for completeness' sake, the exceptions made by the Soviet-type economies to the rule that capital shall have no charge:

(i) Short-term capital in the nationalized sector. The object of this charge is to discipline enterprises, to make them use short-term capital sparingly and to keep down their liquidity—it is a cardinal principle of central planning that enterprises should be as illiquid as possible so that they cannot by dishoarding escape from the pressures of the centre.

(ii) On long-term capital lent to private individuals (e.g. for private house construction) and to kolkhozy. The theory here appears to be that the nationalized sector is a sort of large state capitalist who has every right to make a charge for the funds lent to ideologically inferior sectors.[3]

(iii) On international lending, even inside the Communist bloc. It is not clear what the ideological or practical justification is for this; possibly it simply arises from Stalin's determination to improve the Soviet terms of trade no matter with what trading partner. But the interest rates are kept, for propaganda purposes, low and in compensation the other terms of the contract are normally rather stiff.

---

[1] Cf. Ch. 6, Sec. 13.

[2] Compare Wiles, *Oxford Economic Papers*, June 1957; also Ch. 10, Sec. 4.

[3] Other features of the Soviet economy indicate the same general attitude. Thus turnover tax is not charged by one nationalized enterprise to another, but is charged by the nationalized sector not only to consumers but also to enterprises in other sectors. It is not, then, strictly correct that consumer goods are taxed and investment goods are free of tax; rather is it the case that all goods sold outside the nationalized sector are taxed, including such investment goods as bricks sold to individual peasants or such current means of production as (until recently) petrol used by kolkhozy.

(iv) On the small savings, voluntary and involuntary, of the population. That the state should pay interest to the population might have the same kind of ideological justification as in (ii), or these payments might be simply based on practical necessity.

We thus find to our surprise that only one major class of lending conforms to Marxist ideology in being free of interest: that of long-term capital from the budget to nationalized enterprises. In none of the other cases, however, is interest charged in order to improve the rationality of resource allocation but rather for almost any other end. Surprisingly enough there appears to have been no ideological questioning or defence of these practices.

On substitute and shadow rates of interest compare Ch. 6, Sec. 12.

5. The rule that heavy industry should grow more rapidly than light is an exceedingly important inference from the words of Marx. It merits a chapter to itself (14). Similarly the whole tremendous movement towards Full Communism (Chs. 17, 18) involves an immense economic revolution. Its objects are purely ideological, and it is surely impossible for the most purblind empiricist to deny the importance of ideology now that this movement is becoming a practical programme.

6. We now turn to certain persistent Marxist habits of thought which have no direct result in specific economic institutions as had the items above, but which nevertheless colour the whole of Communist economic thinking and are very worthy of note.

(a) Just as in Marx, so today it is normally assumed that average costs are constant as output changes. The concept of the margin was until very recently quite unknown and remains thoroughly unorthodox. This raises special trouble in mining, agriculture and forestry where, as we have seen, differential rent is not charged even though it is an old Marxist concept. This is far from surprising since Marx himself never seriously considered the function of rent but merely noted its existence under capitalism. This does not mean of course that practical men fail to recognize rising costs. Thus, with a fixed plant, it is recognized that overtime and the over-straining of machinery raise costs. Or on a different scale the drive into the virgin lands met with a great deal of practical managerial opposition, but the law of diminishing returns remains a heresy, and it is most significant that this opposition was defeated. Similarly linear programming has run into trouble for its marginalism.

(*b*) Profit is a source of all savings, i.e. there are no small savings. This assumption stems from Marx's fairly accurate analysis of the class structure of his day, which permitted too low an income to the proletarian for him to save any significant amount. But the consequence of this has been the absence from Communist thinking of any concept of *voluntary* saving: in Marx saving is as it were the plough-back of the capitalist class—indeed the consumption of capitalists is treated as a mere deduction from the surplus value achieved and it is implied that 'accumulation' is the primary end of capitalist production. It thus remains rooted in the Communist (including Yugoslav) tradition that saving is achieved at the point of production, out of gross profits, before any income is distributed to the factors of production. This basic idea has led to the extremely high rates of turnover tax, which are habitually justified in terms of the saving which they make possible, and to the comparative neglect of savings accounts, state bond issues, etc. It could perhaps be argued that this is a more efficient and realistic concept of saving than the opposite one with which Western economists approach the subject: that saving is essentially accumulated voluntarily, by individuals, out of income, and that corporate plough-back and budget surplus are exceptions to this rule. It also seems to be the case that right-wing Communists rely more on voluntary saving out of income: compare the controversy between Preobrazhensky and Bukharin in the 1920's, in which the latter defended the private saving of the kulak while the former wanted the state to 'exploit' the peasantry by means of high prices for industrial goods.[1]

(*c*) There is a strong tendency to begin one's thinking with intermediate, not final, products; thus five-year plan drafts start not with such and such a bill of consumer goods or armaments but with production targets for steel, electricity, oil, etc. This arises originally from the fact that Marx held to a *labour* theory of value; i.e. value derived from the ultimate factors of production and was channelled through the intermediate factors on its way up to the consumer—an exactly opposite notion to the (correct) Western doctrine. Consumption in Marx, and more especially under Stalin, is treated as a drain or leak from the never-ending cycle of production. It is thus ideologically sound to begin all one's thinking with production (Ch. 14, Sec. 11). It will be observed that this preoccupation with intermediate products tends to make an

[1] A. Erlich, *The Soviet Industrialization Controversy*, Harvard 1960.

input/output matrix indeterminate (Ch. 10, Sec. 15). Similarly when a Communist government desires faster growth it does not say, let us cut back consumption to give elbow-room for investment, but let us increase heavy rather than light industry (Ch. 14). It comes, as we see in Ch. 15, Sec. 15, to the same thing in the end; but the Communist naturally first thinks of all the particular intermediate products connected with investment, not with the volume of investment itself. *This habit of thought leads on to central physical planning;* for if production is to be decided before consumption the maker of the intermediate product must be told by someone other than the consumer what to do.

(*d*) Marx wrote at a time when 'production' was still very narrowly defined. It may be recalled that the Physiocrats spoke as if only agriculture were productive, and carried the rest of the economy on its back. Smith and Ricardo expanded this to all material outputs, but still excluded services. Marx took over their definitions unaltered, and services were not included in the concepts of 'production' and 'national income' until after the Jevonian revolution. This ascribed the price of everything to its scarcity, and so could not make any distinction between a service and a good. Albeit services and for that matter goods not exchanged for money still receive short shrift from Western national income accountants. The services of housewives, and the goods they produce such as home-baked bread, are the principal case; and as we see in Ch. 12 these omissions are very important in any comparison with Communism, which permits significantly fewer housewives.

The Marxian definition of the national income excludes services to this day, even in Yugoslavia.[1] The pressure of commonsense and administrative necessity has, however, gradually forced the inclusion of such marginal items as the work of shop assistants and passenger travel to and from work—both of which directly contribute to final material production. Education, medicine, the planning bureaucracy and the armed forces, however, are still excluded. That is, incomes earned in these fields are treated as transfer payments.

One would expect such a definition to be as the philosophers say emotive, to bring into disrepute the excluded activities. Certainly

---

[1] As a rough rule of thumb, add 13% to the Marxist definition to obtain the Western definition of NNP.

F

it has as far as trade and distribution are concerned. But then they are not merely 'unproductive'; they are by their nature 'capitalistic', i.e. responsive to supply and demand, unstable. This sector has constantly suffered from under-investment, low wages and general social disregard. Education and medicine on the other hand have been highly regarded and rapidly expanded. It is thus difficult to be sure how much practical influence this ancient fallacy has had.

PART II

PLANNING AND RESOURCE ALLOCATION

CHAPTER 4

ALLOCATION MODELS AND THEIR INDICATORS

1. THE ground is now cleared for the detailed study of the Communist command economy. In this chapter we do not discuss the rationality of resource allocation, merely the various stimuli and systems which are or can be used to allocate resources.

The communist countries have tried out many 'models' of a command economy, and others yet untried are theoretically possible. Models may differ in many respects; we are concerned here with the differences between models with respect to, not ownership, but the system of allocating scarce resources. The allocation systems using a free market hardly require analysis in terms of separate models except in so far as in some of them it is profit that is maximized while in others it is profit plus the notional salary of the entrepreneur or even profit plus the whole wage bill.[1] There are also cases in which profit is not maximized but some rule of thumb such as a conventional profit margin per article is used. Such matters are familiar in Western economics and receive only cursory treatment in a book essentially devoted to the command economy. We list our models as follows:

(i) Perfect central allocation in physical terms without money. We shall call this Central Command, or CC. Because there is no money consumers and workers cannot be influenced through the market, so they must be included in the plan and receive orders. Labour is directed, wages are unrelated to effort and consumers are given predetermined bundles of goods. This is the ideal at which the Party originally aimed. After it had failed, but not until then, it was dubbed 'War Communism' and abandoned. It is, of course, our model (x) in Ch. 1.

---

[1] In Yugoslav industry since 1958 all wages have been declared abolished, i.e. they have been merged in the profit. This should in theory lead to the maximization not of the enterprise's profit combined with the workers' bonus, but of the whole wage bill plus profit.

(2) The same, but with money. The money in this case would be a purely accounting device and have no significance for resource allocation, even in the markets for consumer goods and labour, which of course are supposed to be directed under system (1). I introduce model (2) simply to point out that money can be passive throughout. Passive money corresponds essentially to what Soviet economists call 'ruble control'. The purpose of passive money is to throw up useful checks on plan fulfilment; typically the bank has a copy of the enterprise plan, and may not clear a cheque that is not in agreement with the plan. Prices expressed in such money may be irrational to the extreme limits of fantasy, for all anyone cares, since they affect no economic decisions and their irrationality in no way makes them less useful for auditing purposes.

In elementary Western textbooks money is said to serve as 'a means of exchange, a standard of value and a unit of account'. When we discard the institutional blinkers of these textbooks we see that the three functions are separable. In (1) there is no money at all. In (2) it is only a unit of account. In the remaining allocation models it is also a means of exchange, which phrase is here taken to mean that the exchangers react to price changes in a normal market manner. As to 'standard of value', it is not clear to me what this is. Presumably it is a measure which statisticians can use with confidence, i.e. which gives 'rational' answers to the particular questions they ask. On this definition, we discuss money as a standard of value in Ch. 12. If on the other hand 'standard of value' means 'store of value' then we are asking whether money is an adequate 'means of exchange through time'; and this raises very well-known questions about the course of prices into which we need not enter. Finally note a new function of money: as a 'means of command'. This is when the command economy expresses its targets in money, and we discuss this at length in this chapter.

(3) The so-called 'centralized market' economy (CM). In this system all decisions as to *intermediate* resource allocations are centralized in a planning office, but the choices of consumers and workers and of the public bodies that allocate land and capital are taken on purely free market principles; and it is the business of the central planners simply to react faithfully to these decisions taken by the ultimate consumers and factors of production. In other words industry is one big public monopoly, distributing its resources on free market *principles* but by central methods of *administration*. This is the 'freest' or most 'liberal' type of central

planning. Psychologically very different from the other models, it is nevertheless by definition a command system since the actual orders, on whatever principles they rest, are given by the centre.

Ideally in such a model wages are settled by individual bargaining, but trade unions are of course practically possible. But the important thing is that, trade unions or no, both consumer and worker are liberated from the command economy and react to it normally on a market. In other words we have moved from model (x) to model (iv) in Ch. 1. Money is a means of exchange at either end of the shrunken planned sector. Inside this sector it is mainly a means of command, but could be to some extent one of exchange, according to the precise degree of independence enjoyed by the enterprises. In any case the prices of intermediate goods are rational, and influence the decisions of the central command.

(4) We can invert the previous model (ICM). Here the initiative lies with the central planners, whose decisions as to the allocation of intermediate resources are the determinants of the whole. Within this sector money is, on the whole, passive, but outside it it remains active as in CM; only it is now used by the central planners to persuade the consumers at one end and the factors of production at the other to conform to the predetermined plan. This is achieved by suitable wage differentials and by a varying rate of turnover tax. ICM, then, is the nearest of the pure models to Soviet actuality since 1928, when there was a reversion to central planning, but money was retained and rationing and direction of labour rejected. However, there has been rationing from time to time and various forms of concealed, and sometimes not so concealed, direction of labour; also capital and land are centrally allocated, which again impairs the purity of the model. Moreover, in the central planning of consumer goods output the Gosplan undoubtedly pays attention to consumer demand as expressed in the shops, so that elements of CM are also present, although they are based on the arbitrary and irrational prices that are to be expected under ICM. It is of the essence of this model that heavy and variegated indirect taxes or subsidies are imposed on whatever factory cost emerges from the accounting system—and this cost itself is likely to be arbitrary. For the retail prices must be so set as to clear the market and must therefore, given that the outputs are predetermined, be unrelated to cost. This necessity finds expression in the Soviet phrase 'method of differences': the turnover tax is not a fixed percentage either of

retail prices or of factory cost but simply the *ex post facto* differences between the two. This model claims most of our attention in this book.

(5) Capitalist war economy (CWE). Here the pattern of final production only is decided by the central planners, and sold off to consumers as in ICM. Managers choose what intermediate goods they want to fulfil their plans, and bid for them in the open market. Intermediate goods are thus assimilated to labour in (4). In this way what is doubtless itself an irrational plan is fulfilled by the allocation of resources that is most rational in terms of it: there are not too many canals as opposed to railways, or too many big tractors as opposed to small. And the chosen method of rationally allocating resources is the free market. The final product-mix may be (a) administratively binding on managers by direct orders or (b) monetarily attractive through a special system of prices ex-factory. The best example of such a model is a war economy in a Western country: the government as consumer of arms determines a large part of the pattern of production administratively (it does not, as in peacetime, bid on the open market for arms or allocate contracts by competitive procedures, since such methods would be too inflationary). The arms manufacturers, however, are free to economize in their use of labour and raw materials for the fulfilment of these orders.[1] This model has been very largely discussed in Western literature and has not yet occurred in industry under Communism. But it is satisfactory to see how it fits in: as a watered-down version of ICM.

Moreover (c) in agriculture this model is very common all over the world: both the Soviet zakupka and the British and U.S. price support programmes, and the many crop valorization schemes of underdeveloped countries, are essentially CWE. The government uses the price mechanism to influence the entrepreneur's outputs, but his choice of inputs is free (much less free, it is true, in U.S.S.R.). The difference is, of course, that the government then sells off the outputs it has bought, as best it may, to the private consumer: whereas in CWE proper (*a* and *b*) the government is the consumer.

Mention of war reminds us that the similarity of war economics to socialist economics is of course a cliché. Improvements in the rationality of both go hand in hand. The accepted doctrines have

---

[1] Albeit in practice scarce raw materials are often allocated administratively, which impairs the theoretical purity of the model.

been that a weapons system should be independent of cost, and that military supply should be centrally planned in physical terms, without leaving possibilities of substitution or profit-maximization open to subordinate military units. These doctrines are now very rightly called in question in U.S.A., especially for minor items. Compare the interesting article of Mr. Norman V. Breckner,[1] which throws up very many coincidences with the problems treated in this book.

(6) Full market (FM). By this is meant the pure competitive system with decision-making decentralized to socialist firms. Capital and land are owned by various public bodies which invest them on free market principles. Price-making is also decentralized and competitive.

(7) Regulated market (RM). This is the same as (6), only improved by a number of indirect controls, which leave the profit motive intact, but canalize its operation. Such controls would be anti-trust, utility rate regulation, etc.—all as necessary in a socialist as in a capitalist market economy, since in both profit is locally retained and can be enhanced by anti-social practices. This is in essence the Yugoslav model, though the imperfections in Yugoslav markets are very great by capitalist standards, and it is not clear to what extent Yugoslav Communists accept the ideology of it.

2. Innumerable mixed systems are of course possible, nor is it even pretended that the seven here presented exhaust the list of pure ones. In a mixed system, the boundary between the two types of model commonly runs along some easily recognized divide. Thus the 'allocation model boundary' is often between investment decisions and current production decisions. In the Soviet Union, investment is almost always on ICM lines while current production contains large elements of CM and (nowadays, with locally fixed prices) even FM. In Poland, which is in so many respects a liberalized Soviet Union rather than an imitation Yugoslavia, investment tends to be CM or ICM and current production RM or FM. This particular model boundary can hardly be drawn in Yugoslavia, where investment projects are rather carefully attuned to the (admittedly, very imperfect) market. Note that we are not talking here of the overall total of investment, but of choices between particular investment projects.

[1] 'Government Efficiency and the Military Buyer-Seller Device,' *Journal of Political Economy*, Oct. 1960.

The boundary may run between macro- and micro-economic decisions. The overall total of investment in Yugoslavia is certainly not subject to the free market, since a high percentage of business saving out of profits is imposed by law. No Communist economy hands over this essential decision to the free market.

Above all, the boundary may run between superior and subordinate units in the chain of command, the lower units approximating more—or less—to FM than the upper. This possibility raises a whole maze of new complications, most of them actualized by Communist attempts at *decentralization*. We treat this topic at length in Ch. 7. *In this chapter we assume no decentralization to subordinate planners.* Every decision is taken either in the capital city or by the enterprise. The allocation models given above describe only how the centre works. There is no intermediate authority. The workings of enterprise are given below, under the heading of 'indicators'.

Finally, of course, the economy is divided into a co-operative and a nationalized sector, and the 'allocation model boundary' as described above may run between them, i.e. along the structural model boundary. May, but not must, for in the Soviet Union co-operative and state trade are subject to precisely the same régime, and co-operative and state manufacturing to all but the same régime.

The most important of all these mixed forms, both in theory and in practice, is that of CM in investment and RM in consumption, which we shall call CM/RM, or *allocation model* (8). For it is used by nearly all underdeveloped countries today and by U.S.S.R. during the NEP. The state invests according to a pre-determined plan, and then hands over the enterprise to be currently used according to the market. The *ex post facto* profitability of the enterprise helps to determine further investment plans. But profit is an ugly word, and more sophisticated investment criteria—most of them quite false—in fact abound.[1] Bad investment choices are then sanctified by tariffs and subsidies, so that the allocation model becomes ICM/RM. Nevertheless when used properly allocation model (8) has the huge advantage of combining a forced *volume* of investment with rational choice of *particular projects*.

3. Clarity demands here a discussion of what we shall call *epiphenomenal planning*: planlike activity in central offices that does

---

[1] Many are listed in Ch. 16. The Pakistani government uses the capital/output ratio as its basic criterion, an absurdity I have attacked in *Economic Digest*, Karachi, Autumn 1960.

not change the situation from what it would have been in a purely market economy. Epiphenomenal planning may be of three sorts: *the merely predictive plan, the currently altered plan*, and both together. Real planning is, by definition, not to predict nor merely to react, but to produce a document and stand by it in the short period at least.

There is a difference, then, between a command economy and a planned economy. The former includes CM, in which the centre tells indeed the enterprises what to do, but in constant, currently adjusted reaction to external events (chiefly technical progress and changing consumers' tastes). CM is precisely the 'currently altered plan', i.e. no plan at all. A planned economy on the other hand can include several sorts of RM, and especially the Yugoslav sort, to which we shortly come. It is possible to hew to a plan by means of indirect controls only.

The 'currently altered plan' may be due to mere inefficiency, not principle. In CM it is a matter of principle, but in ICM and War Communism a currently altered plan would arise from unforeseen technical necessities: the simple failure to use the method of balances leads to bottlenecks which force the current alteration of the plan. On all this cf. Ch. 10, Sec. 11.

The 'merely predictive' plan is commoner. It is fatally easy for the government of some market economy to say in some detail what ought to be done, and publish it under the name of a plan; but provide no enforcement mechanism. We may examine a few instances. The first is the 'control figures'[1] published by the Gosplan during the NEP. These were books of figures for the most important outputs and activities during the coming year. Trotsky said they were or ought to be orders, but there was no enforcement mechanism and enterprises were guided by the market instead. Unwilling to admit their futility on the one hand, or to exaggerate their importance on the other, the Gosplan described them as 'orientation' (orientirovka). This sort of equivocation is precisely what we mean by 'epiphenomenal planning'. There is, incidentally, direct continuity between the 'control figures' and the annual plan of Stalin's command economy. The control figures of 1929 *were* his annual plan, but they were no longer mere orientirovka. The transition to a command economy *consisted* in giving the 'control figures' legal force.

---

[1] Kontrol'niye Tsifri, which is, to repeat, better translated 'check figures'.

To the development under Stalin that under Attlee presents a sharp contrast. The 'Economic Survey for 1947',[1] published in February 1947, had many of the stigmata of a real plan (including of course its arrival after the period to be planned had already begun!). Yet the whole document rested on a basic confusion, as the following passage shows:

> The Government has no direct control over the way in which man-power moves; it can seek to influence the movement in a number of ways, but the ideal distribution of man-power would involve changes of such magnitude that it would be impossible to bring them about by any means short of complete war-time direction. Even if direction were used, the transfer of labour would be limited by lack of accommodation. The following table sets out a distribution of man-power at end-1947. This is neither an ideal distribution nor a forecast of what will happen; it represents the approximate distribution which is needed to carry out the objectives in paragraph 118 and which the Government considers can be achieved if the nation as a whole sets itself to achieve them.

Needless to reproduce here the table of man-power targets. Enough that at the end of 1947 right-wing economists were making fun of the extreme under- and over-fulfilment of the various targets; a thing far from unnatural since no enforcement mechanisms had been provided. Yet the 'Economic Survey for 1948'[2] continued in the same almost self-contradictory strain:

> Labour is not at present, and is unlikely to be in 1948, the limiting factor in economic activity as a whole. Any projected distribution such as is given in Table XXI is therefore largely a forecast of the results of other factors, and if some figures turn out differently it is not necessarily in every case a matter of regret. But the labour forces proposed for coal, agriculture and textiles are targets in the full sense. They are numbers believed to be required to reach specific objectives in the set of output and export targets decided for 1948. The attainment of these man-power targets is among the first necessities in 1948.

Note the apologetic tone, induced by the failures of the previous year. In subsequent years the 'Economic Survey for 194(x)' has said more and more about 194(x-1) and less and less about 194(x) itself, until in March 1954 the word 'for' was dropped from the title, so that now in effect 'Economic Survey 1960' merely means the economic survey of 1959, published in 1960. This, then, is the history of the Soviet 'control figures' in reverse. Both started as 'epiphenomenal planning'; the one developed into the operative planning of a command economy, the other withered away into mere undisguised prediction and then ceased to be even that.

[1] H.M.S.O., Cmd. 7046, para. 128.
[2] H.M.S.O., Cmd. 7344, para. 186.

The Yugoslav example is intermediate. Since 1950 the Yugoslavs have continued to publish an annual plan and to cast material balances (500 of them in 1960). In 1957 they returned to FYPs, which they had abandoned in 1950.[1] Yet the enterprise remains bound to the market, and there is no direct enforcement mechanism. True, it sets up its own 'plan', i.e. expression of intentions. But in the harmonization of state and enterprise plans the latter have primacy. Moreover, the enterprise may diverge from its own plan in the direction of the market, and so *a fortiori* from the state plan. Asked about this, a Yugoslav planning official said to me first, 'Contradictions between enterprise performance and the plan? But the planner has monthly situation reports coming in, so he knows how to plan according to realities'; and secondly, 'You can't argue with an enterprise.' Superficially, then, Yugoslav planning is not only 'merely predictive' but 'currently altered' as well. Yet this is not quite so, for the indirect mechanisms of RM are employed to establish approximately the goals of the state plan. Moreover, the federal government's investment funds are directly allocated in such a way as to further the plan. Thus Yugoslav planning is a complicated mixture of 'merely predictive', 'currently altered' and genuine; and the enforcement mechanisms for the genuine planning are mostly indirect but also in part direct.

Yugoslavia thus does not differ widely from what we have above called model (8). There too we find an investment fund that is really allocated by the centre (a larger proportion of the whole than in Yugoslavia), but a series of material balances the role of which seems to be merely epiphenomenal. There too current operation is exclusively, and investment—even centrally allocated investment—mainly, on market criteria, but a patina of planning overlays the whole. There too the logical status of the very word 'planning' is in question.

But in many cases what seems to be epiphenomenal planning is really *persuasive planning*. This is the making of recommendations, which are not orders but do have real influence. The enterprise or subordinate authority does sometimes reject them, but usually follows them after some argument. Such a type of planning might be the issue of technological circulars by a ministry of agriculture anywhere in the world; or the influence on industrial location decisions sometimes exercised by the British cabinet; or the activities

[1] The formal date of expiry of the first FYP was 1952. On present planning techniques cf. Branko Kubović *et al.*, 'Economic Planning in Yugoslavia,' *Jugoslavija*, Belgrade 1959.

associated with the name of M. Jean Monnet in France; or the relation between any Western Treasury and central bank.

Persuasive planning is not any particular model; it simply describes the 'enforcement' mechanism. In the same way epiphenomenal planning describes the utter lack of any such mechanism. In fact the latter often consists of detailed current output targets on model (4), while persuasion takes the place of actual orders in model (8); i.e. it is used to affect investment decisions alone.

4. What makes the human agents in the economy 'tick' under these various systems? *Any motive or goal influencing the enterprise shall be called an 'indicator', any principle of action influencing the planner a 'criterion'.* An indicator is thus detailed instruction or vague operation order handed down from one's administrative superior, a criterion is the way in which one's autonomous superior guides himself. If, as in models (6) and (7), the enterprise has complete freedom, it is indifferent whether its motivator is called an indicator or a criterion. Thus typical indicators are physical output targets, physical input/output ratios, wage-bill limitations, monetary output targets, etc. Typical criteria are the optimum allocation of scarce resources in view of consumer demand, the preference for heavy over light industry, autarky, the population of unoccupied areas, etc. Profit can be either. This chapter is about indicators, not criteria.

The word 'indicator' (pokazatel') is extremely common in Soviet economics, and it is indeed only a command economy that makes the concept necessary, for in market economies where the firms at the circumference take all the decisions, such as our FM and RM, profit is virtually the only indicator. That is to say, firms must look to their profit as determined by the market and simply cannot afford to set themselves cost targets, physical targets, etc., etc., except in so far as these latter help them to make more profit. But in a centrally planned economy, an establishment may be asked to follow any course of action, any policy, by the central planning organ, and the latter will ensure the physical survival of the establishment, whatever its profit.

We are not concerned in this chapter with whether the decisions, choices and relative outputs indicated are rational; that is largely a matter of criteria, and is discussed in Ch. 5. Our question here is whether the indicators themselves are effective, i.e. the extent to which any given indicator fails to perform its overt function properly. Does it in practice indicate something different from what was really intended by the setter of the indicator, or does it leave obvious loopholes, so that a firm or establishment may fulfil the letter while disobeying the spirit?

5. *Profit*, being to repeat both indicator and criterion, is in a rather special position and deserves prior treatment. Private profit is the greatest *spontaneous* indicator, the one the enterprise will itself choose when no other is imposed on it, the one that (normally) most tempts it to evade the plan.[1] It is notoriously an imperfect indicator from the point of view of the community which may be deemed to have 'set' it, in that private and social profit diverge (social profit is in a sense the 'criterion' of the community). They may do so (a) because of monopoly, which causes profit to 'indicate' a lower output than required by the correct allocation of scarce resources; (b) because it is often technically impossible to make a charge for some cost or revenue. The two stock examples here are, on the one side, factory smoke, the damage of which is, in default of arrangements to the contrary, borne by people other than the owner of the factory; and on the other side, farm drainage, which can benefit a neighbour's farm and indeed might only be profitable if that benefit was taken into account, yet he cannot be forced to pay his share; (c) because private profit is an insufficient incentive, especially for the introduction of new techniques. People do not always in practice maximize their profits; they often merely avoid loss, and therefore tend to prefer the quiet life to the strains of innovation; (d) because consumers are irrational and make the 'wrong' things profitable to produce. The stock examples here are on the one side, alcohol, and on the other, milk; (e) because prices are wrongly set by the government, or based upon incorrect private accounting.

Yet so ingrained in Western economics is the idea that profit is the sole indicator, that when we wish to correct these imperfections we usually do it by seeking to make the right course profitable, i.e. by some tax or subsidy, rather than by issuing an administrative order to the firm to do something else. This is, of course, the essence of our RM.

Non-profit indicators are in fact more common in free economies than we tend to suppose. State schools for instance, and a national health service, can hardly in the nature of things be subjected to the profit motive, though we may doubt if that would be so completely

---

[1] Not, however, when the managerial bonus depends on plan-fulfilment, and profit is not an important indicator thereof. See however Sec. 11 below.

unworkable as enthusiasts for the Welfare State believe. Anyhow, as things are, such social services are little enclaves of CC in FM or RM economies. Targets are set, such as pupil/teacher ratios, success in examinations, average age at leaving school, turnover of hospital beds, reduced incidence of disease, etc., etc.

Nor are non-profit indicators anything like absent in the conduct of capitalist business: even free actors in a market need not be profit-maximizers. The engineer may impose some partial input/output ratio that appeals to his engineering conscience, or the entrepreneur may simply want a quiet life, or a firm may have a policy of very high, or very low, or conventional profit per article regardless of the total profit, etc., etc.[1] Such actors can and do all drive bargains on the market suitable to their own 'indicators'. There is, in fact, no single-indicator economy in practice. Above all, the Rule of Lerneresque socialism, that marginal cost should equal price, is itself a non-profit indicator; but probably not such a one as an enterprise would freely adopt. Its enforcement would undoubtedly mean a degree of CM.

6. Under RM we speak not of indicators but of *controls*. Strictly what we call 'controls' in ordinary Western parlance are only negative; i.e. controls not instilling a new motivation into the enterprise, but canalizing the action of its existing, spontaneous motivations: be they profit maximization or anything else. In CC, however, the indicators, always excepting profit itself, which is what a human being would spontaneously seek in most situations, are *positive controls*; they do not so much stop the manager from doing some of the things he wants as make him do a particular thing. A negative control, we might say, is not an indicator but a counter-indicator.

Not all physical planning is CC, nor all monetary planning RM. Thus building-licences, raw material rationing and consumer rationing are RM: the initiative is still the enterprise's and its motive is profit as usual, but the state intervenes by stopping some of the proposed purchases. Conversely it is CC if a production target is given to an enterprise, but owing to the complicated nature of the product the target is expressed in money terms: e.g. not '10 machine tools of specification 201/Q' but '10 million rubles worth of machine tools, any specification your customers arrange'. This latter is not essentially different from saying: '100 tons of machine tools, any

---

[1] Cf. my *Price, Cost and Output*, 2nd ed., Ch. 5, Sec. 9, Ch. 11.

specification your customers arrange'—and everyone would call that CC. But money clearly tempts the authorities to decentralize some of the decisions. It can leave much more initiative to the enterprise than in purely physical CC, and particularly so if prices are not centrally set.

Again all effective price control is CC, because if a list of controlled prices is published alone, enterprises will concentrate on imperfections in the list—on the articles it happens to make most profitable, or does not include; in particular on new articles, which it cannot include.[1] This disturbs the proportions of the various articles produced so very much that in practice the state must specify quantity and quality as well as price.

In the field of economics Communist totalitarianism has precisely this one great advantage, this one revealing stigma, that it can successfully use positive controls. Actually to tell enterprises what they shall do, as opposed to what they shall not do, requires very great political power; not merely a large administrative hierarchy but a powerful body of auditors and even a network of devoted 'economic informers' to report currently on violations. The whole quality of political and daily life is altered by such a system. This, to repeat, is why the true dividing line in economic affairs runs not between 'planned' and 'unplanned' (CC and RM versus FM) but between 'command' and 'market' (CC versus RM and FM). Of the protagonists of *laissez faire*, who suggest the opposite, it would be most charitable to say that they are blind to the simplest and most obvious facts daily to be culled from the world press.

To the common polarity of 'direct' and 'indirect' controls I can attach no meaning not already inherent in either 'physical/monetary' or 'positive/negative'. Since it blurs the distinction between these two pairs it is not useful.

7. There is, as we have seen, one form of a command economy where, of the free choice of the planners, profit remains the sole indicator. This model we called the centralized market system (CM). In it the government understands the scarcity problem as in a Western textbook, and the same economic theories underlie its actions. Only it centralizes all firms under what is basically one management, so that, for instance, profits and amortization quotas automatically revert to the centre, being only retained by the firm as a privilege; and no major decision may be taken without

---

[1] British, Polish and Soviet experience can tell of very many goods slightly changed and in no way improved, simply in order to beat price control.

reference to the centre, indeed otherwise than at the centre. Essentially, then, these firms are also mere establishments as under CC, branches of the single nation-wide socialist firm. However, labour, land and capital are still hired on a free market, and consumer goods and services are still sold on one. Rent and interest, therefore, remain operative categories, as do wages. Thus the ultimate factors of production and the ultimate outputs are subject to the same pressures as before, only whereas previously all intermediate products were also freely bought and sold, now all are centrally allocated on the profit principle. The government endeavours to make the same rate of profit on all commodities, to respect absolutely the changing desires of the consumer, to allocate capital only in accordance with profitability, etc., etc. Then the government is really only a very large public monopoly of the same kind as a firm in one of the pure market models. So long as its internal accounting procedures are strict, and obey the rules of the free market game, it is simply reproducing the free market results at great administrative cost. The same price, output and location decisions are taken at the centre as would have been taken at the circumference without delay and correspondence. This is approximately the model recommended by Oskar Lange in his *On the Economic Theory of Socialism*, except that here he recommends CM for prices only and would leave outputs to be decided by the managers on the profit principle (location he does not mention). We shall see later that there are strong elements of CM in all Communist economies.

8. But in proper CC all indicators are possible and profit is only one of them. What *makes* managers obey these indicators? In RM and FM the owner-manager simply takes the profit, and that is why it is an indicator. But for the hired manager the problem is different: he is instructed to seek profit, on pain of dismissal. In CC it is the same, only the indicator need not be profit. There is both carrot and stick. The stick is the force of the law (for the plan is a law and to violate it is a civil, in some cases a criminal, offence). The carrot is the attraction of the bonus the manager receives for fulfilling or overfulfilling the indicators. Of the enormously many possible indicators, we shall discuss only the most theoretically or practically important.

(i) The central planners, *on any model from* (1) *to* (5) *inclusive*, might base their directions to establishments solely on detailed physical output targets and specifications. They tell the establishments exactly what to do and that is the end of it. No initiative whatsoever is left to these latter. If at all practicable, this system is the most 'perfect' of all, more perfect indeed than profit itself, in the sense that only that is done which is required to be done (it will be remembered that we have not yet reached the question of whether the requirements are themselves desirable; that depends on the allocation model and on the planners' criteria). The only possible element of establishment initiative is that managers might be able to fulfil their output targets with fewer of each kind of input than laid down—and even that might be excluded specifically by the plan. Certainly the system does not leave room for cost-saving initiative which would entail the use of different kinds of input from those laid down. In this system, there need be no money— money in real life is the product of a degree at least of decentralization. If there is money, it is purely accounting, or passive, money, which has no influence of any kind on output or distribution. But with absolute centralization such money would be an entire waste of time, since equally adequate accounts could be kept *in natura*. When this system is extended from establishments to embrace both workers and consumers it is the original Bolshevik idea now called War Communism. One might wish so to frame one's definitions as to say that here there are no indicators, only direct commands.

9. All other systems of indicators are very complex, since they leave some initiative to the establishment. With indicators of type (i), whatever the allocation model, there is complete centralization of command and no local initiative, however much more liberal or rational some models appear than others. We now devolve some decisions on the enterprise, *irrespective of which model it is placed in*, and see how it uses this freedom. We retain until Ch. 7 the assumption that there is no intermediate planning authority between the centre and the enterprise.

Perhaps within a generally defined category of production, such as nails, which is obligatory upon the establishment, the details of quality, size, shape, delivery date, etc., and similar details of cost and technique of production, are left free. This introduces us to the all-important concept that the Russians call the *sortament*. Central planning is so inordinately complicated, and economic life such an infinite mass of detail, that in practice very many decisions must always be decentralized. It is here that the indicator comes into its own, taking on the character of an operation order rather than,

G

as in (i), of a direct command. The essence of the indicator problem is, what is its influence on the sortament and other decentralized decisions? All indicators have some *bias*, in that they tempt the establishment to misuse its freedom and violate the spirit of the planners' orders while keeping to its letter. This might actually improve the rationality of resource allocation: see Ch. 7, Secs. 5, 6.

Of all the achievements of Sovietology, the analysis of indicators other than (i) above seems the most difficult to codify. The two excellent books on this topic[1] present us with description, and are long enough to help us to empirical understanding. But scientific comprehension is another matter. Reflection tells us why this subject is so Protean: it is like trying to write a simple textbook of tax evasion. The interest and importance of the subject is that the enterprise is trying *not* to do what it is told: sin is multiform, virtue is more easy to generalize about.

In the next section, accordingly, we merely list the main types of output indicator. In Sec. 11 we deal with input indicators, and dispose of an ambiguity in profit as an indicator. In Sec. 12 we discuss the *sistema zakazov*. In Sec. 13 we distinguish the 'rationality' of criteria from the 'effectiveness' of indicators. Finally in Sec. 14 we attempt such generalizations as seem possible.

10. Normally what happens is that a customer or customers is named in the producer's plan and *contract(s)* must be concluded with them and written into the plan. In the Soviet system, it is extremely common for two subordinate units to be forced to draw up a contract with each other concerning details which the superior unit finds too difficult to administer. The contract is then submitted to th superior authority and on approval acquires the force of law. In this way subordinate authorities are compelled to entangle themselves in the general system of centralized command further than that system could conveniently do by itself. During the negotiation of the contract the supplier will press the customer to accept, and the central planners to authorize, delivery of the articles that most easily enable him to fulfil his plan. Once the contract is settled, all establishment independence, of course, ceases, but the damage has been done, the bias toward those articles that happen to be most profitable has been written into the plan. So:

---

[1] J. Berliner, *Factory and Manager in the U.S.S.R.*, Cambridge, Mass., 1957; J. Kornai, *Overcentralization in Economic Administration*, London, 1959. There is an excellent short statement in A. Nove, *The Soviet Economy*, London, 1961, Ch. 6.

(ii) Let the output targets merely specify a weight: e.g. 'produce 10 tons of nails'.

Then if the sortament is free this sets up a bias towards the larger and heavier articles, since concentration on them enables the target to be fulfilled with smaller fabrication costs; and the producer will press his customer to contract for these.

(iii) Suppose then that the authorities, finding that only large articles are being produced, switch to a physical output indicator by numbers, still leaving the sortament free. Then of course the bias is towards producing the smaller articles in the sortament, since this is now the cheapest way of fulfilling the physical output target.

(iv) Many other such elementary systems of erroneous indicators are possible. For instance, an area indicator might be set for window glass, which would then be produced in as thin sheets as possible.

So far in (i) to (iv) we have proceeded without money, or at least without active money. We may now introduce money, but thereby, as we saw in Sec. 6, we do not leave CC. Note that centrally fixed prices are always more likely in a Communist command economy than centrally fixed outputs, owing to the extreme ideological aversion of Communists from bargaining, money profits, etc.

(v) General output targets in some physical unit, then, and sortament left free, as in (ii), (iii) and (iv), but fixed prices for each article in the sortament. Let there be no monetary target formally laid down. Then the producer aims in part at profit, this being the one reliable spontaneous motive that operates whether or not the planners lay it down. But his physical output target remains, so he has two maximands, one official and one unofficial. With the general case of many maximands we deal in Sec. 14. The answer in this particular case is likely to be that the bonus system makes the physical target far more important to the director. He will therefore proceed as in (ii), (iii) or (iv), almost as if there were no money.

(vi) Keeping the disposition of the sortament as in (v), we now change the indicators for the general categories themselves from physical to monetary. Of such the first, and almost universal in the Soviet Union, is gross output. This indicator is used because it is statistically easy to obtain; it means little more than the sales of the establishment. It sets up at least three disadvantageous biases. The first is towards buying in semi-fabricates and adding very little net value to them, so that a high gross output can be obtained with little cost. That is to say, either there would be unnecessary subcontracting, or unnecessarily expensive raw materials would be used. Cases have even been known of a single ministry (for ministries also have their gross output targets) planning for a particular product to be passed from factory to factory, with very little net value added in each factory; this bumps up the *ministry's* gross output. The second bias is that with all prices centrally fixed, only those lines contributing most to gross output (not profit as in (v)) will tend to be produced, and there is no automatic mechanism of supply and demand to reduce their contribution as output expands. Thirdly, it must be remembered that whatever the nature of the output target there is usually a wage fund target; that is, the wage fund must be as small as possible. In this case this reinforces the bias already mentioned in favour of expensive raw materials and unnecessary subcontracting, rather than direct waste of labour.

In very complicated and unrepeatable products, which present no homogeneous unit in which physical output targets can be expressed, and which can be constructed out of many different materials in many different ways, gross output is not only the main but almost the sole indicator. Construction establishments, that is, are told to build factories, dams, aerodromes, etc., costing so many rubles. Their own 'project makers' draw up the plans and these must indeed be passed in detail by the central authority, but at no other place in the Soviet nationalized sector does initiative rest so largely with the periphery. Nor are price relatives anywhere else so influential: money is by no means passive in the field of nationalized construction, and the rationality of prices is a more urgent issue for building materials than for industrial inputs.

(vii) The general target might be net output. This has been proposed, especially in Poland, but hitherto little used, owing to the greater statistical difficulties involved. It eliminates the first set of biases noted in (vi), which are undoubtedly the most serious, but it leaves the second and third biases untouched.

(viii) Then the general target might be profit, as for instance in Polish light industry. There remains, however, a system of centrally fixed prices for the sortament. As in (vi) and (vii) this sets up a permanent bias, this time in favour of the lines that *under the given price tariff* happen to be the most profitable.[1]

11. So far we have dealt mainly with output indicators. But there are also innumerable pure input indicators, both physical and monetary.

---

[1] For an orthodox Marxian view of profit as an indicator compare Edith Varga, 'Improvement or Revision of our Economy?', *Nepszabadsag*, Sept. 8, 1957 (= O-P Oct. 25, 1957).

(ix) If physical they are technical ratios such as kwh per lb. of coal, ounces of mortar per 100 bricks, etc. With the disadvantages of this system any Western capitalist who employs an enthusiastic engineer will be amply familiar. His engineer will persuade him, for instance, to save fuel—at the cost of labour or of a particularly expensive furnace lining. Or the engineer's 'indicator' might be speed, durability, lightness or a dozen other things. In each case, a bias is set up towards extravagance in everything else. Marxist economic thinking lays itself wide open to this kind of fallacy.

(x) A characteristic monetary input indicator is the upper limit on the wage bill, perhaps the most frequently violated of all indicators. Since we have unfortunately no space here for inflation under the Stalinist system we cannot go into the reasons for such violation. What matters here is the influence of this important indicator on price, cost and output: it drives the enterprise to secret sub-contracting (which imposes the wage expenditure on other enterprises) and to skimped work of all kinds. In construction, where the product is unique so that physical measurement is at a heavy discount, there are other money cost limits. They have much the same effects.

(xi) As Stalinist crudity recedes the favourite combination of indicators is now gross, or sometimes net, output plus a battery of input ratios. This is certainly better than the past but still very inadequate and uncertain.

Profit itself is both an output and an input indicator; hence its simplicity and power. But profit is, to repeat, by no means a usual indicator in the Soviet economy, and decentralization does not necessarily enhance its importance. Other indicators tend to govern the decentralized decisions, so that when central planning is relaxed in a multi-indicator planned economy we need not be surprised if bargaining and competition arise of a very curious kind. Thus take the present (1959) set-up in Soviet industry.[1] For 'decentralized commodities' the enterprise has only a gross value of output target, prices centrally laid down, and a radius within which it may sell. True it must mainly sell by long-term contract, and these contracts must be approved by higher authority, but they are essentially the product of bargaining and even, since the enterprise has contracts with many clients, of competition. Then what is the enterprise's price and output policy for 'decentralized commodities?' Profit-maximization? not at all, for the director must still hand over all

---

[1] Koldomasov, *P. Kh.* 4/1959.

the profits, or only apply them in specific ways. Rather, as ever, is plan-fulfilment his policy, since this determines his bonus.

It is vital to grasp this. We saw above that if a manager is subject to no special constraints he will probably take profit as an indicator, spontaneously. But in the most decentralized forms of CC there are still constraints, and typically an output target upon the fulfilment of which a large part (say 30%) of the manager's income depends. Now this managerial bonus might theoretically be paid out of central funds, so that the monetary result of the firm's operation was totally irrelevant. But in fact it must be paid out of the establishment's revenue (Khozraschet). So simply because the source for the bonus for fulfilling any indicator is profit, the role of the particular indicator profit is reinforced. But neither the manager, nor even the trade union or production conference, can indefinitely divert profit to personal use, since the State, as 'ideological owner', controls its appropriation. So the policy is to get *enough* profit to pay the bonus out of, and then so to over-fulfil the plan as to make the bonus payable. In U.S.S.R. today (1959) plan-fulfilment means maximizing gross value of output, subject to certain restraints: the cost plan, the wage plan and, *inter alia*, profit. The kind of commodity the manager will most press on his clients is the one with a high price on the centrally fixed list, and a cost not low overall but low in the particular inputs for which maximum input/output ratios are fixed by the plan. The articles his clients actually want (whether they are shops subject to the consumer or other enterprises subject to their own plans) will be his bait. He will offer such articles as a condition of sale of the ones he wants to make. This is what capitalism knows as 'full line forcing'. Badly chosen indicators, then, produce outputs that the *planners* do not want. But if the plan itself was irrational this might not be an entirely bad thing.

12. So far we have rung the changes on input and output indicators, in physical and monetary terms. A constant feature has been that *the producer has the initiative*. In everything not centrally ordered, in all matters of detail and interpretation, the customer's wishes are quite secondary. Communists accuse capitalism of producing for profit not use, thus failing to see that competitive profit *is* use. A truer accusation is that Communists produce for plan, not use, or in decentralized matters for production, not use. Could an indicator directly represent the customer's wishes?

(xii) The answer is that it would have to be very different from the kind of thing so far discussed, and would in particular suffer from being neither measurable nor overfulfillable. We are looking, in fact, not for a new indicator but a new allocation model (model 7, to be precise). Such a thing is the *sistema zakazov*.[1] In this case in place of the contract the customer or customers have the right to give any orders they please in respect of the sortament. This is a much more flexible procedure, as it cuts out the central planner except in so far as the general category of the good to be produced by the establishment is concerned. We are still, of course, extremely far from *rationality*, because under the centrally fixed prices we have no guarantee that the customer's demands are rational; moreover his demands may be due to centrally fixed output targets as well. But at least he now gets what he needs; the system's *efficiency* rises.

The trouble with this system is that it is inordinately hard on the producer, and interferes with his plan-fulfilment, since it cannot itself be made a statistical measure of such fulfilment. In recent years little has been heard of it.

13. One asks, then, of a criterion, or of a plan based on some criterion, or of a *de facto* allocation of resources, is it irrational? Of an indicator one also asks, is it counter-productive?—does it help or hinder the plan, the achievement of the resource allocation aimed at, however we may wish to describe the latter? A firm grasp of this distinction saves much muddle. If the Soviet price system, for instance, is found to assist in the fulfilment of Soviet plans, that simply means it is not counter-productive. It tells us nothing whatsoever about the rationality of those plans, indeed they might be so irrational that certain counter-productive indicators produced a better allocation.

In this way we can avoid the error of approving whatever a plan does achieve as rational simply because it is 'according to plan'.[2] A plan is rational in so far as it achieves some other end, such as consumers' satisfaction or maximum growth. Of that other end we cannot use the word 'rational', since it is, for an economist as such, beyond technical criticism. The ultimate end is a value judgment, but the plan is a mere technical device for achieving it, and itself by no means an ultimate end or in any way sacrosanct. The words that economists use by custom to say whether this or that technical device is good or bad are 'rational'

---

[1] 'System of orders': cf. Ch. 7, Sec. 7. This was introduced in 1951, and its current status is unclear to me. Cf. Orlov, *V.E.* 8/1953; Orlov, *V.E.* 11/1951; *Kommunist* 8/1953.

[2] Cf. D. Hodgman, *Soviet Studies*, July 1956; Wiles, *Soviet Studies*, Oct. 1956.

and 'irrational'. The words may be loaded, but they are not excessively so, and it would be fearfully inconvenient to seek others at this late date. But below the plan again are the indicators the planners use: these in turn are mere technical devices auxiliary to the plan, which however is itself a technical device. Although 'rational' and 'irrational' would do at this point too, it would clearly be better to seek new labels.

A main difficulty here is the poverty of the English language. Economists have had hitherto but the one pair of words for both criteria and indicators, and this alone may have been enough to cause the confusion. We call indicators 'effective', of which the opposite is 'counter-productive', retaining for 'rational' and 'irrational' their normal Robbins-Lerner meaning, their reference to the criteria used by fully autonomous economic subjects and by planners.

The two principal kinds of counter-productivity in indicators appear to be:

They may contradict each other, as when a wage fund maximum renders an output target unachievable.

They may be very incomplete (they *must* be rather incomplete, for the possible amount of detail is infinite), and at the same time indicate something contrary to the spirit though not the letter of the plan. Such are the examples given in Sec. 10 (ii-iv) above.

Prices and profits, when used as indicators, can be counterproductive in the above ways. Thus a raised price might make profits too easy to make, i.e. the plan too easy to fulfil. Or the relative prices of two products might, by error, not correspond to the planners' true preferences. Or again price controls, in conditions of rising costs, tempt the producer to fraudulent innovation.

14. Thus all indicators have their biases, even profit. The reader will probably agree that non-profit indicators are not intolerably bad, only worse than profit. For in allocation models (1) to (5), as here, none of these indicators, not even profit, directly rewards the producer for *doing what is wanted by the customer*. That would require a change in the allocation model, to (6), (7) or (8), as in Sec. 12. But monetary indicators tend to produce more rational results than physical ones, as we show later under the heading Two Cheers For Khozraschet (Ch. 6, Sec. 6); but each broad type is about as easy to evade, and therefore as liable to be counter-productive. In all cases, further intervention can improve the situation at more administrative cost. In the West when the profit indicator fails, the government steps in with anti-trust devices, smoke abatement laws,

etc., etc., substituting RM for FM. In the East, the faults of (ii), (iii) and (iv) can be corrected by switching to (v) or (xii), i.e. by actual decentralization; or the faults of all these alike are reduced by further subdividing the sortament and establishing physical targets for the various qualities, i.e. by further resort to (i).

This suggests a generalization that is at least attractive. A command economy will begin by decentralizing a fair amount of decision to enterprises, and imposing a comparatively simple set of indicators. The biasses that these set up will compel it either to increase the complexity of the indicators (tendency towards system (i)) or to decentralize the system towards more market-like forms. The most market-like and therefore the most ideologically suspect form which we have met hitherto is a combination of (viii) and (xii), which would differ from a free market 'only' in that prices are centrally fixed and that customers may not change suppliers. Strong as these derogations from freedom are, the system is a very loose one, by Communist standards. The two single-indicator systems, then—the wholly decentralized one of profit and the market and the wholly centralized one of detailed physical outputs—are the best in that they set up fewest objectionable biasses; and a command economy will tend towards the one or the other, being restrained only by its ideological repulsion from one extreme, and by its administrative incapacity from the other.

Where intermediate systems obtain, the presence of more than one indicator at a time is possible, indeed almost certain, and it is also almost certain that they will 'indicate' different things. The choice then arises for the unfortunate manager which of these indicators he shall most obey. In a permissive, essentially democratic society which nevertheless had a command economy for some reason, the solution of this problem would be institutionalized for the manager. He would be allowed to treat it openly as a maximization problem with two variables, just as a consumer subject to the British wartime system of 'points' rationing had to economize both his 'points' and his money, compromising between the different optima they indicated.[1] But in the totalitarian economy of Communism the manager cannot frankly plead the material

---

[1] 'Points' were a special sort of ration card applied to whole classes of goods, e.g. confectionery. Each article was worth so many points, and each consumer received an equal number. The points were thus a parallel currency, required in addition to money. Each consumer had his (equal) points income and faced a system of points prices. Cf. Worswick, *Oxford University Institute of Statistics Bulletin*, Feb. 1944; ed. G. D. N. Worswick and P. H. Ady, *The British Economy* 1945–50, Oxford, 1952, pp. 148–9.

contradiction of his indicators and get the central planners to admit it. Instead, he quietly sets up a *political* system of priorities among his indicators, according to his understanding of the basic ideology of his masters, of any short-term changes in the party line, and of the likely consequences to himself of falling short in this rather than in that respect.

In the past, this system of priorities has been rather stable and could be described as follows: Where there is contradiction, physical targets come first, technical ratios second and money targets third, especially if they are profit targets, as opposed to gross output targets. In conformity with the ideology underlying this, the manager's bonus is principally dependent on the physical output of his firm and he needs only to ensure so much profit as will make it possible for that bonus to be paid.

Moreover, in a very growth-conscious economy like the Soviet, the planned outputs will be impossibly high by whatever indicator they are measured; so that even a single-indicator system is self-contradictory by virtue of what we call in Ch. 13 'planner's tension', the making of impossibly high demands on establishments. Then there arises a choice, not between indicators but between customers to satisfy. Here, too, a political system of priorities has grown up which has long been rather stable: defence customers have priority over heavy industry customers, and light industry and agriculture come at the bottom. Plan-underfulfilment has less serious consequences if only uninfluential customers remain unsatisfied. In recent years, both profit in the first scale of priorities and agriculture in the second (and under Malenkov, light industry) have gained in informal political importance.

CHAPTER 5

RATIONALITY, AND THE PLANNERS' ACTUAL CRITERIA

1. *The importance of being old-fashioned.* In his book, *The Economics of Control* (New York 1946) Abba Lerner explains that in order to obtain the best distribution of scarce resources between competing ends for a given distribution of income, the production of each good or service must be pushed to the point where marginal cost equals price. This is seemingly a very important practical conclusion, which has not in its general outlines often been challenged. Yet somehow in the last fifteen years the centre of economic interest has wandered from it. Smart economic theorists do not like to be heard speaking in those terms. The whole thing seems to be not so much false as unfashionable.

The reason for this is that Lerner's theory makes some highly doubtful assumptions about income distribution and inter-personal comparisons of utility. Changes designed to enforce the Lerner rule redistribute money income among the factors of production and, by altering the relative prices of goods, redistribute real income among consumers with different tastes. Consequently, we cannot be certain that such changes improve overall welfare and indeed we can think up cases in which most people would agree that they diminished it. The attention of the best theoretical minds has thus been shifted from what, to repeat, is the essentially *practical* problem of the allocation of scarce resources to that of identifying an unambiguous increase in the welfare of all persons. If, for instance, no one is worse off owing to a change, but some people are, so to speak, more better off than others, under what conditions is this an unambiguous increase in the welfare of all?

This kind of question, I submit, is scholastic and without practical application in economics or politics. In society, human beings are always making decisions which displease some people and please others, and yet are supposed in some way to represent a greater good of the greatest number. If in family life, in politics generally, or in the drawing up of the state budget such arbitrary procedures were not permitted, there would be no family life, no state and no budget. Social leaders of all kinds would be reduced to the state of speechless scepticism reached by the Greek philosopher who refused in the end to reply to questions, but simply waggled his finger. The coming together of human beings compels us to make arbitrary inter-personal comparisons of utility. That these comparisons are pure value judgments and ultimately without factual or objective basis is very true. Nevertheless, they are made and must be made, and the study of the extremely few cases in which they need not be made is certainly not worth the intellectual gifts that have recently been lavished upon it.

As Arthur Koestler says very justly in another context—or is it another context?

It was easier to reject the utilitarian concept of ethics than to find a substitute for it. Perhaps the solution was to be found in a reversal of Bentham's maxim: the least suffering for the smallest number. But beyond that point lay quietism, stagnation and resignation. To change from Lenin's way to Gandhi's way was again tempting, yet it was another short cut, a toppling over from one extreme to the other.[1]

We have not space here to deal with the problem of what happens when marginal cost is less than average cost, but must still be equated with price. Suffice it to say that there is nothing in Professor Lerner's equations which prevents us from charging more than marginal cost, indeed more than average cost, on intra-marginal purchases; and price discrimination of this kind has always been in practice sufficient to keep an enterprise paying its way in cases where marginal cost is less than average cost. Nor have we space to deal with the treatment of leisure as a commodity. Enough that however this problem is solved, the relative prices of goods and services other than leisure will be settled on the same principles and indeed will remain in the same proportions to each other. And this is the main allocation problem.

I am unable, then, to understand how Mr. J. de V. Graaff[2] arrives at the following conclusion:

Occasionally one encounters the argument that, even if the assumptions underlying the marginal cost principle are rather unrealistic, it can at least be used as a *basis*. Then prices can be raised a little where external diseconomies in production or consumption are thought to be important, lowered where consumption of the good is likely to increase efficiency, and so on. No doubt this is more reasonable. But why not take some other price as a basis? The assumptions which

[1] *The Invisible Writing*, New York 1954, p. 358.
[2] *Theoretical Welfare Economics*, Cambridge, Eng. 1957, p. 154.

would have to be made to prove that price should be K-times *average* cost (or the square root of average cost) are not much more unrealistic than those required for proving that it should equal marginal cost. If a basis is all that we are looking for, we may as well start with all prices zero.

This passage comes at the end of a chapter which correctly sets out all the qualifications to the rule that marginal cost should equal price. There is nothing whatsoever in these qualifications that supports this astonishing conclusion. There is in them no indication whatsoever, for instance, that average cost should equal price, or that enterprises should maximize their losses, or that there should be no pricing system, or that the allocation of resources is an unimportant question; or that there would be fewer qualifications to such rules than to the marginal rule, or indeed that any other rule would so much as cope with some of the qualifications that apply to the marginal rule. Professor W. Vickrey puts it well:[1] 'I had rather stand on a bridge made by an engineer who held that Hook's Law was true under every conceivable circumstance than on one made by an engineer who had chosen a law at random.'

Two practical considerations serve to reduce to its proper status the objection that Lerner did not properly allow for the redistribution of income that would necessarily follow from the enforcement of his Rule. The first is that social services exist. All states are welfare states. In an advanced society, whether communist or capitalist, it is very improbable that the free play of market forces could lead through the reallocation of resources (naturally, we except unemployment) to serious or long-lasting social injustice. And the second is stronger: resource misallocations are permanent; income recipients are mortal. Even if the particular individual losers are not roughly compensated for failing to re-establish themselves (Why should they not be asked to re-establish *themselves*? Why must they be entirely spoon-fed?) the loss they suffer dies with them or, at the very worst, with their children. But the loss that an economy suffers through the irrational allocation of resources continues, by definition, until it is somehow corrected.

2. This book, then, is unashamedly reactionary, even 'classical'. No one privileged, as was the author, to tour Poland in the company of Polish economists in the summer of 1956, in the first flush of the Polish Thaw, could possibly take a sophisticated or blasé attitude to problems of choice. Again and again, entering some building, he was told 'look how high the ceilings are, look at the façade: the

[1] In private conversation.

planners would never pass it now'. Almost no project seemed to have been without waste; almost everything was criticized, and it seemed rightly so.

Bad choices are wasteful. If, for instance, they raise all costs by 5% they waste 5% of the national income, or one or two years' growth. This is an insultingly simple proposition, but it is not psychologically accepted by many of the finest economic minds, East and West. 5% of the GNP is not a small sum, yet false pricing principles could pour it down the drain with the greatest ease.

Note, however, that I am forced to write 'could'. There exists, to my knowledge, no even approximately reliable estimate of how much *is* wasted, in any type of economy. 5% is purely an informed guess. Perhaps no more important task faces the statistician than to improve on this guess. L. N. Kantorovich estimates that 30-50% is wasted in certain industries in U.S.S.R., but he does not show his working, or even indicate that there was any.[1]

3. Such a viewpoint is open to many misunderstandings, especially if strictly and consequentially applied to a Communist economy, which is *both* centrally planned *and* innocent of the rationality concept. Some of the commonest should be forestalled.

(*a*) It is not held that because the only command economies we know are irrational all must be. On the contrary it may even be that central planning can achieve more perfect rationality, with electronic computers and linear programming, than a market economy with monopoly commissions and railway rates tribunals. Cf. Ch. 10.

(*b*) It is not held that public ownership has any logical connexion with either a command economy or irrationality. Connexions there undoubtedly are, but they are psychological and historical. Remember Yugoslavia!

(*c*) The allocation of investment funds is merely one of the types of choice that interest us. The gross irrationality under Communism of current output choices, i.e. of the exact use of fixed assets already installed, is also very important.

(*d*) There is all the difference in the world between the choice of the overall volume of investment and the choice between particular projects. In a market economy the first is, on Keynesian grounds,

---

[1] *Ekonomicheski Raschet Nailuchshego Ispol'zovania Resursov*, Moscow 1959, p. 17. To add such wastages right across the economy would be illegitimate aggregation: if every factory became 20% more efficient the extractive industries could not supply 20% more raw material with equal ease.

seldom such as to ensure full employment without inflation. Although individuals do save a rational proportion of their incomes when there is inflation or unemployment, and investors do still lay out their funds in their own best interests, the macro-economic picture is, whether or not we wish to call it irrational, certainly undesirable. An arbitrary, planned choice is quite *likely* to be better, though it may not be (see Sec. 6).

(*e*) 'Investment criteria', then, is a micro-economic concept. *That projects have external economies does not diminish the need for rationality.* Thus it is true that a project in an undeveloped region may at first be unprofitable, but will render other ventures profitable, which will eventually react back upon it, and justify it *ex post facto*. But in working out such a sequence we need rational prices at every stage. Perhaps there are two such sequences? How choose between them? Or at least two initial projects, each capable of generating the same sequence? How choose between *them*? How know that the whole sequence is worth while anyway? The suggestion that large external economies render the price mechanism unnecessary is nothing but sloppy thinking.

(*f*) It is not suggested that the ordinary non-Communist economy is perfectly rational; merely that however bad it is in this respect—and it is very bad—it is still *much* superior to a (non-Yugoslav) Communist economy. All the writer's Polish experience, and all his reading about other Communist countries, especially about Yugoslavia during the transition to a free market, point unmistakably to this conclusion. But in the total absence of statistics it remains a guess.

(*g*) It is a mere fallacy, however often it is repeated by however high authority, that poverty and underdevelopment give us more excuse for arbitrary choices, while rationality becomes important only when a certain prosperity has already been achieved. Obviously the exact opposite is the case. For arbitrary choices are wasteful choices, and a poor man can afford waste less than a rich. True, a rich man or country faces many more choices, and the subject acquires greater intellectual interest, what with fuel policy, higher education policy, choice between techniques, choice between road and rail, etc., etc. But the dull old choice between bread and potatoes is more important than these in terms of human welfare.

In this book, then, no apology is made for treating the allocation of scarce resources between competing ends as a very important topic. It is not of course the only topic, still less the very definition of economics, as was once supposed. Nor, perhaps, is it a very important topic under capitalism, which has largely solved it and faces the more serious problems of unemployment and insufficient growth. But for Communism it is *the* topic; the failure to solve it leads to fantastic waste and a serious reduction in the current standard of living. Moreover, the manner of the solution of the scarcity problem under Communism has immense sociological and political consequences: shall collective farm chairmen be free to decide their own cropping plan? What are to be the rights of the directors of enterprises? Could not a free market cut the size of the state bureaucracy in half, thus enhancing the power of the Communist Party apparat and reducing the costs of production? What should be the dimensions of East-West trade? Should there be multilateral clearing facilities among Communist countries? Should the ruble be made into an internationally accepted currency? etc., etc.—not to mention the ideological dangers, already outlined in Ch. 3, to which we shall return in Chs. 7 and 10.

4. *Various Definitions of Rationality.* *Consumer's choice* is not the same thing as *consumer's sovereignty.* A man may be free to choose how to spend his income, but unable thereby to influence the producer. This, by and large, is the position of the Soviet-type consumer, who is not rationed.

Consumer's sovereignty is not the same thing as *consumer's satisfaction*, since under FM (which is consumer's sovereignty) the price mechanism fails to take account of all sorts of external economies, or divergences between private and social profit. For example, the consumer's sovereignty obstructs a standardization of products which would cheapen them and thus increase his satisfaction. Or again there are all the usual examples of factory smoke, traffic blocks, etc. Or finally consumer's sovereignty leads to a rate of saving in accordance with the individual's own unforced private time-preference scale; but this has no relation at all to the rate of growth in the economy as a whole that the same consumer might desire—as we can see, when, in the polling booth, he votes for policies involving very high investment. In other words, he even votes his own sovereignty away in order to increase his satisfaction. Thus quite apart from any value judgment we may dare to make it would be a simple *technical* error to confuse consumer's sovereignty with rationality, since it does not even perfectly achieve consumer's satisfaction.

But this in turn is not the same thing as a *rational allocation of resources*. The possibility of the private consumer being irrational is an accepted cliché of Western economies. Here of course we do make a value judgment. We are not now factually pointing out the existence of untapped external economies; we are morally condemning alcoholism, and illiteracy, morally exalting milk, health and what not. In a word we are demanding the substitution of RM for FM.

Note that we have scrupulously adhered in the above purely 'Western' discussion of a free market economy to the always essential distinction between indicators and criteria. In failing to make enterprises exploit external economies which the consumer would have wished exploited the free price mechanism is showing counter-productivity as an indicator; in choosing gin not milk the consumer is using an irrational criterion, his immediate satisfaction. That the economy produces the gin for him shows how *well* the indicator (profit in this case) is working.

'Consumer's sovereignty', as the phrase is used here, normally implies 'worker's sovereignty' too. The marginal disutility[1] felt by workers is from every point of view as important as the marginal utility felt by consumers. If workers are forced into jobs they do not like, welfare diminishes. It is maximized when marginal disutility of work ratios correspond to wage ratios. If consumers want things that are unpleasant to produce they must pay high prices. Consumer's sovereignty unopposed by workers' sovereignty would be a curious form of tyranny, over man in one of his aspects by himself in another of his aspects. The freedom to 'sack the boss' and, perhaps, to strike is not only a basic political freedom, it is also, to pass from the sublime to the ridiculous, an integral but normally neglected part of welfare economics.

The point is not altered if we substitute 'satisfaction' for 'sovereignty'. It does, however, seem to lose much validity when applied to the other ultimate factors of production, land and capital. Our normal value-judgment is that the landlord or capitalist may well be ordered about without much loss of welfare, whereas the freedom of the worker is more important than that of the consumer.

5. How then might *planners' preferences be rational*? We mean by such a rationality not that the planners have accurately gauged consumers' preferences, say by some such allocation model as CM

---

[1] Note 'marginal': intra-marginally work is often of positive utility.

H

(Ch. 4, Sec. 1), but that they have their own system of detailed priorities, which makes sense in its own terms. What does this mean?

(i) that the plans are self-consistent, merely in the input/output sense of equating production orders with consumption orders for each good and service. But this is very elementary, and the number of absurd, arbitrary and wasteful plans that are 'O.K. for input/output' is literally infinite (see Ch. 10, Sec. 14).

(ii) that, at points where the allocation model uses the market and money is active, prices are so fixed as to persuade factors to produce and consumers to buy the planned outputs. But this is as elementary as (i), and equally compatible with an infinite number of absurd, arbitrary and wasteful plans. Indeed, it is only the demand that indicators be 'effective' (Ch. 4, Sec. 13).

(iii) that the allocation of factors and intermediate products, and the choice of techniques, be such as to maximize from available resources the outputs chosen (this implies that the planners must primarily fix the *pattern* of output, and encourage over-fulfilment of all output targets). E.g. transport media must be chosen that carry the planned bill of goods at least cost; highly skilled workers must not be under-utilized, etc. This is a genuine rationality condition, which requires that each factor have a price that reflects its scarcity in view of the planners' output targets. The establishments must be able to bid for the factors, either factually on the market or notionally in the planning office. In Soviet-type economies the factual labour market is of just this nature: the grades of labour are scarce and receive relative rewards precisely in view of the planners' targets, not the consumers' sovereignty; and labour is thus quite rationally allocated according to planners' preferences. But for other factors there is neither a notional nor a factual market of the required kind; so that the pre-determined product mix is not produced at least cost.

(iv) the pre-determined product mix must be intellectually defensible. This certainly does not mean that it must always correspond to that which would have obtained under consumers' sovereignty, or which would most satisfy the consumer. Obviously it is 'intellectually defensible' that a Communist country should forbid the importation of the *Manchester Guardian* and *Confidential*, while subsidizing *Pravda*. The decision to populate Siberia (for the product mix includes a 'location mix') might well be defended on strategic grounds, and the decision to grow at such and such a rate on welfare grounds (having unusually great regard to posterity).

But how would one defend an anti-consumer decision on the proportion of, say, wool to cotton? Neither is ideologically suspect, neither need be imported in Soviet conditions, thus threatening autarky, neither is strategic. Indeed just what *could* be a rational planner's preference that did not aim at maximizing consumer satisfaction in this respect? Long thought has not enlightened the writer, who tentatively infers from his failure that *in the vast majority of small decisions planners' preferences are* ipso facto *irrational*.

6. This is a hard, dogmatic saying with which it is difficult to be satisfied in its *a priori* form. But as a matter of brute fact Communist choices are very obviously irrational. It is astonishing that people with an intimate and accurate knowledge of how the Soviet system works should consider the possibility of operating on the assumption that planners' preferences are in fact rational in a Soviet-type economy. Probably they are confusing rationality of criteria with effectiveness of indicators (Ch. 4, Sec. 13). For it is of course with criteria that the rationality problem becomes really important; indicators only raise it by accident, when they give a little freedom of choice to the enterprise.

Now while Communists choose indicators on the whole for their practical utility, they derive criteria on the whole from their ideology. They are self-critical about the former, and publish much on the subject. They have discussed criteria very little until recently, because as we saw in Ch. 3 their ideology prevents from recognizing the bare existence of a problem of choice. Communist criteria can only be discovered by a sort of psychoanalytical detective work, and what we discover makes distressing reading for those who give rationality some kind of ontological importance in economics.

The location of economic activity, the choice between railways and canals and the revealed official preference for a certain style of architecture (under Stalin) are all demonstrably irrational. Canals, so to speak, are the planner's 'alcohol'. The Soviet press issues a constant stream of instances of irrational supply to the consumer, irrational design of machinery, etc., etc.[1] The micro-economics of Soviet, though much less so of Chinese, investment policy, is

[1] For concrete instances compare: T. J. B. Hoff, *Economic Calculation in the Socialist Society* (London 1949), Appx. C; Wiles, *Oxford Economic Papers*, Sept. 1953, pp. 294–97; Wiles, *Soviet Studies*, Oct. 1955, pp. 148–51; Jasny, *Soviet Studies*, April 1961.

demonstrated to be wasteful in succeeding chapters here. In agriculture Soviet planners have regularly and on their own admission chosen wrong types of crop and wrong climatic conditions. What Soviet literature mainly hints at, Polish literature trumpets abroad, with very convincing details, as we have seen.

Even the choice between investment as a whole and consumption as a whole, where it is customary to give a centrally planned system best, is also demonstrably irrational, since twice in Soviet history it has led to famine (for food might of course have been imported instead of machinery) and once in Poland to serious rioting that shook the régime; besides being a permanent contributory factor to the extreme discontent of the subject masses in all Communist countries. Moreover its intellectual basis is, to say the least, shaky. Thus Imre Nagy found it necessary, as Prime Minister in 1954, to condemn the practice of making heavy industry expand by a greater percentage each year. In other words, Hungarian planners had a law of the *acceleration* of heavy industrial production.[1]

The economist sits in judgment upon the planner no less than upon the consumer, and will only call his system of revealed preferences rational if they do not lead to needless waste or major political catastrophes, and seem in themselves to be based upon some reasoning process rather than pure chance. The revealed preferences of Communist planners have not these attributes.

But an economy can be, either because of its consumers or because of its planners, irrational and yet grow very quickly and achieve striking successes. Irrationality is a serious fault, but not a fatal one (Ch. 11). Permanently irrational systems exist and flourish like the green bay tree—or indeed like the wicked—before our eyes. Economics must develop tools with which to deal with them.

7. Note that a system of '*mixed rationality*' can be conceived of: in which the macro-economic decisions are taken by central planners and the micro-economic decisions by consumers, and both sets or one set or neither run according to a rational system of values. Such indeed is the Yugoslav—or for that matter the British—economy. Some of the more decentralized Soviet indicator systems are also systems of mixed rationality, in which the planners decide the broad lines and the consumers the details. The model CM, however, combines the *institutions* of the command economy with consumer's rationality throughout.

[1] *Imre Nagy on Communism* (Praeger 1957), p. 93.

8. What, then, do Communist planners actually achieve? Obviously they do not achieve consumer's rationality, and equally plainly they do not achieve their own. We can only give examples of the allocation policies (criteria) they do follow.

(i) Enterprise Khozraschet is not only an indicator binding the enterprise but also a criterion forming the plan. This is clearly a major rationalizer of allocations, even when prices are arbitrary and foolish. Cf. Ch. 6, Sec. 6. *Per contra* subsidization leads, even with such prices, to irrationality.

(ii) There are, then, many subsidies, and the central budget is often lightened by putting quite large groups on Khozraschet, such as a whole Ministry or Sovnarkhoz.[1] Little or no objection is then made to internal cross-subsidization of bad establishments by good ones, so long as the money is found by the Ministry or Sovnarkhoz. But however irrational prices are they will probably differentiate correctly between, say, socially profitable and unprofitable mines. This is then not different from a straight central subsidy: it directly encourages the waste of resources within a production branch or geographical area. Of course, physical planning by the centre can correct this, but what if the central planner himself believes that 'branch profitability' somehow escapes from the disadvantages of a central subsidy?

(iii) Heavy industry should be made to expand more rapidly than light. Cf. Ch. 14.

(iv) The habit of using 'leading links' in an input/output matrix or system of material balances makes them the criterion for the non-leading links, and this is certainly irrational (Ch. 10, Sec. 12).

(v) The leading links themselves are politically chosen, and though we do not know the exact criteria the politicians use, our confidence in these or indeed any politicians must be slight.

(vi) Price relatives of goods entering into international trade are set in accordance with capitalist world prices, and then used as criteria, or even as indicators.[2] At first blush irrational, this can be seen to be very sensible, since capitalist world prices are the prices of marginal supplies for Communist countries.

(vii) The proportions of prices and outputs in capitalist market economies are also more generally imitated. In goods and services

---

[1] In Russian otraslevaya rentabl'nost'—the principle of 'branch profitability'. Note that many Western public corporations are forced to operate on this principle.

[2] U.N.E.C.E., *Economic Survey of Europe in 1957*, vi/27; Wiles, *Oxford Economic Papers* 1957, pp. 202–3; Wiles, *Soviet Studies*, 1961.

not connected with international trade such prices will not necessarily be rational, since scarcity conditions differ in all countries,
and to imitate foreign relative *outputs* is irrational under all circumstances. But it is surely better that the American consumer should be
sovereign in U.S.S.R. than that none should be.[1]

(viii) Sheer autarky is a criterion of great general importance, but
so obvious it need hardly be discussed.

(ix) Subordinate units also aim, on the whole with official
encouragement, at autarky. This is the remarkable phenomenon
of excessive vertical integration, or 'subordinates' autarky', discussed
in Ch. 8.

(x) Many other specifically investment criteria are given in Ch. 16,
and the criteria for location are given in Ch. 8.

These, then, and others like them are actual Communist planners'
criteria. They are not an impressive bunch. The best that can be
said of them is that non-Communist planners, in their off moments,
use many of these criteria too. But they are open to correction by
an alert technical press and informed opinion. Nor can they brush
aside the rationalizing influence of the market half so easily.

9. The indicators and criteria influence each other. This is partly
a matter of economic theory and general atmosphere: e.g. if net
profit on rational prices were an indicator the planners of such an
economy would hardly be the kind of people to choose to plough
the desert. There are also techical connexions. Thus if Khozraschet
is an indicator it would be most unreasonable not also to make it a
criterion; i.e. to give the enterprise the general instruction to balance
its budget and then specific planning orders that made it impossible.
Or again if irrational prices of one kind or another are used for
purely accounting purposes by establishments, or *a fortiori* if they
are used as indicators, it is hard for the planners to think in terms of
more rational prices. The same bad prices will tend to serve as
criteria. They need not: there are in fact all sorts of shadow
prices in a Communist economy (Ch. 6). But simplicity and intellectual laziness have their demands, and the use of shadow prices
under Communism lays the planner open to the charge that he does
not trust the government's judgment in price-setting.

[1] For such imitations cf. Wiles, *Soviet Studies* 1954; A. Nove and M. P. Donnelly, *Trade
With Communist Countries*, Hutchinson 1960, p. 31; N. Baibakov, 'Some Problems of Long
Range Planning', *CDSP* Jan. 2, 1957=*Pravda*, Nov. 20, 1956. For yet other foreign trade
criteria cf. Alan Brown, *The American Economist*, vol. V, no. 2.

But prices demand a chapter in themselves (Ch. 6), and the rationalization of the system must wait (Ch. 10) until we have mastered decentralization, spatial criteria and the distribution of goods once produced.

CHAPTER 6

PRICING IN PRACTICE

1. PRICES seem to require far more detailed consideration than they have yet received, or than physical and technical indicators or criteria. But we must not lose our sense of proportion: prices are not—or least until recently were not—more important than these latter. Perhaps they are simply of greater ideological interest to all concerned, or perhaps the mere weight of what has already been written on them gives the subject a momentum no author can resist. Certainly they do influence income distribution, and in this context at least they might be much more important than other indicators—were it not that subsidies, in the nationalized sector at least, invariably make up an enterprise's revenue to the point where it can pay the wages it must. (It will be borne in mind that labour, except in kolkhozy and prisons, is free to move; so an unprofitable enterprise cannot recoup itself out of wages.)

In this chapter we confine ourselves on the whole to the classical Stalinist position, leaving recent reforms mainly to Ch. 10. Thus we do not step out of allocation model (4).

The arbitrariness of prices in general is stated quite openly by Soviet economists, who regard it as one of the advantages of 'socialism' over 'capitalism', in that it gives an extra degree of freedom. That this freedom is the freedom of the boat without the compass is not, of course, perceived. A. N. Voznesensky, at the time (1947) Chief of Gosplan and a Vice-Premier, says:[1]

The price of a commodity in the socialist society of the U.S.S.R. is based on its value or its cost of production. However, in the interests of strengthening socialism and raising the standard of living of the toilers, the Soviet state itself determines the exact price of every kind of commodity produced in State enterprises or marketed in state trade, and consequently it determines the degree to which the retail price of the commodity deviates from its actual value.

Yet even Voznesensky, who was executed in 1949, had too high regard for prices in Stalin's eyes. For in the same book he also writes as follows:

[1] *The Economy of the U.S.S.R. during World War II* (translated Public Affairs Press, Washington), p. 72.

The law of value operates not only in the distribution of goods, but also in the distribution of labour itself between branches of the economy of the U.S.S.R. In this respect, the state plan makes use of the law of value for the proper distribution of social labour between the several branches of the economy, so as to further the interests of socialism. Within the plans for increasing socialist reproduction—and the state economic plans in the U.S.S.R. are such plans—it is necessary to observe certain relationships between industry and agriculture, *between the production of the means of production and the production of consumers' goods,* between the growth of production and the development of transportation, *and between accumulation and consumption.* . . . Thus the law of value in socialist economics is a transformed and most elementary law of the cost of production, distribution and exchange of goods, placed in the service of state planning. . . . The conflict between the value of the goods and the rate of profit has been abolished in the U.S.S.R. In a capitalist economy this leads to the situation that whole enterprises, and even entire branches of production, in which the value or cost of production of goods does not yield the prevailing average rate of profit, perish as a result of crises. As is known, the average rate of profit[1] is not a law in the U.S.S.R., and has no bearing on the development of a socialist enterprise or of an entire branch of production. Occasionally, it was necessary during the Patriotic War to violate the laws of development of the Soviet economic system, and to give them a narrowly wartime character. For instance, it is obvious that a multiplicity of retail prices for the same commodities (a situation connected with rationing) is in conflict with the law of value. After the end of the war economy period the need for rationing disappears, the multiplicity of prices becomes detrimental, and it is in turn discarded. The development of normal trade is assured, and the level of commodity prices is, in the final analysis, established to correspond to the value of those commodities.'[2]

Now in Dec. 1952 Stalin's propagandist Suslov castigated the dead man for 'fetishizing the law of value'.[3] This curious outburst is clearly connected with the recent publication, in October 1952, of Stalin's last work on economics, *Economic Problems of Socialism in U.S.S.R.* There we read:

As to the distribution of labour between the branches of production,[4] it will be regulated not by the law of value, which will lose its force by that time (sc. under Communism), but by the growth of the needs of society. This will be a society in which production will be regulated by the needs of society, and the consideration of the needs of society will[5] acquire first-rate importance for the planning organs.

The assertion that under our present economic régime, in the first phase of

---

[1] This is the Marxian, and indeed Ricardian, law that the profit on capital is the same in every branch of production, owing to competition—P.J.D.W.

[2] Op. cit., pp. 87–90.

[3] Cf. Wiles, *Oxford Economic Papers,* Oct. 1953, p. 312.

[4] To repeat: this, if anything, is the Soviet phrase for our 'problem of choice'.

[5] Implying that this is not yet the case. Perhaps Stalin implies that *raison d'état* governs today, while under full Communism the State will wither away and *raison de consommateur* will govern instead.

development of Communist society, the law of value regulates the 'proportions' of labour distribution between the various branches of production, is also quite wrong. If this were right it would be hard to understand why light industry is not developed in our country at top speed as the most profitable industry, in preference to heavy industry which is often less profitable and occasionally quite unprofitable. . . .

Clearly, following in the footsteps of these comrades, we should have to give up the priority production of the means of production in favour of the production of the means of consumption. And what does the abandonment of the priority production of the means of production signify? *It would mean the destruction of the possibility of uninterrupted growth of our national economy*, for it is impossible to effect an uninterrupted growth of the national economy without giving effect at the same time to the priority production of the means of production. These comrades forget that the law of value can operate as the regulator of production only under capitalism, in conditions where the means of production are privately owned, in conditions of competition, anarchy of production and crises of over-production. They forget that with us the sphere of activity of the law of value is restricted by the existence of the public ownership of the means of production, by the operation of the law of planned development of the national economy; consequently it is restricted by our annual and 5-year plans, which are an *approximate* reflection of the requirements of this law.

Some comrades conclude from this that the law of the planned development of the national economy, the planning of the national economy, destroys the principle of profitability. This is quite wrong and quite the contrary is true. If one considers profitability not from the point of view of individual enterprises or branches of production, and not within the span of one year, but from the point of view of the whole national economy and within the span of, say, 10 to 15 years—which would be the only correct approach—then the temporary and unstable profitability of individual enterprises or branches of production cannot even bear comparison with that higher, stable form of profitability, which the operation of the law of the planned development of the national economy and the planning of the national economy give us, saving us from periodic economic crises which destroy the national economy and inflict colossal material damage on society, and securing for us the uninterrupted growth of the national economy with its high tempos.

In short there can be no doubt that, under our present socialist conditions of production, the law of value cannot be the 'regulator of proportion' in distributing labour between the various branches of production.

This is clearly a blow at Voznesensky. Note especially—it is very characteristic of Marxist thinking—the preoccupation with macro-economics. The passages italicized (my italics) are in especially clear conflict; Stalin denies the 'law of value' *any* validity, even in details, because *one* application of it—on a very broad scale—would get in the way of his investment plans. Note too that, not possessed of our sophisticated terminology, both authors speak of prices as criteria and indicators indiscriminately.

2. It does not always matter under any allocation model that prices are irrational. The aim is to allocate physical resources rationally, not to obey pricing rules. Thus even under FM if supply or demand curves are naturally very inelastic, prices have no re-allocative effect, and it does not matter what they are. The obvious case of this in 'mainstream' economics is the rate of interest, at least in Keynesian theory. In these circumstances prices can only re-distribute income: an effect they are always bound to have,[1] but from which we must perforce abstract. Or at the other extreme under CC model (2) no price ever has a reallocative effect. It follows that in either of these cases there might be central subsidy, intra-ministerial cross-subsidy, irregular rates of turnover tax, etc., etc., without harm.

One of these cases was that of *demand inelasticity*, the other that of *monetary passivity*. This second concept is quite unfamiliar to 'main-stream' economics, and we must explain *how prices are formed when money is passive*. We call money 'active' when it is an indicator: i.e. it affects the decisions of consumers, producers or factors of produc-tion. Passive money, which is used for accounting and auditing purposes only, may yet be a criterion for planners, but it is by definition not an indicator. As we saw in Chs. 1 and 4, an unplanned and therefore monetarily active sector of an economy can subsist alongside an entirely centrally planned sector, which must be monetarily passive. But even within one sector, up and down the vertical chain of production, money can be passive and active alternately. Nay, more, it can be passive and active in the same transaction, according to the way in which we look up or down the vertical chain. Thus in the Soviet nationalized, centrally planned, sector (allocation model 4) money is active *vis-à-vis* the worker, who in the absence of direction of labour, must be attracted to the job where he is required by ordinary market mechanisms.[2] But the enterprise paying out these same wages is simply instructed to do so by the central planners, who also plan prices and outputs so that on the whole the enterprise may be reasonably sure of having enough money to do so. As far as the enterprise is concerned then, the money in the wage transaction is passive.

[1] Rational prices may of course distribute income in a 'worse' way than irrational ones.
[2] The extent to which there is in fact direction of labour in the Soviet Union is discussed in Ch. 7, Sec. 2.

Imagine secondly that this enterprise makes semi-fabricates and passes them on to another enterprise in the nationalized sector. This is done strictly according to plan, but the receiving enterprise must pay a sum in money. In this transaction, money is a purely accounting device, and passive in both directions. These prices, those of producers' goods, we call in this book wholesale prices for short; though in ordinary parlance the word wholesale has a smaller coverage. Now where there is most passivity there is most irrationality. This is not deliberate, merely inevitable. Originally Soviet wholesale prices were the freely settled, moderately rational ones of 1928, and in each satellite they were similarly those of the pre-plan year. But no force operates to *keep* these prices rational, since they are now wholly subject to administrative fiat, and physical planning can rub along whatever they are.

3. They are, for instance, exceedingly sticky. In 1931 the People's Commissar for Finance claimed: 'Is there any ground for talk of inflation when prices of manufactured goods remain stable for the majority of consumers? How can one speak about inflation when the regulated prices on agricultural produce are unchanged?'[1] This was during the worst period of Stalin's inflation! Again during the whole of World War II wholesale prices hardly altered, in face of rampant wage and retail price inflation. When they do change it is by large leaps and in great batches. A particularly striking case is the way in which Soviet wholesale prices were raised by 138% on January 1, 1949, and were lowered again by 16% on January 1, and July 1, 1950.[2]

New goods, on the other hand, tend to receive prices that take account of wage inflation up to the first year of mass production. So these are more rational in relation to wages and less rational in relation to the prices of other goods.

No wonder then that the Westernized economists of Poland held the rationalization of their wholesale prices to be a prime task when the Thaw set in, and they were freer to speak. One of them told Mr. Montias 'They were set at random.'[3] The main method

---

[1] *Ekonomicheskoye Obozrenie*, Jan. 1931; quoted by E. M. Friedman, *Russia in Transition*, New York 1932, p. 337.

[2] Bergson et al., *Journal of Political Economy*, August 1956.

[3] J. M. Montias, *Producers' Prices in a Centralized Economy: The Polish Experience*, Columbia University doctoral thesis, 1958. This work is an immense quarry of detailed information on the absurdity of Communist prices, especially wholesale prices, and the extent to which they influence output. Anyone who still believes there is rhyme or reason in Communist pricing or resource allocation should set himself to reading Mr. Montias's thesis from cover to cover. There is an abbreviated version in his *Central Planning In Poland*, U.S.A., 1962.

of rationalization chosen was to imitate foreign prices. On this cf. Ch. 10, Sec. 5.

4. But however wholesale prices are formed the accounting procedures do build up, out of them and the wages, a money cost for the final commodity. So all the usual problems of cost accountancy are present. Only since this is a Marxist economy, contemptuous of money, they are present in aggravated form: depreciation allowances are too low, joint costs are even more arbitrarily allocated than under capitalism, until recently there was no allowance at all for obsolescence.[1] Be the cost what it may, the product must finally be sold to the consumer on a free market. The consumer has a certain income and must economize his outlays just as in any other type of economy; he is not normally rationed or planned in any way. Consequently, the money in this final transaction is active with regard to him, although passive with regard to the shop.

But since in such a system there is no reason to expect an output pattern maximally satisfying consumers a tax at irregular rates must enter in. Acting as a monopolist of the products of its own nationalized sector, the Communist government simply charges such prices as will clear the market. Between such market-determined prices and the 'full cost' determined costs, which are simply the addition sum of the active and passive money spent on the product, there is a *difference*, which is the state's profit. What it calls the profit is not of first importance: actually the majority of it is called turnover tax, and a sizeable, increasing minority is called profit. The turnover tax is usually settled as the whole expected difference minus the planned profit: this is the 'method of differences'.

The essence of this tax is that it must be irregular. Any attempt to regularize its incidence will bring prices into conformity with costs, which at arbitrarily planned outputs will lead to queues for some things and overstocking of other things. If both the tax were regular and outputs were adjusted to clear the consequential market this would be a change of allocation model, from 4 to 3. The role of the turnover tax is thus absolutely central.[2] The planned profit differs of course from the actual profit according to the accidents

---

[1] Cf. R. W. Campbell in ed. G. Grossman, *Value and Plan* (California U.P. 1960), for an admirable discussion of Soviet accountancy in the nationalized sector.

[2] Hence my suggestion in Poland that the turnover tax be used as an investment criterion (*Oxford Economic Papers*, June 1957). For actual tax rates cf. N. Jasny, *The Soviet Price System*, Stanford 1951, pp. 70–84, 164–7.

of production. Profit is appropriated according to complicated rules laid down by the 'ideological owner' as described in Ch. 1, Sec. 2.

5. Such is price formation in the nationalized sector. In co-operative agriculture there used to be some passive money: the payments for compulsory deliveries to the state and deliveries to the MTS in kind.[1] No kind of cost considerations influenced the setting of these prices, since they were confessedly 'in the nature of a tax'. We may compare the zagotovka price of grain to the wage of a forced labourer: the good (grain) or service (labour) enters the nationalized sector at an exceptionally low price owing to administrative force, in contrast to the price paid for free grain (the zakupka) or free labour. In both cases the price of the final product was designed as usual to clear the market, so the profit or turnover tax was simply greater than usual. At only one point does the parallel break down: forced labourers were deliberately paid only their subsistence, while the zagotovka price was in origin and principle simply the pre-plan era wholesale price, frozen at that level as for all other intermediate goods. It differed from them only in this, that it had a direct and catastrophic influence on income distribution. For in the nationalized sector if a passive price is too low wages must still be paid at the market rate and a subsidy is inevitable. But the kolkhoznik is *adscriptus glebae*, legally bound to the kolkhoz where he is born, and receives in any case a dividend not a wage.[2] So the confiscatory nature of the zagotovka price can determine his income with impunity to the state, and no subsidy is paid. In the satellites and China, where collectivization was less catastrophic and inflation less severe, the zagotovka has never been so grossly exploitative.

Zakupka prices, on the other hand, resemble in principle those paid by any agricultural marketing corporation to farmers, and require no long discussion. They are only interesting in that the zakupka, especially after it entirely absorbed the zagotovka and the deliveries to the MTS, 'has a planned character'; i.e. it is quasi-compulsory, or administrative and party pressure lower the supply curve of agricultural products to the state.

---

[1] These latter became, at the end of the MTS period, the bigger of the two.

[2] The recent transition to a fixed wage does not essentially alter this, as the wage varies with each kolkhoz.

Stalin himself makes clear that prices influence kolkhoz output:[1]

... the confusion which still reigns in our country in the matter of price policy. Here is one of numerous examples. Some time ago it was decided, in the interests of cotton and grain, to fix a price for the grain sold to cotton growers and to raise the price for cotton delivered to the State. In this connexion our economists and planners submitted a proposal which could not but surprise the members of the central committee [sc. of the Party], for by this proposal the price for a ton of grain was about the same as that for a ton of cotton; the price for a ton of grain was thereby made equal to that of a ton of baked bread. To the remarks of the Central Committee members that the price of a ton of baked bread must be higher than for a ton of grain in view of the added price for milling and baking, that cotton is altogether much dearer than grain, as the prices of cotton and grain *in the world market* testify, the authors of the proposal found nothing sensible to say. Consequently the Central Committee had to take the matter into its own hands, reduce the price for grain and raise the price for cotton. What would have happened if the proposals of these comrades had acquired legal force? We should have ruined the cotton growers and we should have remained without cotton.

Moving forward to the consumer from the zakupka and zagotovka we have nothing special to say, as the product has entered the nationalized sector. If we pursue the agricultural product along the third channel, that of the genuinely free kolkhoz market, we are in market socialism or indeed by Marxist standards, capitalism, since the peasant or kolkhoz retains ownership of the product and sells it on a free market to a private person. Of this, too, there is nothing special to say; these are the most rational prices in a Communist economy, and such factors of production as are permitted to be governed by them are the most rationally used. The restriction is important: the kolkhoz itself merely sells its surplus in this market, and hardly plans its outputs according to its prices, except for such minor products as flowers. The kolkhoznik, on his private plot, certainly plans according to its prices, but state, party and kolkhoz impose numerous restrictions on his use of his own time in this way, and obstruct his acquisition of fertilizers, seed and draught power. Above all they continually try to diminish the size of his plot.

6. *Two Cheers for Khozraschet.* Note that criteria can be physical. Thus in Ch. 5, Sec. 8 (iv), (viii), and often (v) are physical. Or monetary: (i), (ii), (vi), (vii); or simply general policies: (iii), (viii), (ix) and often (v). The choice of a monetary criterion by no

[1] *Economic Problems of Socialism in U.S.S.R*, 'Remarks', 3. The phrase emphasized (my italics) is one of the earliest admissions that prices are less rational in the Soviet Union than in the 'capitalist' world; indeed that capitalist price relatives are studied and imitated.

means guarantees rationality, first because it may be anyhow incorrect in principle (e.g. ii), and secondly because it may be based on irrationally formed prices. This latter possibility now claims our attention.

Passive prices, we have seen, have an obvious tendency to be more irrational than active ones. Yet although by definition without allocational effect at the level of the establishment, they need not have been so in the minds of the planners when they were drawing up the plan in the first place. The planners *may* have taken a decision to specify aluminium rather than steel in a particular product on the grounds of the relative prices of these two materials; even though those prices have been determined by some such historical chance as described in Sec. 3, further complicated by inefficient accountancy, and by the presence of free factors of production. For if there is neither rent nor interest, the relative prices of aluminium and steel are unlikely to correspond to their relative social marginal costs, since these two commodities will certainly embody differing proportions of rent and interest. Also there may, owing to historical chance, be a much bigger subsidy for aluminium than for steel.

Precisely these same irrationalities would persist were the economy decentralized and the money made active; for provided only that profit or net output or gross output or more than one of these is among the indicators incumbent upon the establishment, it will certainly take whatever decisions are free to it in view of the relative prices that there are, and it will certainly not bother about the real scarcity of factors not accounted for by those prices. It is then no less desirable that passive money be rational if it is a criterion in the planners' minds than that active money be at all times rational; and the preoccupation of Polish economists in 1958 with the rationality of their money, ascribed by them to the prospect of decentralization, should have been just as urgent had they wanted better planners' criteria.

Nay more, in either case, physical indicators and criteria may actually improve matters. The extreme and obvious case is the zero price, one of the most irrational of all prices conceivable. Clearly almost any *in natura*, rule of thumb calculation of what to do with land, or long-term industrial capital, is better than nothing. Any mere administrator can appreciate their true scarcity, where an economist relying on prices would fail utterly. Indeed one might almost argue that a zero price is better than an extremely irrational price, for the latter could always be mistaken for a true measure of scarcity, the former never.

Nevertheless, in a general practical way, we may be sure that the more attention to money there is, the more rational choices are. For the extent to which interest and rent enter into production costs is not *grossly* different from one commodity to another,[1] subsidies seldom amount to more than 100% of cost, and Soviet accounting practices do not *greatly* distort the truth in other ways. The irrationality of money is therefore limited, while to the irrationality of choice in purely physical terms arbitrary fantasy sets no bounds.

7. That in such a system subsidies should be paid is only to be expected. But it is not necessarily a bad thing. For if moderately rational relative outputs are decided by fiat, irrational prices may obstruct the fulfilment of the physical plan, and subsidies may cancel their obstructive effect. Moreover since wholesale prices can be divorced from wages and retail prices, subsidies have no redistributive effect.

So while in a market economy subsidies are an obvious derationalizer, in a Soviet-type economy there is only a very general presumption against them. In particular cases they may do good. If Khozraschet gets only two cheers, subsidies get only two hisses.

What enterprises do or did receive subsidies in U.S.S.R.? All machine tractor stations, most state farms, many heavy engineering plants and some mines. MTS received subsidies because they were paid in kind by kolkhozy and received in turn from the state for this produce only the ridiculously low compulsory delivery prices. The fact that they made losses, then, was a very special case connected with the absurdities of the agricultural pricing system; it did not prove that they should not exist. The subsidies to heavy engineering were also part of the general policy of encouraging investment at the expense of consumption. That policy accepted, the subsidies are not in general irrational, as we have seen. But they may have been in particular micro-economic cases. The seriously wrong policy is undoubtedly that of subsidizing *some* state farms and *some* mines; i.e. where nature has been niggardly and it is not worth while exploiting her, the Treasury is generous and ensures a permanent misallocation of resources.

For however foolish Communist prices are they are never likely

---

[1] Prof. Hodgman and I give tables for the varying proportion of interest and rent to total cost in U.S. and British industry in *Soviet Studies*, Oct. 1955 and July 1956.

I

much to misstate the comparison between two enterprises. Enterprises pay *about* as much as each other for raw materials, and *about* the same wage-rates. Long-term interest and rent, which are not charged, are not a very large cost, nor if they were charged would their cost differ *greatly* between enterprises in one branch. Consequently it is the micro-economic subsidies that earn our condemnation. Whether the subsidy is found from profits earned elsewhere within the branch or comes from the central treasury (Ch. 5, Sec. 8) is of course irrelevant. Only in agriculture are prices so irrational that one cannot compare efficiency between enterprises.

In general, however, Communist governments dislike subsidies. Thus the MTS were an obvious element of irrationality in the system from a managerial point of view; but, as we saw above, they suffered also from a financial irrationality more apparent than real: had they sold their grain at zakupka prices they might well have been on Khozraschet. However they were not, and the necessity to find tax revenue to cover their deficit must have weighed heavily against their continued existence. In general, too, there are campaigns against subsidization every few years, spear-headed always by the Ministry of Finance. A large part of any Communist budget speech is taken up with the costs of the nationalized sector— a very natural preoccupation of the Minister in view of the subsidy habit. He is always a rather junior Minister, but it must not be assumed that the views he represents are uninfluential.

It must not be thought that without Khozraschet there is no check on enterprise performance, no incentive to economize. On the contrary, subsidized enterprises also have their cost plans, and the ways in which they spend the money they get from the Treasury are just as closely supervised as in a normal enterprise the expenditures of short-term credits from the Gosbank. The bonus system also remains in full force, and instead of a profit target there is a subsidy minimization target.[1] Thus in allocation model (4) subsidies are compatible not only with the rationality of the physical orders given but even with efficient management. But the compatibility is precarious at both points: Khozraschet does improve rationality, and the failure to cover costs does create a lax atmosphere.

8. We can now generalize about wholesale prices and their reform, in allocation model (4). In a free market the mere alteration of prices independently of outputs is broadly speaking impossible.

[1] Described for the MTS by I. Kuznetsov, *V. E.* 9/1955. Tr. in *O-P.* 48/1955.

In perfect competition it can be temporarily achieved by a change of speculative sentiment, and in imperfect competition within the margin of tolerance that each buyer has for small price changes. Also quite large changes are possible when there is a queue, i.e. when the price/output combination is not on the demand curve in the first place. But this is as nothing to what can be done for wholesale prices in model (4). In Western terminology, the command economy renders demand and supply completely inelastic, so price is indeterminate with respect to output.

Consequently it becomes possible to change prices for reasons other than changing outputs: perhaps for reasons of fiscal convenience, or to redistribute income, or simply in order to change prices. Fiscal convenience is largely the abolition of subsidies in one place at the cost of lower profits elsewhere. Income is redistributed when we change wholesale prices that affect kolkhozy.[1] Changes in prices can also be an end in themselves for slightly unorthodox Marxists, who resent the arbitrariness of the prices and wish to tidy them up, but do not perceive that it is useless to do so unless outputs are also changed.

We can now analyse the main types of wholesale price change in model (4). Assume that retail prices, and all outputs, are constant. Then:

(a) the perfectly simple case is that, say, yarn is produced at a loss and cloth at a profit.[2] We add enough rubles to the price of yarn per kilo to abolish the loss. In so doing we have transferred X rubles in all from cloth factories to yarn factories, and lowered the profit per metre of cloth by a corresponding amount. This is broadly speaking a book-keeping transaction between two branches of the single great socialist enterprise. It is worth doing as it simplifies fiscal administration.

(b) Chemical fertilizers are produced at a loss. We raise their price and kolkhozy have to pay more (by hypothesis they may not purchase less). We have now transferred X rubles from distributable kolkhoz income to the budget, and that is a change

---

[1] Wholesale prices and factory profits in the state sector have virtually no effect on income distribution, even though they finance certain fringe benefits; for a factory that makes a planned loss is permitted to pay from its gross revenue into the 'enterprise fund' the same sum as it would have paid if it had made a planned profit. The tariff of permitted payments from above-plan profits is also the same as that from the extra revenue accruing in the case of under-plan losses.

[2] 'Profit' in this context includes the turnover tax.

of great importance unless compensatory fiscal measures are taken somewhere else.

(c) It is generally agreed that the zagotovka price of wheat is too low for social justice; so the state simply raises it. This is the opposite of case (b).

(d) We decide to abolish the deficit in steel production. In so far as steel is a raw material for consumer goods this is case (a). But in so far as it is a raw material for investment goods there is no turnover tax and little profit: the price of machinery will have to go up in its turn. On inspection this also is essentially case (a) only with an intermediate stage. The ultimate buyer of the machine is like the cloth manufacturer: a sum of money is transferred from his profits (via higher amortization quotas in this case) to the deficitary producer. The machine-maker in the middle simply pays and receives higher prices.

There are in all cases statistical side-effects. In (d) investment appears to rise relatively to consumption, and in (d) and (a) dept. I gains over dept. II. In real terms of course nothing of the kind has happened, and to the greater monetary expenditures there corresponds an equal and opposite price increase. In (b) and (c) similar changes affect the statistics of agricultural (kolkhoz) production. These too are without 'reality', but there is a shift of resources from other uses into or out of the consumption of kolkhozniki.

9. One special feature of Communist price formation is the way in which *prices are used to accumulate capital*. In classical price theory, before imperfect competition and the managerial revolution were recognized, capital was accumulated out of income only: all saving was individual, not corporate, and it was not even 'business' saving, since it was due to the abstinence of consumers, not the ploughing back of entrepreneurs. It therefore all entered the market, to be borrowed by entrepreneurs, into whose costs there entered only interest and amortization. This kept the capital market perfect, and the analysis simple. Tatters of these assumptions clothed even Keynes' General Theory, with its stress that savers and investors are not the same people, so how can Say's Law be true?

But none of this was ever realistic, even before the managerial revolution. For businessmen have saved *qua* businessmen and ploughed back into their own businesses since Adam, and as competition has also been imperfect since Adam they have constantly enjoyed high profits through innovations and windfalls. They have, too, always been able simply to raise their prices so as to plough back more. They have covered not only the costs of interest and amortization but what we shall call the 'accumulation margin', the much greater 'cost' of business saving out of profits.

Moreover, this procedure is highly advantageous. Thus suppose a businessman wishes to use £100 for 10 years. He can borrow it all at once, which with interest at 6% will cost him about £13 p.a. Or he can tax his present customers for it, taking perhaps two years over the process, at say £50 in the first year and £47 in the second. If he does this he pays no interest (indeed he receives a little in the second year), and no amortization, since the £100 is a permanent gift to him. If the asset he buys is in either case able to earn the interest and amortization on its initial value, in the second case he can pocket both.

It may be objected that it is he himself who has now saved the £100—was it not at his disposal and might he not have consumed it? Indeed since he is maximizing his profits in any case, he will surely collect the £100 from his customers whether or not he wants to invest them. So in pocketing the £13 p.a. he is only paying himself the market rate for his own abstinence. But the business is not identical with its owner, even in pre-managerial days; and profits are not so mechanically and reliably maximized but that a stagnant business may charge lower prices, since it requires no accumulation margin. And with state price-fixing, as in the Communist allocation model (4), the difference between what prices are since there are high accumulation margins and what they would otherwise have been[1] becomes very great indeed.

We may be sure, then, that since most prices are to some extent arbitrarily determined by producers, even under capitalism their ideal relations are upset by decisions to borrow here, to finance oneself there. The burden of future investment is irregularly and capriciously imposed on some consumers, while others are let off. Some are only paying interest and amortization on the capital that is now producing for them, others are involuntarily accumulating, at much greater rates, capital that will probably produce for others. Some pay current cost, some pay current cost plus a tax for posterity. Yet at the same time all, via the vestigial capital market, are freely abstaining and lending for the rewards that that market offers.

[1] 'Otherwise' includes at least two alternative systems: indirect budgetary accumulation through the income tax and an 'above the line' surplus, and voluntary accumulation through a Stock Exchange. The latter would not provide enough money, the former would discourage work.

But in market systems at least this can be said, that competition reduces the arbitrary power of business over prices, especially in the long run. The accumulation margin arises much more through the very process of the market than from deliberate monopolistic action; it is more Schumpeterian, arising through windfalls and innovation, than Robinsonian, imposed by monopolistic machinations. Many, perhaps most, of the customers who pay the accumulation margin are simply paying the correct scarcity price for a new product, more of which *could* not have been produced at the time. In this way capital is accumulated to be ploughed back into precisely those expanding firms that, had they been able only to borrow, would have borrowed.

Not so under Communism, in the way in which it has historically used allocation model (4). Not only is the accumulation margin in general very high, reducing the role of income tax and voluntary saving; but it is also imposed most severely where expansion is least. If we treat the nationalized sector as a whole we *might* say that the single great enterprise 'taxes' the consumer of a very large accumulation margin and 'ploughs it back' via a budget which is not only the budget of the state but the central account of the enterprise. In these terms we can simply say that Preobrazhensky wanted a high margin, and Bukharin a low one coupled with some private saving (Ch. 3, Sec. 4). In detail, however, it is at points of low expansion that the margin is high, and vice versa. Light industry behaves 'monopolistically', heavy industry 'competitively'.

It might be argued that mostly this is a macro-economic point: the margin is high on all consumption goods and low or negative on all producer goods. Therefore such a price policy is only as irrational as the saving/consumption ratio to which it gives rise, and, as we have seen, no protagonist of free markets is in a position to cast the first stone. But this is not so: seemingly nothing speaks against high margins on producer goods, so that these branches may finance themselves, while the consumer industries pay high prices for their machinery and basic materials, charging the same consumer prices as before, and collecting lower margins. For as we saw in Sec. 8 the high prices are no disincentive to investment in a command economy, and since the ultimate prices of consumer goods are unchanged all we have done is alter the circulation channels of mere accounting money. Nevertheless, the official explanation why margins are high on consumer goods and low on producer goods is always given in terms of the price mechanism, as if Soviet-type economies were not command economies at all. This comes out clearly in the quotation from Stalin in Sec. 1: he claims to be afraid of substitution effects if the price relatives are changed.[1] Doubtless his point has substance for a very few decentralized decisions, but in so crucial a matter as the general volume of investment it is difficult to take seriously the proposition that prices might override planning commands.

Again there are administrative and fiscal differences. If margins are high where expansion is low and vice versa much more money flows through the Treasury. This might be considered a good thing in that it increases central control, or a bad thing in that it is cumbrous and wastes resources.[2]

Be that as it may, the very great difference between margins on general classes of goods generates an atmosphere very unfavourable to micro-rationality: if the general rate of turnover tax is 100% on one category and 0% on another why, asks the economically uneducated politician or civil servant, shouldn't 100% be just an average in the first category, ranging from 200% to 10% on particular consumption goods?

10. There is no strict reason in a command economy why planners, or for that matter auditors and statisticians, should operate with the prices actually paid by or to workers, establishments and consumers. Indeed even establishments may receive as indicators prices other than those they pay or receive. Hence arises the very common phenomenon of *shadow prices*. They are not even limited to CC and ICM. Any public investment programme under RM, say the FYP of some underdeveloped country or the aid plan of the World Bank or Colonial Development Corporation, may easily be based on shadow prices because the free market prices are held for one reason or another not to represent social profit. Or such shadow prices may be precisely an attempt on the part of the civil service to get closer to the free market despite some government control imposed by the electorate; e.g. the administration may plan with higher prices than the actual controlled or subsidized prices of the market place, or with lower prices than those

---

[1] It has always seemed to me that this was the precise quarrel with Voznesensky, and connected in some way with his execution. On Jan. 1, 1949 wholesale prices were raised very considerably. On about March 14, 1949 Voznesensky was executed. On Jan. 1, 1950, and again on July 1, 1950, wholesale prices were lowered, though by no means the whole way back. Cf. Martin Ebon, *Malenkov*, London 1953, p. 64, Bergson *et al.*, op. cit.

[2] On all this compare R. W. Davies, *The Development of the Soviet Budgetary System*, Cambridge, Eng. 1958, pp. 144–152; albeit Mr. Davies seems not to appreciate that a command economy can override any structure of relative prices.

brought about by some protective device the administration hopes shortly to remove.

Thus far our shadow price has been a planner's criterion only. But it might also be an enterprise's indicator, where indicators are used at all. And there might, as we see below, be one criterion shadow price and a quite separate indicator shadow price at the same time! Moreover, statisticians interested in special definitions of welfare or in international and intertemporal comparisons, also use a variety of shadow prices as measuring rods: base-year prices, foreign prices, pre-plan prices, etc., etc. In a word a shadow price is any price not actually paid.

In an ideally adjusted RM there will be very few shadow prices. The marginal utilities of the final consumers, and the marginal disutilities of the basic factors of production, will have the same ratios as the prices actually paid. Since it maximizes growth if social profit in the most ordinary sense is pursued,[1] no special investment criteria are required for development. Factory smoke and all other external economies of the classic types are, of course, fully accounted for: that is the purpose of RM. Indicators are identical with criteria. Only the statistician, making comparisons with other times and places, will use shadow prices in the sense of past and foreign prices.

Under FM there are equally few shadow prices, but there is far less excuse for this lack. In other words there ought not to be FM, and criteria or indicators should be being used that differ from the market. Or, since that would be impossible, RM should be introduced. RM may be described as the making real in the market place of the correct shadow prices, that under FM remain the playthings of the economist's imagination.

CC however provides the most luxuriant variety of shadow prices. Prof. Grossman[2] lists most of them:

2. Index (constant, unchangeable) prices used for aggregating planned or actual output of the enterprise, of groups of enterprises, of branches of industry, and of industry as a whole. At some historical point the index prices may be identical with the transfer prices, but tend to diverge from them, in level and internal structure, as the two evolve separately (though the index prices are of course supposed to remain constant, allowing for the introduction of prices for new commodities at the appropriate level, until replaced by a new set of index prices).

5. Estimate prices (smetnye tseny) at which construction cost estimates are prepared, though not necessarily at which finished products of construction are

[1] Ch. 16.
[2] *American Economic Review*, May 1959, pp. 53-4. Cf. R. Campbell, ibid., p. 79.

transferred from builder to customer. Estimate prices may also serve as a sort of index price for the construction sector.

6. Planning prices; that is, prices at which calculations in the course of planning and project making (engineering design) are performed. These may be identical with some of the above-listed classes, or may differ by the application of 'co-efficients of deficitness' to the transfer prices of certain goods, or by elimination of the turnover tax where the transfer price includes it.

7. Price surrogates, where the use of prices in the conventional form is doctrinally repugnant. The best known of these are the minimum admissible recoupment (pay-off, pay-out) periods for additional investment in choosing between alternative technological variants of unequal capital intensity.

(Numbers 1, 3 and 4 in this list have been omitted as they are actual prices in money and in various forms of barter.)

It is thus evident that neither criterion prices nor even indicator prices need actually be paid. Where money is active the actual price paid is of course necessarily an indicator. Where it is passive it is equally by definition not an indicator, but that does not prevent some shadow price from occupying this role. The most celebrated shadow price indicators were the 1926–27 prices used in Soviet industry until 1950.[1] Actual wholesale prices, although they evolved so slowly as we saw in Sec. 3, nevertheless came in course of time to differ very greatly, and in no certain way, from these indicator prices. So that towards 1950 there was an extremely complicated situation. Accountancy was, by definition, in actual prices. But so also was the profit plan, so that these prices were not wholly without influence as indicators on the producing enterprise.

They certainly did influence one type of consuming enterprise: that engaged in construction. For buildings are a too heterogeneous class of object to have standard prices, so that they have always been planned and valued at cost. So the builder's output target was always couched in current rubles, and he was always interested in what he paid for his raw materials, altering his purchases accordingly. The 1926–27 prices on the other hand were the measure of output for calculating the plan-fulfilment bonus. So usually he decided big matters on the basis of them; they were and were meant to be his prime monetary indicator. And at the centre equal confusion reigned. The building planners used actual prices as a criterion for their input plans and the choice of methods of

[1] Cf. D. Hodgman, *Soviet Industrial Production*, 1928–51 (Harvard 1954), Chs 1, 2; M. C. Kaser, *Economic Journal*, 1950; N. Jasny, *The Soviet Price System*, Stanford 1951; N. Jasny, *Soviet Prices of Producers' Goods*, Stanford 1952.

construction. Industrial planners probably thought *in natura*, with little reference to any monetary criterion.

Prices are not only accounting units, indicators and criteria. They are also weights for measuring purposes. Where actual prices and/or outputs become very irrational the prices cease to be adequate measuring rods, and the statistician must look elsewhere. Soviet statisticians used to use the 1926–27 indicator prices as measuring rods, but these became in the course of time still less rational than actual wholesale prices. Being wrong indicators they were also wrong weights. A quite separate set of shadow prices is often required for measurement. This issue is discussed at length in Ch. 12.

10. The monstrous irrationality of this system needs concrete illustration.

In 1933 (says N. Jasny,[1] writing of actual wholesale prices) the price of kerosene for technical purposes, f.o.b. destination, was raised about 10-fold, to a level of about 45-fold that of good Donbass boiler coal, f.o.b. mine. In 1949 the same kerosene cost not quite 6 times as much as coal. . . . In 1949 important types of rolled steel cost about 5 to 6 times as much as coal; in the second half of 1950 only about 3 to 1. . . . The official rates for transportation with horses are about 3 times as high as those by truck.

Until 1950, as we have seen, output value targets were calculated in 'unchangeable 1926–27 prices'; that is, a factory producing miscellaneous small articles would receive a target not in detailed physical quantities but in a global sum of 1926–27 rubles. Now qualities of goods produced in that year—a pre-plan year in which there was little industry—continued to be valued at their then price. But inflation drove up the actual wholesale prices paid about $2\frac{1}{2}$-fold by 1940 and sevenfold by 1949.[2] Yet new goods and new qualities of old goods were given notional 1926–27 prices (or, after 1940 similar 'accounting prices') on the basis of their actual cost in the first years of their mass production. These could in individual cases be 10 or even 20 times the price of the obsolete quality so that

it becomes better business to over-fulfil plans for secondary and over-priced, but actually less expensive categories of output so as to overfulfil the overall sales plan calculated in 1948 accounting prices.[3]

Unnecessary changes of quality were made deliberately, merely in order to obtain a new price. A good example is given by S. V.

[1] *The Soviet Price System*, pp. 9–11.
[2] Bergson *et al.*, op. cit.
[3] Marshev, *Neftyanoe Khozyaistvo*, 12/1948, reproduced here from Kaser, *Economic Journal*, 1950, p. 89. The '1948 accounting prices' are a modified form of the 1926–27 prices, and evidently open to the same objections.

Marshev.[1] The following table shows the relative prices of a given quantity of petroleum products, the price of light petroleum products being taken = 100.

	1926–27 'escalating' prices	1948 accounting prices	1947 current plan prices	1948 new corrected prices
Petroleum Coke I	124	33	11	40
Petroleum Coke II	124	33	6	11
Fuel oil	17	16	6	15
Gas	30	2	2	11
Varnish	41	21	7	17
Polymers	1	9	3	15

It should be remembered that the 1926–27 prices quoted are those reigning in 1948, not necessarily those found in 1926–27!

Such wholesale confusion led, of course, to very curious retail results. Thus washing-machines have been sold at a loss several times their retail price.[2] Or again the pricing of gas appeared equally arbitrary to Professor Jewkes in Moscow in 1936:

> Apart from an insignificant number ... all consumers pay a standard rate. ... The officials were not inclined to attach much importance to multi-part tariffs. Apparently these have not even been considered in Moscow. There seemed to be no great interest in the view that, since the cost of providing gas to some consumers was higher than to others, there might be a case for graduated prices. ... When I inquired why, with such high profits, the price of gas was not reduced, the answers made it clear that the officials were not accustomed to think in terms of the relationship between the two. Their answer was that they 'thought the price of gas was low enough'. When I asked whether it was considered equitable to gas consumers, as against those who burnt wood in stoves, to make large profits out of them which would go to the revenue side of the local budget, it became quite apparent that I was discussing the question of prices in terms which were strange to the officials. ... The officials appeared to think that gas and electricity prices were fixed quite independently.[3]

The pricing policy of public utilities is of course quite peculiarly important and complex, since marginal is usually below average cost, and the difference has to be allocated among users—or possibly among taxpayers—in some rational way. Yet Soviet railway rates know nothing of this problem. The accepted proposition that rates should vary between marginal cost for marginal users and

---

[1] Loc. cit., quoted Kaser, loc. cit., p. 89.
[2] Arakelian, *Oktyabr'*, 1/1954.
[3] *Moscow in the Making*, ed. Sir E. Simon, London 1937, pp. 75–6.

'what the traffic will bear' for intra-marginal users is flatly rejected. 'What the traffic will bear' is monopolistic and capitalistic:
rates are and must be based on 'cost'—meaning in the context
average cost. What this presumably means is marginal cost plus
an equiproportional mark-up for all users, but our source is not
perfectly clear on what it does mean. Thus the principal problem
is not perceived, and the solution preferred—if we can speak of the
solution to an unperceived problem—is mistaken.[1]

11. It will also be helpful to contemplate a particular reform of
industrial wholesale prices during Stalin's lifetime. Some, indeed
many, price relatives are set by no means on arbitrary grounds
but in order to promote some special end of fancied economic
rationality. As when more democratic governments intervene in
pricing, only too often the exactly opposite result occurs and prices
are rendered less rational. Thus Maizenberg[2] tells us of the reforms
in 1949 and 1950:

First we must note the measures for ensuring the unity of wholesale prices for
a single product. The law of costs in its transformed aspect[3] finds its expression
in the conscious establishment by the socialist government of prices of commodities based on the socially necessary costs of their production. This presupposes the necessity of unified prices for a single product. Disparity of prices
for a single product hinders the planning of industry, undermines the calculation
of its cost and also the rational projection of new construction. This is why the
working out of the new lower wholesale prices took into account the necessity
of establishing tariffs by kinds of product, including the whole output of a given
product irrespective of its departmental subordination, so as to ensure a single
price for a single article. Note, however, that this task is not finished.

Further, the relationships between prices on individual goods were changed
in order to strengthen the interest of enterprises in the more rational use of the
material resources of the national economy.

The prices of coal have a structure designed to stimulate the extraction and
economical use of coking coals. To expand the use of Moscow-region coal, on
January 1, 1950 its wholesale prices were lowered 25% while the wholesale prices
of coal coming from further away were left unchanged; also the freight rates for
these coals were lowered by 50% within the zone of their rational use.

The relation between the prices of iron, steel and non-ferrous metals was changed
so as to stimulate economy of non-ferrous metals. Within the iron and steel
complex the price-relationship of ordinary and low-alloy steel was improved,
prices of the latter being lowered more than ordinary steel prices. This was to
stimulate the introduction of low-alloy steel into construction work.

Price-relationships between various groups of building materials were improved. While the price of construction timber was lowered 10%, that of bricks

---

[1] Chernomordik, *V. E.*, 9/1948.
[2] *P. Kh.* 6/1950, pp. 61–2.
[3] I.e. under socialism not capitalism—P.J.D.W.

went down 24% and that of cement 20%. At the same time lime prices were lowered still more than cement prices.

The reform also suppressed the practice of allocating standing timber to the lumber enterprises without cost, for this discouraged them from penetrating into the depths of forest massifs and was an obstacle to a rational felling policy.

In working out new rail freights a stimulus was given to shippers to shorten the longest hauls. The new tariff applied more thoroughly the principle of differentiation with regard to distance. Thus it is known that as the length of haul increases the cost of a ton-km. falls. Nevertheless for many articles the new tariff provides no tapering of kilometer rates but actually raises them as the normal length of haul is increased.

Thus for mineral building materials freights rise from a distance of 250 km., and for timber from 350 km., and so on. For rolled steel, oil and its derivatives, victuals, and manufactured consumer goods freights cease to fall at a certain distance, taken to be the limiting distance over which transportation is rational.

To ensure a more rational use of rolling-stock the new tariff introduces a sharp rise in freights over short distances, where road haulage is more suitable. With this end the freight rates ruling before January 1, 1949, for less than 50 km. were raised 2 to 4 times. At the same time road haulage rates were lowered from July 1, 1950.

To encourage water haulage on stretches parallel to railways water and rail freights were made to agree. With this aim, too, rail freights alone were raised during the canal navigation season. A number of discounts and penalties were also introduced to stimulate the better use of transport (a discount for haulage on parallel routes, a penalty for despatching loads under the volume or weight capacity of the rolling-stock, a discount for the use of wagons returning empty, a penalty for cross-hauls, etc., etc.).

It can easily be seen that while some of these reforms are rational, others are the greatest folly. Thus it is very right that prices should be unified, provided they are c.i.f., not f.o.b., and unified only for each several locality. But the price of Moscow-region coals is lowered, in flat violation of this correct principle. The 'zone of their rational use' is only to be discovered if a single c.i.f. price reigns in Moscow for coal from all coal-fields, and if transport rates subsidize no particular locality. It will then doubtless be discovered that Moscow-region coals cannot sell even in Moscow, and the 'zone of their rational use' is nowhere at all. Again it may or may not have been right to discourage the use of non-ferrous metals more than the old relative prices discouraged it, or to stimulate the use of low-alloy steel more than before. That would depend on the cost structure, and are not told whether the old or the new wholesale prices corresponded to this more closely. The 'limiting distance over which transportation is rational' will certainly not be discovered by raising instead of tapering haulage rates in direct contradiction of cost behaviour, and the raising of railway rates during the navigable season for canals is almost conclusive proof that these canals should never have been dug.

Note how throughout Maizenberg's description relative prices do influence relative outputs even in the planned sector; doubtless chiefly because prices are criteria for planners, more than because they are indicators for enterprises.

12. Turning to shadow prices, the most celebrated Communist shadow price is that which does duty for the *rate of interest on long-term capital in the nationalized sector*, the 'coefficient of relative effectiveness' (CRE). Celebrated, that is, in the West. It is typical of our tendency to project our own preoccupations on to Communism that a minor issue has been so much inflated in the Western literature. Its interest much exceeds its importance. The formula is that if

$$\frac{I_1 - I_2}{C_2 - C_1} < CRE$$

where 1 and 2 are alternative techniques of obtaining the same output over the same number of years, and $I_1 > I_2$, $C_1 < C_2$, technique 1 should be chosen. I is the initial expenditure, and C the current operating cost *including amortization*. The two kinds of capital equipment may have different physical durability, but must be amortized in the same time. But this is at first sight formally identical with using the 'capitalist' rate of interest (i): for in a non-Communist economy the annual cost of each technique would be reckoned at $I_1 i + C_1$ and $I_2 i + C_2$, and the cheaper would be chosen (remember that C includes amortization). Just as a high external rate of interest would incline us towards technique 2, so does a low normative CRE incline them. We are tempted to say simply CRE = 1/i, but this is not quite true, since the formula applies 'interest' to the whole initial cost, and not merely to the unamortized balance. This is a common error among elementary students of interest: it would appear that the unknown inventor of the CRE fell into the trap.

The formula is not often used, precisely because it is a shadow price, and because, being formally identical to the rate of interest, it is most un-Marxist. Nor is the same CRE used on all occasions, so that there is no single rate of time discount or price of abstinence, even when the matter is considered at all. Naturally it would be very difficult for a Marxist to see why there should be only one CRE, since both time discount and abstinence are notions wholly foreign to him. Nor could the CRE do the whole duty of the rate of interest even if it were rightly used, since it can only choose between alternative ways of doing a thing already decided on; whereas a real rate of interest might knock a project out altogether, in any combination of initial and current costs.

The CRE is thus neither useful nor ideologically sound. In 1946–50 it was the subject of much controversy. Orthodox Marxists, however, never denied altogether its validity as a criterion of choice between project variants; while its supporters, the unorthodox economists and, very significantly, the practical engineers, never demanded a full-blown rate of interest that would actually be paid. Their principal demand, for a single economy-wide CRE, was turned down. The CRE continues in a minor way.[1]

The CRE has no profitability criterion built into it (it is merely a cost formula). As such it could not be used to choose between two different outputs, but only between ways of doing the same thing, whether that thing is worth doing or not. Latterly, however, with the invention of input/output and linear programming, a genuine rate of interest has necessarily been included among the 'electronic shadow prices' recommended by its advocates. It is interesting to see how this awkward ideological corner is turned. The principal advocate of linear programming, Kantorovich, uses the same ingenious argument as was put forward much earlier by an advocate of rational pricing in a different model.[2] This is that since capital (i.e. initial expenditure) is a substitute for labour, or in Marxian terminology dead is a substitute for living labour, the former must be given a technical substitution ratio in terms of the latter. With such a ratio one will know how to optimize the input proportions. Naturally since 'labour is the source of all value' the ratio must express capital in terms of labour, and since one is a stock, the other a flow we must first take some annual percentage of the stock. But this percentage has purely planning, not monetary, significance.

---

[1] Cf. Kaplan, *Journal of Political Economy*, Apr. 1952; Grossman, *Quarterly Journal of Economics*, Aug. 1953; Wiles, *Oxford Economic Papers*, Oct. 1953; Novozhilov, *International Economic Papers*, No. 6; Miller, Eason, Zauberman, Meek, Bettelheim, *Soviet Studies*, Oct. 1949, Apr. 1950, July 1950; Leader in *Voprosy Ekonomiki* 3/1954, tr. in *Soviet Studies*, Oct. 1954; Hunter, *Review of Economics and Statistics*, 1950; Zauberman, *Review of Economic Studies* xvi/7–10. These articles make extensive references to the original Russian sources. There is also a very considerable Polish literature on the same topic with which I am unfamiliar.

[2] A. N. Novozhilov, who wanted a rational rate of interest to be included in all cost estimates; in works of 1939 and 1946, translated in *International Economic Papers no. 6*. Cf. Grossman op. cit.; Campbell, *Slavic Review*, Oct. 1961. For Kantorovich cf. Ch. 10, Secs. 16, 17.

There is very little flummery, and that quite harmless, in this chain of reasoning. Dogma is satisfied by relieving the percentage of any actual financial consequence, and by saying that capital is a substitute for labour, not the other way round. Even so, however, both Kantorovich and Novozhilov have had trouble with the concept. Even Poland does not (1961) actually use a genuine rate of interest, paid by enterprises to banks on their long-term capital. That distinction remains reserved for Yugoslavia alone.

13. The other free good is *land*. *Urban land* receives, so far as the author knows, not even a shadow price in any Communist country, except, of course, Yugoslavia, where it is freely bought and sold. Elsewhere it is physically allocated, even in Poland, by Heaven knows what political bargaining. *Agricultural land* is freely bought and sold by private and public bodies, in Poland and Yugoslavia. Elsewhere it is but seldom reallocated between agricultural users. The shrinkage of private plots is, of course, a political act, quite unrelated to the relative efficiency of private and co-operative use; indeed it would be political suicide to raise such a question. And since kolkhozniks' plots are legally a concession out of kolkhoz land—the kolkhoz owns all the land—no money passes when the concession is withdrawn. Inter-sovkhoz transfer of land is a mere administrative swap of the state's assets from one branch to another. Only when a kolkhoz is engaged, either with another kolkhoz or with a sovkhoz, could money even conceivably pass; but it does not do so, since the land is nominally nationalized in the first place.[1]

Latterly agricultural rent has been discussed a great deal in U.S.S.R. The starting-point is complaints about income-distribution. For since rents are not charged they are absorbed into profits. But in the kolkhoz system the labour-day is the residuary legatee of profit, since labour is paid on the dividend principle. So the failure to charge rents causes inequalities among kolkhozy. Thus we meet again a prime characteristic of prices in the kolkhoz sector: their importance as income-distributors.

Now this situation could have once been met by output-discrimination on the part of the zagotovka organs: which simply took larger deliveries, at the penal price, from the richest kolkhozy. But this method would have been very clumsy, even if consciously

---

[1] 'Sovkhozization' (Ch. 17, Sec. 3.) involves the transfer of land from the old kolkhoz, but since the latter is thereby abolished no money passes. Its members become Sovkhoz workers and thus in theory improve their lot anyway. If their kolkhoz was a particularly rich one, so that sovkhoz wages are actually lower than trudoden payments, they must console themselves with their higher class status.

applied. And actually it was not: the zagotovka organs merely took as much as they could where the harvest happened in any year to be best.[1] In today's set-up a possible remedy is price-discrimination on the part of the zakupka organs. But this would have catastrophic results for resource allocation, lessening the profitability of output on good land. By contrast a true rent is a fixed cost, zero at the margin[2] of profitability which should govern decisions. Nevertheless rent is in a general way condemned by Marx,[3] and there has already been, indeed there has always been, some price discrimination. So this system is likely to expand: i.e. of the three ways in which incomes could be equalized, that one will be chosen that most disturbs resource allocation.

Were actual rents to be charged—as opposed to shadow rents in planning offices—it would be logical to apply them to sovkhozy, forests, mines and oil-wells, if not to all land whatsoever in the nationalized sector. This has been proposed,[4] but it is very un-Marxist indeed, and quite unlikely to be adopted. Here again differential pricing is common, and indeed has been more thoroughly applied than among kolkhozy. Such pricing leads, of course, to individualized rates of turnover tax, since the product of all mines sells at about the same price. The heavy profits tax also helps, and in any case there is almost no effect on income-distribution since wages are separately fixed.

14. The *rate of foreign exchange*, on the other hand, is an actual price, and a very passive one. Like other passive prices it gets stuck at a historical moment and then changes only very rarely. Since Communist economies normally suffer inflation, and foreign exchanges are everywhere a prestige issue, the rate normally much overvalues the currency. But except in Poland there is no shadow rate for deciding what shall be exported and imported; this decision is taken arbitrarily,[5] and the importing corporations make profits which pass into the central budget, while the exporting corporations make losses which are separately subsidized from the same source.

---

[1] Cf. Wiles, *Soviet Studies*, Oct. 1955, pp. 150–51.

[2] A *fixed* low-price zagotovka would not affect the margin.

[3] *Das Kapital*, Book 3, Chs. 45–7. He does not say, but he certainly implies, that there would be none under socialism.

[4] It is implicit in Kantorovich, but missing in normal discussions of agricultural rent.

[5] Wiles, *Soviet Studies*, Oct. 1952; E. Klinkmüller, *Die Gegenwärtige Aussenhandelsver-flechtung der Sowjetzone*, Berlin 1959 *passim*; M. P. Donnelly and A. Nove, *Trade with Communist Countries*, London 1960, Chs. 1–4; Wiles, *Oxford Economic Papers*, 1957, pp. 199, 202–3; Alan Brown in *The American Economist*, Nov. 1961.

K

The covert reduction of the Soviet rate of exchange to near purchasing power parity (Nov. 1960) may herald its use as a criterion, if not as an indicator, in foreign trade, and the abandonment of other more irrational criteria.

CHAPTER 7

THE DECENTRALIZATION, FORMAL AND INFORMAL, OF A COMMAND ECONOMY

Once when I was driving along the Kharkov-Rostov road I stopped at a petrol pump to fill up the tank. Several cars were waiting in front of me. It seemed that the petrol station was not selling any petrol. On the office door was the sign 'NO SALE OF PETROL TODAY'. I was surprised by this notice. No sale? What were the cars on the road to do—wait till tomorrow? I went in as though there was nothing unusual and asked to have my car filled up.

'Can't you read?' A man with a bristling little moustache looked up at me with surprise: 'It's written in black and white, "No Sale Today".'

'Haven't you got any petrol, then?'

'There's any amount of petrol. Baku is functioning properly, I'm glad to say.'

'Then why won't you fill up my car?'

'We've fulfilled our plan for today.'

To tell the truth, I was disgusted. 'How on earth,' I exclaimed, 'can you expect a daily planned quota of petrol sales, if you can't plan the number of passing vehicles?'

'What d'you mean?' My interlocutor rose menacingly from his table: 'Are you opposed to State Planning, then? . . .'

Izvestia, Jan. 6, 1957.

(1) In an unplanned business things just happen, i.e. they crop up, life is full of unforeseen happenings and circumstances over which you have no control. On the other hand, (2) in a *planned* business things still happen and crop up and so on, *but you know exactly what would have been the state of affairs if they had not.*

Mark Spade, Business for Pleasure, Ch. 3.

1. WE first consider in greater detail the actual day-to-day working of Stalin's system, the *informal* pressures it built up and the loopholes through which they escaped. We then take the various non-Yugoslav roads to *formal* reform, i.e. we try to combine planning and decentralization.

A primary feature of Stalin's system (allocation model 4) is the *tension between the periphery and the centre*, between the planner and the consumer or worker (Ch. 5, Sec. 4). We saw in Ch. 4 that the variable turnover tax is the main means whereby this tension is resolved, enabling the planner to set at the same time such wage differentials as will induce labour to where he wants it, and such price differentials as will induce the consumer to buy whatever he decides to produce. We saw further a subsidiary weapon in the

131

planner's hand: the queue. If price and output are too low, he can simply leave it that way and let a queue develop. But the contrary is much less likely: if price and output are too high he is likely to do something about it, to avoid the more obvious waste of indefinite stock accumulation. There is, too, the resort of official advertising, now on the increase.

This, then, is the pure theory of the thing.[1] Note that there is no such tension under War Communism (allocation model 1), since neither worker nor consumer is in a market at all. It is the *intermediate degree of decentralization* in Stalin's model that causes the trouble. And of course trouble is greater in some areas than in others. In the decision of the overall total of investment and in the allocation of funds to particular purposes, the state wins easily. But the more we approach direct contact with the worker or consumer, and the more detailed the choices made in this area, the less power the state has. By theft, embezzlement and 'speculation', by refusing to buy this and refusing to work there, even perhaps by complaining and queuing, the citizen fights back. Moreover, there is more decentralization on principle in these smaller matters.

So in practice there were many other ways of resolving the tension, which cut across the theory of the model as defined. We shall examine successively two reactions by the authorities: further centralization and further decentralization; and the most important evasive or distorting actions taken by the population, which may be distinguished into anti-plan and essentially pro-plan (violating it in detail in order to fulfil it in fundamentals).

2. *Further centralization by the government.* First, in periods of famine and war the consumer has been rationed, much as in any other country. Of this little need be said, since rationing in Communist countries does not differ in principle, or even much in practical detail, from what it is elsewhere. As elsewhere it is accepted as an emergency measure only.[2]

But if consumer rationing is a rarity, its mirror image, the direction of labour, is not. We saw in Ch. 2 that formal labour direction is indissolubly connected with the name of Trotsky. Therefore, fortunately for the history of the world, Stalin had to avoid it, and for the most part he genuinely relied on the labour

---

[1] The pure theory is of course mine, not theirs. It has been set up by myself to ease our conceptual grasp of the various possible systems. The definition of what features are pure theory, and what are practical exceptions to it, are mine alone, and have no relation to Marxism.

[2] Cf. Ch. 9, Sec. 14.

market as his tool. But the extreme temptation to direct labour, to which any totalitarian planner is subjected, has not been resisted. The informal methods may be briefly noted:

(i) high labour turnover has been attacked, especially in the early 'thirties, by evicting 'quitters' from their houses, if these are owned by the factory, and by deprivation of social service benefits. That is, labour is 'directed' to stay wherever it has in the first place chosen to go.

(ii) Party members have always been liable to direction by the Party.

(iii) students leaving technical schools and universities, and—while they lasted—State Labour Reserve Schools[1]—are directed to a given post where they must remain for a number of years.

(iv) the Komsomol brings a great deal of pressure to bear, during particular campaigns such as that for the Virgin Lands. This applies especially to high school leavers and soldiers being demobilized.

(v) during the War direction of labour was official, as in many non-Communist countries.

(vi) the concentration camp system is a most complete form of labour direction for those who fall into it.

(vii) administrative exile is under one aspect a geographical direction of labour. Moreover the exile is often in practice directed to a particular place of work.

(viii) the minor punishments for infringing the labour code have the effect of labour direction; especially the punishment of 'forced labour'—work at very low pay in one's present post.

Of these methods only (ii) and (iii) are at present (1959) in full vigour, though (iv) may at any moment be revived. This clearly proves that direction of labour is no essential part of Stalin's model. The European satellites have indulged in these exceptions less, China however has used them very much more. It would hardly be unfair to say that in 1960 most Chinese labour, even outside the People's Communes, is directed.

3. On the other side the régime has had moments of unaccustomed 'liberalism'. In the first Five-year Plan the balance of payments crisis led to a number of exceptional measures, among them the setting up of luxury shops at which anyone could buy for gold

---

[1] A kind of elementary technical school.

or foreign exchange, and no questions asked. Foreigners and ex-bourgeois were thus painlessly relieved of their valuta, in addition to other methods.[1] Similar shops came back during the war, when the prices were marked (at astronomical levels) in rubles. This time the object was simply to mop up surplus purchasing power. On both occasions one may say that the state decided to participate in the very high profits occasionally to be made on the free market.

Again in the middle 'thirties Stalin permitted entirely private-capitalist gold prospectors to operate once more, as 'socialist' geologists had proved inefficient and he wanted the territory of Siberia more thickly populated. At the same time and for the same reason he permitted the establishment of individual peasant farms on virgin soil along the Manchurian border.[2]

These exceptions are very distinct from the decentralization on principle, intended to be permanent, that set in with Stalin's death. This we deal with below. They differ also from Stalin's own use of indicators that leave a certain initiative to the producer or customer. These were a common and official part of his model, and have already been discussed at sufficient length in Ch. 4.

4. *'Pro-plan' violations by peripheral agents.* Never was system more certain to be violated, even though it had the force of law, and law the threat of terror. The causes of these violations may be analysed into:

(i) the pressure of the planners' impossible demands, which we shall call 'planner's tension' and describe at more length in Ch. 11.

(ii) dilatoriness, inefficiency and over-centralization;

(iii) competition for labour.

We take (i) and (iii) together in this section. The planners always ask, as we have seen, for more than could possibly be done. The 'method of balances' cannot assure supplies unless other enterprises fulfil their (also impossible) plans. As the output targets are always the most important part of the plan, and the director's bonus depends mainly on his fulfilment of them, he is always violating the rest of the plan for their sake. Black markets, or rather black bilateral transactions, occur in raw materials and labour, and firms secretly barter services among each other (you repair my furnace, I'll lend you some aluminium until next quarter). All

---

[1] People suspected of holding gold were tortured. Gold teeth were knocked out. The relatives, living abroad, of would-be emigrants were blackmailed. Foreign bank-notes were forged. Cf. R. O. G. Urch, *The Rabbit King of Russia*, London 1939, Chs 1 and 25; W. G. Krivitsky, *I Was Stalin's Agent*, London 1940, Ch. 4.

[2] J. D. Littlepage and D. Bess, *In Search of Soviet Gold*, N.Y. 1938, Ch. 11.

expenditures are extremely tightly controlled, and directors can even now spend only minimal amounts on their own initiative. So these activities mean squaring the accountant and probably also the auditors, and in reply the authorities constantly reshuffle directors and accountants before they get to know each other.

Further enterprises try to corrupt higher headquarters by various means which need not be listed, and in particular send or hire permanent agents or representatives at these offices. These 'tolkachi' are supposed to know exactly whom to talk to, which forms to use, etc. The main objects of this activity are to reduce the plan targets and expedite or increase supplies.

It is certainly not surprising, but may seem a pity, that such activities were illegal, although they are directed towards plan fulfilment. For they are clearly acts of indiscipline, tending to reduce the general enforceability of all plans, and they do disturb *priorities*. For within the State plan there is a whole series of somewhat unofficial priorities, and since the authorities know that not everything can be performed they want to 'rationalize' plan underfulfilment, i.e. to see it occurs in the 'right' branches of the economy. Hence if all enterprises can be kept short of stocks and money they will always be dependent on the centre for everything, and this is better than violation of the plan even for the plan's own sake.

One kind of tolkach, however, is very difficult to suppress: the factory cell and the local organ of the Party. These people are as interested as any in the success of the enterprise, since their own prestige and promotion depend on it. They carry far more moral weight than the lay tolkachi hired directly by the enterprise, and their activity is hard to condemn as anti-social. So the peculiar situation arises that the Ruling Party, the Vanguard of the Proletariat, that can make or break any director, and upset the most important economic decisions, goes grubbing around for belting and sulphuric acid on the director's behalf.[1]

Labour is in short supply like any other commodity, particularly if skilled. Planner's tension ensures this, but the difference here is that it has to be obtained on a free market. Competition is formally impossible as all wage rates and the total wage bill are rigidly fixed. But in fact it goes on all the time, and the wage regulations are

[1] Gerry Hough, *The Role of Local Party Organs in Soviet Industrial Decision-Making*, Harvard University doctoral thesis, 1961.

simply broken.[1] Moreover, from 1928 to 1947 in U.S.S.R., and in later years still in some of the satellites and China, the cost of living kept rising, and mere humanity demanded that wage maxima be exceeded during these years. Competition became at one time so severe in U.S.S.R. that even the labour of prisoners was bid for by rival prison camps; in a few cases the individual prisoner was approached while out on his day of leave.[2]

5. So much for detailed violations directed towards general plan fulfilment. Others are *anti-plan* through and through, and aim directly at the satisfaction of the consumer. The prevailing monetary inflation leads at most times to a general excess of demand, and the irrational pattern of allocation ensures that there will always be excesses in particular lines. There is a certain amount of 'black' production of things in very short supply: the classic case is the light engineering factory that did secret overtime producing sewing needles, which were sold at great profit, until the director and the accountant went to prison. But there is very much more 'black' marketing, or 'speculation', in that people with time on their hands will queue up for scarce consumer goods (preferably after getting special prior information of the arrival of a consignment), buy at state prices and resell at a profit. This activity might well be of great social benefit where the speculator provides the services of storage or transport. But Marxists are violently hostile to all private profit taken from trade, which they hold to be essentially unproductive and thus to generate a quite different order of profit from, say, private craft production. So the very multifarious activity of this kind that always goes on is severely repressed. Black production is of course contrary to the plan, since it uses materials and equipment contrary to instructions. Black marketing violates no plan except in periods of rationing; but it violates the law of the land and the ethos of the constitution. Free and black markets are so highly imperfect and localized that one can earn a very large income in this way until one is arrested.

6. As to *sheer crime* it suffices to say that scarcity, social conditions, the breakdown of religious sanctions, the failure of the new 'socialist' morality to take root, the immense complexity of economic laws and the large profits to be made out of the contradictions they involve, all give rise to economic crime on an

---

[1] Not so much by paying illegal bonuses as by upgrading jobs. Grades and their pay are laid down by the centre, but the classification of people into these grades is left to management.
[2] J. Rounault, *My Friend Vassia*, London 1952, Ch. 49.

unprecedented scale. Ordinary burglars and such flourish and multiply, accountants divert funds, workers steal materials, and above all peasants steal kolkhoz property. This latter branch of theft forms an important source of peasant income. Yet at least these crimes have their counterpart under capitalism, even if that system does create so much temptation and necessity for them.

But over and above these types of crime come the 'crimes' of disobeying the plan. For the plan is law, and its violation by worker or manager is a minor legal offence. Hence that vast new branch of law, the Soviet labour law, which is without capitalist parallel. Hence, too, a number of managerial offences such as gross negligence, wilful non-fulfilment of the plan, refusal to penalize workers according to law, economic sabotage. These, too, are without parallel.

Plainly crime also operates against the plan. But may not all three of these phenomena, crime, black marketing and black production, improve the allocation of resources, whatever their relation to the plan? Once this solemn question is put it can only receive one answer: crime of the types recognized as such under capitalism does not improve resource allocation, but nearly all other violations of Communist plan and Communist law do. If we violate minor provisions in the plan in order to fulfil major ones we are probably at least improving efficiency and avoiding waste. If we simply violate *tout court* we must be doing so to satisfy the consumer, as otherwise it would not be profitable. If we violate labour law we are attending to that desideratum so neglected in Western theory, workers' sovereignty. Deleterious in their long-run effect on state discipline and social morality, nearly all these violations improve the allocation of resources here and now; though probably most of them divert effort from investment to consumption, and so lower the rate of growth.

The more ruthless and totalitarian a Communist system is, the fewer violations there are. Thus, in China, persuasion and terror have reached such heights that there is probably less crime, even including economic crime, than in the advanced countries of Western Europe.[1] In U.S.S.R. in the first FYP, when the system was new and the control mechanisms undiscovered, there was far more. In liberal Poland there is more than in Stalinist Poland, since the old pre-Communist moral restraints cannot be brought back,

[1] U.S.A., with its wave on wave of racially heterogeneous immigrants, is of course no fair comparison.

while the new merely terroristic restraints have been abandoned. These are mere impressions, of course, devoid of statistical backing.

7. But for all these qualifications the system was desperately over-centralized, and increasingly so right up to Stalin's death. This was particularly true in the field of 'distribution', as explained in Ch. 9. 'We must refer it to Moscow' was the invariable refrain. In so terroristic a system the first rule of survival was to avoid responsibility. On this Krokodil had a classic cartoon:

Departmental Head: Why do you bother me with these trivialities? Can't you settle them yourself?

Assistant: Oh no, comrade, we don't want to bother you. If you'd just put your signature here. . . .

D.H.: My signature? I'll clear that with the Minister.

The moment Stalin died the trend was reversed, and every sort of attempt was made to square the Communist circle, i.e.:

(i) to abolish bureaucracy;

(ii) to decentralize, and to raise local initiative;

(iii) to retain planning, and avoid the 'anarchy of the market'.

The rest of this chapter is devoted to the incompatibility of these three aims, first in theory, then in the various practical attempts.

(i) and (iii) are quite incompatible, i.e. the market saves a very great deal of paper-work. This may seem obvious, but the exercise of proof is most enlightening. First, a market does not require much less *knowledge* in its participants than a central planning system. For in the former it is enough for the participants to know their own costs and outputs, and *guess* at the *changes* in behaviour of their rivals and customers; while there is no central authority that needs to know anything. Under central planning each participant must pass up its knowledge to the centre, but is spared the pains of guessing about rivals and customers. If the centre is administratively expensive, so are market intelligence and speculation. Again the necessities of accounting and audit are in both cases the same. Even on the side of demand there is no special need for more bureaucracy, since the central planners *can* proceed by trial and error just as the market can. So, secondly, the immense extra apparatus is required for *communicating and enforcing orders*. For in a market no apparatus is required to give orders—the profit motive does that, and therefore no apparatus is required to enforce them. Planners' orders will, moreover, be unpopular and disputable, giving rise to evasive action, legal complications, precautions against corruption, etc., all infinitely more severe than in a market system, which offers far fewer temptations of this kind.

Moreover, thirdly, the system requires *technical knowledge* at both the receiving and the giving ends. For it is no mere clerk or economist who can give such orders, but a trained technician is needed at the centre. This waste of technical training is an acutely felt disadvantage of the system.[1] It is one of the most surprising fallacies among Sovietologists that the command economy economizes in technical experts: the one trained man can sit at the centre and run everything. For the principal function of a technologist is to deal with crises on the spot, to keep the machinery running. Central planning removes one or more of these men to the centre, where he must spend his time quarrelling with those who remain on the spot, so that they cannot get on with their proper work. This is undoubtedly the main reason why the U.S.S.R., giving merely rather more higher education than advanced Western countries, trains in particular very significantly more engineers. The excess of Soviet engineers is not so much a Cold War victory as a comment on the efficiency of a market system.

Yet again the products are not sold to the highest bidder, but must be 'distributed' according to yet another plan—for which the market offers no parallel. On 'distribution' compare Ch. 9. I cannot resist, however, quoting here an account of the bureaucracy it still involved in U.S.S.R. in 1960.

... a characteristic example, when in order to get ball-bearings from the First state ball-bearings factory indents, accounts and allocations from the motor-factory 'Likhachev', situated next door, take a long journey: via 14 all-republican and all-union depots and planning organs, in each of which a laborious work is undertaken of circulating, verifying and formalizing documents. The weight of all the documents formalizing the yearly supply of ball-bearings from First to Likhachev was 200 kg.[2]

In general it seems impossible to deduce from Soviet figures the increase in bureaucracy caused by the command economy. The regime has every ground for concealing it, but with the best will in the world it is difficult to keep occupational statistics comparable over time or place. Thus there are about 1 million *fewer* 'clerks' in U.S.S.R. than in U.K., but about 2 million more 'watchmen and

---

[1] N. deWitt, *Educational and Professional Employment in the U.S.S.R.*, National Science Foundation 1961, pp. 508–11.
[2] Yu. I. Koldomasov, *Planirovanie Material'no-Tekhnicheskogo Snabzhenia*, Moscow 1961, p. 22.

guards',[1] and many hundred thousand more 'engineers'. Moreover Soviet communications workers do more on behalf of the economic administration and less on behalf of the final consumer. So while the above a priori argument makes it reasonably certain that the command economy *is* more bureaucratic, we cannot tell by how much. *Moreover the market system's whole gain may be wasted on 'uninformative' advertising, and most Stock Exchange work is also waste.* It is only perfect competition that is certainly superior.

8. Decentralization and planning, however, are compatible: the subordinate authority is given powers to command the enterprise hitherto reserved to the centre. If this is done, however, bureaucracy is in no way diminished: it merely changes its seat of operations. If since Stalin died bureaucracy has at all diminished in U.S.S.R., it is not because Khrushchev has substituted Sovnarkhozy for Ministries, but because—mainly against his will—more powers have gone directly to enterprise managers, to the detriment of Gosplan and Sovnarkhoz alike. Indeed if more scope is not given to the market decentralization merely multiplies planning authorities and actually increases bureaucracy.

There are several ways of decentralizing a command economy without making it into a market economy. We shall know them collectively as DC ('decentralized command').

What, strictly, do we mean by this at all? There are few trickier concepts. We shall mean here a transfer of allocative sovereignty in the sense of Ch. 4 from the central to the subordinate 'body'. We mean a redistribution of functions and competences, without reference to the efficiency wherewith they are discharged. Thus we do not mean an increase in the geographical distance between authorities; the 'body'-government link is not decentralized if Sovnarkhozy are substituted for Ministries, *ceteris paribus;* but it is if as a result of this increased distance control is informally relaxed. *Per contra,* however, the 'body's' control over the enterprise will be informally tightened by its new geographical propinquity, and that is a centralization of the 'body'-enterprise link. So the net effect, on the enterprise-government link, may well be nil. Nor do we mean a change in the number of subordinates referring to one centre: thus if 100 Sovnarkhozy grow where 25 Ministries grew before this makes control more difficult, but that is not automatically more decentralization. On the contrary, if the government insists on

[1] Nove, *Manchester Statistical Society,* Jan. 1962.

having as much control over 'bodies' as before it will merely lead to greater inefficiency, in which case there will be complaints of an *increase* in centralization!

Nor do we mean any special change in the number of people in central offices. For, as we have just seen, the same division of functions and competencies can seem more centralized the less efficiently the centre plays its part. Just as great physical distance reduces this efficiency, so will a decrease in the numbers, equipment or ability of the central officials. So for that matter will an increase in their numbers, if it reduces their efficiency. For there is here an optimization problem: too few officials will become a bottleneck through sheer incapacity to cope, too many will delay decisions while they consult each other. Either way, enterprises will complain of excessive centralization. But if a smoothly functioning 'perfect computation' issues very many more orders, only punctually and without self-contradiction, they will complain less. Though centralization has risen, overcentralization has diminished.

Thus it is just possible that U.S.S.R. uses fewer central 'bureaucrats' in proportion than UK.[1] It would then follow either that Soviet bureaucrats were more efficient as individuals; or that they fulfilled their (vastly greater) functions less efficiently, or less justly, or on the basis of less information, or with greater delay; or that British staffs were too big, and therefore less efficient for that reason.

Again in other contexts decentralization might mean a change in ideological or proprietorial sovereignty, in the sense of Ch. 1. But so long as we remain in a command economy the state remains in this sense sovereign, takes the lion's share of residual profit, etc.

Another confusion about decentralization springs from the self-deceiving and indeed self-contradictory Communist notion of 'democracy'. Communists, as is well known, believe in totalitarian democracy, the spontaneous and rational unanimity of all citizens with each other and their government. The Plan occupies the position of Rousseau's General Will.

'In drafting proposals for improving the system of indices, special attention is devoted to bringing this system into closer accord with the new organizational forms of management, with the principles of democratic centralism. Only these principles ensure the unity of the centralized planning of the economy with the development of local initiative by management and by the wide masses of the working people.'[2]

---

[1] Nove, op. cit.   [2] Yefimov, *Kommunist*, 4/1961.

Local initiative and centralization seem to the earthbound Westerner perfectly contradictory: you can mix them by assigning to each its separate function, but you cannot enjoy them both in any one function simultaneously. But Communists continually square this circle by using the phraseology of Rousseau and Marx. They thus avoid having to admit one of the doctrines upon which this book is based: the logical necessity of a market in the absence of a command economy (Ch. 1, Sec. 6).

So since decentralization is a mild hurrah-word, and bureaucracy a definite boo-word, in the Communist vocabulary there are a number of bogus systems of decentralization, whereby its form is captured and its content eschewed. To such bogus systems belong:

(i) 'Operative' functions are decentralized, but 'planning' functions are not. Now to plan is to give orders and to operate is to carry them out, so taken literally this is a mere platitude. But if we twist the words a little we can discern two concrete meanings. First the central plan is loose and general, and the *planning* of the details is defined as 'operation', and so decentralized. This is perfectly genuine, indeed the very definition of DC, and we return to it. Or, secondly, the central plan is tight and specific, but the *responsibility* for its execution rests on the local man. This is a typical piece of Stalinism: the, say, manager is told he has more initiative but in fact he only has more burdens. Moreover, under this system the planner is relieved of responsibility for the good sense of his orders. Initiative at the centre, responsibility at the circumference: the thing is the autocrat's ideal, and very much Communist planning resolves itself into only this.

(ii) The local elected organs are incorporated in the planning hierarchy. This, too, may or may not be bogus. It is bogus if the elected organ is simply treated as a local branch office under orders, like a French mayor. For after all it is always possible, though not very logical, to elect a man to a purely administrative post, where his actions are not beholden to his electorate. But the decentralization is not bogus if, in consideration of the organ's elected nature, it has a certain freedom of decision. And informally it is bound to have just that. Thus the Sovnarkhozy are appointed by the republics in which they are,[1] but subject to Gosplan orders. The new (June 1960) Supreme Sovnarkhozy of the republics, which seem so unnecessary, are probably an attempt to cut down the competences

---

[1] Though through Party channels the chief officials are subject to vetting at higher levels, i.e. are mostly on the nomenklatura of the Central Committee.

of the local Gosplan offices at that administrative level, and are therefore a move in the direction of particularism.[1]

9. Turning to genuine DC we must first divide economic decisions into 'big' and 'small'. 'Big' decisions include the choice between consumption and investment, or between broad categories of products, or between basically different techniques, and the location of major plants. 'Small' decisions affect mainly the sortament and minor technical change. This distinction is so drawn that a big decision could not with sanity be decentralized while a small one was still centralized. The bare logical possibility of such a thing remains, but need not detain us.

We abstract for the time being from the production/territorial distinction, and call the intermediate bodies upon whom decision-making is devolved neither Ministries nor Sovnarkhozy but simply 'bodies'. There are two basic cases.

First the 'bodies' receive all the planning functions, and the centre is simply abolished. Then, owing to the 'logical necessity of a market', exchanges between the 'bodies' must be ordinary market transactions, however oligopolistic or imperfect. Their internal prices and resource allocations are their own affairs, and may or may not be relevant to their 'international' trade. This relation is a complicated matter to which we return.

Alternatively, a centre remains which makes the 'big' decisions, but devolves the 'small' upon the 'bodies', who also issue commands, thus putting detailed flesh on the generalized skeleton. Then the enterprise receives as detailed a plan as ever, but each 'body' determines, not as in the former case of DC everything, nor as in pure CC nothing, but its own sortament, without reference to any other body. *Note that in this case 'big' decisions must include all inter-body trade, down to the smallest detail.* For if this is not all exactly laid down by the centre the 'logical necessity of a market' reasserts itself: the bodies must bargain with each other, and that is not CC. This is an exceedingly important proposition—the author holds it to be a tautology—about DC: where the system of command is maintained throughout, relations between 'bodies', however trivial, must be reserved for the centre.

Thus there are two pure types of decentralized planning, in which

[1] Strictly, they have only 'operative' functions while the Gosplan retains 'planning'. But the line is, as we have seen, impossible to draw, and there can be no doubt that these new bodies will encroach on the Gosplan.

the allocation models used by the centre and the 'bodies' respectively are:

(a) FM and DC;

(b) CC and DC.

In pure CC there are only the centre and the enterprises, in pure FM only the enterprises.

10. Still confining ourselves to theory, how would the rationality of the economy differ under these systems from what it was under CC? With big decisions part of our answer is simple: in CC/DC they are taken just as under pure CC. So, if central administrative enforcement is not impaired by the strengthened political influence of the 'bodies', these systems require no further discussion. With FM/DC on the other hand the big decisions look very different. The main questions here are how the prices on the 'inter-body' market are arrived at, the extent to which the 'body' maximizes its profits on the market; and whether it has internal allocation procedures that tell it what its profits really are. This is exactly the problem in international trade between Communist countries, which thus appears as the very paradigm of FM/DC.[1]

Does the 'body' maximize its profits? Common sense would tell us that subject to ideological and political restraints it surely does. Certainly nothing to the contrary emerges from the example of trade between Communist countries, the only actual case of the model. Limited only by the political power of Moscow, every satellite maximizes its profits.

The more difficult question is how it knows what its profits are. In that special form of the command economy we have called CM (Ch. 4, Sec. 1) the 'body' hews strictly to the market, using rational accounting prices and adapting its outputs to the market as if it were a large capitalist enterprise. In this case there is no difficulty. In all other cases the 'body' cuts its relation to external prices: under ICM by taxes and subsidies, under CC by physical orders that neglect monetary considerations, etc., etc. Unless very sophisticated

---

[1] International trade is outside our competence, but note that in this particular case there is not a separate Communist 'inter-body' market, since at most points non-Communist supplies are, and are seen to be, alternative to Communist supplies. Consequently prices are world prices, even though the quantity of trade across the Iron Curtain is kept down by administrative means; so that relative marginal costs are not the same in Communist countries as in the world as a whole. But in the hypothetical case of FM/DC within one nation's boundaries the centre might still put a ring-fence of tariffs or quotas around the 'inter-body' market, and thus cut it off from world scarcity relationships. Cf. Mendershausen, *Review of Economics and Statistics*, May 1960; Wiles, *Soviet Studies*, 1961; Holzman, *Review of Economics and Statistics*, 1962.

forms of activity analysis are used, each 'body' plans irrationally, and with a different irrationality from all other bodies.

Now it is not necessarily a bad thing that irrationality differs from 'body' to 'body': if under CC there is too much steel and too little aluminium in every part of the country it may be an actual improvement that under DC there is here and there too little steel and too much aluminium. This is especially the case if we take black markets into account: for now the black marketers have something to work with. What *is* wrong with FM/DC is that the 'bodies' will surely tend to autarky, and (if territorially defined) sacrifice economies of scale. This is a very grave disadvantage, that makes the model effectually unemployable.

FM/DC is not unknown under capitalism. Especially when it is large, the enterprise is tempted to pursue unprofitable courses, and in particular to cross-subsidize bad products out of good, to mis-allocate joint costs, etc. This is like the ICM of a planning 'body', while a perfectly rational large enterprise corresponds to a planning 'body' on CM.

11. We finish the theory of decentralization with a word on 'small' decisions. These are decentralized in nearly all practical systems simply in order to save administrative cost and delay. If there were very few of them they could certainly be taken at the centre along with the 'big' decisions. And the arguments for doing so are just the same: to avoid autarky and to exploit the economies of scale. For in the choice of sortament these remain considerable. Thus if it is a 'big' decision to choose between thick steel pipes and thin steel pipes it is still extremely wasteful if every diameter of the latter is produced by every plant in the thin steel pipe section; specialization could well go a great deal further, and on a free perfect market it would certainly do so. Imperfect com-petition is like decentralization: both stop specialization short of the ideal point. The former restrains the cheaper, specialized firm from driving out its less efficient or specialized rival from its particular line. The latter allows 'subordinate autarky' (Ch. 8, Sec. 5) to flourish.

So there are good grounds why the centre should supervise even the tiniest details. It is here that the indicator comes in. An indicator is, after all, an operation order, in place of a specific instruction, to a subordinate body, telling it how to handle some detailed question in a large number of instances. If, as in Ch. 4, the centre imposes indicators on enterprises it can certainly do the same to 'bodies'.

L

12. In the foregoing sections we discussed the decentralization of decision-making. Now suppose something less drastic. *Initiative* is decentralized, in that planning proposals always come from below, while decision remains centralized. The function of the centre is to correct and reconcile, not initiate, proposals. We have stumbled here across an important tacit confusion in our notion of the command economy: that *formal and effective command coincide*. In fact they need not. Thus a free market system is obviously very decentralized, and a plan drawn up by a few people in Moscow *on their own wishes* and enforced by them regardless is obviously very centralized. But suppose the central plan is a mere summary of local proposals? If the 'bodies' are territorial and so fairly autarkic the proposals even in their original form will nearly satisfy the 'method of balances', and require little central co-ordination on technical grounds. In any case they may reach agreement among themselves about inter-'body' exchange, without prior reference to the centre; and merely seek the latter's rubber stamp. Or suppose the central plan contains large tolerances, outside of which the localities would not in any case wish to go? Or suppose it is easy and common to alter the plan during the course of the period it covers, and 'bodies' can secure such alterations at will?

These possibilities have nothing to do with CC/DC as above defined, but are rather a sluggish and imperfect RM of the initiative-holders, be they 'bodies' or enterprises. To the extent that the initiative-holders make contradictory proposals, or run against whatever aspects of public policy the centre retains, the reconcilers will have more to do, and the system veers towards pure CC. But if the initiative-holders can bargain successfully among themselves beforehand, and present a coherent scheme, or if they happen to agree with the centre's notion of public policy, the system veers towards RM, with a sort of epiphenomenal planning bureaucracy giving everybody formal permission to do what he says he is going to do. There are now elements of such a situation in U.S.S.R., though they must not be exaggerated and they may well not increase in strength.

CHAPTER 8

SPATIAL RATIONALITY AND THE TERRITORIAL PRINCIPLE[1]

1. EVERY production decision is a location decision, since all economic activity possesses ubiety, is somewhere. Even to use existing capacity is to locate, in this way rather than in that, current production. Resources must be rationally located as well as allocated. Rationality of outputs is far too often discussed as if it were a major subject separable from the minor appendix of spatial rationality. But in fact there is no such thing as a rational output programme independent of location. For the choice of location must be permitted to determine the choice of output, and vice versa. They are co-variables, presenting a simultaneous equation.

This simultaneous equation is automatically and correctly solved for us by perfect competition: if all entrepreneurs maximize their profits in current production and in investment everything will be so located and transported that production (c.i.f.) is as cheap as possible. Of course external economies heavily complicate this generalization, in a way that they do not complicate the choice between products; but it remains true for the overwhelming majority of 'small' decisions and the majority of 'big' ones. Nor can the external economies be rationally allowed for unless there are proper prices (Ch. 5, Sec. 3). Again it is true that the interests of national minorities are far more heavily vested in the locational than in the allocational aspects of economic choice. But we cannot tell how much these vested interests cost us without proper prices; so we can make no sensible decision about them in an arbitrary economy.

Under 'perfect computation' the location problem would also be solved *ambulando*. But what of all the intermediate allocation models? Under imperfect competition the degree of monopoly varies arbitrarily between firms that, of course, possess ubiety.

---

[1] The principal Western sources on location theory in general are: John G. Rice, *Ideological Theory Underlying the Distribution of Industry in the U.S.S.R.* (Unpublished memorandum of the Department of Geography, University of Washington, Seattle 1959. This is easily the best source); H. Hunter, *Soviet Transportation Policy*, Harvard 1957; H. Chambre, *L'Aménagement du Territoire en U.R.S.S.*, Paris, Mouton 1959; A. Popluiko, *Munich Bulletin*, January 1956; F. Holzman, *Quarterly Journal of Economics*, August 1957.

So space is wrongly used. Under imperfect computation things are considerably worse, for the arbitrary allocational criteria of, say, the Soviet system of imperfect computation are not even able to serve as bad locational criteria. Thus profit, even under imperfect competition, at least gives an automatic answer to the location question, even if a wrong one. But such Soviet criteria as heavy or light industry, national autarky, mere modernity, maximum capital-intensity, say nothing about location. To be as preoccupied, then, as Soviet economists are with spatial economics, to try to evolve special location criteria for normal cases uncomplicated by external economies or local vested interests, is implicitly to admit that one's general allocation criteria are unhelpful. Indeed it would very much surprise a thoroughgoing Marxist to be asked for a criterion that did double duty.

2. A good instance of this is Soviet regionalism. In free market economies regionalism is a demand, *inter alia*, for regions more autarkic than they would naturally be. 'Diversify', 'prevent emigration', etc., are possible slogans, but hardly 'specialize'. The regionalist wishes to protect or develop some politically or culturally defined entity. But the Soviet regionalist is quite as likely to demand rationalization and specialization. In other words he is worried about the mere economics, as well as the politics and sociology, of his subject: he feels that establishments are *economically* mislocated by the criteria in use—a feeling to which few are prone in a market economy.

Why have economic regions at all? In a market economy the location of each enterprise is separately determined by its profit. There is no regional economic authority, since there is no authority at all above the enterprise. *Ex post facto* we may draw some regional boundary or other, corresponding perhaps to a political administrative unit, or the territory of a national minority, or to the notions (so contradictory!) of this or that economic geographer; and see whether the profit motive is populating or de-populating, specializing or diversifying, this entity however defined. But this is not the centre of our interest. Even when we interfere with free location we do not always do so in the sacred name of some kind of regionalism. The local political authority, especially if dominated by a national minority, has indeed its pull, and in some cases should have. But for the rest we interfere to bring work to the workers, to cure local unemployment, to prevent the growth of Megalopolis, etc.; and this is only indirectly regionalistic, since it is aimed at particular people for their own sakes, who *happen* to live concentrated in one region.

But now establish a command economy, and abolish the profit motive. Moreover, on good Marxist grounds, refuse to recognize the scarcity problem or rational prices at all. Then why locate anything anywhere? There is no longer any general criterion, embracing all decisions. Strategy helps some, national minority pressure determines others. We still want to prevent the growth of Megalopolis and prevent local unemployment. But these criteria leave a huge vacuum of indeterminacy. In the Soviet case what has flooded in is bogus regionalism. Basically this is because the desires of the local political unit are the only constant left, so the planner naturally turns to some regional concept when he makes his location decision.

Then, too, regionalism is not only an intellectual standby, but also an administrative necessity under CC. For the central planner has to think in broad categories, lest he be bogged down in details. So just as he must think of steel, not bicycle wheels, he must think of regions, not the location of a given plant. If his problem is to be administratively manageable he must delegate decisions about bicycle wheels to trusts; so also the placing of plants to regions. With ideal communications, indefinitely much information and good computers—i.e. with perfect computation—the central office can dispense with all such intermediaries and delegation, as we have already seen (Ch. 4, Sec. 2). It can deal directly with a given establishment, telling it to go to the north-eastern suburbs of Vinnitsa and make bicycle wheels. But life is not like that yet. Imperfect computation requires not only regional*ism* but regional *authorities*.

3. The necessity to think in such broad terms has very unfortunate results at the margin. The planner must lay down quantities of 'steel' and 'aluminium' without ever knowing whether the marginal bicycle wheel plant is as profitable as the marginal saucepan plant. Under perfect computation these two are directly compared, and production in each line is pushed until it is equally profitable; the demand for such general items as steel and aluminium is determined solely by the demand for such particular items as bicycle wheels and saucepans. But the use, under imperfect computation, of intermediate authorities for steel and non-ferrous metals limits the equalization of profit to alternative outputs within each branch

separately.[1] So also with regions: it may well be approximately right that Ukraine should have so many new factories, but we cannot tell whether specifically Vinnitsa should have a bicycle factory until we know what R.S.F.S.R. is doing about bicycle factories. Ideally, under perfect competition and perfect computation alike, the regional distribution of new plants to Ukraine is visible only *ex post*. I.e. it merely results from the location of specific plants to specific places. The failure to understand this ideal, or to try in any way to approach it, is the crux of Communist regionalism, and the reason for both its excessive importance and its lamentable confusion.

3. For Communist locational policy is particularly irrational, even compared with allocation policy. We possess, in stark contrast to the paucity of material on allocation, many direct statements about these criteria. Their effect, not only if taken in the mass but even if taken individually, is to leave us in very great perplexity.

The following criteria[2] have been or are used:

     i. regional autarky,
     ii. regional specialization.

These two directly contradictory criteria are often given in theoretical works in the same breath, without any trace of consciousness that they are indeed contradictory. Their special necessity for a command economy has been explained above. This once accepted, to a Western-trained economic mind such a conflict suggests an optimization problem. But to the Marxist mind so sophisticated and moderate a notion as an optimum is anathema. Rather is the Marxist—and indeed the Russian—temperament maximalist. Of two conflicting goods both must be maximized, and the contradiction is not resolved. Nevertheless in practice there have been swings between these criteria. The second was most dominant in the first and second Five-year Plans, and the first before and after that period. If (ii) be held to mean that some areas remain agricultural it is deeply un-Communist, since industry as such is a good thing, and the difference between town and country must be abolished.[3] There is also quite good authority for the view that even industrial

---

[1] Cf. my criticism of *a priori* sectoral allocations, as opposed to plant-by-plant comparisons, in Pakistan: *Economic Digest*, Karachi, Autumn 1960. It is argued that the sectoral allocation should arise *ex post* from the choice of individual schemes.

[2] There are no locational indicators, since location decisions are made rarely enough to be wholly controlled by the centre.

[3] Cf. Ch. 17, Sec. 1.

regions should not be specialized.[1] The brief dominance of (ii)
came during Stalin's maximal insistence on large plants, administered on the production principle.

There follows another contradictory pair of criteria:

iii. minimization of transport,
iv. maximization of scale of enterprise.[2]

This contradiction is handled in theoretical works as above. In
practice (iv) goes with (ii) and (iii) with (i), as we have just seen.
The great period of gigantomania was also the great period of
regional specialization. However, (iv) has a special effect on
agriculture, which it tends to push into virgin lands. For it is easier
to found a large farm on virgin soil than to amalgamate villages
in settled areas; and the labour-extensive sovkhoz on virgin soil
is more obviously and satisfactorily large than the amalgamated
kolkhoz. Hence we find not one but two virgin lands campaigns:
in the early 'thirties, as part of the general gigantomania, and again
in 1953–56 as an independent phenomenon. As to (iii) transport
has to be minimized because it is ideologically suspect: it is not
material production, so in some refined way it is wasteful.[3] However absurd this may seem, it is a genuine and permanent criterion,
of special force during the third Five-year Plan.[4]

A third unresolved contradiction is that production should be:

v. near the consumer,
vi. near the raw material.

These criteria derive, common sense apart, from one of the very few
incursions of post-Marxian Western economics into the system of
thought: A. Weber's *Ueber den Standort der Industrien* (Tübingen
1909). Often condemned, Weber's influence nevertheless has
survived. It is particularly attractive since Weber wrote in physical
terms, instead of saying simply that location should be guided by
profit—which is all his doctrine amounts to. A few authors have
flatly recognized, as did Weber, that we have here an optimization
problem.[5] Most have slurred it over with the ambiguous phrase,
'near the consumer and the raw material'. A peculiar emphasis
within (vi) was placed in early days on the possession of a separate

[1] V. I. Lenin, 'Sketch of a Plan for Scientific-Technical Work', April 1918; *Sochinenia*
1950, vol. 27, p. 288.
[2] Cf. Ch. 16, Sec. 3.   [3] Cf. Ch. 3, Sec. 6.d.   [4] Cf. Ch. 6, Sec. 11.
[5] E.g. I. G. Aleksandrov in 1924, quoted by Chambre, op. cit., p. 41.

fuel base for each area. Regional autarky in fuel, and the exploitation of local fuel reserves however poor, were especial desiderata. This quirk of planning is traceable back to Lenin, and his passion for electricity.[1]

So much for the contradictions, and for the criteria to which Western economics provides no parallel.

vii. *Profit* itself, or rather cost, has invariably been a minor criterion, but of course at the arbitrarily set central prices. Indeed, on occasion these are arbitrarily *changed* so as to justify a location decision. Cf. the example of Moscow coal in Ch. 6, Sec. 11.

viii. The most important of all Communist criterion by far is *local political pull*. Plants go to areas where local officials, especially Party officials,[2] are important or unscrupulous. Many indeed are the unofficial descriptions of the pressure that they bring to bear in the capital to this end. This is so deep-rooted a feature of Communism that it has carried straight over into the Yugoslav quasi-RM. In Yugoslavia the capital market is not only 'marred' by imperfections but also by large elements of CC; and Yugoslavia is perhaps the classic country of such local political pressures.

ix. This is almost unconnected with the Titoist deviation of socialist RM. It arises quite simply from the acuteness of the *national minority* problem in Yugoslavia. Now it is a basic Marxist demand that humanity be uniformly developed under Full Communism. Hence the rapid development of backward minorities is a principal criterion of location. Morally this criterion is most ambivalent, since Russian and Chinese Communists use it to swamp minority areas with Great Russian and Han immigrants. Thus development is cynically equated with assimilation. Similar problems, we must however admit, attend industrialization almost everywhere: e.g. the Scottish Highlands and the Italian Tyrol. Economically the criterion is of course very wasteful indeed, since backward minorities live in uneconomic localities almost *ipso facto*. One may speculate that the comparative rationality of Yugoslav prices makes the waste more evident, hence the problem more acute.

Our next two criteria, the 'white spots' fallacy and the forced

[1] Cf. Chambre, op. cit., pp. 22–6, 38–9. There is an amusing passage in Lenin, not on location but on electricity as such, which throws a flood of light on the arbitrariness of Communist planning: *Ob Yedinom Khozyaistvennom Plane*, Soch. 1953, vol. 32, p. 118.

[2] The Party rather than the State is the decisive locator of economic activity. Cf. Gerry Hough, *The Role of Local Party Organs in Soviet Industrial Decision-Making*, Harvard doctoral thesis, Feb. 1961, Chs 4, 5.

labour fallacy, are intimately linked and require more extended treatment.

4. Natural resources are all too often unemployable, and it is only right to leave them so. If labour does not wish to mine in sub-zero temperatures, if the desert is inhospitable to seed, it is economic to employ the labour somewhere else at lower wages, or to thicken sowings on better ground. It is also economic to substitute some other activity: should the mineral only be available in the perma-frost we will get it more cheaply by exporting what we are best at and buying it abroad. Should all cultivable land be already taken up we can best increase food output by manufacturing fertilizers, not by ploughing the sand. The point is of great simplicity and follows directly from the most elementary principles of economics: waste of resources means misallocation, not disuse; or, since factors of production must combine to produce, one factor may quite easily be wasted simply by our insistence on using the other at all. The full employment of natural resources, or the 'obligation' to 'fill up the white spots on the map' has either a non-economic rationale or none.[1]

The use of this criterion has specially tragic consequences, since it is so intimately connected with Stalin's use of *deportation* and *forced labour*.[2]

Now forced labourers receive specially low wages. In principle these, being piece-work, may rise quite high, but in practice they vary about subsistence.[3] Deportees also receive less than the market rate. Yet the principles of price formation are not affected by all this. The Soviet authorities do not neglect to charge the cost of guards and administration against forced labour, so that 'social cost' is also duly covered,[4] or at least the more obvious parts of it. Even so such labour is often held to be cheaper, in efficiency units, than free labour. Whether it is so or not is a large question beyond our purview. But such is or was the authorities' belief, and they acted on it by sending it to the frozen North, where it undertook tasks that free labour would not, and made Arctic enterprise apparently profitable. Now it may be argued that this was almost certainly a correct

[1] Cf. Wiles, *Soviet Studies*, Dec. 1956.
[2] I mean not the official Russian term (*prinuzhdennaya rabota*) for the minor punishment of labour at the normal place of work at low wages, nor exile (*vysyl'ka*), nor normal imprisonment, but deportation to a specific place (*ssyl'ka*) and confinement in 'corrective' labour camps or colonies.
[3] Since about 1950. Previously they were below subsistence level, and death-rates were well above those for the civilian population.
[4] I take this from a detailed and unpublished MS. of my own.

decision, since in addition to all previous calculations free labour would have required an Arctic supplement. But not so, for in reality forced labour also required and received an Arctic supplement, in better food, heating and clothing than it got in Southern camps. The fact of the Arctic supplement cuts both ways.

Clearly if forced labour is always cheaper than free it has no special advantage in any particular location. If free labour is mis-allocated in the Arctic so is forced. The whole tragedy and horror of Stalin's conquest of the Arctic rests on an economic fallacy. If it is desirable to put the camps where they cannot be seen, Central Asia and Southern Siberia are ideal, and indeed many were placed there. Forced labour, as a violation of 'worker's sovereignty',[1] leads to mislocations of labour, not only from its own but also from the social point of view. For as in other spheres so here private and social utility tend to coincide.

Since Stalin's death most of the forced labourers have been released, but very often they have been 'deported' to the location of their erstwhile camps. Thus the horrors have greatly diminished, but the Arctic fallacy remains. Into the other aspects of forced labour, and especially into its general rationality as an economic institution, we cannot here enter, as they are very political. It has played a much smaller role in other Communist countries except China. Chinese forced labour is of no special economic interest, as firstly there is no Chinese Arctic, and secondly free labour is so commonly directed that there is not sufficient difference between the two categories for comment.

5. We turn to the *effect on location of the territorial principle*. First we must define some new concepts. A by-product of 'planner's tension' (Ch. 13, Sec. 2) is the desire of every subordinate and intermediate unit to ensure its own supplies. That is, they want a supplier under their thumb, who when his production inevitably falls short of plan will give priority to their own requirements, both inside and if need be outside the plan. So enterprises manufacture their own spare parts and repair their own buildings, ministries manufacture their own machinery and truck their own goods.

'Subordinate autarky' then is a criterion of all intermediate and lower authorities, and many of them have considerable planning powers. It is greatly enhanced by decentralization, even if only of

---

[1] Ch. 5, Sec. 4.

initiative rather than of decision. It is also clearly a universal psychological tendency, operating even in the absence of planner's tension, and even on a capitalist free market.[1] In a command economy the centre is mostly very hostile to it, since it likes subordinates to be powerless against its orders. But such autarky has nevertheless received official encouragement from time to time, notably under Stalin, who permitted whole autarkic empires to grow like cancers in the body economic: the gold trust, the railways, and above all the forced labour camps. These organizations even had their own schools and shops. Indeed during the famine period of 1932–33 many factories took over small state farms, or established 'patronage' links with individual kolkhozy, in order to ensure the rations. In general wherever a special effort was required Stalin would appoint a trusted trouble-shooter like Kaganovich or Beria, and grant him a great deal of 'subordinate autarky' for the time being.

It is of the essence of this phenomenon that there is a main and an ancillary activity, e.g. gold-mining and the movement of gold-mining officials, railway operation and the education of railwaymen's children. Control over the ancillary activity is decentralized to the intermediate authority; it will not be looked on as an end in itself, and will probably be conducted inefficiently. The main inefficiency is in fact locational, and that is why the subject is treated here at such length.

To whom are the ancillary activities subordinated? On what principle are the intermediate units of command organized? Infinitely many principles are possible. Some are political. Thus in South Africa holding companies tend increasingly to divide by nationality, in Sweden it matters whether the owner is capitalist or co-operative, etc., etc. We deal here with only three principles, all purely economic: production or horizontal, territorial and vertical. Most Soviet industry was arranged under Ministries, each interested in one product wherever the enterprise might be, until summer 1957, when Khrushchev abolished them and substituted Sovnarkhozy, separate local authorities that administer every enterprise in their territory. The first, called by Communists the production principle, is none other than the 'horizontal

---

[1] Under capitalism it is specially strong when there is inflation and full employment, which correspond to planner's tension.

integration' of the Western textbook. The second is the territorial principle. Vertical integration differs from either of these, as can be seen from its pure form: several competing factories offer their goods to the public through several competing shops, each wholly owned by one of them. The gold trust, the railways and the forced labour camps, previously mentioned, were all examples of vertical integration. So are the specialized distribution outlets maintained by some Soviet producers to this day.

Many combinations of enterprises, in all sorts of economy, are mixed forms between these three. Thus if under capitalism two horizontal monopolies combine this is a vertical integration carried out in order to strengthen the units' monopoly power—and monopoly power is by definition a horizontal concept. Or *some* kinds of vertical integration demand local propinquity, as of a blast-furnace and a steelworks in order to conserve heat; and these are facilitated by the territorial principle.

With our concepts established, we may proceed. Now as far as the product-mix goes, subordinate autarky and the existence of ancillary activities are rather uninteresting: if there are to be railways the employees' schoolchildren must be educated, if gold is to be mined the directors need aeroplanes, and from the standpoint of scarcity economics we care little who organizes the teaching and the aeroplanes. In particular, a Sovnarkhoz would not seem to differ greatly from a vertical trust or a Ministry. But location and the use of transport are another matter. If the textile industry is under one management, and makes its own, say, electricity meters, these meters will of course be made in only one factory and will be transported immense distances across the country; which is a clear waste since they might have been produced locally in every major industrial centre and sold to non-textile consumers as well. And the same applies to nearly every ancillary service. *Per contra* if the Leningrad region runs its own textile industry, not merely meters but textiles themselves become, on our definitions, ancillary. The region will reduce its textile output to a size sufficient only for its own purposes, and divert the resources into some locally deficitary product; then economies of scale in textiles will be sacrificed.

Were it not for subordinate autarky and ancillary enterprises economic activity would be located in the same single most profitable way however it was organized. Thus suppose activities A and

C are final products and share the outputs of activity B, in a nation with three regions, 1, 2 and 3. The most profitable location is:

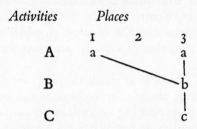

and the market would establish this by competition, or the central planners by rational computation, whether production was in the hands of Ministries A, B and C or Sovnarkhozy 1, 2 and 3, or any combination thereof; because only so would these units maximize their profits. This would remain true even if the intermediate units were vertical trusts: for they would *ex hypothesi*—remember this is either perfect competition or perfect computation—be willing to sell and buy surplus and deficitary intermediate products among themselves.

Now introduce subordinate autarky, and declare B an 'ancillary' industry under the production principle, i.e. it receives no Ministry of its own. Then the ideal suitability of 3 for B is forgotten, and we get, for instance:

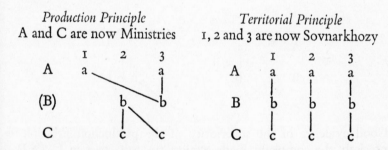

In this example Ministry A feels the same advantages of location as previously, and maintains two a plants and a smaller b plant in the same places as before. But Ministry C perceives, perhaps quite correctly, a better niche for a *small* b plant in 2 than there now is in 3, since A already has one there. This leads C on to establish a small c plant in 2 as well. C may still be maximizing its profits, but the restraint on merging the two b plants has upset everything.

The superficial observer sees at any rate cross-transportation, with A's b passing from East to West through region 2 while C's b covers part of the same route in reverse. It is obvious that b made in 2 should supply regions 1 and 2, while b made in 3 supplies 3, But it is less obvious that the b plants should be merged into 3; and still less obvious, though equally true, that the C plants should be merged into 3.

The territorial principle is much simpler: we declare 1, 2 and 3 to be Sovnarkhozy, abolish the Ministries and sit back. Quickly everybody will be producing everything, regardless of cost. The concept of an ancillary industry has no meaning here, or, better, all industries are ancillary. The resulting location is normally worse, it would seem, than under the production principle.

It is of particular interest that the production principle would give rise to no special location problems if b were not 'ancillary'. If a B ministry were kept going subordinate autarky could not act to mislocate it. By themselves 'Ministries' will always locate fairly rationally, and the production principle is superior here to the territorial.

Vertical integration would produce a different result again, probably better than the territorial principle and comparable in badness with the production or horizontal. Thus divide the economy into four vertical trusts, two for each final product A and C. Then there will be some such location as this:

	1	2	3
A	a		a
B	b		b b b
C		c	c

Good evidence of the superiority of the production principle is precisely the complaint made against the Ministries in U.S.S.R.: they neglected backward areas and concentrated on the developed parts of the country! Granted the already considerable wastage under Communism in developing the backward parts of a country (see Sec. 4), this is high praise.

7. So much, then, for resource allocation or product-mix, and for location or space-mix. But we have finally to fit in the economies of scale (i.e. horizontal integration) and of vertical integration.

Clearly the former suffer from the territorial, the latter from the production principle. Then, too, most technical improvements are 'horizontal', since they concern one phase of production only and need to be spread to all enterprises thus engaged. So here again the production is better than the territorial principle.

8. We may now turn from the theory of the thing to the actuality of the Sovnarkhozy (Ch. 2, Sec. 8). They are an immensely important change, but it is absolutely false to speak of Khrushchev's measures in summer 1957 as deliberate decentralization. Rather is the barbarous name of 'territorialization' correct. Formally 30 ministries have died and 102 territorial substitutes for them been born: if the distance between Moscow and the next subordinate authority is longer, and there are more of them to control, the distance from that authority to the enterprise is shorter and it has fewer to control. Khrushchev certainly did not originate his reform in order to relax central control, but for various reasons given below (Sec. 10). In practice, however, the 'territorial principle' contains two strong elements of decentralization.

First the new planning authority corresponds to the territorial Party unit (Union Republic or Oblast'); indeed, this is its *raison d'être*, it is a way of transferring power from civil servants (the Ministers) to Party bosses. But if the units of State and Party power correspond they are together very strong. All sorts of local economic interests were formerly held in check because the Ministers did not agree with the local Party bosses. But now the centre cannot prevail against the combination. 'Subordinate autarky', strong under the Ministries, is now almost irresistible. And although this autarky is formally planned—in the sense that the central plan itself is distorted by the local authorities, rather than directly defied once drawn up—it must be called an element of decentralization.

Secondly, the territorial principle involves daily choice between commodities. Accept, that is to say, that there is DC at all: 'small' decisions are left to *some* kind of 'body'. A Ministry could usually think in terms of physical units of its product. A Sovnarkhoz must compare products all the time. Hence the role of money is enhanced, quite independently of the will of the authorities to enhance it, merely by the administrative set-up they have chosen. In strict theory an economy based not on physical calculation but on money could be very centralized; but where money is influential it must be rationalized, and when it has been rationalized why should the centre reserve even 'big' decisions to itself any more? The centre is strong if prices are arbitrary or non-existent because decentralization would then be so irrational. But put the means of decentralization (rational prices) at the disposal of the economy, and the centre will lose prestige and *raison d'être*.

Formally, however, the territorial principle makes no difference. Indeed, things are becoming more centralized (Ch.9, Sec.13), since the authorities are increasing year by year the class of 'funded' commodities, subject to physical output targets and delivered to named customers in quantities centrally laid down. These are, of course, the more important commodities. Moreover, as we see in Ch. 9, Sec. 6, in one respect the territorial principle actually centralized things, since in the initial year the intermediate category, the erstwhile 'planned' commodities, that used to stand between the 'funded' and the 'decentralized', had all to be added to the 'funded' class. The Ministries used to be trusted with the 'distribution' of this category of good, but a Sovnarkhoz cannot be. Indeed, it would be technically impossible, for a Sovnarkhoz is not a monopolist of any commodity.

Nor is this the only way in which the territorial principle leads to greater centralization. There must be somewhere in U.S.S.R. an office that bothers about the quantity of steel, not the volume of all industrial output in Kiev; and indeed about new techniques in steel-making. So in practice the departments of Gosplan have been very greatly strengthened.[1] In 1957, for instance, the Sovnarkhozy were permitted to transfer raw materials allocated to them from one type of output to another; in 1959 this privilege was withdrawn. 'The production principle is dead, but technology forbids it to lie down.'[2] Hence a duplication of experts even greater than before. For previously these functions could be performed, along with the control of the enterprises, at the Ministries. But now separate experts are required: at the Sovnarkhozy, to control the enterprises, and in the Gosplan to think about the overall totals.

9. Let us now try to sum up the pros and cons of the territorial and production systems, with CC at both stages of decision-making,

---

[1] 'You boys think you've got rid of me,' Mr. Nove heard a minister say to a group of managers after dinner in summer 1957, 'but you're quite mistaken. From now on I'm sitting in the Gosplan, doing the same thing as before.'

[2] I quote, here and elsewhere, my contribution to (ed.) G. Grossman, *Value and Plan*, California University Press 1960. Further Western sources on the territorial principle are: Kaser's contribution to the same volume; O. Hoeffding, *American Economic Review*, Papers and Proceedings, 1959; Laskovsky, *American Slavic and East European Review*, Feb. 1958; Swearer, *World Politics*, Oct. 1959; Hough, op. cit.; Wiles, 'La Territorialisation de l'Economie Soviétique', in *L'Economie Sovietique*, Brussels (Institut Solvay) 1958.

the centre and the 'body'. We cannot expect an exact symmetry of gain and loss, because at the end of it all it is not places but products that are made and sold; so a place-wise command hierarchy will not have the same internal logic as a product-wise one. A shift, then, from 'production' to 'territorial' will bring about:

Gain	Loss
Economies of vertical integration (but there are not very many of these)	Economies of horizontal integration (these are very important indeed since they include long runs, standardization and technical collaboration)
Fewer long hauls and cross-hauls from one plant in a ministry to another	Sovnarkhoz boundaries interrupt previously existing rational hauls
	Much greater 'subordinate autarky'
Amalgamation of enterprises in industries hitherto 'ancillary' (e.g. building, local transport)	Splitting up of enterprises in the 'octopoid' industries (e.g. railways, electricity)
	Mobile enterprises hampered (e.g. specialized construction, seasonal agricultural labour)
New enterprises no longer concentrated near capital owing to personal preference of Minister (but this is a small point)	Sovnarkhozy of areas not worth developing push through crackpot schemes
'Body'-to-enterprise communications easier	Gosplan-to-'body' communication more difficult
	Greater administrative apparatus

Perhaps above all the loss of technical collaboration is important. Indeed, it is so important that the Soviet Union violates the territorial principle at this point, by maintaining a large new central technical committee (the *Gostekhnika*). A minor offset to this loss is that a Ministry, being in some sense the monopolist of a product, may prefer to sit on innovations, and persuade the planners they are no good. But among a hundred Sovnarkhozy there may well be a risk-bearer, prepared to brave the wrath of Moscow if things go wrong in order, perhaps, to acquire a larger investment allocation in that product if things go right.

It is of course best to have a production-territorial compromise, as until Khrushchev was deemed natural. But of the two extremes the table shows conclusively that 'production' is far better. Only the decentralization of some decisions to below Sovnarkhoz level, to the enterprise itself, and the recentralization of others into the Gosplan, makes the new system workable. In the actual historical experience of the Sovnarkhozy, other things have not been kept

M

equal, and their defects have been masked by simultaneous though irrelevant improvements.

10. *The territorial principle must be stringently distinguished from regionalism* in the Western or even in the Communist sense. Regionalism looks at an economy primarily from the point of view of *large* areas, attempts to make them more autarkic[1] than they would be in a free market, and gives them great powers of initiative and decision. Under both the production and the territorial principles the economy is viewed as a whole, but for the convenience of the planners a 'reference grid' is imposed on it. The 'co-ordinates' of this grid are either product categories or geographical areas. The chain of command still begins at the centre and runs downward, either through Ministries or through Sovnarkhozy. Either type of body might receive or wrest great independence; if Ministries did so, it would look like British nationalization, if Sovnarkhozy did so there would be an approach to 'socialist regionalism'.

During the French Revolution the Abbé Sieyès proposed to abolish all local government units and divide France into squares. This is how Khrushchev thought of the Sovnarkhozy, when he made them too small to be autarkic with propriety, and carefully kept them distinct from the local organs of state, lest the combination be too strong. But the 'slide into regionalism' is gradual and irresistible, for many reasons:

(a) the local organ of the Party runs both Sovnarkhoz and Soviet, as described; and this is the centre of power;

(b) the superior intermediate organ, the Republic, is better able to dominate the Sovnarkhozy on its territory than any Ministry in Moscow, even with the existing planning hierarchy;

(c) but in the larger Republics a new organ has now been interposed (summer 1960) between Gosplan and Sovnarkhoz: the Supreme Republican Sovnarkhoz. True, this has the nominal powers only of 'operation', not 'planning', but we saw in Ch. 7, Sec. 8 how thin this distinction is. The point is that the new body is the creature of the Republic, not of the Gosplan, and must cut into the latter's competences.[2]

(d) Furthermore there is quite independent pressure towards genuine regionalism. Soviet geographers, and before them Russian geographers, have a long intellectual tradition of regionalism. The

---

[1] Or is it *less* autarkic?! Cf. Sec. 1.
[2] In small Republics there is only one Sovnarkhoz anyway.

economy under War Communism and indeed before that was divided into Sovnarkhozy, under that very name, much larger than those of today. The Goelro used eight large regions for planning purposes. The Gosplan has used regions since its inception,[1] and since the beginning of the third FYP (i.e. since Stalin eventually took regional questions seriously) 13 regions. In May 1961 this number was increased to 19,[2] and, characteristically for Khrushchev, they acquired local offices. Previously the large region had been merely a figment of the Gosplan, with no independent administration. Even the new regions remain occupied with perspective, not current, planning, and possess no executive power.

There is thus every reason to expect an ordinary regionalism to emerge from the territorial principle, but almost none to trace them to a single origin. The Sovnarkhozy owe their name, and their separation from the normal organs of state, to the Sovnarkhozy of War Communism. They would appear to owe nothing whatsoever to the lucubrations of academic geographers, who have consistently thought in terms of units about eight times as big. Their true origins are as already suggested:

(i) Khrushchev's interest in Yugoslavia, and therefore in the Komuni of that country, which he visited in 1955 (cf. Ch. 2, Sec. 10).

(ii) Khrushchev's experience with agricultural planning, in which the local Soviets were—and still are—the agents of the Ministry of Agriculture.

(iii) Khrushchev's hatred of bureaucrats and city slickers, his desire to clear much people out of Moscow, his obscure appreciation of the dangers of a 'Managerial Revolution' (cf. Ch. 2, Sec. 10).

(iv) The identification of his enemies Malenkov and Kaganovich with such people.

(v) The resistance of the Ministerial apparatus to Khrushchev's virgin land campaign, which was fresh in his memory.

(vi) Khrushchev's need to bribe the oblast' Party secretaries, in order to get their support against his enemies, the Anti-Party Group, at the critical juncture.

---

[1] Chambre, op. cit., *passim*, but especially Ch. 1; Popluiko, op. cit.

[2] Strictly two single-Sovnarkhoz regions (Moldavia and Belorussia), and 17 multi-Sovnarkhoz ones, of which two (Transcaucasia and Central Asia) embrace several republics, one (Kazakhstan) corresponds to a republic, and the rest subdivide republics. Cf. *Ekonomicheskaya Gazeta*, 28 May 1961. The functions of the region are discharged in Moldavia and Belorussia by the Sovnarkhoz that corresponds to the Republic, and in Kazakhstan by the republican Gosplan.

(vii) The undoubted duplication in the 'ancillary' activities of building and transport under the old system, and a ludicrous mis-understanding of its causes.

(viii) An entire failure to appreciate the more serious faults of the new system.

11. The contrast between production and territorial principles appears even in Yugoslavia. We saw (Ch. 4, Sec. 4) that the so-called 'social' plans of enterprises, which are on the whole mere projec-tions of how they will fare on the market, are submitted to the higher political organs, which are also planning organs in the normal sense—in so far as there is any normal planning in Yugoslavia at all. Now these organs are of course territorially organized: hardly a political authority in the world is based on the production principle.[1] So it is no surprise to learn that the 'social' plans are dis-cussed first in the chambers of commerce. These are, exactly as under capitalism, nation-wide associations of the enterprises engaged in particular trades.

Their role in planning is further proof of the *primacy of the production principle*; if you are going to plan at all you can get away with neglect of location, but not of output. Location is economically *secundus inter pares*, it owes its unexpected importance in the decision-making process to a simple political fact: there are always subordinate territorial units in any political set-up, seldom productional units. Moreover, when it comes to political influence rather than formal political structure, the territorial interest is usually stronger and better defined.

---

[1] There are traces of such a thing in Fascist Corporatism and Guild Socialism.

CHAPTER 9

THE 'DISTRIBUTION' OF PRODUCTS

1. IT is not enough to know what the enterprise produces: we must also know who gets the product. The determination of this is, in Soviet parlance, 'distribution' (raspredelenie, raznaryadka). It has been strangely neglected in Sovietological, and indeed in Soviet, literature.[1] There is no more horrible maze than this subject, nor any chapter with which I am less satisfied. The very notion of a rational analysis of distribution procedures seems hardly to have occurred to anyone. Nor have I any confidence in the accuracy of the descriptions given. Furthermore they are in a continuous flux.

The schema that follows is not meant to be logically exhaustive, but it is meant to cover indiscriminately the procurement of agricultural materials, the distribution *proprement dite* of industrial semi-fabricates, and the methods whereby the final consumer obtains his wares. The treatment is more exhaustive than for production planning itself, because there is no other introductory literature to which the student may be referred. The writer also asks the charity normally extended to those who try to map uncharted seas.

We begin with a major generalization: *distribution is seldom more centralized than production, but it may be much less.* Indeed this seems to be not so much a generalization as a tautology, for if a director's distribution plan did contain more detail on who should get what sort of article, than his production plan gave on the production of these articles, his distribution plan would be, *inter alia*, a supplementary production plan. Nor is this a merely theoretical point: the wholesale organs of the Soviet Ministry of Trade do—or did—largely determine the distribution of the so-called 'Decentralized' commodities, produced by enterprises under local control; and in so doing it is stressed quite officially that they are the prime determinants of the production plans of these enterprises.[2]

---

[1] The great exception is Herbert Levine's 'The Centralized Planning of Supply in Soviet Industry in the U.S. Congress, Joint Economic Committee's *Comparisons of the U.S. and Soviet Economies*, Part I, U.S.G.P.O. 1959. It contains a full bibliography. A fair subsequent account is given by Yu. I. Koldomasov: *Planirovanie Material'no-Technicheskogo Snabzhenia*, Moscow 1961. It is, however, not at all analytic. Cf. also D. Granick, *The Management of the Industrial Firm in USSR*, New York 1954, Ch. 8, Appx. C.

[2] See footnote 1, p. 172.

2. Imagine, then, first a fully command economy, whether CC or DC, in which the enterprise receives exhaustively detailed orders, and has little freedom of decision; and that the users of the product are similarly compelled to purchase only planned quantities. Then at least four different distribution systems are possible:

I. *Distribution by the centre from enterprise to enterprise:* (a) producer direct to customer named in plan by the centre; (b) producer to customers named in plan by the centre via a wholesale depot, which merely provides physical services such as warehousing and transport;

II. *Distribution by the centre through a 'body' or a wholesaler:* the producer delivers to an intermediary named in his plan by the centre; the latter then re-distributes to customers named in *its* plan by the centre the similar articles delivered to it by many producers on some system or other. Such systems might be:

(a) with homogeneous goods: it then does not matter what system is used;

(b) with heterogeneous goods: these may be redistributed at random, by corruption, or in some way dependent on state policy.

III. *Distribution by the producer himself:*

(a) by Kontraktatsia, among a number of potential customers named in his plan by the centre;

(b) a centrally planned bill of products can be 'distributed' or rather simply sold by its producer entirely according to his private profit, to buyers whose intake is also centrally planned, but who are not bound to 'distribute' their purchases in any special way.

IV. *Distribution by intermediate 'body',* whether Ministry, Sovnarkhoz wholesaler or local Soviet:

(a) within the sphere of authority of that body;

(b) over the whole economy, i.e. as the agent of the centre and nominally with regard to the national plan, not profit.

V. Then comes the intermediate case in which production remains centrally planned, but there is *no distribution plan at all,* because the purchaser is not planned in any way (as opposed to III(b), in which the purchaser is at least under orders to buy a certain amount of the product somewhere). Such a purchaser is the final consumer.

3. *Per contra* if production decisions are totally decentralized it is yet possible to centralize some distribution decisions. In this case:

VI. The producer is tied to a particular customer, and vice versa, but their production and prices are in part or in whole their own affair. This is generically the procedure of decentrally determining the *sortament*, in cases where the basic categories of output are still centrally fixed. We may distinguish two sub-groups, in which the standard procedure gives the last word as to what shall be produced (a) to the producer, (b) to the consumer. (a) was the original Stalinist procedure, (b) is the *sistema zakazov* ('system of orders') that grew up in the last years of his life for consumer goods. The shop could not order elsewhere—it was as tied as the producer—but the producer did have to do what it asked (cf. Ch. 4, Sec. 12).

VII. An intermediary intervenes in VI. This wholesaler is then a statutory monopsony, acting on producers either (a) purely through the price mechanism or (b) through some quasi-planned system of kontraktatsia. In either case he has an enforceable claim to dispose of their whole output. Of course the monopsonist may *redistribute* the product according to some other principle. Note that under capitalism the sales office of a cartel is very similar.

In this whole list of possibilities VI and VII are the odd men out, distribution being more centralized than production. But this is only correct in a Pickwickian sense, for, as we have seen, the distribution plan cannot specify *how much* output shall be transferred to the named recipient in greater detail than the production plan, without *becoming* a production plan. What we mean in these two cases is that the specification of the *identity* of recipients is more centralized than the specification of *quantities* of output.

VIII. We come finally to completely decentralized production decisions on a free market. Then either (a) the producer produces to the order of the customer, or on spec., and then distributes accordingly; or (b) here, too, a wholesaler may intervene, especially if production is on spec., although it can only act as a transmitter of the customers' orders.

There are of course very many other possible arrangements. Note, for instance, that *prices* could be more or less centralized than production, and have a great effect on distribution. We deal with this point when we come to describe each category in detail.

4. Next it will be asked, to what particular Communist institution does each formal category correspond? It is helpful to set this out very briefly before proceeding, at the cost of some repetition.

I and II apply to 'funded' commodities: the most scarce and important for which Gosplan draws up the raznaryadka.

IV applied to the next most important, the 'quota' or 'planned' commodities, and to the 'decentralized' or least important commodities; but in both cases before the Sovnarkhozy were set up. Today there are no 'planned' commodities, and

III(a) is the way in which 'decentralized' commodities are primarily handled today under the Sovnarkhoz system.

III(b) is the Chinese system of 'free choice'.

I to IV apply to wholesale transactions within the nationalized sector of a Soviet-type economy. It is to these only the Communists, unlike the present writer, apply the word 'distribution'.

V applies to transactions between retail shops and final consumers.

VI describes the settlement of the sortament under I, II and III(a).

VII describes the zakupka, i.e. quite generally the acquisition from the private or kolkhoz or other unplanned sector of materials for the nationalized sector.

VIII is free market socialism, as throughout the Yugoslav economy or in the Soviet kolkhoz market,[1] or during the Soviet NEP.

5. So far we have presented a purely formal analysis that gives equal weight to each item. Pursued for more than a certain length this method is sterile and misleading. We now turn to say what other things need to be said, without too much thought for a formal pattern.

I(a) is the ideologically basic, the archetypal method. Every single product is ordered and distributed by the centre. Under War Communism this was very common. It still applies to large capital goods. Yet in one way it is not so simple as it looks. For suppose an enterprise producing a good is ordered to despatch it in various quantities to other named enterprises, and the output is not homogeneous? Batches might vary in quality, or there may be a production delay, which will have to be imposed on some particular customer. The manager is not told how to proceed in such cases, and must decide somehow for himself. This is the general problem of *'unplanned heterogeneity'*, which complicates the raznaryadka at every point. There are many informal ways of dealing with it,

---

[1] Strictly the kolkozniks' private sales on this market are capitalism; consequently private VIII(b) is prohibited, since a capitalist working on his own at 'production' is tolerable, but a capitalist making profits out of 'distribution' puts too heavy a strain on the Marxist conscience. Latterly, however, socialist wholesalers have been permitted in this market; i.e. the co-operative network may sell goods on commission for kolkhozniki.

and since they are nearly the same in every case I have listed them all under II, which is the most interesting case.

I(b) is identical with I(a), but the literature may easily confuse it with what follows. It is in Soviet parlance 'transit turnover without use of own capital' (transitny oborot bez vlozheniya sobstvennykh sredstv). The article still passes from named supplier to named customer, using perhaps only the warehouse facilities of the intermediary.

II is 'transit turnover with use of own capital'. Here the intermediary plays an active role, drawing resources from many suppliers, mixing them up and passing them out on its own distribution plan to many customers. At this point we shall list, as completely as possible, the various solutions to the problem of *unplanned heterogeneity*. If (a) the goods are homogeneous, the customer will not care whose goods he gets, and the intermediary's redistribution procedure is of no interest. A good case is the redistribution procedure of the zagotovka and zakupka organs[1]: no miller cares which kolkhoz's wheat he gets to grind, so long as the due discounts for moisture, etc., are allowed. But if (b) the goods are heterogeneous the customer is *ipso facto* interested in which particular articles he gets, so the intermediary's redistribution procedure acquires some importance. Nothing in the literature tells us what the procedure *should* be, but perhaps ideally it should be neutral. Then (i) the intermediary hands out his products at random, or first come first served; or (ii) he may consider it fair or neutral or desirable to impose on each customer a quota of bad commodities as a condition of getting any good ones: a sort of 'socialist full-line forcing'. However, he may abandon neutrality and play a positive role. Then (iii) he may take bribes, or distribute according to the political rank of his customers. Or (iv) there may be possibilities of price-differentiation open to him, whereby he can restore his customers' indifference between his wares. No case of this, however, is in practice known to me. Or (v) he may increase his purchases from preferred producers and diminish those from the less preferred. But there is little tolerance for this in the plan, and this can be no permanent solution. So perhaps (vi) he asks the planners to alter the current plan in this sense. Then if they do just that, we have a slow-working, essentially *un*planned, consumers' sovereignty. Or they may order technical improvements among the

---

[1] Though these would not be referred to in Soviet parlance as 'transit turnover with use of own capital', since the phrase is reserved for wholesalers of finished products.

less preferred producers; this, too, is a sort of planned consumers' sovereignty. But under (vi) the problem remains of how to dispose of existing, heterogeneous, stocks. Finally (vii) the intermediary may act according to his general vision of the Party line: if he read, for instance, in yesterday's *Pravda* that aluminium is specially important he will give the best qualities to his customer who directs an aluminium factory.

I have had the very illuminating experience of discussing this mystery with a Czechoslovak and a Polish economist. The Czech at first refused to understand the problem: 'this question does not arise, we order the bad producer to improve his product'. 'Yes, but in the meantime you have a bad consignment to allocate, and in any case the good producer may still further improve his product. Indeed, in general, highly fabricated goods are never homogeneous, however hard you try.' To this no answer was forthcoming. 'I wonder if corruption is the answer.' 'There is practically no corruption in the Czechoslovak economy.' The Pole took the problem at once, and without waiting for me to mention it said the solution was corruption. He might also have admitted the existence of 'socialist full-line forcing', as the Chinese have (Sec. 7).

The extent to which any of these things happens is unknown to me at this point, owing to the sparseness of the literature. This at least can be said: that when 'funded' commodities are homogeneous (coal, oil, wood, cement) the centre is content with system II; its own raznaryadka extends no lower than the 'body'. But if they are heterogeneous, and the producer and the customer are subordinated to different 'bodies', it distributes from enterprise to enterprise (iron and steel), or from the producer enterprise to the 'body' responsible for the consumer enterprise (chemicals).[1] For the corresponding possibilities in retail trade there is more evidence—see V below.

6. Turning now to models in category IV, we enter the 'decentralized command economy' of Ch. 7. Without a grasp of that chapter, models IV cannot be understood.

IV(a) is simple and obvious. It is in distribution the parallel to decentralized system CC/DC in production.[2] If ever there was an obvious 'small' decision it is the distribution of commodities produced by some enterprises of a 'body' among the other enterprises

---

[1] Koldomasov, op. cit., pp. 33–4.   [2] As described in Ch. 7, Sec. 9.

of that same body that wish to use it. Thus a Sovnarkhoz may devote its above-plan outputs to such internal uses as it decides.[1]

IV(b) is altogether more strange and interesting. It is a decentralized procedure for dealing with the 'export surplus' of a 'body', and appears to be—if the sources are to be trusted, and they are very explicit—what used to happen in U.S.S.R. with 'quota' or 'planned' commodities. It is a strange system, since it presupposes such dedication and virtue on the part of the intermediate economic authority. Suppose, for instance, this authority is itself a consumer of its own 'quota' commodity. Will it not help itself to the lion's share, and let the rest go hang? The temptation must also be very great simply to maximize profits in drawing up the plan. Be that as it may, it seems from the literature[2] that under the old 'production' principle the Ministry which was the main producer of such a commodity did draw up the all-Union plan for its distribution, i.e. the functions of Gosplan were delegated to it. It faced, therefore, all the problems of unplanned heterogeneity listed under II above.

Under the territorial principle no 'body' is any longer the monopolist of a commodity, so that IV(b) would mean competition in a market between Sovnarkhozy. So the whole category of 'quota' commodities lapsed. Some became 'funded', i.e. are distributed by Gosplan, a few became 'decentralized', the third category.

This third category, of 'decentralized' commodities, presents no difference in principle from the second. It was, and is still after the introduction of the Sovnarkhozy, also effected on model IV(b), but at a lower level in the hierarchy. 'Decentralized' commodities were *not* supposed to be produced on principles of market socialism, but according to the decentralized plans of local authorities. But in practice something very like market socialism can arise: imagine a 'decentralized' consumer good, the production of which is supposed to be planned by the local Soviet, but of which there is no export surplus. The temptation merely to 'plan' to follow consumer demand, perhaps at prices equally 'decentralized', will be very great. It requires the eye of faith to distinguish the 'decentralized planning' of the local authority from the behaviour of a Yugoslav enterprise. This remains true even when, as very often happens, there is an export surplus; for we are officially assured that

---

[1] Volin, *Kommunist*, 3/1959. Incidentally this shows how little power has been decentralized to Sovnarkhozy, since it follows that most of the production according to plan is distributed on the orders of the centre.

[2] E.g. D. Granick, op. cit., p. 136.

the wholesale organ's raznaryadka, and not the local planning commission's orders, is the principal determinant of the enterprise's plan.[1] Indeed, we saw above that when the raznaryadka is more detailed than the production plan it is itself a supplementary production plan. However, under the territorial principle it seems that 'decentralized' commodities, hitherto planned if at all by local Soviets, have been largely taken over by the Sovnarkhozy. This has doubtless of itself tended to diminish the influence of the wholesale organs, now that they have a more powerful planning body to deal with, and the problem of the export surplus is diminished by the mere increase in the size of this body.

On the other hand, it is difficult to be very sure what at any moment is the relative influence of planner and shop with decentralized commodities, as the Soviet and Bulgarian examples below (Sec. 11) show.

7. We now hand over initiative to the enterprise. III(a) is instantiated in the new (1959) Soviet system, whereby an enterprise receives in its plan a named list of possible purchasers, or an area (the 'transport-economic region') within which it must sell; and an output target in money terms. Thus competition is let in, not at the stage of plan execution but at that of consultation and kontraktatsia when the plan is drawn up. All this applies, of course, to 'decentralized' commodities only. Thus Mr. Kaser writes:[2]

I readily take your point that the mutual agreement between enterprises for delivery of a 'decentralized' commodity represents a form of 'bidding' since enterprises will seek to sell and buy goods that get them past their output targets at minimum cost and will choose their clients or suppliers with that end in view. But the degree of freedom afforded the enterprise is fairly low: under the new system it will be compelled to choose one within its planned transport-economic region (previously often with the enterprise designated by the ministerial *glavk*). Moreover, there are controls over disbursements by the State Bank aimed at eliminating price competition between enterprises in the course of such contract negotiation and the network of decentralized mutual-settlement systems run by the Bank tends also to restrict choice of client and supplier to those established in the current year. Of course the price differentiation controls are not always effective.

The problem of unplanned heterogeneity should not arise in this case, since the parties take account of heterogeneity at the moment of kontraktatsia. III(b) is the most decentralized of all command

---

[1] Cf. Granick, loc. cit.; ed. Rubinshtein *et al.*, *Ekonomika Sovetskoi Torgovli*, 1950, X/5–6; S. V. Serebriakov, *Organizatsia i Tekhnika Sovetskoi Torgovli*, 1956, p. 230.

[2] Of UN/ECE, by private letter of September 29, 1959.

systems, and often difficult to distinguish from the market socialism of VIII. It is common in U.S.S.R. for above-plan production, and for surpluses that bad planning has piled up locally in the trade network, to be hawked around on free market principles. Since these things were originally produced according to plan, and the trade organizations that buy them are also to some extent planned, this is perhaps best classified as III(b). But as a serious and deliberate system III(b) has to my knowledge only been instantiated in China, where in connexion with the general relaxation and legalization of late 1956 the so-called system of free choice or selective purchase was introduced.[1] The system of free choice applied to both industrial materials and finished products. Important consumer articles of simple sortament and bottleneck materials were still to be distributed according to plan. For the rest the centralized raznaryadka was evidently to be abolished, and any factory or trade organization could buy or sell anywhere in the country; in particular any shop could buy from any wholesaler. This also applied to above-plan surpluses of the 'funded' commodities. At the same time production planning was to be decentralized, but only for private and mixed companies, and quite clearly not for the same range of goods as the very wide range embraced by the free choice system. Ch'en Yün has since[2] proved to be far to the right in Party councils, and his whole policy in 1956, embracing as it did a deconcentration of craft co-operatives and an enlargement of peasants' plots, is strongly reminiscent of the NEP. Nevertheless, the free choice system is not exactly market socialism or the NEP, since it did apply to enterprises whose production remained under central command. It is, again, not the same as IV(b), since in that system the raznaryadka remains, being planned by some intermediate authority.

An advantage claimed by both Ch'en Yün and Chou En-lai for the free choice system was that it would stop the forcing of bad products on to customers along with good ones. In other words 'free choice' was directed against the 'socialist full-line forcing' of II(b)/ii (Sec. 5). 'Full-line forcing' establishes in a sense that undesirable 'anonymity' of products discussed in Sec. 8 here.

[1] Ch'en Yün, Speech to the 8th Party Congress, New China News Agency, September 21, 1956 (in *Ost-Probleme*, October 19, 1956). Chou En-lai, Speech to the Same (in *People's China*, November 1, 1956; esp. pp. 16, 19). Tseng Shan, written Statement to 8th Party Congress, Jen Min Jih Pao, September 28, 1956 (= *Current Background* 423).

[2] In late 1959, as a result of the renewed drive against rightists. Cf. Durdin, *New York Times*, March 31, 1960.

It seems that it was never intended to apply system III(b) to rigidly planned outputs, but to permit output sluggishly to follow demand. But III(b) was definitely meant to cover the nationalized sector. Although I can find no single flat statement to this effect—evidently the matter was controversial—the many discussions are only comprehensible on this assumption, and there is far from being any statement to the contrary. Perhaps clearest in his own mind on this point was Tseng Shan[1]:

> With reference to this category of products, there should not be rigid plans relating to output and specifications, and factories should be permitted, according to market needs, to change from time to time their production plans as far as varieties, patterns and specifications go. The state may only exercise adequate control through the allotment of raw materials, to prevent blind development.

Thus Tseng Shan seems really to have wanted system III(b) in the short run, VIII in the long.

I have had great difficulty in establishing the extent to which these proposals were ever implemented. In a sense they were not new, since there had been something similar until 1953, and even thereafter a small proportion of nationalized and centrally distributed intermediate products was allocated to the market by the planners. This goes even for such articles as non-ferrous metals and machine-tools.[2] No doubt, however, these were at least sales to unplanned buyers—the private entrepreneurs; they would fall here under system VIII. What was new in 1956 was that there should be free sale between a planned buyer and a planned seller.

Certainly the practical extent of the system must have been minimal, if one of the central material distributors could write a whole article on his functions and experiences in 1956 without mentioning it.[3] Of course such a person would see in III(b) a threat to his own job, but even so he would have made himself ridiculous by passing the whole subject over in silence, had it seemed important. On the other hand some sales under this system did occur, since wholesale trade on the free market, or 'the sales made by peasants to industry direct and the uncontrolled sales made between industrial departments' rose from Y 11·8 md. in 1955 to Y 16·6 md. in 1956, largely in the fourth quarter of 1956[4] (i.e. after Ch'en

---

[1] Op. cit.
[2] *Tung Chi Kung Tso*, May-June 1957 (ECMM 97).
[3] Men Cho-min, *Chi Hua Ching Chi*, 2/1957 (ECMM 80).
[4] Wang Ping, *Tung Chi Kung Tso*, 11/1957 (ECMM 91).

Yün's speech). This is a very large sum, in a national income of about Y 100 md.

Apart from the usual neglect by all sources of the raznaryadka question, the Ch'en Yün proposals were further obscured by being part and parcel of a much wider decentralization, which had much more important aspects. In particular, as Wang indicates above, he revived the 'kolkhoz market', and the new III(b) market was seen as simply a part of it, and not the most important part. This is as if the Soviet trade fairs (see model VIII in Sec. 11 below) could be freely attended by kolkhozniki. Also the production planning of the enterprises in mixed and private ownership was reduced, so that clearly in so far as they entered the new market this was pure market socialism, and not III(b) at all. Thus this sort of sentence must have been intended for such enterprises only.

> The production of goods permitted to be purchased and sold freely is governed by the law of value. To minimize the blindness of the free market and ensure the normal development of production, the competent departments of State should, in the light of their knowledge of market conditions, make proposals concerning production as a guide to producers in arranging their production plans.[1]

Thus while Ch'en Yün undoubtedly had III(b) in mind it is certain that it never came into being in pure form. For it is one thing to set output and input plans to a *part* of an economy, and allow it to effect the necessary exchanges on a market mainly occupied by the unplanned sector; and quite another to insist that these exchanges occur, albeit freely, but only among the enterprises subject to central command.

It would certainly appear that selective purchase had been much modified by April 1959, when the Minister of Commerce said that

> ... the commercial agencies, seriously upholding the principles of the State plan and the slogan 'procure whatever type of product has been produced, and procure whatever amount has been produced', have exerted great efforts to seek raw materials for industrial production, to find markets for industrial products, to prompt agencies to improve their production quality.[2]

This slogan emasculates the essence of selective purchase, which is that low quality products shall be refused if unsaleable. But it still leaves the administrative structure intact: there is no detailed raznaryadka of products, either for the factory that sells or for the commercial organ that buys.

[1] Sun Yi-min, *Chi Hua Ching Chi*, 12/1956 (ECMM 77).
[2] Cheng Tzu-hua, Speech to 1st Session of 2nd NPC, April 25, 1959 (CB 580).

Constantly in the literature of all Communist countries attention is drawn to the *simultaneous existence of local surpluses and deficits* in the warehouses of Trade organs. III(b) is a commonsense way of dealing with these: let the commercial organs freely buy and sell with each other; it does not disturb the production plan, and the raznaryadka is not so important. This regional equalization does however, lead on to a market influence on production itself—system VIII; and is therefore 'dangerous'. But by laying the emphasis on concomitant local surplus and deficit the sources divert attention from the far more important and equally common phenomena of overall surplus or overall deficit, which no amount of III(b) can cure. For that we need full-blooded VIII. The difficulty is dealt with more fully in Sec. 11.

There are in any case serious ideological objections to III(b). Is it not that evil capitalist thing, 'commodity turnover',[1] rather than undefiled socialist 'goods exchange'? True, the outputs are planned, but in view of 'unplanned heterogeneity' the worse goods will simply not get sold unless prices are flexible. That surely turns these articles into 'commodities'? Anyhow it is rather to be doubted if a transaction could by definition be 'goods exchange' unless it took place according to a proper raznaryadka.

See the appendix to this chapter.

8. Then in model V there is no raznaryadka, since the customer is now the final consumer, who is quite unplanned. But since production does not immediately follow supply all phenomena of 'unplanned heterogeneity', listed under II (Sec. 5 above) repeat themselves—all the more so since there is no restraining plan. The consumer expresses his preferences with much emphasis: he knows which factory's biscuits are best, and queues for them. Information as to the *origin* of a new consignment of consumer goods (*Czech* shoes, *Leningrad* biscuits) is very precious, and a potent source of *blat*. The well informed head the queue when the shop opens. Price differentiation, corruption, full-line forcing are all possible weapons in the hand of the shop.

Here we must digress to speak of the important distinction between *anonymity* and *homogeneity*. A homogeneous product is so by nature: wheat of a given sort is what it is because nature has so decreed, and man can do little about it. Heterogeneity is the automatic and inevitable product of human fabrication: it can be

[1] Ch. 3, Sec. 2.

made greater or less by conscious effort, but only in very simple
cases (? pins) can it be abolished.[1] But producers of heterogeneous
products can preserve their anonymity, in the quite literal and simple
sense of not putting their mark or name on the product. Textiles
are an excellent example, so much so that a British textile manufacturer, struggling against this anonymity, advertises 'Look for the
Name on the Selvage'. Much of Western imperfect competition theory is really about deliberate 'individualization', not
inevitable heterogeneity.

Now in Soviet-type economies 'material interestedness in production' is a great cry. In any economy a producer may prefer anonymity,[2] but in the Soviet Union, where penalties are so great, it
must be particularly popular. Individualization, identifiability,
which seem good to *some* capitalist producers, are in U.S.S.R.
a weapon of the authorities against all producers. Wherever
physically possible, goods must be identified, even if only on the
packaging, with a 'production mark'. Of this it has been said: 'This
makes it easy to establish the actual producer of the product in
case it is necessary to call him to account for the poor quality of his
goods. For this reason, it is one of the most effective weapons in
the battle for the quality of products.'[3] Thus the authorities themselves encourage expressions of consumers' preference, though for
reasons of their own. That is, they make precious little effort to
accommodate the planning mechanism to consumer preferences,
but they do use them as a stick to beat producers with.

9. Model VII is important in capitalism and in market socialism.
In U.S.S.R. it is exemplified by the Zakupka, the nominally
voluntary state procurement from kolkhozy on a nominally free
market. The Zakupka is not formally different from the British
Milk (or Egg) Marketing Boards. In all three cases the 'distribution'
by the producer of his product is very simple—he must sell it to a
statutory monopsonist, at a price fixed on the market by the interaction of the many producers and the one monopsonist. Thereafter,
however, there is indeed a difference: the 'redistribution' by the
British boards is again on market principles, i.e. they sell to the
retailers and wholesalers who bid highest, while the Zakupka

---

[1] Cf. my *Price, Cost and Output*, 2nd ed., Oxford 1961, Ch. 2.
[2] It is by no means obvious that differentiation is always profitable, and imperfect competition theory errs hugely in making this suggestion. Cf. Wiles, op. cit., pp. 18, 65–6.
[3] D. M. Gen'kin and M. A. Fial'kov (ed.), *Pravovoye Regulirovanie Gosudarstvennoi Torgovli
SSSR*, Moscow 1957. I owe this quotation and the whole idea of 'anonymity' to Mr.
Marshall I. Goldman, *Journal of Political Economy*, 1960.

authorities must 'redistribute' according to a plan, since with them the grain has entered the socialist sector and become a funded commodity.

In China VII plays a very large role indeed, since it applies not only to agriculture but also to small industry.

10. Model VI may be passed over as sufficiently familiar, since our whole discussion of multi-indicator systems presupposed this particular distribution procedure. In any of the other procedures here mentioned the details of the sortament are likely to be settled along the lines of VI(a) or VI(b). VI(b), the *sistema zakazov*, differs only from VIII in that the buyer is bound to a particular seller. He cannot choose where, only what, he shall buy; so the sellers do not compete.

11. Model VIII is chiefly used as listed above (Sec. 4). More interesting, however, are the unexpected uses of it in the Soviet economy. As this is written (1960) it seems to be in use among Sovnarkhozy in respect of 'decentralized' articles. Kaser writes (ibid.) 'some Sovnarkhozy despatch to other Sovnarkhozy circulars and even catalogues, listing commodities they have for sale'. It is important to see that this is an 'export' matter; at every stage in the Soviet hierarchy procedure VIII affects an organ's relations with its equals, not with its superiors or inferiors. This goes for any intermediate authority (trust, Ministry, Sovnarkhoz, Republican Gosplan).

VIII was also effectively the model for 'decentralized' articles under the old Ministries, though it was not supposed to be. See under IV(b) above, Sec. 6.

It is also the model relevant for intra-bloc trade, for here, too, the 'bodies' (countries in this case) are formally equals, and the articles exchanged are 'decentralized', since there is no supranational planning authority.

Another Soviet use of procedure VIII is, or may be, the disposal of above-plan output *by the enterprise*. We have already seen in IV(b) that if a Sovnarkhoz may freely dispose of above-plan output internally it is nothing remarkable. Market socialism only rears its ugly head when Sovnarkhozy freely sell their above-plan output, or indeed any output, to each other, as above. Free sale by the enterprise, which has so few internal uses for its own products, is another case. Mr. Herbert Levine brought back from U.S.S.R. a most surprising statement on this.[1] Directors may now 'sell the above-plan output of the enterprise and often are permitted to dispose of unneeded materials and equipment without *notifying* the Sovnarkhoz' (my italics; doubtless he means without getting permission from). The order *re* unneeded materials and equipment goes back to 1955, and will not be a big matter. But above-plan output is an everyday occurrence. If this can indeed be disposed of by method VIII the enterprise is almost as free as Kolkhoz. Levine himself says his informant

seemed bright and knowledgeable, yet some of the things he said I knew to be incorrect. These I dropped from the report on my own. This statement on the disposition of over-plan output startled me and I tried to make sure I understood him by having him repeat it. . . . I have found no confirmation of this statement anywhere else. On the contrary, it appears from other sources, that as far as the Gosplan-distributed goods are concerned, the republican council of ministers controls the distribution of all or at least the significant part of over-plan output (*Sovetskaia Litva*, Dec. 26, 1957, p. 2, and *Rabochaia Gazeta*, Nov. 21, 1959, p. 3). Perhaps [he] meant only the sovnarkhoz-and/or the republic-distributed goods.

Yet Levine's questionable informant may after all have been right, and the matter is certainly (early 1960) in a state of flux. In late 1959 there was in Moscow an

inter-republican exhibition and sale of goods. There took part in it: the wholesale bases of the trade ministries of all union republics, the consumer co-ops, many wholesale enterprises (torgi), and [and this is what tends to confirm Levine's story] more than 20 industrial enterprises. The exhibition was given three tasks: first, to ensure a broad inter-republican exchange of goods not planned by the U.S.S.R. Gosplan; secondly to agree on the *sortament* and delivery dates of haberdashery, cultural and household articles planned by the Soyuzglavtorg [a wholesale trading department of Gosplan]; and lastly the sale of superfluous goods by wholesale and retail trade organizations.[2]

R.44 md. of goods were bought and sold, which is no less than the staggering proportion of 6% of all retail trade turnover in 1959.

Now clearly the first task of the exhibition is our distribution system VIII, and it demonstrates that bodies of equal planning status, when not brought under subordination to a higher one, must trade on free market principles, however imperfectly. Of the third task, sale of surpluses, it is specifically stated later that some of the

---

[1] Private letter, 22 Dec., 1959.
[2] A. Smirnov, *Sovetskaya Torgovlya*, January 9, 1960.

surpluses were of 'funded' commodities. The participation of factories is also important. The experience of one is described thus:

the hat factory 'Record' had earlier supplied to the metropolitan base Rostorgo-dezhda R.36 mn. worth of goods. The latter agreed only to take R.30 mn. worth, and refused the rest on the ground of alleged non-correspondence with the sorta-ment. But at the exhibition the enterprise sold the remaining hats literally in a few days.

The author, Smirnov, is manager of the Soyuzglavtorg. He recommends a wide extension of this system of sales. Unfortunately he does not make clear how prices were fixed. Neither does the latest trade textbook, which also has a section on trade fairs.[1] As it came out earlier (Sept. 1959), the textbook was still able to say that 'funded' commodities 'cannot be the object of free sale at fairs'. The textbook, which is of course very *bien pensant*, implies that there are and always have been many fairs. Smirnov almost writes as if there had never been any before. The 1950 edition of the textbook, and a 1956 handbook, make no mention of trade fairs; but they attribute very similar functions to the 'commercial intermediary offices' (torgposredkontory).[2] These offices existed in the late 'thirties, were wound up during the war, and started again in 1949. The sources make it clear that they rarely handled funded commodities, but do not actually exclude it.

In Bulgaria the same system has been—but for how long?—formalized. On July 25–26, 1960 the Central Committee and the Cabinet decided, *inter alia*, that

industry may no longer make any goods without order from a trade organization. Trade organizations on their side may accept from now on no goods which are qualitatively inferior or for which there is no demand. Further, the Ministry of Internal Trade is empowered to forbid the purchase of consumer goods from enterprises that neglect these rules. Further, it can with immediate effect dissolve existing contracts between shops and factories, if the latter do not fulfil their obligations. Further, the Ministry must strengthen its performance as regulator of trade in the whole country; to which end a central wholesale office is created in the Ministry with marts (Handelsumschlagplätze) and branches in all industrial centres.

Further, the Minister of Trade has power with immediate effect to move certain goods from one county to another, and the county trade organizations have the same right and duty with regard to retail trade.[3]

---

[1] *Ekonomika Sovietskoi Torgovli*, 1959, pp. 226–7.
[2] Ed. Rubinshtein, *et al.*, op. cit., X/6; Serebryakov, op. cit., pp. 241, 290.
[3] My text is a translation of the condensed report in *Hinter dem Eisernen Vorhang*, Munich, August 1960.

12. It is important to see that procedure VIII has little connexion with what is formally called the 'decentralized' distribution of commodities. Allocation by local government organs is simply a special case of allocation by bodies inferior to Gosplan, and comes under IV(a). The whole ethos of 'decentralized' distribution is local procurement for local needs; within the locality there is supposed to be 'central planning'. But no 'body' can be wholly autarkic, so the problems posed by IV(b) always arise. The territorial system makes them vastly more acute, so that *for decentralized commodities VIII is taking the place of IV(b)*. For the old ministries were few in number, and located in Moscow, and each had a very large 'export surplus' of comparatively few commodities. They could work the queer hybrid IV(b) system. But the Sovnarkhozy are many, difficult to control, and pre-eminently 'multi-product'. In such conditions VIII is natural, unless the commodity is 'funded' under the Gosplan.

Between III(b) and VIII the line is even thinner. The trade fairs and torgposredkontory certainly originated as III(b): as free market ways of redistributing what the plan had caused to be produced, and then itself wrongly distributed. *Par excellence* their object is to even out local surpluses and deficits in the trading system. Again it is plain that the surplus hats in the above example had been produced according to plan; and any 'funded' commodities finding their way into a fair will of course have produced according to a plan. So the sale of surpluses and the evening out of local surpluses and deficits, the third of the overt objects of the fair, is III (B). But the first object, 'the broad inter-republican exchange of goods not planned by the U.S.S.R. Gosplan', is surely VIII.

13. After the tedious sifting of evidence and building of schemas, let us dare to draw a few more interesting conclusions and comparisons. Certainly anyone who has read—or written!—thus far, deserves a change of diet.

What governs the degree of centralization of the raznaryadka? First, perhaps, sheer intellectual torpor: the feeling that if production is centrally planned distribution must be too. System III(b), which puts centralized production plans and decentralized distribution into such awkward proximity, comes as a shock to the naïf observer. Second, ideology: there are periods of high centralization for its own sake. In U.S.S.R. the first of these was War Communism, and the second was late Stalinism. In 1952 the number of 'funded' articles reached its peak, and the officials concerned wrote as if this were a good thing and would further increase.[1] With Stalin's death the number instantly sank, and has continued to do so until the Sovnarkhozy were imposed. In 1958, as we saw, 'planned' articles were assimilated to 'funded', so the number rose many times. Thereafter one would have expected a fall again, but in fact the number has continued, for whatever reason, to climb.[2] A third factor is of course the sheer administrative capacity of the planners to do the work. This must have weighed with Ch'en Yün in 1956.

Most interesting, however, as a cause of centralized distribution is the presence of excess demand and/or planner's tension. Planner's tension is discussed in Ch. 13; enough to say here that it is the excess of administratively ordered output over capacity output. It can exist together with or separately from the excess of money demand over capacity output at given prices, which is also a normal feature of Soviet-type economies (especially of course in consumer markets but also, in so far as money is active, in inter-enterprise transactions).

Now with whichever of these two we have to deal, centralized distribution is at bottom a form of rationing, a response to shortage. Historically, the very method of balances itself arose after 1928, out of the need for an orderly raznaryadka, when articles became scarce. 'Funded' articles, we read in every source, are not merely the most important in a general way, nor merely the easiest to administer centrally, but also the scarcest. 'Planned' articles are less scarce, 'decentralized' ones still less so. And this is all simple common sense. System III(b) will plainly work best where there is no excess demand or tension at all; it is no accident that its introduction in China accompanied a deliberate reduction in tension, after complaints that it had been particularly bad in 1956. *If there were neither excess demand nor planner's tension, a command economy without a raznaryadka could be quite normal*; though ideology would undoubtedly stand in its way. The raznaryadka is technically justified only as a means of ensuring the observance of priorities when there is tension. The general slackening of tension since Stalin died will not of itself decentralize production planning, but it is likely to—and has—decentralized distribution.

System III(b), then, was an invention of Chinese right-wing Communists. Technically bound to such other right-wing moves

---

[1] Levine, op. cit., pp. 157, 159.
[2] Koldamasov, op. cit., pp. 23–4. Cf. United Nations, Economic Commission for Europe, *Bulletin* XII/1, footnote 23.

as a reduction in planner's tension, it is psychologically part of a whole syndrome, extending from a revival of peasants' private plots and the 'kolkhoz' market to the evocation of the Hundred Flowers and the Spirit of Bandoeng.

Finally, decentralized distribution is a weapon against bad quality. On this our Chinese sources (advocating III(b)) and our Bulgarian sources (advocating VIII) are very explicit. So, too, is the Chinese renunciation of III(b), also quoted: when they reverted to the slogan, 'procure whatever type of product has been produced, and whatever amount has been produced', they were renouncing a weapon against bad quality.

14. Now under capitalism excess demand leads to *rationing*. What is the connexion between this and the raznaryadka? The input plan of any enterprise is, in a sense, rationing: it is administratively prevented from buying more than so much. But unless the rationing ties the buyer to a particular seller it is not a proper Communist system of distribution. When during the war the British consumer had to register with a particular butcher that was a sort of voluntary raznaryadka: once the shopkeeper accepted the registration it was difficult to change. Even here, however, the voluntary, unplanned nature of the original 'contract' reduces the parallelism. Milk-rationing was a better case, since if one lived in a certain street, one had to use the milkman who 'had' that street— though of course the 'sortament' of the milk remained to be settled between buyer and seller! On the other hand there were forms of rationing even less similar to the Communist distribution systems than that of meat. These were the rations that could be used in any shop, and over a wide 'sortament': the 'points' described in Ch. 4, Sec. 14. In wholesale transactions much the same applied to steel, where the 'points' were called 'M-forms'.

It is surprising how little any of this resembles Communist systems of distribution—except of course the consumer rationing that is occasionally forced on Communist countries too.[1] Nor is it a clear technical impossibility for a command economy to distribute steel by means of M-forms. M-forms could easily be superimposed on any decentralized system such as III(b) or VIII. The dissimilarity seems to arise from very deep causes. When there is excess demand

---

[1] Consumer goods are rationed during wars or at other times when it would seem normal in any country: e.g. in U.S.S.R. in the famine and its aftermath, 1932–35, in DDR during the food-shortage caused by the flight of farmers to the West.

or, in wartime, planner's tension,[1] we in the West instinctively work from the side of demand, by deflation or by some kind of rationing. Both are restraints on purchases. Communists instinctively work from the side of supply, telling the producer to whom to deliver how much. The input plan of the consuming enterprise is merely the mirror image of the producer's output plan. It is quite secondary in Communist thinking.

This is not to say, however, that there will never in future be more Western types of rationing.

15. The types of distribution throw up a number of parallels with the types of imperfect competition under capitalism—a romantic subject upon which too much stress should not be laid. Under market socialism this is not of course surprising. System VII, for instance, approximates 'pure' competition (many sellers, homogeneous product)—though in the presence of a monopsonist and the absence of easy entry[2] we can certainly not say 'perfect' competition. With VIII it is plain that all types of competition can be expected.

In a command economy on the other hand it would be absurd to say that any particular distribution system *is* such-and-such a well-known type of imperfect competition; for enterprises follow orders. But there are a number of resemblances, which shed new light on both imperfect competition and Soviet-type distribution.

Thus with I there is no direct, or market, competition. Enterprises may 'compete' in the minds of the planners, and influence next year's plan by producing cheaper than others in the same branch. But that is all. In II and III there is limited 'imperfect' competition as already described, but the producers are severely hamstrung by the restraints upon their outputs. IV(b) is an imperfect oligopoly of 'bodies' in a very genuine sense. In V the 'producers' certainly compete with each other: i.e. the shops compete for customers. Latterly, shops in U.S.S.R. even advertise against each other. VI is bilateral monopoly, subject to such restraints as the central plan may impose on it, e.g. by fixing prices.

In all this there is a certain correspondence with capitalist conditions: the things that are most perfectly competitive under

---

[1] There was considerable planner's tension for steel in wartime Britain, which took the form of a so-called 'M-form inflation': not only was there too much money, there were also too many M-forms, chasing too little steel.

[2] Entry is not easy because the kolkhoz cropping plan is so strongly influenced from outside.

capitalism show most tendencies that way in U.S.S.R.—agricultural commodities; where we advertise most they advertise most—shops and their wares, etc., etc. This is of course only to be expected, since it arises from the nature of the product.

Particularly illuminating has been the discussion of the planners' attitude to product differentiation. Not only is this inevitable in a highly manufactured commodity; it is also, in rational and moderate forms, actually desirable. If several factories produce identical products without distinguishing marks, and a consumer has a complaint, he cannot bring it home to the culprit. By abolishing 'anonymity', the planners fix responsibility on producers. This has clear applications in Western economics, and is another nail in the coffin of the old simpliste doctrines that products are differentiated only by an evil conspiracy of capitalists, that differentiation lessens consumers' sovereignty and productive efficiency, etc. It is on the contrary to 'anonymity' that these strictures apply, in all types of economy.[1]

Again tension and excess demand have effects akin to those of excess demand in a market economy, in creating a 'seller's market'.[2] The producer can choose to which customer he delivers first, he can lower his quality, take bribes, etc., etc. That is, all the informal non-plan bargaining counters lie in the producer's hands when there is tension, just as in a market economy all the informal non-price bargaining counters are with the producer when there is excess demand and sticky prices.

16. In conclusion there is one more reason why the raznaryadka is of crucial importance. For while it is often in fact a supplementary production plan, narrowing freedom of decision on the sortament, it always effectively determines the transport plan. For when we decide who shall send what to whom we are of course locating all the outputs and saying how far they shall be shipped. All Soviet sources show awareness of this, and demand that the raznaryadka be such as to make the most rational use of transport. In this connexion there is also a trend in U.S.S.R. to making the producer, not the consumer, pay the transport cost. In conditions of planner's tension or excess demand the consumer is willing to pay very high transport

[1] Cf. Goldman, op. cit.   [2] Cf. Wiles, op. cit., pp. 67-8.

costs, and this leads to irrationalities. Although the point is easily made, only a longer treatment would do justice to it.[1]

APPENDIX TO CHAPTER 9

Extracts from Chang Shih-chang's 'Answers to Questions on the State-led Free Market', *Hsueh Hsi*, Nov. 2, 1956 [ECMM No. 66] [Note: 'socialist market' means the total market in China; 'socialist unified market' means the sphere of planned distribution; 'state-led free market' means the exchanges on system III(b) plus what corresponds to the Soviet kolkhoz market.]

As we know, the form of production of commodities decides the form of distribution of commodities. Since in production there is need for planned production to be supplemented by free production within the scope permitted by state plans, then in the unified socialist markets of the country, with the state markets as the main body, there may also be created free markets led by the state within definite limits. The reason is also very clear. Such free markets, being led by the state, are subordinate to the socialist unified markets, and are a constituent body of the socialist markets, capable of remedying the deficiencies of the socialist markets, capable of remedying such defects of the socialist markets as the tendency to deal chiefly in goods having big sales, the failure to supply the type of goods needed, and the untimely supply of goods. Because there are still the socialist markets as the main body, these free markets are basically different from capitalist free markets, and will not develop into capitalist free markets.

In undertaking selective purchases of certain industrial products which are daily necessities, instead of the planned distribution of such products, the factories will be made to show concern for the market of their products, and must needs take steps to raise their quality, and increase their varieties. The stores, in order to enable their stocks to be sold in good time, must needs strengthen their investigation and study of the needs of the residents, and select the goods suited to the needs of the residents. All these help to

---

[1] For a pre-mathematical treatment of the problem of minimizing transport costs by means of an optimal raznaryadka see Koldomasov, op. cit. Ch. 6; more sophisticated treatments by L. V. Kantorovich and others are listed in United Nations, Economic Commission for Europe, *Bulletin*, XII/1, footnotes 60 and 66.

improve production and the expansion of the circulation of commodities. With the abolition of unified purchases of certain agricultural by-products, and the permission of their free purchase, the production of such items will be stimulated and the needs of the urban and rural population met.

It will thus be seen that the existence of the free markets led by the state not only does not undermine the socialist unified markets, but will also further promote economic activity, the growth of production, and the solution of the possible contradiction, in a planned economy, between supply and the people's needs. This is also a good measure for combining planning and elasticity. If this is not done, the superiority of socialism will not be fully revealed in the field of the satisfaction of the daily-growing needs of the people. . . .

In the free markets, can prices be freely fixed? Will commodity prices undergo violent fluctuations?

This question involves the role of the law of value in the free markets. As we know, the law of value still plays an active role within the scope of the socialist production of commodities. Especially in the regulation of supply-demand relations, the law of value still plays a very important role. As long as we fully understand this law, we can utilize it to serve socialism, and prevent it from having an undesirable influence. In our practical economic life today, many facts have shown that the use of the law of value for a correct grasp of price policy will have an active influence on the stimulation of production and the regulation of supply and demand. On the contrary, in some areas where there has not been properly implemented the policy of better prices for better goods, lower prices for inferior goods, or where there has even been a downward pressure on prices in the purchase of supplies, there would be a reduction in output and a stagnation of the market.

Accordingly, in the free markets led by the state, the law of value should be employed in an even better manner, permitting the free fixing of prices, and resolutely implementing the policy of grading goods and pricing them according to quality. Goods of good quality produced at greater costs may have their prices appropriately raised, while goods of inferior quality should have their prices lowered. This will stimulate the producers into turning out more goods of better quality, which is beneficial to both producers and consumers. Comrade Ch'en Yün has stated correctly, 'At the present moment when there is the tendency for the quality of certain commodities to drop, the advocacy of the policy of better prices for better goods in effect will lower prices.' If goods to be purchased through free selection still are subject to price restrictions, the significance of free selection will be lost, and there will not be produced the effect of stimulating production, raising quality, and increasing varieties. . . .

Recently in certain large cities there has been reported the situation in which purchasing units from the outside had resorted to blind and competitive buying, freely raising prices, and there were even retail stores in some areas proceeding to Shanghai and other large cities to buy what they thought they needed. As a matter of fact, goods bought in such a way would not necessarily fully meet the needs of the people, and because the cost is high, and expenses great, not only will the burden of the consumers be increased, but the enterprise itself may find itself suffering a working loss. Such a situation can only happen during the first stage of selective purchasing, when professional experience is still lacking. After a certain period, the situation must be improved.

After the enforcement of selective purchasing, and pricing according to quality, it is entirely possible that certain factories, due to their backward equipment, technique and management, will find the markets for their products affected, and experience difficulties in securing liquid capital and in attending to production. This must make the industrial departments take steps to rapidly improve the equipment, technique and management of such factories, and the aim of selective purchases will thus be realized. Naturally there may be individual factories that are so backward and are incapable of being improved, so that they may have to face the fate of elimination. This is unavoidable. However, under existing economic conditions in our country, workers in factories may be placed under employment in a unified manner by the special trade companies, and may thus get work in other factories, so that the closure of their original plant will not render them unemployed. Accordingly, the enforcement of free purchasing provides an active factor in urging the backward factories to improve their production, and will not have a detrimental influence.

CHAPTER 10

HOW TO RATIONALIZE A COMMAND ECONOMY[1]

1. THE arbitrary mess that Marxist economics and Stalinist institutions make of resource allocation can be corrected in three ways, which without much distortion we may name after Lerner, Lange[2] and Leontief. The first is that of *perfect competition*, the second that of *perfect central adjustment*, the third that of *perfect computation*. In terms of our allocation models in Ch. 4 these correspond to (7), (3) and (4) respectively.

First, what have all these methods in common? They all allot prices to all factors of production, including land, capital and foreign exchange, and to as many final goods and services as is humanly possible. As we have seen, in this sense prices are measures of scarcity and therefore a *logical*, not merely a practical, necessity. Rationally, to solve the scarcity problem is to solve it by measurement; and the measures are prices. What is not logically necessary is that there should be a market in the sense of people higgling with each other or paying money across the counter. Electrical relays can higgle just as well. If *their* interactions are properly called a market then a 'market' is also a logical necessity: if not, not. Thus a market is either 'human' or 'electronic'. One or other is a logical necessity for rational allocation, but for arbitrary allocation we may of course dispense with both.[3]

2. Now turning to what is different, perfect competition is very familiar and need not detain us. One attaches prices to land and capital, makes the turnover tax uniform, abolishes subsidies, establishes free trade across the borders, decentralizes decision-making, and sits back. Naturally the transitional problems are very serious, and the ideological ones equally so. The changes, to my mind definitely heretical, that the Yugoslavs have made in their ideology are discussed in Ch. 17. The practical transitional problems that they faced are nowhere described, but it should be noted that

---

[1] This chapter assumes in the reader an elementary acquaintance with input/output.

[2] The reference is to Lange's early work, *On the Economics of Socialism* (Minneapolis 1948). Latterly Lange has inclined to the 'Leontief' position.

[3] Consequently this is not the same as the assertion of Ch. 1 that a market is a logical necessity if there is no command economy. Reference there was, implicitly, to a human market.

still (1960) tax rates are not uniform (in which country are they?), and the foreign exchange market, owing to the makeshifts imposed by the perennial balance of payments problem, remained a jungle of special provisions until early 1961. The remaining elements of central planning in the system have been briefly adumbrated in Ch. 2. This model principally differs from the others in permitting enterprises to fix their own prices (that is why there is competition). Note that Lerner differs from Lange in this respect, and there is no such thing as the single 'Lerner-Lange model', sometimes referred to in writings on this subject. But plainly the Lerner (or Tito) model cannot be called a command economy, so need not be further considered in this chapter.

3. Perfect central adjustment is model (3) of Ch. 4. It has not hitherto been discussed since it has hardly been exemplified. But the theory of it, and to some extent the practice, are live issues in Poland. It requires no 'electronic market' but it does make necessary the other elements in perfect computation: the swift communication of innumerable data. For in this case the changes in profitability brought about by shifts in tastes, resources and technology must be reported at once to the centre, and the relevant orders as to new production sent as quickly back. *It is, in essence, the problem facing any large vertically integrated firm.*

The attempt to rationalize a Stalinist economy in this way shows four special features of some interest. First, we cannot simply equalize the rate of turnover tax everywhere and leave the resulting private profits and losses to do their work; for we have *ex hypothesi* deprived entrepreneurs of the power to decide production. Rather must we treat the tax as 'socialist profit', and ourselves proceed to maximize its yield by investing most where it is highest, and reducing production where it is low or negative. This will in the end equalize the tax everywhere. In other words the turnover tax becomes the principal investment criterion (cf. Ch. 6, Sec. 4).

4. Secondly, in practice the variability of the turnover tax has a greater percentage effect on market price, and therefore on output, than the absence of land-rent and long-term interest charges. For as time wears on more and more recourse is had to the 'method of differences' and actual outputs diverge more and more from the ideal.[1] If, then, rationality refers only to the relative outputs

---

[1] Or, as in Poland, the country emerges almost directly from a destructive war into Communism, and the method of differences is used to sanctify whatever relative capacities to produce there happen to be.

of goods it seems more important to equalize the turnover tax than to introduce the missing charges, and our second special question is whether this is really so. For rationality also refers to the choice between techniques, and it might be thought that on this ground the absence of the missing charges was more important.

Thus let the supply of land, labour and capital be fixed, and it be our aim fully to employ least one. Then by charging no interest we do not create any more capital, we simply misallocate what there is. We may well be aiming at greater capital-intensity (cf. Ch. 16), but we shall only attain it in one enterprise at the expense of another. The law of diminishing returns tells us we should produce more if we allocated the capital more evenly. With constant output-proportions of final goods, a misallocation of factors between enterprises would lead to an unambiguous physical short-fall in every line of output. Is not this more important than a wrong choice of final output pattern? It would not appear so, for reasons of rather fundamental economic philosophy. By 'technique' we normally mean the way in which factors are combined to produce goods. But it might equally mean the way in which goods are combined (i.e. the pattern of final output) to produce satisfactions. A wrong combination of factors lessens the output of goods, but a wrong combination of goods lessens the output of satisfactions. Diminishing returns, then, is neither more nor less important than diminishing marginal utility. Irrational factor-pricing is not *a priori* more important than irrational output-pricing: the 'perfect central adjuster' must tackle them with equal urgency.

5. Then, thirdly, the system of perfect central adjustment requires correspondence to prices in the capitalist world market, since these are marginal opportunity costs in a Communist economy. It has in the past been claimed as evidence of the irrationality of Communist prices that capitalist international prices are used in trade between Communist countries.[1] But not so, for there is only one world market, not two, even if the link is rather tenuous. The price of marginal supplies to a Communist country *is* the capitalist price, and there is no such thing as the special scarcity relationships of the Communist world, except in non-traded commodities or those subject to either side's strategic export ban.

So a good aim under this method of rationalizing ICM is to set the prices of traded commodities at world prices—or if for prestige

---

[1] E.g. by myself, *Oxford Economic Papers*, Oct. 1953.

reasons an overvalued exchange rate is preferred, then domestic *relative* prices should be brought into correspondence with foreign *relative* prices, and exports should receive a flat proportional subsidy while imports pay a similar tax.[1] But, needless to say, mere correspondence of prices must be backed up by output changes: both domestic outputs and exports and imports must be adjusted until marginal costs are equal to these prices. As ever, the mere correction of prices is a sterile academic exercise; rationalization *means* adjustment of outputs.

There is, however, one important practical qualification. A Soviet-type economy is normally required to keep the percentage of its foreign trade that goes across the Curtain down to 30; and doubtless a higher and less definite limit applies to each commodity. Accept this limitation as being beyond an economist's criticism. Then perfectly free and rational trading will tend to exceed the limit for certain commodities, and marginal supplies will be Communist supplies. So to some extent there really are 'two world markets', and 'special Communist scarcity relationships'. If all other Communist countries are pursuing rationality too, this presents no problem. If they are not, the problem of rational international prices is posed in earnest. It is not enough, as has been jokingly said by Communist planners, to 'keep one capitalist country going, so that we shall know what to do'; for that is the solution only where capitalist supplies are marginal. We are not bound to solve every problem facing Communism, and shall leave this conundrum standing. The case of there being no capitalist supplies at all (i.e. either there is a total trade ban or Communism has taken over the whole earth) is clearly of no special economic interest; the question is, are the supplies marginal?

6. Note, fourthly, that perfect central adjustment has at least two major forms. In one, prices only are centrally set in detail, while outputs are governed by the Lerner Rule, mc=price. This rule becomes then the indicator for all enterprises, and is enforced upon them administratively or perhaps by fulfilment bonuses. There is thus no direct central command over output. In the second form the outputs also are centrally calculated, and the enterprise receives direct orders as to both price and output. Communist experience of perfect central adjustment is, as we have seen, very meagre. But broadly speaking the first form corresponds to capitalist policy

[1] Cf. Wiles, *Soviet Studies*, 1961.

on public utilities, and the second to arms procurement in a capitalist war economy. Mere anti-trust is of course part of RM, not CM.

Is the more liberal of these two forms viable? Capitalist experience has often been that price control is unworkable without output control: if you control the price of a particular line it will disappear from the market because the capitalist switches to some other line, so you must compel him to produce the controlled line. And much Communist experience backs this up. Enterprises are for ever putting out new lines, within the tolerance of the sortament, in order to circumvent price stops on existing lines. What consolations can we offer on this to the more liberal form of central adjustment? First, it is not always true of large and respectable enterprises: e.g. public utilities, nationalized industries in Britain. Secondly, competition in regard to quality, on the lines of the Chinese system of free choice (Ch. 9, Sec. 7), is quite compatible with this model. Thirdly, output restriction can be stopped, and therefore price control evasion kept to a minimum, by at least two devices: the tax on unused capacity, as in Yugoslavia, and the general output target in money terms, as in Poland.

7. So irrational is a Stalinist economy that to introduce perfect central adjustment is to bring about a major upheaval in relative prices and outputs. For this initial stage some central computation, as in the next section, may well be desirable; thereafter, of course, one proceeds à tâtons. Such a use of central computation is often advocated in Poland; it must be distinguished from what follows. The essential difference is that central adjustment, as its name implies, does not infringe consumer's sovereignty.

8. Perfect computation is of course the correct use of input/-output combined with activity analysis. It could either be used on ICM (model 4), omitting the worker and consumer from the range of its sovereignty; or on model (x) of Ch. 1 and (1) of Ch. 4—a communitarian socialism embracing the whole nation. In the former case real money would have to be used at least at the periphery of the planned sector: prices that genuinely persuade worker and consumer to conform. This differs very definitely, but in a way not easy to grasp, from perfect central adjustment, just described. In the latter the central authority decides prices and outputs in *reaction* to consumer demand. In the model now under consideration the authority computes what quantities are good for consumers and sets such prices as will make them want to buy

them. In the second, 'communitarian', case of perfect computation there is no need at all for real money, but the planners have of course extra allocation and distribution problems that in the first they can evade: everyone must receive his due task and his due ration from the computer. In either case the planner is telling the consumer and worker. The centre is, by definition in every case we call perfect computation, sovereign. Indeed it is more sovereign than in the historically experienced Stalin model, since that delegated so many decisions to intermediate bodies and enterprises. Our theoretical concepts of central adjustment and computation both include such perfect communications that all delegation is unnecessary.

9. It is obvious that all forms of perfect computation are at present technically impossible. Not only is the information-gathering wholly outside our present capacity: there are problems of computer accuracy as well, since in such long calculations very small initial slips have catastrophic results. But in the end we must surely reckon that perfect computation may become, in terms of administrative cost, competitive with perfect competition. For the market also has its administrative costs, and the more perfect it is the higher they are: both in the physical plant and information network necessary to run a perfect market, and in the anti-trust department necessary to stop imperfections. Or, since technical progress will surely lower the cost of both, it is enough that the cost of perfect computation remain higher, but society be rich enough to afford it. One can then imagine that the random or speculative fluctuations of prices in perfect markets, coupled with the ever-present danger of market imperfection, will be judged by very undogmatic people to be a far greater disadvantage than the high administrative costs of perfect computation.

Let us step aside then, briefly, from our train of thought to contemplate the irony of history: economic structures, which determine or—let us not be too Marxist—at least influence and justify political and social structures, depend on such trivial details as filing systems, communications technology, matrix algebra, etc. To instal a command economy before the requisite inventions have been made one must be a Communist, tolerant of bureaucracy, hostile to private enterprise and insensitive to rational choice. But once the inventions are made the rationality of choice may well change sides, and the cost of bureaucracy so diminish as not to weigh in the balance. The issue would then be simply between capitalism and the command economy, with the political accompaniments of each.

In our present context it is enough simply to pose this question. In concrete terms, when a young graduate of applied mathematics at Columbia or Manchester can tell a button manufacturer in Akron or Kidderminster what to do, and when experience has shown the manufacturer that this advice is sound, why have a free market of any kind? so why have private profit? so why not a socialist command economy? The answer would have to be political.

10. But our task here is rather history than prophecy. It is evident from Ch. 3 that Marx had no notion of perfect computation, or rather that he held all computation to be perfect, since he could not distinguish arbitrary from rational choice. At any rate he favoured *some* kind of command economy. So did his successors: apart from Tito, what kinds of computation have they used?

Under War Communism and the first FYP, it would seem, none. There was simple chaos. Then, however, came the *method of balances*. 'Balance' is a Soviet word meaning a properly drawn up budget for anything, and the method consists in drawing up budgets for a very large number of materials and types of equipment and labour. It is calculated what consumption of a particular raw material is entailed by the issue of such-and-such production orders. Consumption, stocks at end of period and exports are then balanced against production, stocks at beginning of period and imports. The reader may imagine to himself what things were like before even this crude procedure was gone through!

We have now arrived at the problem of circular repercussions. Suppose the material to be coke. A short-fall in the *ex ante* balance may be considered a good reason for erecting another coke oven rather than adjusting some of the consumption items downwards. But this means more steel. And the production of more steel means more coke. There is, then, a problem here, either of an infinite[1] series of iterations, or of solving simultaneous equations. Hitherto (1961), the Soviet policy has been to calculate the most important of the first two or three iterations above, and to put the weight of all the minor or more indirect repercussions on stocks and the

---

[1] Many loose thinkers speak of '*the* problem of infinite equations'. This might be taken literally, in which case it could mean (a) that iteration is an infinite process, or (b) that quality, time and place should be so very narrowly defined that the matrix should be infinite. And in any case their reference might be either to input/output or to activity analysis. But it is clear that in all cases one can obtain useful results from a finite number of iterations.

'mobilization of internal reserves' (i.e. the simple demand that producers make up the difference by squeezing more out of the resources they have). This is as much as to say that answers have been arrived at by mere empirical manipulation.[1] Mathematically sophisticated methods, i.e. simultaneous equations, have been eschewed, partly because they are ideologically suspect and partly, no doubt, because they would not have been very useful in the immense complexity of real life planning.

11. But however crude may be this merely empirical method of adjustment, the fact remains that without it there is utter chaos; as indeed there was in the early periods. Nor will the current *ex post facto* adjustment of the plan to emerging bottlenecks do, for that would be to give up a basic characteristic of ICM or War Communism: that they possess a *plan*, a document that says what shall in future be done.

Indeed this is what we called in Ch. 4, Sec. 3 the *currently altered plan*. If the plan is currently adjusted, as a matter of principle, to both physical bottlenecks and shifts in taste, instead of currently predicting or successfully moulding them, we have CM. If it is currently adjusted to physical bottlenecks alone then we have the very inefficient forms of ICM or War Communism known until the Second FYP. In the former case the lack of a plan in a command economy is natural and logical; in the latter a laughable catastrophe.

For any kind of efficiency, then, the bottlenecks must be anticipated, not reacted to. Naturally there must be some current adjustment if only because unforeseen inventions will be made or unforeseen political changes will occur. It is not implied that there must be perfect foresight of everything. But if quite ordinary technical difficulties and bottlenecks of the sort described arise all the time and are solved by adjusting the plan, then there is no real plan, and furthermore in the resulting chaos the consumer will probably take over. Consequently planner's sovereignty entails almost by definition the successful use of the method of balances, so that the plan really does govern the economy for at least some short period ahead.

In other models of socialism or capitalism—for example, FM and CM—the method of balances is merely useful. It enables one to *predict* the changes in the material structure of production likely

[1] Cf. Herbert Levine, source as in Ch. 9, Sec. 1.

to be brought about by this or that change in demand. The actual adjustment to these changes, however, is and is meant to be made currently, as the prices of inputs and outputs rise and fall.

12. As we saw in Ch. 5, the method of balances gives rise in a sense to some criteria of output choice. Planners must start somewhere, and cannot indefinitely hesitate like an ass between two bundles of hay. So certain 'leading links'[1] are chosen, such as heavy chemicals, aluminium or whatever may be the current priority material, which function as the system's determinants. Other outputs then follow by technical necessity. But these other outputs have also their scarcity, and should at the margin be just as socially profitable as the 'leading links'. In other words the whole concept of the leading link is wrong: no output has the right to determine any other, all must mutually determine each other. Not less important, however, who chooses these leading links in the first place, and why? We know only that it is a function of top government, a fact that would in any country shake our faith in the rationality of the choice. That a Communist government, unguided by a free price system and neglectful even of its own arbitrary prices, should make the choices, implies that virtually all leading links are more or less ill chosen.

13. *Input/output* achieves the same thing at the method of balances, only far better: by simultaneous equations, and the special mathematics of matrices, rather than by tedious iteration. From the present equilibrium of all material balances we can discover how to move to a new equilibrium of all balances which incorporates both the desired extra quantity of, say, steel and all the infinite regress of consequential changes. When the Russians began to take an interest in this improvement N. Nemchinov[2] claimed that Wassily Leontief's first glimmerings of input/output derived from his study of Soviet planning problems, and were published in *Planovoye Khozyaistvo*, December 1925 ('The Balance of the National Economy of U.S.S.R.: A Methodological Critique of the Work of the Central Statistical Administration'). Such a claim is almost essential if input/output is to be accepted by the ideologues, but it is unfortunately quite untrue. For Leontief was then already in Germany, and his article is a translation of one he published in *Weltwirtschaftliches Archiv* in October 1925. Nor does it deal at all

[1] In Russian vedushchie zvenya, or vedushchie otrasli (branches).
[2] *Voprosy Ekonomiki*, 10/1958. Cf. H. Levine, *Bulletin of the Association for the Study of Soviet-Type Economies*, 1960; Campbell, *Slavic Review*, Oct. 1961.

with input/output, since the crucial element of solving a large number of simultaneous equations is wholly missing. We can at most say that the author, owing to his Soviet experience, had already developed interests which later led him to his discovery. In fact his first published venture with many simultaneous equations was an article in the *Review of Economics and Statistics*, August 1936: 'Quantitative Input/Output Relations in the Economic System of the United States.' *This* is the article correctly cited in the standard textbook[1] as having originated the technique; and certainly from then on input/output was at home in the West, while in the East the seed had fallen on stony ground.

14. Now input/output is itself a very crude tool, sharing many crucial disadvantages with the method of balances itself. First, both assume fixed coefficients: so many tons of steel require so many tons of coke, neither more nor less. In real life an increase in steel output raises the price of coke, perhaps more rapidly than that of labour or blast-furnaces; so it would be best to economize in coke more severely than in labour or furnaces, thus altering the input/-output coefficients. And this is but a poor and crude example of the infinitely many subtle readjustments any economy, command or market, makes to a given change.

Secondly, input/output does not tell us whether it would be a good idea to have more steel in the first place, rather than more of something else. The giving of such information has always been the privilege of the price mechanism; and so it remained even after input/output itself was in full flower. For both it and the method of balances tell us only what plans, what relative outputs are consistent with each other. There are infinitely many such self-consistent bills of goods, and neither method gives us any idea at all whether any one such 'bill' or 'mix' is better than another. Clearly we are better off with a device that tells us something about this latter and more important question, even at the cost of some material inconsistency. With high-speed computers, however, this is perhaps not very serious: one can propose a very large number of 'bills' of final output at random, and find oneself left with a fair number that the matrix has proved technically possible, between which one may then exercise choice. The criteria of choice, though, must be separately determined and applied. They have no connexion with the matrix and its mathematics.

[1] H. B. Chenery and P. G. Clark, *Interindustry Economics*, Wiley, 1959, pp. 3, 9.

Thirdly, one cannot deduce a single, determinate bill of outputs from a list of available factors. This clearly follows from the fact that each factor can make many products, in contrast to the assumption that each product requires only one set of factors (fixed input coefficients).[1] Without information as to demand one is powerless here.

Finally, it is most significant that the method will grind out the same answer *whatever* prices are used, since it is basically a set of physical relationships. If a ton of steel requires two tons of coke then we can put the prices of steel and coke at 50 to 1 or 1 to 50; so long as they are constant over the operation they will tell us the same answer in tons. Indeed money is not necessary at all for an input/output table: it might just as well be made in tons or square feet, or even a mixture of money, tons and square feet. For so long as each commodity is measured in the same unit throughout there will be valid fixed coefficients that yield the same answer as a table based on rational prices.[2] A technique that is insensitive even to astronomically ridiculous prices is not of much use. I cannot but think that the mathematical charm of this device has led many grossly to overstate its utility.

15. But for Soviet-type purposes it would have been extremely suitable! Soviet-type prices *are* ridiculous, Soviet-type planning *is* conducted with fixed input/output coefficients and in physical terms. With the method of balances alone, this kind of planning was arbitrary and difficult, with input/output it could be arbitrary and easy. The technique would have merely been the coping-stone on the method of balances, enabling each material balance to be brought into harmony with all the others in the most elegant and convenient way—and all to produce a quite arbitrary set of outputs by a rather arbitrary allocation of inputs. As previously, there would have been no indication that this was the best set of final products, nor that this was the best way to produce it. It would merely have had the virtue of not contradicting itself.

[1] Obviously without such fixed input coefficients the matrix is indeterminate both ways—which is the case in real life.

[2] It may be asked, what would be the relation of the national income to the input/output table if the prices in the latter were irrational? The answer is that the national income would emerge at the same place in the matrix, only at irrational prices. And if the table were in whole or part physical the national income would emerge as a mixture of money, tons and what not. Such national incomes would of course have very little meaning, although they might be usable in growth series; but the matrices themselves would continue to function perfectly.

In fact input/output has not yet (1961) been put to serious practical use in either Poland or U.S.S.R. That is, no current plans have yet been derived from it, though in Poland at least it has been used, with a very few rows and columns, to give planners an idea of what the economy would look like if certain large changes were made.

Has it any more practical uses? It surely has. Coherence or feasibility is not at all a small virtue in a plan. It lowers administrative cost, and ensures the punctual arrival of the document by reducing the amount of objections to it. In a book on a rather abstract level, the tremendous fact that plans are always unpunctual has been under-emphasized. Yet in real life it is one of the greatest problems. Provisionally, the director extrapolates from what he did in the last quarter, but this may not be what the centre really requires. Moreover where there is imperfect feasibility there are bottlenecks, and a bottleneck in one input means a superfluity of another. Therefore perfect feasibility means a fuller employment of resources, and more output. Again it means less 'planner's tension', or at least a more rationally distributed tension.[1]

In conclusion input/output has an interesting relation to the curious Marxist habit of beginning the plan with intermediate products. We already saw the psychological or ideological reasons for this in Ch. 3, Sec. 6c: the labour theory of value derives value up from factors, not down from products. Now strictly such an attitude would tempt us to begin with labour and capital targets, and work forward from them. It is perhaps a measure of the folly of beginning with factors at all that Communists do not do this; instead they set themselves intermediate product targets, and use these as determinants of their plans. Improper to say 'as determinants of their matrices', because proper matrices are hardly yet in use. But a system of material balances has determinants in just the same sense.

Now what is the effect of this? If all final products were also intermediate products (as are some agricultural commodities) then to fix all the latter would also be to fix the final product mix, since the whole includes the part; and the whole system would be determinate. But this is far indeed from being the case. To fix intermediate products is merely to determine the requirements of less fabricated intermediate products, and of the ultimate factors of

[1] Cf. Ch. 13, Sec. 2.

production. It hardly helps at all to determine final products, since although it puts some mixtures out of court it leaves infinitely many still possible. The essence of input/output is the not wholly ridiculous assumption that each input can make many kinds of output, whereas each output needs a fixed bill of inputs. Therefore determinacy can only begin with final outputs, not somewhere in the middle of the chain of production: a steel target is only in a very restricted sense a determinant.

16. But whatever the usefulness of this method, it was not in fact a native product. Ironically, in addition to not inventing a system that would have suited them very well, the Russians did invent an important refinement of it that introduces the price mechanism. It is possible by a further considerable complication of the mathematics to meet the objections voiced above to input/-output, and by means of prices to discover, not merely the many self-consistent solutions, but also the one optimal solution to the problem of how to use the economy's resources. This is 'linear programming' or 'activity analysis'. Much of it was developed by the Leningrad mathematician L. V. Kantorovich in 1939.[1] But, as before, the seed fell on stony ground, and it was left to two Americans, Koopmans and Dantzig,[2] to develop the whole technique quite independently some years later.

The use of prices, and the making of rational choices, is of the essence of activity analysis. Basically it is just a practical technique for making multi-dimensional production-possibility surfaces and indifference surfaces. However abstractly mathematical, it rigorously entails a quite different attitude to economics from input/output. Arbitrary allocations and meaningless prices are ruled out by the very procedures. Now Leontief's first, path-breaking book on input/output (*Studies on the Structure of the American Economy*, 1941) began to circulate among Soviet economists in an unpublished Russian translation in 1955 or 1956.[3] But already by that time input/output had become inextricable from its more sophisticated successor, and in fact the two techniques have been taken over together and are taught and applied together. A slightly different

[1] In his book *Matematicheskie Metody Organizatsii i Planirovania Proizvodstva*, Leningrad 1939 ('Mathematical Methods of Organizing and Planning Production'); there is a full translation in *Management Science*, U.S.A. 1961.
[2] G. B. Dantzig, 'Programming of Interdependent Activities: II. Mathematical Model', *Econometrica*, July-Oct. 1949. Cf. Dantzig and Koopmans in ed. T. C. Koopmans, *Activity Analysis of Production and Allocation*, 1951.
[3] According to Leontief himself: *Foreign Affairs*, Jan. 1960.

chronological sequence, and input/output would have been an indisputably Russian achievement, so well evolved by, say, the end of the NEP that Stalin would have accepted it as a 'creative development of Marxist economic science'—which is not far from what it is. Then in 1955 activity analysis, with its chatter of prices and rational choice and optimum solutions, would have been an evil, formalistic, subjectivistic bourgeois perversion. Which again is not far from what it is. For it strikes at the root of Marxism: placing, just as would perfect competition and perfect central adjustment, prices on land and capital as well as labour, dealing in marginal not average magnitudes, striking down the arbitrary power of political authority to decide investments without due thought. It is a corrosive acid indeed that the fissure in the monolith has admitted; though not more corrosive than the rather different acid Tito admitted in 1950.

17. Kantorovich's original contribution was not especially 'deleterious'. For he began with a purely local, seemingly only technical, problem—of the optimum allocation of the existing scarce resources (i.e. equipment) available to a particular engineering factory. Given its production plan and its sortament, how could the factory so use its machines as to overfulfil that plan, keeping to the proportions laid down in the sortament? Not Stalin himself could object to calculations of that sort. Doubtless Kantorovich had no notion of what an explosive mixture he was handling.

Clearly, too, such very micro-economic problems are common to all systems and models. That the mathematical genius should arise who could solve them in U.S.S.R. was pure chance: it might equally have happened in Peru, or—as it later did—in U.S.A. We can only say that the larger the firm the more numerous the internal choices and possibilities of departmental conflict, so the more urgent the problem.[1]

The real difficulties begin when the scarcity problem is seen to apply (a) outside the enterprise and (b) to the goals for final outputs laid down in the plan. Take (a) first. If we consider more than one enterprise together then they must both have the same shadow prices, and be prepared to exchange. This means that the central plan must enforce the same shadow prices on all, and must adapt its own requirements of intermediate goods to those prices. This means

[1] Cf. Jack Hirshleifer, *Journal of Business*, July 1956, April 1957. Mr. Hirschleifer's transfer prices between departments present precisely the same problems as Communist wholesale prices.

a sharp change in methodology, though hardly in institutions. It means, as we saw in Ch. 6, Sec. 12 in connexion with the old rate of interest controversy, that all decisions except as to final outputs must be subjected to the price mechanism. Neither planner nor politician can any more arbitrarily say what he likes, and in particular the old Marxist habit of beginning with quantitative goals for major producers' goods must be abandoned (Ch. 3, Sec. 6).

In his second book[1] Kantorovich is much bolder and advocates all these things. But he still rigorously accepts the planners' final output pattern, and explicitly condemns consumer's sovereignty. He must thus be described as an advocate of perfect computation under ICM, deriving his shadow prices from the factor-scarcities induced by the plan. The outputs, incidentally, are in all his models imposed upon the enterprise by the planner along with the shadow prices, though there appears to be some independence as to sortament.

18. What kind of people, then, are likely to support which of these three solutions? Stalin is dead, and that something must be done about the present irrationality is being admitted by more and more administrators and economists, especially young ones. But there are many solutions to choose from, ideologically, politically and sociologically very different, and even varying in their economic effects.

In Yugoslavia, Stalin died early. Tito made the choice he did in 1950 mainly because, as we see in Chs. 2 and 17, of his ideological diagnosis of Stalinism: the State's planning bureaucracy has become a new quasi-capitalist class, and this is the root of all evil. We must substitute for it workers' control. Ideology, however, was not the only reason, for Kidrič, the practical man, added to this prescription his own of market socialism, i.e. a competition which with setbacks has been growing more and more perfect to this day. We must bear in mind that 1950–52 was early days for a vision of perfect computation; the Americans had only used linear programming in a practical way for the first time in late 1949, when they retrospectively predicted the economic consequences of the Berlin airlift. So the immediate technical choice lay between central adjustment and competition; essentially the former was tried in 1950–52 and

---

[1] *Ekonomicheski Raschet Nailuchshego Ispol'zovania Resursov,* Moscow 1959 ('The Economic Reckoning of the Best Use of Resources'). Cf. Ward, *Journal of Political Economy,* Dec. 1960; Campbell, op. cit.; United Nations, Economic Commission for Europe, *Bulletin,* XII/1. This book was apparently written during the war, but its publication was for obvious reasons delayed.

found incompatible with workers' control. Moreover, Yugoslavia had special historical reasons predisposing her to a decentralized solution: in her national minorities problem, with no one nation really dominant and recent bitter memories of fratricidal, nay genocidal, strife. There was only one truly Yugoslav political force: its Communist Party. How natural, then, for this one force to conserve its strength for the major political decisions, and try to relieve itself of responsibility for the economic ones.

19. The Polish choice has not been finally made. But everything points to central adjustment as the 'Polish Way'. First, it is in the tradition of Polish economics. For instance, we have seen that the most distinguished pre-war protagonist of this model was Professor Oskar Lange. Lange's personal influence in 1956 was negligible, but even then the writer detected very strong currents of this kind of thinking; and in subsequent years Lange himself has not been behind others in recommending this sort of solution. Politics and history have also contributed very largely. A homogeneous country with no minorities, modern Poland has no political stimulus towards federalism. A central bureaucracy in Yugoslavia means a clique of Serbian monarchists oppressing the other nations. In Poland it is a prideful expression of Polonia Restituta, the negation of the years of partition and the previous years of anarchy under the *liberum veto*. True, there were Polish Titoists, but a Titoist is, above all, an idealistic Communist, and any kind of Communist is pretty scarce in Poland. Hence there was little ideological hostility to bureaucracy, and few influential people wanted workers' control. On the other hand there was a sharp reaction against the lunatic over-centralization of Stalin—computation, as it were, without computers. Finally, the sophisticated northern Slav has no special respect for the uneducated Balkan Slav. So central adjustment seemed in 1956, and still seems, a suitable compromise.

20. U.S.S.R. differs again. Its nationality problem is serious, but not hopeless like the Yugoslav. That Soviet federalism should exist but be bogus, while Yugoslav federalism is genuine at least in economics, expresses well the different positions occupied by Russians and Serbs. The latter must make genuine concessions, the former must do something but need not do much. A more important influence is surely the Messianic futurism, the vaulting science-fiction ambition of the Russian people, that makes them the ideal centre of world Communism. Computation of some kind, preferably on the communitarian lines of model (x), cannot but appeal

to them. It is more *grandiose* than other models. So while Marxism was still uncontaminated by the rationality concept there were two attempts at imperfect computation. And now that rationality has been admitted its proponent (Kantorovich) is trying to sell it in a form that would not alter the present degree of centralization.[1]

Albeit there are certainly others, both in Poland and U.S.S.R., who defend far more decentralized schemes, though without worker's control. Such sentiments are particularly evident among the managers of Soviet trade. They have immediate practicability on their side (remember that *perfect* computation is still far off), but ideology is against them. Where Marx wanted central and arbitrary planning, they propose rational decentralization. Where Tito places the local organs of the working class, they place that unglamorous figure, the director. Clearly the proponents of perfect computation have a better pitch. Moreover, these latter have a further advantage in that they can wrap up their unorthodoxy in mathematics. One can put very unorthodox, indeed very doubtful, things across in sufficiently symbolical terms.[2] Again they ask for little institutional change, they threaten nobody's job.

So of these extremes there is little doubt which is preferred in U.S.S.R. But central adjustment is a very strong contender, since it is immediately practicable. It is also more attractive than computation to enterprise directors, a very important class, without being offensive to planners. One version of it (Sec. 6 above) is to switch to general output targets in money terms, and rational wholesale prices. That switch can be observed almost as much in U.S.S.R. as in Poland. Of course a major ideological difficulty is that this model is not, strictly speaking, planning. It is a command economy without planning (Ch. 4, Sec. 3). But sufficient controls and interventions of all kinds would survive to make it acceptable to a Marxist.

---

[1] A few basic shadow prices would be laid down by the Gosplan, and the rest calculated by each Sovnarkhoz independently in the light of its own conditions. But should any of these later differ between Sovnarkhozy that might profitably exchange such goods they must be equalized by the centre, so that exchange may take place rationally. This means of course the *constant* intervention of the Gosplan in Sovnarkhoz planning, though Kantorovich does not say so (op. cit., 1959, p. 167).

[2] A good Western instance of this is Keynes' simultaneous multiplier: an evidently self-contradictory concept that would have been laughed out of court had it been put honestly into words.

PART III

GROWTH

CHAPTER 11

CHOICE VERSUS GROWTH

A system—any system, economic or other—that at every given point of time fully utilizes its possibilities to the best advantage may yet in the long run be inferior to a system that does so at *no* point, because the latter's failure to do so may be a condition for the level or speed of long-run performance.

—J. Schumpeter, *Capitalism, Socialism and Democracy*,

New York 1947, p. 83.

1. This chapter's main concern is with the tension between growth and choice, or the question of *balanced growth*.[1] What light does Communism throw on that?

What exactly is imbalance? It is customary to divide it into a supply and a demand side, but this is difficult to sustain. An imbalance that is not *between* supply and demand, but affects one alone, is like the Zen Buddhists' clap of one hand. Perhaps what is meant is that you can either produce finished goods that consumers do not want ('demand' imbalance) or intermediate goods that producers do not want ('supply' imbalance)? But that is only a difference of degree: consumers' elasticities of substitution are usually much greater than producers', so what are in the one case 'relatively high scarcities' are in the other 'physical bottlenecks'—concepts not essentially different. Only in an economy on the Stalin model is there a serious difference, since there the one kind of imbalance can be corrected *either* by changing outputs *or* by changing prices; while the other can only be corrected by changing outputs, since it is in the command sector. It is more correct to say that the distinction lies between imbalance in the products market and in the factors market.

Even so it is hard to see a real difference in a market economy. Why should a shortage of TV sets be less, or more, growth-promoting than a shortage of steel? In nothing that follows is it

[1] In what follows I am deeply indebted to Streeten, *Oxford Economic Papers*, June 1959.

really clear. What *is* certain, however, is that *imbalance is by definition a situation contrary to short-run private profit*: it is simply a new-fangled word for old-fashioned disequilibrium.

We see at some length in the succeeding chapters that there is little to be said for certain kinds of imbalance: the violation of the 'welfare' equations in the name of greater capital-intensity or in order to force heavy industry ahead. There are other more desirable kinds of imbalance. We shall classify them here as either necessary in order to have rapid growth, or inevitable results of it. The first concern mainly market economies, the latter planned economies.

2. In a market economy unbalanced development is a valuable stimulant. If a technical leap forward occurs in spinning there will be investment and research in weaving, as in Britain, *c.* 1800. If the government presses ahead with a railway every other kind of investment will follow at the places through which it passes. If private enterprise crowds into a particular town, sooner or later government will bestir itself to build a new waterworks. Both private and public investors are hesitant: bottlenecks and lopsided-nesses make the opportunities for them large and obvious. This is the case that Mr. A. O. Hirschman has made his own[1]: enterprise is often the scarcest factor of all, especially in underdeveloped market economies, and imbalance, which is, to repeat, simply another word for the classic 'disequilibrium', creates large profits at particular points. It thus calls forth initiative from the unenterprising, and increases the rate of growth. With this argument it is difficult to quarrel.

But what relevance has this for a command economy? Suppose the incentives to invest affect only a very few people in the capital city; they pass large investment plans out along the chain of command, to which others must indeed, at the circumference, add the details. But these others have the overall magnitudes from above: those figures are *their* incentive to invest. Then it is logically conceivable that the central decision-makers will react positively to bottlenecks, or even to a low rate of interest, or excess demand, or the accelerator effect. A centrally planned non-Communist society could be imagined in which the central planners, at least in this matter, behaved like private capitalists. But in a Soviet-type economy the 'Hirschman' effects go into limbo along with the

---

[1] In his *Strategy of Economic Development*, Yale 1958, Chs. 3, 4.

more orthodox stimuli listed above. The overall volume of investment is a political decision. Ideology will always make it very big,
and it is scarcely possible that any particular bottleneck should
make it bigger.

It is of course pointless, with decisions thus centralized, to try
to stimulate enterprises by micro-economic imbalance. If material
supplies are wrongly allocated in the light of the output plan
that can only hinder production—the fact that his product is scarce
cannot, at least officially, stimulate a manager whose incentives are
the plan and the fulfilment bonus. If there is a queue for this
consumer good and a large stock of that one, or if there are very
different rates of turnover tax, this stimulates no greater production
overall than a more rational product-mix.

The deliberate creation of imbalance, then, is not a necessary
stimulus to Soviet-type growth, as it is to free market growth.
Nor has such a claim ever been official Communist doctrine. Much
rather is imbalance a necessary result, (a) of rapid growth in general,
(b) of central planning in general, and (c) of Communism; so that
hostility to it is in fact, 'objectively', hostility to growth.

Points (b) and (c) have received more than adequate attention already, and we need only add here this, that quite apart from their
neglect of scarcity considerations many specific practices of the
Communists lead directly to imbalance. The first of these is that of
'drives' and 'campaigns'. Heavy chemicals, virgin lands, maize,
Chinese domestic steel; whatever it may be, the Communists
cannot bear to do it by halves. The military metaphors of 'thrust',
'advance', 'campaign' obsess their thinking. They could, within
their system, quite as easily 'advance on a broad front'—imbalance,
to repeat, is not a stimulus; but they find it *psychologically* easier to
advance on a narrow one. Propaganda, both for the masses and
for the bureaucracy, should relay only a few messages at a time.[1]
The very concept of dialectics demands that there be thesis, anti-
thesis, synthesis: balanced growth, it is not fanciful to say, is un-
dialectical. *Intellectually*, too, imbalance is easier. It is simpler, if we
use the method of balances and not input/output, arbitrarily to
define a few goals—the 'leading links' of Ch. 10—and stick to them;
adapting everything else to these, instead of readjusting them in the

---

[1] As the Chinese apparently found in 1958, when successive campaigns for domestic
steel, for forming Communes, for joining the militia, etc., followed each other so thick and
fast that the cadres became confused: and extreme imbalance followed, in that basic tasks
like harvesting were neglected.

light of the first-round adjustments in other branches that the setting of these goals demanded. And this is of course imbalance. Finally, at the micro-economic level enterprises produce most if they are encouraged each severally to over-fulfil their plans, although it leads of course very directly to imbalance. In this case enterprises are stimulated to, not by, imbalance.

3. But there is more than imbalance. Some of the schemes may not, in fact, be technically feasible; they may be 'groundnuts' schemes.[1] These are of course not the same as failure to predict demand or errors in the estimation of scarcity relationships. Such simple waste is very likely to increase as investment is forced, merely because money is difficult to spend. Any system, that is to say, has a rising 'marginal propensity to waste'. Under Communism, where political pressure builds up behind any scheme once it gets into the plan, and the government is further likely to have committed itself by advance publicity, such schemes are inevitable; and especially in agriculture, where nature is most resistant to technical change and estimates, being most subject to uncertainty, are easiest to fudge. Soviet agriculture has been one long 'groundnuts' scheme, from collectivization itself through the domestic rabbits craze,[2] the initial occupation and abandonment of the virgin lands[3] in 1929–33, the kok-sagiz[4] campaign, the great Stalin re-afforestation plan of 1949–51 and the re-occupation of the virgin lands in 1953–55, to the maize campaign of 1956–58.

But while British Socialism confined its groundnuts to agriculture Communism can plant them in industry too. Two examples may be quoted from first-hand experience, to give the feel of the thing. In 1930 an engineer reported to Victor Serge that he was building a large sovkhoz:

Really, I ought not to build it. I cannot get materials, they arrive late, their quality is awful. If I refuse to work in this madhouse they will call me a counter-revolutionary and send me to a concentration camp. So I build as best I can, with what I've got, and fudge all the drawings. Any time I may be accused of sabotage. I shall be late on the plan, which once again makes me a saboteur.

[1] The reference is to the Overseas Food Corporation's expensive failure to raise ground-nuts on an uncultivated tract in Tanganyika (1948); it plunged right in, without a pilot scheme, and found it virtually impossible to grow groundnuts at any cost.

[2] R. O. G. Urch, *The Rabbit King of Russia*, London 1939, *passim*.

[3] N. Jasny, *The Socialized Agriculture of the U.S.S.R.*, Stanford 1949, pp. 242–4, 254–5.

[4] Kok-sagiz is a plant from which rubber is supposed to be extracted. It was forced upon farms in the Western districts, under great publicity, after the late world war. It is no longer grown.

P

I send detailed memoranda to my superiors and they tell me I am taking bureaucratic precautions against them, and that we live in an epoch of out-and-out struggle: your duty is to surmount all obstacles.[1]

In 1939 Kravchenko just managed to prevent a rather larger fiasco:

> When we saw the site where our factory was to be erected, we were horrified. It was a huge naked stretch of muddy riverfront a considerable distance from town (Stalinsk), without electric or gas lines, without railroad tracks or a trolley line, without so much as a negotiable road. . . . The terrain was wholly unsuitable for a metallurgical establishment. One did not have to be a construction engineer to observe that the ground would not support big buildings and the heavy machinery called for by pipe-rolling. . . . Equipped with photographs, charts and other materials, we returned to Moscow. It was a heart-rending task I faced— to unsell the government on a widely ballyhooed enterprise which had the imprimatur of the highest authorities and involved the reputations, perhaps the freedom, of scores of big and little officials whose bureaucratic indifference or technical illiteracy was at the bottom of the inept project. . . . Everyone stared in stupefaction. All of them, it was evident to me, thought only how to extricate themselves from what might snowball into a political catastrophe. The picture I drew was too clear, too detailed to be wished away. Besides, it quickly appeared that voices had been raised in warning before, but had been silenced by fear.[2]

On a very much larger scale still, the Grand Turkmenian and the Danube-Black Sea canals, vast projects upon which resources had already been prodigally spent, were both dropped before completion after Stalin's death in 1953.

Of 'groundnuts' the same must be said as of imbalance. We may call them both, generically, waste. The Communists, then, aim at certain targets in certain ways. Waste, macro- and micro-economic, is the direct and obvious result both of the volume of money that they try to spend and of their special psychology. But they do not aim at it or desire it; indeed they make constant efforts to avoid or correct it. Waste, then, is no stimulus to them, merely an inevitable and vicious by-product of their system. To cure it, however, would radically alter the system, reducing somewhat its capacity to grow.

4. So much for bottlenecks as incentives. Then there is often a case for immediate or partial imbalance in the light of a longer or wider view, such as a large firm or government might be able to take. I refer here to such obvious imbalances as occur when one tries to take advantage of large external economies, or to bring about the demonstration effect.

---

[1] V. Serge, *Mémoires d'un Révolutionnaire*, Paris 1951, pp. 269–270.
[2] V. I. Kravchenko, *I Chose Freedom*, London 1947, pp. 325–6.

Notoriously in a free market migrant labour and new enterprise will locate itself next to old, since all sorts of external economy will be lost if it goes off on its own. But if something intervenes to make it do so, and if a few other activities can be similarly forced into the new place, a new pole of attraction is created with external economies on the same scale as the old. The imbalance is thus only temporary, and is worth incurring in order to avoid the external *dis*economies of the continued expansion of Megalopolis. As to the demonstration effect, it may well be worth while to found some unprofitable project simply to shock people into a realization of what modern technique can do; we deal with this in Ch. 16, Sec. 9.

The correct attitude to these cases is that of Stalin, quoted below in Sec. 7. Beyond question a command economy has a great advantage in the pursuit of such schemes, and a market economy needs regulative authority ever watchful for such missed opportunities. But such schemes are at bottom only a *temporary* violation of the rules, whose justification is precisely a more exact basic observance of them. We face here at bottom merely another divergence between long- and short-run profit. The subject is important, but of doubtful relevance in a chapter entitled 'Choice versus Growth'.

5. Next, the insistence on continuously balanced growth can lead to the wrong kind of institutional set-up and general atmosphere.

For a start, it can cause us to prefer a market economy! And within a market economy we may be led to concentrate political effort on choice-improving controls, instead of growth-promoting initiative; on anti-trust rather than promoting inflation or super-highways. Theories are even developed, by the protagonists of balance, to prove that inflation in a market economy, which so manifestly interferes with choice, throttles development: or that a healthy balance of payments is more important than rapid development. To these the short answer is quantitative: are not the costs and distortions of exchange control or tariffs a very small price to pay for 1% p.a. on the rate of growth of the national income? Would not that same gain outweigh the remediable injustices and trivial inconveniences of inflation? *Can* a fully employed economy actually produce less than a slightly deflated one?

In economic theory the anti-growth bias comes out clearest, of course, in classical welfare economics. Perfect competition, as every undergraduate knows, is the organization of industry that best ensures consumer sovereignty. Hence many lyrical passages in the textbooks, ending in an almost theological O *Altitudo*. And the accepted case against monopoly is that it restricts output below the competitive level. Now empirically this case is quite unproven since the Managerial Revolution. And even if it were proven it would be unimportant, since it would be only a violation of the 'welfare' equations. The real criterion for judging the organization of an industry is whether it promotes investment and technical progress: and the Managerial Revolution has clearly brought monopoly from the lowest place in this order of merit to the highest—which it shares, let us hasten to add, with any oligopoly of sufficiently large firms.

It is useless to protest that perfect competition is supposed to be the most efficient form. For in this context the word efficient takes on an entirely new and indeed bogus meaning: 'responsive to changes in consumer demand' (not necessarily to changes in long-run scarcity relationships—monopoly might perceive these better). This has little to do with technical progress or with growth, nay even directly hinders them. Extreme responsiveness of this kind is a disadvantage, leading to low investment and low profitability, and therefore stifling technical research. Also it can hardly exist in conjunction with large scale, which is, of course, a condition of efficiency *proprement dit*. Efficiency—meaning low real cost—is the micro-economic duty of man; given that, growth follows, either spontaneously or through planning that uses up the resources set free. It is characteristic of our growth-blind economics that we blur this vital concept by making the word do duty in the field of 'scarcity' too.

This type of theory must in the long run have seriously influenced our political and economic institutions. In a Communist economy on the other hand the consumer is lowly regarded in every way. He is not, as we have seen, technically 'sovereign'. Factories producing for him have—or had under Stalin—less pull, even given the priorities fixed by the plan. There is none of that extreme preoccupation with delicate readjustments of existing resources so as to satisfy him most completely out of whatever is available. These things are a brake upon the growth of the sheer volume of production. Faced with a choice between producing A or B, they lead us to postpone investment until next year, when it is clearer which the consumer prefers: and even then we shall probably try to produce both instead of concentrating on the mass production of one. Why does a non-Communist economy suspend and distort the price mechanism in time of war if not because it is in a hurry? The Soviet economy is always in a hurry, and its cavalier attitude to the consumer enables it to be so.

6. These considerations are particularly important when we weigh the pros and cons of forced saving and forced investment. Both are clearly inevitable if the actual rate of growth is to exceed the 'natural', 'warranted' or *laissez faire* rate of growth, whether in undeveloped areas proper or in mature backward areas like Great Britain. This is very far from saying that forced saving and forced investment are the only desiderata for such growth, but they do raise 'scarcity' problems that other expansionary measures do not.[1]

Suppose that allocation model (8), the institutional solution least disruptive of our present political, social and economic structure, is adopted in order to effect this programme of forced investment. Model (8) has received very little attention so far, because its detailed workings are no mystery to Western economists, and because it is not a pure type. But it bulks fairly large in Communist economic history: the Soviet NEP and modern Yugoslavia, both very successful ventures; and in some form it is universal among capitalism's protagonists in the growth race: Japan and the Common Market countries. In discussing economic growth this model is crucial.

Current production, then, is sold on a free market, or at least on a market as free as that which we now have. Much greater funds than now are made available for investment by a large budget surplus above the line. A central committee is set up which in any year must allocate the investment funds that private enterprise has not spontaneously taken up. In practice it will almost certainly do this 'irrationally'. Ideally, of course, this need not be so. But, in fact, what with human fallibility, the haste with which decisions must be taken, political influence and corruption, the direction of these investment resources will be irrational. Then within twelve months the errors that have been made will be sufficiently clear. In the first instance private enterprise will step in to enlarge the bottlenecks and correct the disproportions created by the planners' previous errors, and these latter will invest the new year's surplus funds in such a manner as to create bottlenecks and disproportions elsewhere. Making *different* errors every year, they will make no serious errors.

---

[1] We assume throughout this book that investment, however directed, has some positive effect on growth, even if small. So much is admitted even by Colin Clark (*Growthmanship*, London 1962, p. 49). Cf. Ch. 13, Sec. 3.

Again, precisely because of economic growth, really serious over-investment in any particular branch of the economy is unlikely to occur. Provided that a project is technically feasible—that it is not a 'groundnuts' scheme—aggregate demand, growing through additional investment in other directions than this, will after an interval float off a particular mistake and render it an *ex post facto* necessity.

Thirdly, even absolute waste—and of this there must be some—is merely a necessary by-product of the superior prosperity that the system brings. Conceive, that is, a project that will become useful neither when completed nor at a later date, but never, no matter how much growth there is. This might be either because it is a technical failure (a groundnuts scheme) or something simply not demanded. Now a fashion house must buy some clothes that turn out to be unsaleable. Champagne manufacturers must make some bottles which explode.[1] If they knew which clothes or which bottles they would of course be able to lower their costs. But they do not sit down and produce nothing at all because they do not know; they write off this loss as a cost of production. So the growing economy may write off the irremediable errors of its programme of forced investment as a cost of growth. Suppose a purely numerical example, entirely without empirical warrant: owing to the programme 30% of the national income is invested, instead of 15%, and wasted projects instead of being 2% of the old investment are 6% of the new. I.e. there is a rising 'marginal propensity to waste'. Then something like an extra $1\frac{1}{2}\%$ of the national income will be wasted every year. But the rate of growth rises, let us say, from 2% to 3% compound—we suppose rather sharply diminishing returns to the new investment; and already in two years the national income is greater than it would otherwise have been. Thereafter, of course, the excess becomes very great indeed, though consumption takes a good deal longer to catch up.[2]

Fourthly, it is not true that this sort of planning requires an impossibly long view of the future structure of demand. Such foresight, it is objected, is more than is vouchsafed to the wisest of us. Statistical exercises, whether governmental or private, in

---

[1] F. H. Knight, *Risk, Uncertainty and Profit*, London (LSE) 1933, p. 213.

[2] Let P be the present and F the future national income as now expected. Then $(P1 \cdot 02)^n = F$, where n is any number of years. Under the new dispensation we start with $0 \cdot 98P$, owing to the wasted investment projects, and $0 \cdot 98P(1 \cdot 03)^n = F'$, the new terminal national income. Then $F' = F$ when $n = \dfrac{\log 0 \cdot 98}{\log 1 \cdot 02 - \log 1 \cdot 03}$. Compare, however, Sec. 10.

demand prediction are often simply bogus.[1] Now while this is perfectly true it does not affect the case for investment planning here put forward. The planner is not asked to estimate future demand for a longer period than the life of the particular capital asset he is at any moment considering. If it happens to be very durable he must of course, just like a private entrepreneur, make a long-term estimate; if not, not. No new problem of forecasting has arisen. Indeed, one problem has fallen away, and actually less, not more, forecasting is required. For since the economy is growing more quickly than before, the likelihood of an absolute decline in any branch of production is smaller than before. Now when there is the possibility of an absolute decline, not only extensive investment (expanding capacity at present costs) but also intensive investment (reducing costs at present capacity) becomes a doubtful proposition. Suppose that the marginal firm is normally profitable. Then to justify extensive investment we must be sure that demand will increase. For intensive investment it suffices that demand will be constant. In a stagnant economy only intra-marginal firms should make such expenditure, and it is a matter of prediction to know just how many—and which—*are* intra-marginal. All this problem is much reduced by greater growth, so that we may fairly claim that investment planning of the type proposed actually reduces the amount of crystal-gazing required.

The amount of misallocation can be exaggerated in yet another way. When investing we make an allocation not only of all the ordinary scarce resources but also of 'capital', i.e. of 'waiting'. A programme of forced investment need involve the misallocation of 'waiting' only. For there is always at any moment an enormous number of profitable schemes that ought to be undertaken one day, 'when the capital is available'. There is no need to undertake unprofitable schemes: the more modest proposal suffices that all the profitable schemes be put in hand at once. Just as an investment cut, imposed by the Government, means merely that schemes are postponed, so an increase means merely that they are accelerated. The direction of investment in allocation model (8) is still determined by the market, or by direct welfare considerations: the

[1] That they are indeed bogus is amply demonstrated by Professor Devons, in *Lloyds Bank Review*, July 1954, pp. 30–5. Compare also the 'fuel gap' and 'fuel crisis', extrapolated for many years ahead by West European governments in 1956, with the manifest overproduction of all types of fuel only three years later—also freely extrapolated (the red face is visible beneath the official whitewash in the OEEC's *Towards a New Energy Pattern in Europe*, Paris 1960; especially in its comments on *Europe's Growing Needs of Energy*, OEEC 1956).

amount only is increased over what would naturally have occurred.

7. There is a certain tendency for 'welfare' economists, when contemplating the rate of interest, to say: 'here is this list of possible schemes; the rate of interest tells us in which order, and, indeed whether, they should be undertaken.' This is too static a view: there is no finite list of schemes, nor need there be any such thing as the exhaustion of capital opportunities. Investment causes growth. So long as there is land and labour available the investment can be merely extensive. So long as superior foreign techniques are available, it can be merely intensive. Thereafter, it must be in research as well. But in all three cases *capital expenditure increases the number of capital opportunities*, for the growth of the economy makes some schemes more desirable than before, others desirable for the first time, and some of both classes technically possible for the first time.

Extra funds for investment should then be fearlessly extracted from the consumer and splashed about. 'Scarcity' will not suffer greatly—as Stalin said so very rightly:

> Some comrades conclude from this that the law of the planned development of the national economy, the planning of the national economy, destroys the principle of profitability. This is quite wrong and quite the contrary is true. If one considers profitability not from the point of view of individual enterprises or branches of production, and not within the span of one year, but from the point of view of the whole national economy and within the span of, say, ten to fifteen years—which would be the only correct approach—then the temporary and unstable profitability of individual enterprises or branches of production cannot even bear comparison with that higher, stable form of profitability, which the operation of the law of the planned development of the national economy and the planning of the national economy give us, saving us from periodic economic crises which destroy the national economy and inflict colossal material damage on society, and securing for us the uninterrupted growth of the national economy with its high tempos.[1]

8. Growth conflicts, then, at certain points with consumers' sovereignty and even with 'scarcity' itself.[2] It is quite wrong to throw either wholly overboard, however. The advantages of each must as far as possible be quantified, and a balance struck. To correct an important and permanent misallocation of resources is in itself economic growth; for unwanted production is not production at all.

---

[1] *Economic Problems of Communism*, 1952.

[2] This conflict is quite separate, be it noted, from the possibility that one day economic growth will have gone so far that resources will cease to be scarce at all. This is the question of 'Full Communism', for which see Chs. 17–20.

Thus in a starving community a 10% per annum rise in industrial production combined with a 1% fall in agricultural production—the two being of roughly equal value to start with—may truly be called on grounds of 'scarcity' not growth at all but diminution. That is, the rise in the Laspeyres index of production, which weights industrial and agricultural products by the scarcity relationships of the initial year, will be outweighed by the fall in the Paasche index, owing to the very great weight the latter would give in such circumstances to agricultural products. This indeed is what might fairly be claimed on welfare grounds for the planned economy in Stalin's lifetime.[1] Or again, in any economy staggering sums can be wasted by misallocation, especially on a level of high policy. The restriction of road haulage in favour of railways, the cross-subsidization of bad coal-mines by good, the protection of declining industries: such things can waste a few percent of the national income every year.

On the other hand, the violation of the welfare equations is not an absolute, unconditional crime; it depends how long and how great the violation is. On any commonsense view of interpersonal or intertemporal utility comparisons a certain increase in growth is worth any amount of minor allocation errors. Rapid growth diminishes the harm done by violation not only of consumer sovereignty but also of rational allocation in general. There are three main reasons for this.

First, rapid growth eases the problem of forecasting and floats off many of the inevitable errors, as just described. Secondly, there is the 'hairbrushes and nailbrushes' argument. As I have said elsewhere:

in the Soviet economy there are, as it were, always too few hairbrushes and too many nailbrushes in view of the resources available, while in a 'capitalist' economy this proportion is always more nearly right. But the production of both these articles is growing at about 10% per annum in the U.S.S.R. and at about 2% per annum in 'capitalist' countries. In the end the Soviet citizen will be supplied better even with hairbrushes.[2]

The mere fact of growth then floats off even a *permanent* misallocation of resources. But, thirdly, the misallocation need not be permanent. 'Scarcity' need not be violated always in the same direction. Those who object to planning, monopolies, cartels,

---

[1] Though if we were to base our prices on strategists', not consumers', preferences the Paasche index would show quite as great a rise as the Laspeyres.
[2] Wiles, *Oxford Economic Papers*, October 1953, pp. 315–16.

imperfect competition, etc., on 'scarcity' grounds, implicitly assume that these things always exert their malign influence on resource allocation in the same place in the economy; but if monopoly, planning, etc., crop up in different places as time passes—and they do do so—then in the long run the relative quantity of hairbrushes and nailbrushes will vary about the 'scarcity' optimum. If stocks in the hands of the users are large relative to current purchases no great harm at all will be done by these fluctuations, and even if they are not, the right proportion must often be hit as the pendulum of planning, monopoly, etc., swings from one side to the other.

9. There are, then, good arguments as well as bad for deliberately unbalanced growth (Sec. 3) and there are arguments for not worrying too much about imbalance if it is the by-product of a greater good (Secs 4 to 8). But the whole matter must be looked at soberly. While it is absurd to die in the last ditch of 'choice' it is still foolish to go a-whoring after the new bitch-goddess, growth. In particular poverty does not excuse such a shift of affections. For if poverty makes growth more necessary it also makes waste more intolerable. If a previous passage[1] has stood up for the old verities, the new must, of course, have their turn. In a previous piece under the title of this chapter, the author put it this way:[2]

'Plenty, not scarcity, is the essence of economics.' There is a sense in which this phrase is the cheapest of unscholarly rabble-rousing. But it contains a great truth. For while an emphasis on choice and scarcity is logically compatible with due insistence on growth, it is not psychologically so. Its implications are all wrong, and economists who are interested in choice are not in fact interested in growth, as Mr. Colin Clark taught us long ago in his brusque but salutary dismissal of the classical economics.[3] Mr. Clark is of course as he would be the first to admit, theoretically unsound, but how much healthier than the spectacle of Professor Robbins wringing his hands:

'The time at our disposal is limited. There are only twenty-four hours in the day. We have to choose between the different uses to which they may be put. The services which others put at our disposal are limited. The material means of achieving ends are limited. We have been turned out of Paradise.'[4]

For Communists paradise lies ahead, and we may fairly reply with Karl Marx:

[1] Ch. 5, Sec. 1.
[2] 'Growth versus Choice,' *Economic Journal*, June 1956. I have used certain other passages from that article here without quotation marks.
[3] *Conditions of Economic Progress*, preface to the first edition. The withdrawal of these strictures in the second edition seems a shade premature: that funds are now available for the study of national income brings us only a very short way towards an economics of plenty.
[4] *The Nature and Significance of Economic Science*, 2nd Ed., London 1946, p. 15.

'The philosophers have only *interpreted* the world, in various ways; the point, however, is to *change* it.'[1] This means, of course, that economists should make value judgments. But Professor Robbins is most explicitly in favour of that activity, denying to it only the name of economics. His error is merely one of misplaced emphasis, and this article has no other object than to shift that emphasis. It contains, so far as its writer is aware, no concrete innovation. 'Scarcity', then, is an effective reply to the redistributive, democratic socialist of the West, whose one idea is to squeeze a quart out of a pint pot. But the totalitarian, growth-conscious socialist of the East has a shattering rejoinder: 'Why aren't you making a quart pot, like me?'

Inconsistent? I think not. We face two desiderata, not one, and an optimization problem. Over all our micro-choices there hangs, as the logicians would say, a meta-choice. The satisfaction of the welfare equations is itself a competing end.

10. So far nothing has been said which should be taken as favouring *a priori* a large initial sacrifice followed by more rapid growth over slower growth without the sacrifice. This is not at all the same question as whether sub-optimal choices in some way quicken growth. We face now, on the contrary, a very deliberate policy of present sacrifice and ask whether this particular choice between present and future may not be, on the most simon-pure classical principles, optimal.

There is a great deal of elementary confusion on this issue. It is certain that in allocation models where Say's Law does not apply (principally FM) individual choice of a savings proportion is not necessarily translated into a corresponding community choice; it may merely result in unemployment. But that does not mean we cannot apply very ordinary welfare analysis to whatever savings proportion does emerge. Moreover, as we saw in Ch. 5, Sec. 6, the supervention of a different allocation model does not magically debar the use of that same analysis to whatever proportion is arbitrarily imposed.

Now welfare analysis operates with a futurity discount. The end of all production is consumption, so we simply compare the consumption streams resulting over a period of time from the two investment policies. Thus let savings rates, once chosen, be constant. Then if we consume C in the base year we attain an investment proportion big enough to ensure the rate of growth α in both consumption and investment. While if we consume kC, where $k < 1$, the investment proportion is and remains greater, and the rate of growth is β, where $\beta > \alpha$. Let the community's rate of futurity

[1] *Theses on Feuerbach.*

discount stand unchanged at γ. Then for any n future years the
present value of the first stream of consumption is $\dfrac{C(a-\gamma)^{n+1}-1}{a-\gamma-1}$;
and of the second stream $\dfrac{kC(\beta-\gamma)^{n+1}-1}{\beta-\gamma-1}$. So if n is sufficiently
large, present sacrifice appears to be always worth while.

This line of reasoning seems to justify any degree of Stalinism,
however monstrous. But it rests on one very questionable assumption: that γ remains constant (a) as the consumer contemplates the ever
more distant future, and (b) the poorer he is in the present. This
is surely quite false: on the contrary γ rapidly increases as n increases,
so that effectually there is a limit to the number of years for which
a consumer is willing to look ahead. In this case there is also a
limit to the size of k that he will tolerate. The textbook assumption
of a constant rate of futurity discount serves only to simplify the
textbook's mathematics. It has no empirical warrant.

In another way the argument points up an essential fallacy to which
many succumb who would justify Stalinist investment policies:[1] a
present sacrifice is not repaid by attaining a high consumption
level in some one future year, it must be compared with the total
consumption stream over all future years. Fallacious, then, to
justify 1928 by 1984. 1929–32 also resulted from 1928, and must be
reckoned to its account. In any case, we may add, consumption
takes a very long time to recover from an initial sacrifice. Thus if
we take the numerical example in the footnote to Sec. 6 it is not
until the twenty-third year that consumption equals what it would
have been in the same year under the old dispensation, and not
until the eighth year that it regains the level obtaining when the
change was introduced (always supposing we continue to invest
30% of the national income; naturally if we invest less after a while
we can easily consume more than we should have been able to
under the old dispensation). Furthermore the sums of the two
consumption streams, suitably discounted for futurity, do not
approach each other for a still longer period. In these dreary
lengths of time lies the explanation of very much Communist
economic history.

The argument from points, not streams, of time is only valid if
we abandon the consumer for the strategist. The strategist does

[1] I owe this point to Prof. A. Erlich.

think of points. For war is not continuous, and even if war preparations are, they consist of 'investment', not 'consumption'. Weapons
obsolesce very rapidly, and we often require not weapons but the
capacity to make them. In many strategic situations—and particularly
in those that Stalin had to face—present strategic weakness is trivial
compared with future strength. From this point of view Stalinism,
with its eyes on the future and not the path to the future, is clearly
justified.

CHAPTER 12

MEASUREMENT PROBLEMS

1. THIS is not a chapter that can be skipped: unless, of course, it is ill written or incorrect. Elementary economics takes far too little account of measurement, as may easily be seen from the greater attention allotted to, say, indifference curves than to price indices in the textbooks. Yet by any sane sense of priorities indifference curves are utterly trivial compared with price indices. To take but one example, it is *quite meaningless* to say that the Soviet economy is growing more rapidly than the American without knowing what the words 'Paasche' and 'hedonic' stand for. Dull and technical subjects do not magically lose their importance so that the weaker brethren may understand the modern world. If economic competition is the essence of the cold war—a view the writer does not wholly share—the outcome of the competition is for the economic statistician alone to assess, and this chapter touches the most important questions in all economics.

The Sovietologist faces many special measurement problems:

(i) dishonesty and even falsification in the official statistics;

(ii) lacunae;

(iii) the correct choice of weights where outputs are irrational;

(iv) the critique of peculiar Communist procedures which do not fall under (i);

(v) special pleading by Westerners who dislike his statistical results.

Indeed Sovietology casts new light upon all economic measurement, and has made very many striking contributions to the subject.

2. As to (i), even falsification has its theories and principles. We must distinguish between *misreporting* and *mishandling* of data. The former is mainly micro-, the latter mainly macro-economic.

In a command economy with 'planner's tension' (Ch. 13, Sec. 20), and in which managerial bonuses depend on fulfilment of the output plan, there is enormous temptation to misreport data. It is too often simply assumed that the temptation is to exaggerate, but the situation is more complicated. In the very short run exaggeration pays, but it has very serious costs in the next planning period, when the very principle of planner's tension is that more output will be demanded than that currently *reported*. Suppose, as is typical, that the rate of bonus is zero for all plan under-fulfilment, 20% of basic income for fulfilment itself and then 5% for each succeeding 5% of over-fulfilment; let X be planned output in year 1, and the planner's known habit be to screw up targets to 105% of the previously reported output. Then the manager, who has in fact produced say 0·99 X, will do far better to report a mere 1·01 X of output in year 1, thus obtaining his 20% bonus that year and a target of 1·06 X for next year; if he thinks he can in fact produce 1·07 X in that year, or at least report it on the basis of an actual production of 1·05 X. For he will then draw his 20% bonus again. If he is greedy and short-sighted he will report 1·05 X in year 1 and draw 25% bonus. He is then faced with a target of 1·10 X in year 2, which presents him with an insoluble production problem and a very difficult falsification problem. He will only choose this second procedure if he is likely in any case to receive a transfer or retire, or expects shortly to replace his present chief accountant with his brother-in-law, or needs the cash to buy a dacha. For he will lose all bonus in the second year, or have to falsify so hugely as to run the risk of legal proceedings.

It might even be best to under-report. Suppose his actual output in year 1 was 1·04 X, and his brother-in-law was already his chief accountant but the Party cell secretary suspected this arrangement and had arranged a transfer for the latter. Then the correct play is to report 1·01 X, thereby assuring the 20% bonus now and a 1·06 X target for next year, which represents a mere 2% increase in actual output: something that the incoming accountant may easily be persuaded to vouch for, indeed that may even happen.

Misreporting, then, is a problem in micro-economic motivation with many and amusing variables. But it seems probable that it is on balance in an upward direction, since in the presence of planner's tension plan fulfilment is seldom easy, and the bonus for it is greater than for over-fulfilment; so that much misreporting must be simply claims of 1·01 X when 0·99 X has been produced. Whereas if output is 1·04 X there is little incentive to exaggerate it, and some to understate it, thus building up a reserve for future years; but such outputs are rare.

The foreign observer is powerless to correct micro-economic misreporting: he cannot personally count every brick a Soviet brickworks makes. But he must not lose his head. *If the degree of such misreporting is constant it does not affect growth measurement*: i.e. it will certainly have affected our view of Soviet growth in 1927–30, when the system that causes it was introduced, but subsequently it cannot have greatly mattered. And the same applies to every other Communist country. We may, however, dimly guess at other factors influencing the amount of misreporting: the improvement in Soviet auditing procedures after 1930, the exceptional fear of being caught out during the Great Purge (1937–38),[1] the increase in planner's tension during war and reconstruction in U.S.S.R., its diminution in China, Poland and Hungary in 1956, its increase in China in 1958, etc. In a given year such things may be important; thus in the most notorious case of all they exaggerated Chinese agricultural production in 1958 by about 80%; and the rate of growth by about the same amount. But if we neglect such bad years and concentrate on the rate of growth over a period, rather than on absolute levels at a date, they are insignificant. Indeed, between certain years their influence is negative. Thus any comparison of official Chinese data that takes 1958 as a base year, or of official Soviet data to the base 1930, will certainly underestimate the rate of growth, even though some exaggeration was present in the given year too. Clearly micro-economic misreporting is only important in the context of production, international productivity comparisons, etc.

3. It is doubtful if the central authorities or others who publish data misreport what is told them. No case of such deliberate falsification is known to the writer, and the captured 1941 Plan—a secret document—is strong evidence against it. The Plan worked on the published figures. Mishandled, however, the data certainly are: they are aggregated in very questionable and even downright wrong ways, which nearly all tend to exaggerate achievements.[2] Here the foreign observer can and must intervene, but the corrections he applies are of little theoretical interest, and must be mainly omitted here. Each problem is a separate 'whodunit' on its own, and the beginning student does wrong to get himself bogged down

---

[1] Can this be a reason for the very slow growth of industrial output in that period?

[2] The only mishandling known to me which understates an achievement is the Soviet index of industrial production, 1945–46. This shows a greater fall than any foreign estimate. But compare also Sec. 10 on the Soviet agricultural index.

n a particular one, such as crop estimates on the root,[1] or 1926–27 prices in Soviet industry.[2]

4. We therefore turn to one of the points of *general* statistical interest, that arises out of Sovietological studies: *it is better to guess a weight than to omit a growth series*. Suppose there are two commodities, of which the growth indices are A and B; A has a known weight k, while B's true weight t is unknown. Then the true index T is $\frac{Ak + Bt}{k + t}$, but the statistician must either guess a weight g for B, or leave B out. I.e. he must choose between $\frac{Ak + Bg}{k + g}$ and $\frac{Ak}{k} = A$; between guesswork and 'timidity'.

If $t > g$ or $t > k$ all values of g will clearly improve the accuracy of the index, even infinity or values very close to zero. The interesting case, however, is where $g > t$, $t < k$. Then the accuracy of the index is improved, of course, by guessing if guesswork is closer to the truth than 'timidity':

$$\left| \frac{Ak + Bg}{k + g} - \frac{Ak + Bt}{k + t} \right| < \left| \frac{Ak + Bt}{k + t} - A \right|$$

This inequality[3] reduces itself, where $g > t$, to:

$$g < \frac{2kt}{k - t} \simeq 2t\left(1 + \frac{t}{k}\right)$$

This expression is most easily understood when $k = \infty$. It is then intuitively plain that just as we do better with g anywhere between o and t, so we do better with g between t and 2t. Values like $-t$ and 3t will clearly impart inaccuracy. The expression $\frac{t}{k}$ shows us that as $\frac{t}{k}$ increases, i.e. as B becomes more important in the index, it becomes more important to include it: so ever wilder and wilder guesses are tolerable. Thus if $A = 120$, $B = 150$, $k = 6$, $t = 3$ the correct

[1] N. Jasny, *The Socialized Agriculture of the U.S.S.R.*, Stanford 1949, Appendices G and H; A. Kahan, *Journal of Political Economy*, June 1956.

[2] D. Hodgman, *Soviet Industrial Production*, Harvard 1954; F. Seton, *Soviet Studies*; N. Jasny, *The Soviet Pricing System*; *Soviet Prices During the Plan Era*; *Soviet Prices of Producer Goods* (all Stanford 1951–52); R. Powell, *Sources of Industrial Growth* (privately circulated, May 1961).

[3] I have taken arithmetical rather than geometrical differences as the mathematics of the latter is beyond my powers. Where B-A is small it does not matter. I am indebted for help to my colleague Mr. K. A. H. Gravett.

answer is 130. Even so wild a guess as $g = 10$ gives 138·8, a more accurate answer than the 'timid' one of 120.

Nothing in this section, however, excuses the guessing of a growth series!

5. The Sovietologist is again and again faced with a synthetic official output index that he must check for mishandling against a large selection of the individual physical series from which it was built up. These latter can only have been misreported,[1] and are therefore a firmer base. As Prof. E. Domar has put it:[2] if you go into a bad restaurant where you mistrust the cooking you do not order hash or fruit salad, you order bacon and eggs or a banana.

In checking the synthetic against the individual series we face two problems. First, how shall we weight these individual series? To this the answer has already been given in part: we must be bold and weight them somehow. It follows that foreign weights, pre-plan base-year weights, retail price weights, wage-bill weights, any imperfect system, is better than none. We return in Secs. 7–9 to the choice between these weighting systems.

Secondly, we have only a *selection* of the individual physical series. There are three possible biases here: (i) the physical series chosen for publication will be those showing greatest growth, (ii) precisely such series will be suppressed, for security reasons, and (iii) those showing greatest discontinuity and quality change will naturally not be shown. (ii) induces a downward bias for any economy, since the areas of greatest quality change are normally those of greatest physical growth, and quality change is itself growth, as we show in Secs. 19–25. But apart from any possibility of systematic bias the main fact is that the number of physical series published can hardly, in the nature of things, represent more than a small fraction of total output, so that random bias is very probable.

Agriculture, transport and construction do not suffer from these problems, since there are only a few major physical series in each of them, and quality change is slow. So either one has them all and can proceed, or not.[3] But in industry the problem is acute, indeed much

---

[1] As a rule: though physical crop statistics were also mishandled in pre-war Soviet year-books; for the barn yield before collectivization was presented in direct continuity with the root yield after collectivization and no warning was given.

[2] In conversation.

[3] Thus Messrs. D. G. Johnson and A. Kahan find their Soviet agricultural output index gratifyingly insensitive to weight change: *Comparisons of the U.S and Soviet Economies*, Joint Economic Committee of Congress, U.S.G.P.O. 1959, Part I, p. 204.

more than is generally realized, since the production of armaments is never published and is exclusively industrial, so that a large part of the industrial total fluctuates according to the political situation, yet is quite unknown. These factors have led Mr. Francis Seton[1] altogether to reject the attempt to reconstruct the synthetic index from the individual series in favour of an empirical correlation between the synthetic index and the output of a very few primary industrial inputs, such as steel, electricity and coal. Surprisingly, he can establish a single excellent correlation for a wide variety of non-Communist countries, developed and undeveloped; and the question arises why we should not use it to infer industrial output in any Communist country from these same primary industrial inputs— which of course *are* published, and subject only to misreporting.

6. The logic of Seton's method is that the degree of fabrication (i.e. the amount of value added to his primary inputs) rises or falls everywhere by a percentage dependent only on the percentage increase of those inputs: it is independent of the degree of maturity of the economy and, he hopes, of Communist planning. The absolute degree of fabrication may of course differ greatly by country and by year, but it does not affect the correlation of the rates of growth. Thus to take arbitrary numbers we might find such a correlation, in terms of percentage increase per annum:

three basic industrial inputs	5	10	15
total industrial production	6	11	14

Never mind why this is so, simply accept it as a proven fact. Then, if such proportions hold good for Turkey, Italy and U.S.A., why not for Czechoslovakia and China? It is difficult to think of anything in a Communist economy that might destroy this correlation, except at the point of take-over of power. It is noticeable that Seton's index for U.S.S.R. closely resembles other Western recalculations, except in 1928–31, when it shows a greater rise than any of them.[2] In this period craft industry (which hardly uses these inputs) was very rapidly destroyed[3] and planner's tension, hitherto

---

[1] *Manchester Statistical Society*, 1957; *Soviet Studies*, Oct. 1960. The remaining literature on Soviet industrial production is enormous. We may list: Hodgman, op. cit.; Jasny, opp. citt.; Nutter, *American Economic Review*, May 1958; Kaplan and Moorsteen, *American Economic Review*, June 1960; Shimkin and Leedy, *Automotive Industries*, U.S.A., Jan. 1958.

[2] On 1928 = 100 Seton gets 1932 = 181; Kaplan-Moorsteen make it 154, and Shimkin-Leedy 148 (interpolating from their 1934 figure). Hodgman (at 172) is weak on small industry, and Nutter (at 139) on large, so they may be neglected.

[3] It is a world-wide tendency to exaggerate the growth of industrial production by omitting the declining craft output from the total. Under Communism the decline is merely more radical and sudden, so that the problem differs only in degree, not kind.

altogether absent, was raised to heights never afterwards attained.
Furthermore in those heroic days most indicators were for output
only, and in the crudest physical terms at that; so that in the absence
of cost, quality and technical restraints input/output ratios rose
alarmingly. It is even likely that the degree of fabrication fell,
since the output of spare parts, repairs and high quality lines shrank
catastrophically.

All these factors must have upset the relation between output
and the three basic inputs in the same direction; and events of this
kind have no parallel in non-Communist economies. So it would
certainly be wrong to accept the Seton method for the take-over
period, even in other Communist countries where it was slightly
less brutal.[1] We see, not for the first or last time, the important
statistical distinction between the take-over and the subsequent
period.

The Seton procedure must, then, be accepted as normally superior
to an ordinary index based on few physical series, especially if
armaments are omitted or guessed. But Communism is subject
to sudden drives, to periods of abnormal waste and administrative
panic. This is one thing that the procedure cannot cope with.

7. However, in an area of such great uncertainty, no reasonable
alternative should be neglected; and the problem of compiling
a normal synthetic index from physical series is in any case important
since Comminust statisticians themselves face it. Now normal
statistical theory unhesitatingly uses for weights either market
prices (as representing the relative marginal utilities of consumers) or
factor costs (as representing the relative marginal costs of producing
enterprises). Either way the values are marginal transformation
ratios between one good and another, and these make good commonsense weights.[2]

But what if outputs are irrational? The superficially surprising
answer is that *irrational prices may well be the best weights for irrational
outputs*; since in certain allocation models they still represent marginal transformation ratios. This is notably true of the Stalinist
allocation model (4). We are of course, in this as in all other cases,

---

[1] A sole exception here might be China, where the market, craftsmen and even capitalists
were only very slowly liquidated. But China in 1958 was very like U.S.S.R. in 1929–32.

[2] The factor costs of finished goods do not, of course, represent the marginal disutilities of
the inputs of the ultimate factors of production; since the costs are the costs of goods, not
factors. Factor cost is thus an output index weight. Wages, rent and interest are suitable
weights for input indices, and must of course be applied to quantities of labour, land and
capital. An employment tax or a land tax would create the same distinction between 'factor
cost' and 'market price' in an input index as do other taxes in an output index.

interested only in weighting and summing the actual physical outputs that there are, not some hypothetical set of rational outputs. We measure what is, and the irrationality of what is is under no circumstances an absolute bar to measurement; least of all in this case.

Thus suppose that there is consumer's choice (not sovereignty), and all outputs are sold on a free market at prices sufficient to clear the market without queues; but that relative outputs are nonetheless arbitrarily and stupidly planned, so that the difference between price and marginal cost varies. Then retail prices represent consumers' marginal transformation ratios as much as before. Suppose further that labour, land and capital are all bought on a free market, the prices being fixed just so as to attract them to the right enterprises in order that these may fulfil the plan; then factor costs represent entrepreneurs' or managers' marginal transformation ratios as much as before. All that has happened is that the two sets of marginal transformation ratios no longer coincide, or m.c. no longer = price. But this is a perfectly unremarkable state of affairs, applying in practice to all non-Communist economies too. The only differences between Communism, or allocation model 4, and the rest are irrelevant: e.g. that the irrationalities are much greater, and arise not from enterprise policy or market imperfection but centrally, and perhaps out of a system of physical not monetary indicators. The fact remains that under Stalin's allocation model the state is one large monopolist operating between a factors' and a consumers' market. If capitalist monopoly does not render retail prices unusable as weights, neither does Stalin's.

There can thus be no general doubt that Stalin's retail prices make suitable measuring rods in general. There are, however, certain qualifications. First, take national income deflators, cost of living indices and purchasing power parities, for all of which it is correct to use retail prices. If there are queues for particular products, but not equal queues for all in proportion, relative prices no longer represent consumers' transformation ratios. Common to all economies, this is particularly serious in Soviet-type ones. *Per contra*, if certain goods accumulate unsold in stocks, we may call these negative queues, and these goods are as much overvalued by retail prices as those are undervalued for which buyers queue. So rigid and irrational is Communist planning that even in the worst periods of shortage and inflation there have been such stocks.

Often, again, needed goods are not produced at all. There is then, of course, no queue. This, however, is part of the much graver problem of variety and new goods, which needs lengthier treatment (Secs. 19–25).

8. *Factor costs* on the other hand represent merely the marginal transformation ratios between *products* (not, to repeat, factors) for enterprises. It is difficult to see why they should be of any special interest to the statistical theorist, since the entrepreneur's or manager's valuations of his products have far less status in welfare economics than the consumer's valuation of them; the consumer, not the entrepreneur, represents 'social benefit'. Consequently the taxes and subsidies that separate these two valuations distort factor costs as a measuring rod, not market prices. For, as we have just seen, the latter are satisfactory measuring rods so long as they merely clear the market, no matter how irrational outputs are.

The factor costs of products, then, are a very inferior substitute as weights for the retail prices of products. This leaves them, seemingly, just one useful sphere: the determination of the overall ratio of investment to consumption. On a free market this ratio might just as well be expressed in output prices (consumption foregone) as in input prices (factors released). But as Stalin handled prices 'consumption foregone' is no longer meaningful: the prices of investment outputs are administratively determined. They are, as it happens, kept very low, but as we saw in Ch. 6 they could have been much higher without affecting the prices of consumption outputs. So we are forced back on to 'factors released' (input prices). Ideally then we want to compare the inputs devoted to investment with those devoted to consumption. But in the absence of adequate input statistics we must use the next best thing: and that is the factor costs, not the market prices, of finished goods and services. If the factor cost of investment output rises relatively to that of consumption output this is an almost unambiguous indication that the community is putting more factors of production into investment. This would only not be so if at the same time factors used in consumption became more efficient, or if taxes on factor use were altered. But since the relation is contemporaneous the growth of efficiency is not a disturbing element: the factor cost of goods accumulated versus the factor cost of goods consumed is a perfectly valid measure.

9. Then, of course, as the practical Sovietologist must never forget, data are scarce and one cannot always pick and choose. As

a *pis aller* we may very well sometimes be glad of factor costs in most inappropriate circumstances. Thus, if Hodgman's index of industrial production uses 1934 wage-bill weights we may well object to his claim of superior rationality; but we are still left with the task of supplying better weights.

Factor costs present, not in the strict logic of allocation model (4), but in Communist reality, a complication: land and capital are not bought by the government on a free market, but confiscated and—with the many exceptions noted in Ch. 3, Sec. 4—administratively allocated. It is thus impossible to know how scarce they are, and we are forced back on arbitrary devices, which have given rise to interesting controversy.

First one might omit land and capital altogether, and use wages and salaries alone as measures of net value added. But enterprises and industries use exceedingly different proportions of land and capital to labour, so it is clearly most unsatisfactory to weight by labour alone, although equally clearly much better than nothing.[1] It might be an improvement to take the percentages of value added by labour to all value added in various Western industries, and apply them to Communist values added by labour. It is certainly false, but probably not very false, that capital—and land—intensity varies about the average in much the same way in all economies. It is hard to deny that such weights would be slightly better than labour-weights alone.

Thirdly, one often has statistics at least of the book value of the capital used, and in agriculture of the physical quality of land. With even rather inefficient accountancy it is certainly justifiable to apply Western amortization and interest rates to the book values; and a reasonable guess as to the value of the land is better than none, as has been demonstrated. This is probably a still more accurate approach to the 'true' factor cost of products. The procedure is also used to compile input indices.[2]

But inside the nationalized sector in this model, and throughout allocation model (2), money is not one-sidedly but two-sidedly passive. It need then have no serious correspondence to relative scarcities (whether from the state's or the consumer's point of view), i.e. it need not express marginal transformation ratios at all. It may not even exist. It is here that *foreign prices* become preferable.

[1] Cf. D. Hodgman, op. cit.; Wiles and Hodgman, *Soviet Studies*, 1955-6.
[2] E.g. A. Bergson, RAND paper, P2148, of Nov. 29, 1960.

This recommendation certainly does not imply that foreign prices correspond to the existing[1] relative scarcities; only that they may well get nearer to them than prices developed by purely passive money on the spot. A study of some of the sources quoted above will readily convince the reader of this. Obviously, again, where there are no prices the statistician is very well advised indeed to use foreign ones for measurement. Had 'War Communism' ever worked it would certainly have thrown up this particular measurement problem.

But prices arising from doubly passive money are not utterly unreliable if they are *random*. I.e. the more irrational they are, down to the last detail, the better they are for measurement. They are least reliable when the government has pursued some general policy about them. Thus, if, for instance, new goods have higher prices than old,[2] or particular branches of industry are subsidized[3] the probability is that the output of these will have grown systematically faster than the rest, and be systematically over-weighted (in the first case) or under-weighted (in the second).

The absence of rent and interest from factor costs also sets up a bias in the system of wholesale or factory prices: it gives greater weight to labour-intensive commodities. On balance this will be to the commodities least favoured by the régime, so here is another downward bias.

10. Even if prices or costs are rational, many problems arise from the Communist use of *gross indices of output*. Gross rather than net indices are constructed when the sales value of each enterprises output is simply added to that of all the others, without eliminating the double counting that arises from the sale and purchase of intermediate goods. It is entirely natural, and even in a small way desirable, to pay attention to gross output in a centrally planned system; since gross output is the most obvious, operative and easy to enforce of all output targets. It would be absurd to eliminate it from the enterprise plan. The objections, raised in Communist and non-Communist countries alike, are to its use in statistics referring to the past or to comparisons with other countries, and to its uncorrected

---

[1] Note again that we are of course interested in weighting the actual physical outputs that there are, not some hypothetical set of rational outputs.

[2] As in the celebrated Soviet 1926–27 prices: new goods were given notional 1926–27 prices which corresponded to their current costs, and were thus much higher than those of old goods, fixed before the inflation.

[3] As in Soviet current prices for machinery.

use as an indicator. No doubt here Marxist ideology has played a part,[1] and also sheer Stalinist crudity.

Certainly if we add up the successive vertical stages of output without 'netting out' we get a larger total, whether in current or in constant prices, than by the correct procedure. It is common to infer that this exaggerates Communist rates of growth *vis-à-vis* those of countries that use correct procedures, but that does not follow, for as usual the exaggeration of absolute values has no connexion whatsoever with the exaggeration of rates of growth.

Take two branches of production, in one of which production— or at least the reporting of production[2]—is vertically disintegrated into an intermediate branch d (say fodder) and a final branch D (say meat); while the other branch I (say wheat) is vertically integrated. Then the use of gross as opposed to net indices will cause no exaggeration if all three branches rise in unison, say by a factor k. For then

$$\frac{kI + kd + kD}{I + d + D} \text{ (gross)} = \frac{kI + kD}{I + D} \text{ (net)}. \tag{i}$$

There will be exaggeration if D and d grow faster than I, since

$$\frac{mI + kd + kD}{I + d + D} > \frac{mI + kD}{I + D}, \text{ where } m < k; \tag{ii}$$

or if without warning or statistical adjustment there is a switch from net to gross reckoning:

$$\frac{kI + kd + kD}{I + D} > \frac{kI + kD}{I + D}; \tag{iii}$$

of if once the gross system has been accepted there is further vertical disintegration, or a multiplication of vertical reporting stages not adjusted for (let the gratuitous new reporting stages be called i' and d'):

$$\frac{ki' + kI + kd + kd' + kD}{I + d + D} > \frac{kI + kD}{I + D}. \tag{iv}$$

The factors k and m might be real or monetary. If the latter they would have to be deflated in the normal manner.

Note especially that gross indices may understate growth. Thus in (ii) m may > k. For instance, in the 1930s Soviet crop farming,

---

[1] Cf. Ch. 14, Sec. 5.
[2] I.e. it is not how the industry is actually subdivided for management purposes, but the mere number of reporting stages that counts.

which is more integrated and presents fewer intermediate reporting stages, held up better than livestock farming; and since 1953 the latter has gone ahead more. So, if the use of gross indices is the only disturbing factor, the combined index has exaggerated first the fall and then the rise in agricultural output.[1] Or again in case (iv) the number of intermediate reporting units may be diminished.

However, in the case of Communist indices of industrial production there can be no doubt that the bias has been upward, owing to a combination of (iii) and (iv), setting in at the moment when the system is introduced and, on the whole, increasing ever since. The mere increasing complexity of modern industry is enough to ensure this: more and more difficult components simply have to be sub-contracted out to specialized enterprises. Or again so simple a thing as the end of a war increases gross output more than net; the supply position improves and enterprises are more willing to trust sub-contractors, farms specialize in fodder for sale, artificial fertilizers are bought and sold, etc. And thirdly, as explained in Ch. 4, the use of gross output as an indicator encourages every intermediate authority to increase mutual sub-contracting among its subordinates.[2]

11. It is a singular feature of both price and output indices, in all economic systems, that the *Laspeyres index normally exceeds the Paasche*. The amazing size of the possible discrepancy was discovered in a Sovietological context. In his celebrated *Dollar Index of Soviet Machinery Output*[3] Prof. Alexander Gerschenkron demonstrates this for U.S. and British machinery output, using in each case domestic prices. He does not demonstrate it for Soviet output, which he values only in U.S. prices of 1939. It is, he says, because the degree of fabrication increases with technical progress: think of tractors and sickles—the base year price of the tractor will be very high and that of the sickle very low in comparison with the prices of the given, more technically advanced, year, when there

---

[1] Unless the weighting of the two sub-indices has been adjusted in some way to counteract this.

[2] For a Soviet estimate of the exaggeration of industrial output indices brought about by gross reckoning cf. S. G. Strumilin, *Ocherki Sotsialisticheskoi Ekonomii SSSR*, Moscow 1959, pp. 234–6. Reckoning from 1928 = 100, Strumilin gets a net volume index in 1956 of 1461, in contrast to the official gross index of 2290. There exists also a detailed comparison for 13 Australian food industries over a number of years (Karmel, *Journal of the Royal Statistical Society*, 4/1954). In altogether 142 pairs of years gross output increased more rapidly than net 61% of times, less rapidly 37%, and as rapidly 2%. Great, indeed distressing, variability was shown within each year and industry.

[3] RAND Corporation, Santa Monica 1951; esp. Ch. 4.

will be more tractors and fewer sickles. Value added per pound of metal, he says, is much greater for tractors than for sickles.

But while he has established the fact—and the differences between the two indices are very striking, ranging from 40% over 17 years to 800% over 40 years—it does not follow that he has given the correct reason. He nowhere says *why* an increase in the degree of fabrication should have this effect, and it is indeed far from obvious. For if fabrication increases wage-costs increase, and with technical progress goes prosperity and an increase in wage over material costs. It is precisely the things with the highest degree of 'fabrication' that strike foreigners as having the highest prices in U.S.A.: e.g. hair-cuts, domestic service. Value added per pound of metal is infinite in both cases, so that by Prof. Gerschenkron's explanation they should be exceptionally cheap.

But perhaps an increase in the degree of fabrication means that more of all factors of production are applied per unit of raw material, not more of labour alone?[1] We must now ask whether it is indeed true that articles are more 'fabricated' in advanced economies. Are sickles? *or tractors*? Surely the whole meaning of economic advance is that there is reduction of inputs per unit output. And doubtless most such reduction is precisely in new goods like tractors. Such goods are indeed highly 'fabricated' in a backward economy and less so in an advanced one.

Note however that, relying on the fabrication theory, Prof. Gerschenkron infers that international comparisons will behave like intertemporal ones: the prices of a backward country will always favour the advanced country, and vice versa. This was confirmed by U.S./West European comparisons made after he wrote.[2]

But even the success of this inference does not strengthen the fabrication theory, as it can be otherwise explained. Consider for instance two countries or one country at two times, both possessed of the same general level of technique and natural resources. Let chance will it that the base year (or place) specializes in A, and produces little of B, but in the given year (or place) the specialization is reversed. Then if there are increasing returns base factor costs

---

[1] Prof. Gerschenkron tells me this is the meaning he himself attaches to the phrase.

[2] D. Paige and G. Bombach, *A Comparison of National Output and Productivity*, OEEC, Paris 1959; M. Gilbert and I. B. Kravis, *An International Comparison of National Products*, OEEC, Paris 1954; the same, *Comparative National Products and Price Levels*, OEEC, Paris 1958. The same holds for U.S.A. versus U.S.S.R. Cf. Bornstein in *Comparisons of the U.S. and Soviet Economics*, Joint Committee of Congress, 1960, Part II, p. 385.

favour the given year (place) and vice versa. But in machinery-making returns do increase, specialization is very considerable, and alterations of structure are very pronounced. So, confining our-selves to factor costs not market prices, this is probably a sufficient explanation of the Gerschenkron effect.

Fabrication, to repeat, is likely to have the opposite effect. In so far as an advanced economy specializes in more fabricated things it will be using more of that resource which costs most in advanced economies: labour. This is most categorically proven by the prices of services in U.S.A. Prof. Gerschenkron himself admits that in textiles the degree of fabrication has happened to decline, in that dress styles, at least for men, are simpler. But it has surely also declined for machinery. It is not 'tractors' that have a high degree of fabrication, but tractors in backward economies. In advanced ones there is mass production and automation, so the move into *erstwhile* much-fabricated lines does not raise labour costs. If in any industry the degree of fabrication does not decline the article's relative cost increases as the economy advances: compare not only services but, say, high-class cuisine in China, France and U.S.A.

12. Now factor costs are conceptually incorrect, as we have seen, as weights for output indices. If we switch to market prices the Gerschenkron effect may easily not hold at all in a market economy, even though we still assume increasing returns. For demand may have outrun supply or the degree of monopoly have increased, so that profit margins have risen enough to offset the fall in costs. This is suggested by Mr. Ira Scott,[1] who tries to demonstrate it from the output of non-mechanical consumers' durables in U.S.A. between the same dates as chosen by Gerschenkron. For these goods over long periods of time the Laspeyres index is only insignificantly higher than the Paasche. The main reason must surely be that in Mr. Scott's list—cottons, woollens, linoleum, glass, etc.—there has been far less structural change and economies of scale are far smaller.

However, the Laspeyres index remains higher, in all of Mr. Scott's four cases, and we may suggest three reasons for this: (i) if the full-cost principle is used, or (ii) if there is competition, prices follow costs up and down, and there are slightly increasing

---

[1] *Review of Economics and Statistics*, 1952.

returns in these industries too; (iii) a subsidiary reason is that what a country does not specialize in it may well not produce at all but import; and this adds to its price the greater costs of international transportation and merchandising. In sum the Gerschenkron effect is only not likely to operate in a pure agricultural comparison, where everything is subject to diminishing returns. Indeed it would then be reversed.

13. The effect can in fact be reduced to a logical necessity. Let the four elements of the two indices, prices and quantities in the base and given years, be as follows for two commodities:

Q_0	P_0	Q_1	P_1
A	Y	jA	kY
B	Z	lB	mZ,

where P is market prices or factor costs and j, k, l, m are any factors of increase or decrease we care to name. Then taking indices of output first, we put Laspeyres = Paasche + X, or

$$\frac{YjA + ZlB}{YA + ZB} = \frac{kYjA + mZlB}{kYA + mZB} + X.$$

Then $kl + mj = ml + kj + \dfrac{X}{ZBYA}$,

or Laspeyres — Paasche = $(m{-}k)(j{-}l)$. The Gerschenkron effect can now be defined as being that if $k < m$, $l < j$ Laspeyres is always $>$ Paasche. Note that a difference between j and l, i.e. structural change, is absolutely essential.

14. If we take price indices instead of output indices it is easy to prove that the same result emerges, so that Laspeyres is still greater than Paasche in the same circumstances. It follows that a real income index, which moves as does the reciprocal of a price index, shows the opposite behaviour to an output index. I.e. where there are increasing returns to all products and prices follow costs, a Laspeyres index of output exceeds a Paasche, but a real income index based on a Laspeyres price index is smaller.

Elementary algebra takes us a little deeper here, towards a surprising result. We have seen that the Laspeyres output index $\dfrac{\Sigma\, q_1\, p_0}{\Sigma\, q_0\, p_0}$

exceeds the Paasche index $\dfrac{\Sigma\, q_1\, p_1}{\Sigma\, q_0\, p_1}$ in ordinary circumstances; and so does the Laspeyres price index $\dfrac{\Sigma\, p_1\, q_0}{\Sigma\, p_0\, q_0}$ the Paasche $\dfrac{\Sigma\, p_1\, q_1}{\Sigma\, p_0\, q_1}$. Now a real income index is the money income index $\dfrac{\Sigma\, p_1\, q_1}{\Sigma\, p_0\, q_0}$ divided by one or other price index. But this means that the Laspeyres real income index is identical to the Paasche output index, and vice versa!

One of the great classic instances of Laspeyres > Paasche is precisely the Soviet *cost of living* index during the period of maximum structural change. On the base 1928 = 100, Laspeyres gives 1937 = 701, Paasche 495.[1] It is then no surprise that predominant over the misleading upward biasses of the Soviet index of industrial *production* based on 1926–27 prices is the very natural upward trend (we must not call it bias) implicit in Laspeyres. Mr. Raymond Powell has recently shown that one can explain virtually the whole of the excess of the Soviet official index over Western recalculations by the fact that the Soviet statisticians consistently applied the Laspeyres formula in circumstances of great structural change.[2]

The singularly great discrepancies between Laspeyres and Paasche in Gerschenkron and Chapman should give all statisticians pause. The lack of such discrepancy in Scott is hardly reassuring until it is explained. We now turn to ask whether the discrepancies are accompanied by pro-Communist bias.

15. Similar, then, to the Gerschenkron is the 'Nutter effect',[3] namely the claim that ordinary processes of measurement favour Communist growth because Communists invest more in industries of increasing return and/or greatest technical progress.

Let there be two investment strategies, I to put money mostly into good B, where returns increase more *and* there is more progress, II to put it mostly into good A where there is less of each (but some[4]). In the first case (i) let market prices rise and fall with

---

[1] Chapman, *Review of Economics and Statistics*, 1954.

[2] R. Powell, op. cit. The old story was that the principal cause of the excess was that for new goods, introduced after 1926–27, Soviet statisticians used notional 1926–27 prices. These were the current prices in the first year of mass production. But since there was strong inflation until 1948 these current prices were far above what would have been the price in 1926–27 had the good been new then; and since the Soviet economy concentrated heavily on new goods, especially machinery, this greatly exaggerated the rise in output. The new story is that in fact current machinery prices were stable, and the above 'escalator effect' only applied to a few consumer goods; moreover, a Western recalculation on strict Laspeyres lines reproduces the Soviet result.

[3] Levine, *Journal of Political Economy*, Aug. 1958. I owe this whole passage to Mr. Levine's inspiration. Cf. Nutter, ibid., Feb. 1957, esp. p. 62.

[4] I make this condition partly for its realism, partly in order to retain increasing *relative* returns, and so curves convex to the origin.

costs, or let costs be directly used as weights. In fig. 1 let movement
from Q, the initial position, up the ray from the origin represent
policy II, and movement to the South East policy I. We can move
up the ray to S or V with the same effort as off it to M or N, which

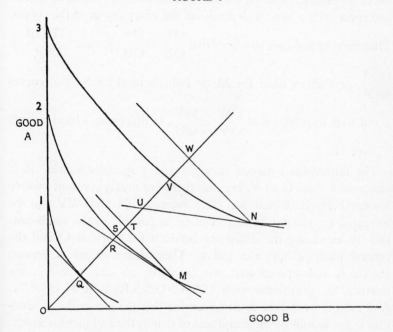

are on the same production-possibility curves but embody more
of the good that is easier to produce. Now at S and V Paasche =
Laspeyres, since, according to our previous notation, j = 1. With

M and N Paasche indices $\dfrac{OR}{OQ}$, $\dfrac{OU}{OQ}$ are always less than the indices

for S and V, and Laspeyres indices $\dfrac{OT}{OQ}$, $\dfrac{OW}{OQ}$ always greater.

That follows immediately from the convexity of the curves to the
origin. It would appear that far too much discussion of this kind is
conducted in terms of Laspeyres alone.[1] Remarkable biases one
way or the other can be shown with *one* of the two basic indices,

[1] Both Nutter and Levine are guilty here.

but the other has a strong tendency to show an equal and opposite bias. We have to be flat footed and conscientious, and go through all the prescribed procedures.

Our real question, then, is with Fisher's Ideal:[1] if that shows a consistent bias in favour of M over S, or N over V, the Nutter effect is genuine. Our figure shows that there is no logical reason to expect such a bias: it depends on the exact shapes of the curves.

Thus curves 2 and 1 are so related that $\dfrac{OT}{OS} > \dfrac{OS}{OR}$; so that $\dfrac{OT.OR}{OQ^2} >$ $\dfrac{OS^2}{OQ^2}$, or Fisher's Ideal for M $>$ Fisher's Ideal for S. But curves 3 and 1 are so related that $\dfrac{OW}{OV} < \dfrac{OV}{OU}$, so that Fisher's Ideal favours V over N.

The differences between curves 2 and 3 are very subtle. R is closer to S than U to V, because there are nearly constant relative returns between S and M. The distances TS and WV can be increased by placing M and N as far as possible to the south-east, and by increasing the difference between the slope at Q and the general pitch of curves 2 and 3. These delicacies are at present absolutely non-operational: we can have no idea whether, for instance, in comparison with U.S.A., U.S.S.R. is at M or at N. And even if we did we must remember that the bias in the production index would be the reciprocal of that in the real income index.

16. We now (ii) turn to market prices as weights, cutting the bond that ties them to costs. So consider next the same outputs, irrationally priced. Suppose the planners refuse to reduce the price of B, on which they have concentrated, but force people to buy more of it than they want: or suppose that B is subsidized but the statistician wrongly discounts the subsidy. Put, as an extreme case, unchanged relative prices. Then taking M or N in fig. 1 indifferently, Laspeyres is as before greater than for S or V, and now Paasche is equal to it. So Fisher's Ideal is greater than for S and V, and greater than what it would have been for M and N with rational prices, and there is indeed a 'Nutter' bias.

[1] That is, the square root of the product of Laspeyres and Paasche. For a recent discussion of the virtues of this index cf. R. Marris, *Economic Arithmetic*, London 1958, pp. 240–6.

17. Suppose next (iii) that outputs are irrational, but the prices of expanding outputs are lowered and of contracting outputs raised so as exactly to clear the market. This is allocation model (4), and with it we begin to approach Communist reality.

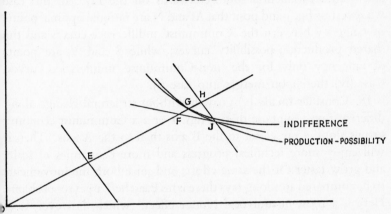

FIGURE 2

Fig. 2 shows this. Starting at E, the economy can with equal effort arrive at J or G. The point of highest utility on the production-possibility curve JG is G, but the easy statistical triumph is preferred of concentrating on B to the neglect of A. The price-line FJ represents the relative prices necessary to sell the combination J: it is tangential at J to a lower indifference curve, not shown, which cuts the production-possibility curve at J.

Points E and G are shown, as before, along a single ray, so that Paasche and Laspeyres are the same for G. Laspeyres for J $\left(\frac{OH}{OE}\right)$ is clearly greater. Paasche for J, however $\left(\frac{OF}{OE}\right)$ is smaller than all of these, and we are back in the situation of fig. 1, with one important difference. This is that any indifference curve at J is almost certain to be flatter than the production-possibility curve there. This is because G is a rational optimum, so a point of tangency; therefore unless the curves are kinked the indifference curves will be more horizontal than the production-possibility curves going south-east. It follows that if J here were M or N in fig. 1 FG here would exceed RS or UV in fig. 1: the Paasche index would be

R

smaller and Fisher's Ideal smaller. Thus in case (iii), which is the all-important case for Soviet-type reality, the Nutter effect is less likely than in case (i).

(iv) Now suppose both economies are rational, only the 'Communist' one is luckier, since its indifference map is not the same, and guides production south-eastwards off the ray. In this case we revert to fig. 1 and posit that M and N are rational optima, points of tangency between the 'Communist' indifference curves and the shared production-possibility curves; while S and V are points of tangency only for the 'non-Communist' indifference curves. Case (iv) thereupon merges into case (i).

18. Consider finally (v) growth without structural change along different rays. Suppose that in figs. 1 or 2 a Communist economy grows along a ray closer to the B axis than to the A axis. Then it will enjoy more technical progress and more economies of scale, and grow faster for the same effort; and since both the movements to be compared are along rays there is no Paasche/Laspeyres problem. Here is a most unequivocal Nutter effect,[1] which, however, does not apply overmuch to the Communist/capitalist comparison. For both Communist and capitalist countries are (eventually) industrialized, and both even concentrate to about the same extent on capital goods,[2] which are supposed to enjoy increasing returns and technical progress most. Rather the bias favours industrial over agricultural countries; it is indeed a widely known theorem in colonial economics.

In sum the 'unfairness' of Soviet performance lies elsewhere. The use of given year prices, without any check from rational end-year prices, really is an unfair advantage in output indices, but one that can be corrected by conscientious pursuit of all the correct procedures. And the rapidity of structural change exaggerates this effect. But in real wage indices the effect is reversed. For the rest there are indeed valid 'Nutter' effects, but none of them is relevant to the Communist/capitalist comparison.

19. Next a very different problem, also raised by Mr. Nutter: that of *new goods*. This may also be called the problem of *variety* or of the *hedonic price index*. Can an economy hostile to variety

---

[1] It is indeed the original one: Nutter, op. cit., p. 59.
[2] Cf. Ch. 14, Sec. 14.

and innovation[1] be satisfactorily compared with one that favours them? The question raises issues far beyond mere Sovietology, and demands a general excursus for which little apology is made.

All price and output indices compare like with like, so unlike must be reduced to like in order to fit it in at all. With some very simple quality changes this reduction is not arbitrary, will be accepted by the politicians and trade unionists who use the index, and so is practised. Thus if orange-juice is strengthened by 10% and its price rises 10% the cost of living is held not to change. The statistician proceeds confidently here because he knows that no one will seriously question what he has done.

But take a greater quality change: from silk to nylon in women's stockings. Both stockings offer essentially the same services: a modicum of coverage and a certain type of appearance. Only nylons are both cheaper and more durable: say twice as durable and four times as cheap. Then clearly the cost of covering women's legs in a certain way has been divided by eight. But no official index dares say so, even though both price and durability are objective characteristics, and one would have thought the reasoning irrefragable. Moreover, there are more subjective differences, which happen in this particular case to be less important than the objective ones, and to add to the advantage of the new good. One thinks, for instance, of washability.

As 'quality change' increases to become beyond a peradventure 'new good', the subjective factors usually gain in relative importance.[2] Take, then, a third change, the introduction of TV. Already the comparison between watching TV and going to the cinema is complicated enough: though perhaps only of the same order of complication as nylons and silk. But what of TV and going to the races? One can go to the races in person, and see the crowds, hear

---

[1] Strictly we have three basic possibilities: (a) a constant number of static types in both times or places compared, but larger in one than in the other; (b) the same constant number of shifting types in both times or places, obsolescence taking out as much as innovation puts in, but the rates of turnover being unequal; (c) no obsolescence, and expanding numbers of types, but one rate of expansion greater than the other. A full analysis would also have to consider permutations and combinations. Here we simply speak of 'variety and innovation'. The seminal work on this subject appears to be that of Mr. A. T. Court: 'Hedonic Price Indexes with Automotive Examples', in *The Dynamics of Automobile Demand*, General Motors Corp., N.Y. 1939. For the rest I am aware (1961) of only three works: a privately circulated paper of Mr. Meyer Burstein (Northwestern University, Evanston, Ill.); Zvi Griliches, in *Government Price Statistics*, Joint Committee on the Economic Report, U.S. Congress, Jan. 24, 1961; Zvi Griliches and Irma Adelman, *Journal of the American Statistical Association*, 1961. This chapter was written more or less independently.

[2] This is not necessarily so. Thus an aeroplane is very different from a ship, but air and sea travel are very easily comparable, the objective factors being of overwhelming weight.

the bookies, get the feel of it all, get one's feet wet, etc., for the price of a return ticket to Newmarket. Or one can go to the races on TV, missing both sunshine and rain, and having a far better view of the horses, for about one penny. Taking all subjective factors into account these are perhaps equally satisfactory and essentially comparable experiences; and one costs 1/1000th of the other, for a family of four and a distance of forty miles. Or consider finally TV news: here is a genuinely new experience, essentially incomparable with reading a newspaper, listening to the news on 'steam radio' or seeing it in the cinema. A man to whom this possibility opens up is richer, but not in any measurable way. There are, that is to say, genuinely new goods which no stretch of imagination or bold statistical procedure can render comparable.

20. Neglect these for the moment, and concentrate on the rest: in increasing order of subjectivity, stronger orange-juice, nylon, telecast horse-racing. Normal procedures include stronger orange-juice in the manner indicated. But nylons enter the index only in the second year of their mass production, receiving the weight of the first such year; and all that is considered is the change in price or output from the first such year, i.e. *the change from silk to nylon receives no consideration at all*. Treat, then, nylons as if they were a kind of stronger orange-juice, and enter them as 'silk equivalents'. Very conservatively, put one nylon stocking as worth two silk stockings. Then the true index of stocking production is simply that of the sum of silk-equivalents; and the index of the cost of buying stockings is that of the average price of silk-equivalents every year, i.e. the index of expenditure in money divided by the true production index:

	Output or Sales in pairs (Price in shillings)		Nylon in silk	Index of production (Cost-of-living index)	
Year	Silk	Nylon	equivalents	Orthodox	Hedonic
I	100(32/-)	0(—)	—(—)	100(100)	100(100)
II	60(32/-)	25(8/-)	50(4/-)	78·8(100)	110(60)
III	20(25/-)	50(8/-)	100(4/-)	57·5(80)	120(43)
IV	0(—)	65(8/-)	130(4/-)	48·8(80)	130(12)

In this table year II, the first year of mass production of nylons, is taken as base throughout, and the indices are thereafter converted to I = 100. Thus, for instance, the orthodox output index for year IV is $\dfrac{\Sigma\, q_4\, p_2}{\Sigma\, q_2\, p_2}$, and the hedonic output index is $\dfrac{Q_4}{Q_2}$, where Q is silk-equivalents. Or again the hedonic price index for year III is $\dfrac{\Sigma\, p_3\, q_3}{\Sigma\, p_2\, q_2} \cdot \dfrac{Q_2}{Q_3}$. At all times $Q = Q_a + l\, Q_b$, where a is the old and b the new good, and l is the factor of 'quality linkage', in this case 2.

The difference is horrifyingly great. Yet nylon *is* a silk-equivalent of that order of magnitude, so the orthodox procedure is undoubtedly wrong by that order of magnitude. With telecast horse-racing, of course, the same procedures bring about still more fantastic differences: e.g. the 'cost of seeing the races index' would in the end-year be, say, 100 (orthodox) and about 0·1 (hedonic), if all race-goers switched to TV.[1]

If 'standard of living' means anything it means that such changes raise it. If numbers such as real wage indices are to mean anything they stringently require that all three changes described be quantified. Therefore they must go into cost of living and production indices. I.e. if we are to quantify changes in the standard of living the cost of living index must tell us the purchasing power of money over utility, not goods, and the production index the output of utility, not goods.

21. Why has this rather obvious point not hitherto been met? It is objected that the suggested procedure is hopelessly arbitrary, that opinions might legitimately differ a great deal about the value of l, that the research required for such an index would be lengthy and expensive, and that it would not command sufficient confidence for wage negotiations. None of these objections is in the very least relevant on the present plane of argument. Moreover, the first two could not under any circumstances have substance at all, and this can be simply shown. Our present procedures deliberately neglect the effects that innovation must have. But innovation is well known to be in progress. Therefore our present procedures seriously distort the indices. They are more arbitrary than any arbitrary allowance for innovation, made in good faith, would be likely to be. If such-and-such quality linkages between television and rail fares are established, other statisticians may well protest over details. But at least then a serious attempt would have been

---

[1] Actually it so happens that they do not. TV is a very imperfect substitute for race-going, and rather draws in a whole new class of 'race-viewers'. If in the end-year new race-viewers plus those who switch to TV from race-going equal in number those who still go, the 'cost of seeing the races index', is 50·5.

made to eradicate a major bias. How much more necessary it is to protest against failure to begin!

We have not, then, to choose between an established accuracy and a new inaccuracy. The dilemma is one much more familiar to economists: do we want precise answers to the wrong question or imprecise answers to the right one? This is the problem that we faced in Sec. 4, and the answer is the same: better to guess than to omit, for to omit has the same effect as guessing zero, and that is quite certainly wrong.

Into practical ways of establishing the correct quality linkage we cannot enter here. The main difficulty is that it differs from person to person and time to time. When nylon first comes on the market ignorance, prejudice and fashion may well make $l = 0·8$. It will gradually rise until it is $2·0$ for *most* people. But there will be a minority, say, of those allergic to silk, for whom it is $10·0$, and another minority, say the diehards with maids to do the washing, for whom it is $0·1$. The demand of this latter minority can keep the price of silk quite high, if supply is adjusted quickly enough. Therefore the price ratio is no measure of l, even in a perfect market.

22. What, then, can be the meaning of 'the general value of money' or 'inflation'? Our reformed price indices measure the purchasing power of money over utility, not goods. This is clearly correct for real values. But perhaps for assessing the worth of monetary policy, the aggressiveness of trade unions, etc., it is the prices of physically similar goods that matter? Perhaps the 'true' degree of inflation is different from money's loss of purchasing power over utility? It is difficult after even the longest consideration to make much sense of this. All we need to say is that monetary policy has been so lax that even after so much technical progress the cost of living has gone up, or that if it had been less lax technical progress would have lowered the price index. The prices and weights of goods of unchanged quality are so much influenced by those of new goods and goods of changed quality that their behaviour on their own has little significance. For instance, a price index of such goods alone certainly does not tell us how all prices would have moved had there been no technical progress. A rapid rate of successful innovation is just as deflationary as a rapid increase of productivity in existing lines of production.

To put it another way, there is no such thing in economics as a production index of 'sheer volume'. With qualities constant, we do not add tons of steel to tons of cement and call it an index; we weight them by their prices, i.e. by their utility to the consumer. This gives the 'economic volume' of steel and cement. Once this is admitted there is no stopping-place short of total admission that every improvement in quality adds to the consumer's utility and is thus an increase in 'economic volume'. The hedonic price index *entails* a hedonic output index. Either both are right or neither is.

23. We have undergone in the preceding sections a disagreeably large revolution in statistical theory. Its consequences, if correct, will reverberate very widely, since it demonstrates that nearly all existing output and cost of living indices are wrong. The latter rise much too rapidly and the former much too slowly. This is not the place, nor is the author the man, to revise them all! In particular, however, Communist economies differ from others in their rates of and attitudes to quality change and innovation. Therefore they cannot be compared with others until our revolution has been squarely accepted—or defeated. For to raise the question in our context is to raise it in all contexts. But we are interested here in comparing rates of change and growth: have the previous sections indicated any bias as between one rate and another? First we answer the question generally, then in its Sovietological context.

(i) There is less innovation in extractive industry than in transport or building, and less in these than in manufacturing and non-transport services (I assert this because it is 'obvious', not because it has been proved. To prove it would be, of course, to undertake the statistical work of computing orthodox and 'true' indices). The main reason for this is that Nature does not permit rapid change in her direct products. Indeed, in the case of minerals it is logically impossible since a mineral is by definition something untouched by man. *Quality change and product innovation increase with the degree of fabrication.*

(ii) By and large the rich happen to benefit from innovation more than the poor. This is simply because basic necessities are the more or less direct products of Nature, and bulk larger in the budgets of the poor. Moreover, it so happens that of the fabricated things clothing is subject to less innovation than durables and entertainment. Thus let the prices of unchanged goods remain constant between two years. We then obtain significantly different hedonic cost of living indices for the rich and the poor:

	Weights				
	Base	End	Orthodox (Laspeyres and Paasche)	Hedonic (Laspeyres)	(Paasche)
The Poor					
Food, Fuel	50	50	300	300	
Clothing	30	25	300	200	
Household	15	15	300	100	
Entertainment	5	10	300	50	
Total Index			300	227·5	220
The Rich					
Food, Fuel	30	20			
Clothing	25	20			
Household	15	15			
Entertainment	30	45			
Total Index			300	170	137·5

This raises many questions we cannot here answer. Notably, *are* the upper and middle classes in post-war Britain any poorer? Has the increase in progressive taxation, in so far as they have not evaded it, even so much as compensated for the advantage they derive from innovations? Assess them on a crude sumptuary basis— their new cars, their wines and spirits, their holidays abroad, the expansion of private education—and it is evident that the official statistics are inexcusably misleading.

(iii) But poor countries differ from poor people. They have in this context an 'advantage of immaturity' which is indeed only part and parcel of the whole advantage of that ilk. For if one normally thinks of technical progress as the cheapening of existing lines it is, of course, equally the making of new, superior lines. So orthodox indices underestimate the progress of countries that are *poor and industrializing*. On the other side they unduly favour the poor and stagnant over the rich and stagnant, since the latter are already industrialized, and that by itself raises their rate of innovation.

(iv) Some industries and countries are afflicted by *unnecessary innovation*, e.g. the oligopolistic motor-car industries of the advanced capitalist nations. This is easily taken care of by giving the 1961 model a one-for-one quality linkage with the 1960 model, i.e. by refusing to recognize any change. One needs, then, to be on one's guard against a superficial impression of dynamism here. Clearly the stable-quality Volkswagen and Moskvich are much more dynamic than Ford or General Motors. Similarly in producer's goods imperfect competition needs unnecessary variety, monopoly excludes it.[1] Variety is far less important in producers' goods, though innovation remains vital.

(v) In other cases again newness is an essential part of the product, and if on a constant volume there is no style-change output must be held to decline. One thinks here of women's clothing and entertainment. In these cases physically similar goods should have a less than one-to-one substitution ratio as time passes, and new goods a one-to-one ratio in most cases.

(vi) All this applies inter-spatially as well as inter-temporally. A country where variety is large or there has been much innovation suffers in productivity comparisons and purchasing power parity calculations made on orthodox principles.

24. Such, then, are the general biasses. How do they affect comparisons between Communist and non-Communist? Contemptuous of consumer's sovereignty and mystically enamoured of mass production, Soviet-type economies undoubtedly allow much less product-differentiation and are very dilatory about introducing entirely new goods. As usual we have no figures whatsoever, not even much of an idea how one could compile figures, for the number of qualities or the extent of innovation. The basic thinking on this whole subject has simply not been done. We have merely a broad impression of monotony and standardization.

In inter-spatial comparisons then the result is clear. There is no (iv) in Soviet-type economies but also no (v), and quite generally too little variety. Therefore orthodox comparisons in terms of similar goods only crassly understate Western superiority in standard of living and productivity. So when we read that Soviet GNP per head is 40% of U.S. in 1959, we know this is a terrible exaggeration. But just how terrible? Should we say 35%? 30%? 25%? We do not know. So primitive as yet, and so unbalanced in its development, is economic science.

Inter-temporally we can be more definite and more interesting. In the period of Communization, e.g. 1928-31 in U.S.S.R., or 1949-50 in the European satellites, orthodox measurement greatly

---

[1] Compare my remarks on British and Swedish electric generators in *Oxford Economic Papers*, June 1951.

overstates the rate of growth. To reduce variety is to reduce output, and in our present ignorance we cannot be sure whether this does not altogether cancel the increase in physical volume of similar goods and services. In particular the liquidation of artisans is not merely a loss of physical volume but also of variety. For one's impression is that while an advanced manufacturing sector produces greater variety than artisans an immature one produces less.[1]

The 64-ruble question is as to the rate of innovation during the succeeding period of sustained Soviet-type growth. If this is notably lower than in the West the whole thesis of superior Communist growth is shaken.[2] Obviously at any moment there will be less variety than in the West, indeed less variety than in a less advanced economy such as the Japanese, which produces about as much physical volume per head. But our question is as to the rate of growth of variety. Here we can only admit we are entirely in the dark, thrown back on purely literary sources and impressionistic methods. The writer's own feeling is that, starting from so very small a base, Soviet-type variety grows at about the same rate as Western. But he might well err widely—in either direction.

25. We turn to *absolutely new goods*, for which old-good-equivalents cannot be found at all. These are those that bring a quite new satisfaction, 'adding', as the advertisements so elegantly phrase it, 'a new dimension to living'. These must indeed be simply 'chained in' at some price or other, in the absence of all quality linkage. But at what price? In the Soviet industrial index the notional 1926–27 prices were factor costs, which is clearly inappropriate, since a new good probably yields more utility per unit cost than an old one (it *might* not). Nor are market prices much better, as we saw in Sec. 21. It is evident that both values normally understate the utility of the completely new good.

We turn, then, to the agnostic's standby—it is better to guess a weight than to omit an item. A good lusty guess is the best answer I can suggest.[3]

---

[1] Much of an important nineteenth-century ideology—that of William Morris—was based on the fact that industrialization initially reduces variety; *pro tanto* it has been exploded by twentieth-century developments.

[2] This holds whether we use the normal or the 'Seton' technique of compiling indices (Sec. 5), since both are insensitive to variety and innovation.

[3] Note, incidentally, that when Soviet statisticians before the war gave grossly exaggerated weights to new goods, because they chained them in at inflated current prices, they did better than they knew. In a haphazard way they may have given a truer picture of the hedonic reality than by any orthodox procedure! But the same should have been done for all countries.

26. The labour of housewives presents problems only less grave than those hitherto discussed. We saw above (Sec. 22) that we must measure utility, not goods. Now a loaf of bread is an intermediate good: only slices of bread and butter on a plate provide utilities. Yet between the loaf and the plate how very much production remains to be done! The walk to the shop, the queue (in U.S.S.R.) at the counter, the second queue (long in U.S.A.,[1] very long in U.S.S.R.) at the cash desk, the walk back home, the cleaning of the breadknife, the wait (in U.S.S.R. at least) for the place in the shared kitchen, the actual cutting and buttering: it might amount to half a woman-hour in U.S.A. and two woman-hours in U.S.S.R. The 'hedonic revolution' cannot stop short of counting all this in. If shops become more frequent, if supermarkets post more accurate internal sign-posts, if cashiers become more competent, the efficiency of the housewife rises, or—it is the same thing—the hedonic cost of living falls. If consumers' durables are part of the national capital, unpaid domestic labour is part of the national labour, and in every country in the world the labour force, that gaseous body, is under-estimated.

This problem is more familiar than the others here dealt with. We need say no more in general than that such labour adds about equally, in normal cases, to national input and to national output. But with Communism in particular there is much more to say. With their anxiety for merely statistical success, their contempt for services and the family, their yen for investment and the equality, as they see it, of women, Communists take innumerable actions prejudicial to housewives. They give them fewer domestic tools, they cram them into far fewer shops, and they force them out into the labour market. The ex-housewife's new work is of course statistically recorded, but the services she has ceased to render, or now renders partially and inefficiently, never were. Suppose a town with 100 inhabitants of working age, and a 'town income', defined in a normal way, of £60 a day, produced by a 'labour force' of 60. The other 40 are engaged in unrecorded domestic and voluntary work at two-thirds of the productivity of the 'labour force', so that the true 'town income' is £86·7. The onset of Communism squeezes 20 women out of the home into the 'labour force'. Suppose further that, owing to their inefficiency in this new work, the housewives' productivity is now only one half of that of the normal

[1] I am thinking of supermarkets: a type of shop that might come off very ill in a proper hedonic calculation.

'labour force'; and that this is statistically recorded. So apparent normal 'town income' is now £70, and apparent labour inputs have risen 33%.

All that the naïf statistician sees is 'remarkable growth due to the mobilization of female labour'. Really, however, the housewives were rather more productive in their old 'jobs', and did as long a day's work as their husbands; and really, too, they react to their 'mobilization' by working longer hours in toto. They continue to perform half their old domestic tasks, and put in altogether $1\frac{1}{2}$ normal days' work per day. Then the true 'town income' has risen merely from £86·7 to £90, while the input of labour-hours has risen 10%. So trivial an increase in income is surely not worth the human frustration.

But all this is a transitional loss. Once the Communists have remade society, growth measurement no longer suffers from this distortion. Interspatial comparisons with non-Communist countries, however, continue to exaggerate the Communist position on this account.

CHAPTER 13

WHY THEY HAVE GROWN FASTER

'Give me good politics and I shall give you good economics.'—Talleyrand.

1. MUCH the most important feature of the Soviet economy, then, indeed one might almost say of the Soviet Union at all, is its extremely rapid rate of growth. Industrial production rises very approximately by 10% per annum (latterly by 7%), and the real national income per head as a whole by approximately 5%. It is, of course, agriculture and the service trades that bring down the average so much. But this average, which has been held *without interruption* (except by German occupation) since 1932,[1] has seldom been attained at all by the average capitalist state, at any stage of its maturity. A growth of real national income per head of 5% per annum over a substantial period was until recently quite without parallel in the world's economic history. Moreover, all other Soviet-type economies show about the same rate of growth, except China since her agricultural catastrophe began in 1959. Many questions pose themselves: can the achievement be explained away as teaching no important lessons, about institutions or policy, to the free world; how is it achieved; and can it go on?

In Sec. 2 we baldly enumerate many suggested reasons. Note that we do so not in terms of the abstract institutional and allocational models previously set out, nor in abstraction from the political and ideological environment; but historically, in view of what has actually happened and is continuing to happen.

2. A wholly unprecedented rate of economic growth is achieved because:

(a) The whole of society is dedicated to just this end. 'Communism', its ultimate goal, is principally an economic concept, and it means a state of such plenty that everyone can—literally—have as much as he wants (Chs. 17–20). The Soviet Union achieves economic growth as Medieval Europe achieved Christianity.

[1] I choose this date, rather than the customary 1928, because I am firmly convinced that orthodox measurement procedures are helpless against the various subtle diminutions of 'production' or 'welfare' brought about by the initial Communization of an economy, listed in the previous chapter.

Both societies have their creed, their priesthood and their inquisition; for attendance at Mass we must now substitute plan fulfilment and for the City of God 'Full Communism'. We must also postulate a much higher degree of administrative efficiency, totalitarianism and cruelty. Leisure, tolerance, scepticism, amusement, humanity, present comfort—none of these things is permitted to stand in the way of economic growth. The 'Capitalolatry' of Ch. 3, Sec. 3f should also be borne in mind.

(b) It follows that the government is more continuously interested in the tiniest details of economic efficiency than any other government. Take almost any speech of Khrushchev: the bad accounting practices of, for example, such-and-such a kolkhoz, the waste of metal in factory A, the intolerable localism of Sovnarkhoz B, more maize, more chemicals, more this, more that—in what non-Communist country, even if totalitarian, could the Prime Minister make even one such speech? Let the reader exercise his imagination: Mr. Macmillan is addressing the assembled workers at Dagenham; he passes the world situation briefly in review, and after a few words on the government's Grow More Potatoes Campaign, presently stealing the headlines in the daily press, he gets down to brass tacks. The automation of engine assembly, the new sand they are putting in the moulds in the foundry, Brother X, the shop-steward who started the last unofficial strike, the standardization of windscreen-wipers—they are all there, he has been well briefed. Exhortation follows criticism, and the peroration, reminding the audience that they have never had it so good, concludes with a repetition of the Party's pledge to double the standard of living in twenty-five years. He is warmly applauded, and next day *The Times* carries it verbatim. *Moreover, windscreen-wipers are instantly standardized, and there is not another unofficial strike for twelve months.*

Enough, I think, has been said to show that non-Communist governments have an infinitely more complacent view of their economic functions. Soviet planning means tightening things up. The Soviet power is not a 'Government', standing at arm's length from the nation's economy; it is the entrepreneur himself. Khrushchev is not only Party Secretary and Prime Minister; he is also the Managing Director—and shop-steward—of every enterprise in the country.

(c) And when the master's eye is turned there is the permanent double-bass of 'Socialist Morality' to keep everyone in line. Enterprises must help each other to advance the plan: as Mr. Volin puts it in the party journal:[1]

> More than that: certain economists try to deny that the definition of socialist productive relations as relations of collective co-operation and mutual help has any scientific significance. Thus Dr. Econ. Ya. A. Kronrod asserts that this definition makes no attempt at scientific accuracy, that it is not more than 'a metaphor used for propaganda purposes, directed to people's feelings'.... Looking at socialist productive relations as they really are, it is impossible not to observe that their main economic content, immediately flowing from the rule of common ownership of the means of production, consists in collectivism, co-operation and comradely mutual help.

The author proceeds to slate by name a number of enterprises that have violated this principle.

If it is naïf to take this kind of talk at its face value, it is a quite false sophistication to deny it any practical influence.

(d) Then the volume of saving is much higher than in free economies. In theoretically possible conditions this would be an immense advantage, but as things are we have to take away defence expenditures. It has always appeared to the writer plainly absurd to treat any form of defence expenditure as consumption. Indeed only in a very qualified sense is any defence expenditure investment either: we can only say that some defence research and defence installations have joint civilian products which fall under the heading of investment. Defence is defence, a third category.[2] Saving = investment plus defence, and if it is an advantage of the Soviet system that the population can be forced to abstain, this advantage can as easily express itself in defence as in net investment expenditures. The margin is indeed so great that even if the armament effort is greater than in a free economy there is room also for a greater investment effort. Moreover, since the national income per head is lower than in the advanced free countries it is all the more remarkable that a higher proportion of it is saved; it is as if a poor man paid more income-tax than a rich.

(e) Given an equal volume of investment in a Communist and a non-Communist country, much more funds are directed towards

---

[1] 'Co-operation and Mutual Help are the Basis of Socialist Relations Between Enterprises', *Kommunist*, 3/1959.

[2] Some Soviet economists now make this distinction, with an 'accumulation fund', a 'consumption' (potreblenie) fund and an 'annihilation' (iztreblenie) fund. Cf. Li Hui-hung, as quoted in Ch. 14, Sec. 10.

uses that promote further economic growth. We discuss in Chs. 14–16 the limitations on this policy as a growth-promoter. They are in fact so severe as to cast doubt on this item's importance altogether.

(f) The effect of the abrogation of consumer's sovereignty upon growth also falls to be discussed separately (Ch. 11).

(g) Another brake upon the expansion of a free economy is uncertainty as to the future: the risk that there will be no market owing to general depression, or that a little more output will easily saturate the present market since demand is inelastic. The risky thing to do in the Soviet Union is to disobey the plan; the market is not the enterprise's responsibility. In other words it is risky *not* to expand. Economic uncertainty gives way to political. In the Soviet Union there are no depressions nor any trade cycle,[1] and the individual market cannot normally be saturated in circumstances which would affect the manager's livelihood. For in the immediate future demand is always perfectly elastic, the price being set in the plan, and more remotely if consumer resistance does set in the government takes the rap for any unsold surplus. Meanwhile the manager continues to receive commendation and bonuses, not for profitability, but for fulfilling the plan, even if it calls for goods that are not wanted. To this, however, there have recently begun to be exceptions. A recent traveller reports (1960) that a television factory has been for some time on a three-day week. As we have seen, the consumer is at least to this extent sovereign, that he can refuse to buy what is produced, even if the Ministry of Finance is prepared to lower the turnover tax; and since in such cases goods are not stockpiled indefinitely a highly specific factory may well have to face short time until its equipment is adapted to something different.

(h) Then there is the absence of patents and commercial secrets. In principle an invention becomes the common property of all managers or enterprises interested in it. This is clearly far more effective than our own system for spreading the knowledge of techniques, so long as there is some financial stimulus to invention. Such a stimulus exists. Large prizes are given, tax-free, to inventors, and to the enterprise where the inventions have been made. In principle, then, there are no patents; in practice, if thanks to a more

---

[1] Assertions to the contrary are occasionally made; I can see no evidence for them of any kind. There are from time to time, to be sure, politically motivated decelerations of growth, but they are in no sense cyclical, and have no effect on the above argument.

advanced technique one can over-fulfil the plan with unexpected ease, it is most profitable to keep this discovery secret, not merely from other enterprises, but from the planners. Indeed, once the latter get to know of an invention, they insist on a tougher plan assignment. However, they usually do get to know—they have their spies—and the absence of patents is undoubtedly important.[1]

(i) Another factor favourable to growth, it might be argued, is the absence of any restrictive policies by managers. Monopolies and cartels are forbidden; setting them up is regarded as sabotage. Natural and everyday practices in the Western economies, openly discussed in specialized trade journals, are considered sabotage in the U.S.S.R. and punished accordingly. Now in the very tight and terroristic economic system of China innovation is positively demanded of everybody, and it is dangerous not to try out suggestions. So the foregoing may be the last word on this subject in China, but in more liberal places like U.S.S.R. there are very strong counter-forces. For the Communist command economy induces an all-pervading *fear of responsibility*, as readers of V. Dudintsev's *Not By Bread Alone* will know. This militates, not against inventions, but against their practical application at all levels of the hierarchy, from Minister to director. It is thus far from clear that capitalism is inferior to Communism when it comes to trying things out.

(j) Equally important was Stalin's emasculation of the trade unions, which I consider to be a necessary condition of economic growth in any economy. In fact, trade unions can have, on growth, nothing but a retarding influence. Their wage claims reduce the profits out of which progress must be financed, and—worse still— they actually oppose technical improvements in the name of job stability. True, unions exercise in free economies an upward pressure on costs which stimulates technical progress; and certainly if like *some* American unions they did nothing but ask for higher wages it would not be too bad. But this pressure could more suitably be generated by taxes or by the competition of other firms. And the point has in any case no validity for a Soviet-type economy,

---

[1] There does however still exist on the statute book an ancient law enabling a foreigner, or even a Soviet citizen, to take out a normal capitalist patent. Foreigners do in fact use it. That it continues formally to be available to Soviet citizens merely expresses the fact that when Stalin wound up the NEP he did it by informal violence alone, never legalizing his actions or repealing the old laws. For the same reason the Charter of a Soviet enterprise dates from June 1927 (Volin, *Kommunist*, 3/1959), and the labour code from 1922.

S

in which there are plenty of other stimuli to technical progress, and profits, large or small, are not among them.

(k) The stick behind is sharp and heavy by any standards, while ahead looms the carrot, gloriously succulent at least by comparison with the Soviet average. Labour discipline is very severe indeed, and the penalties for defaulting managers and collective farm chairmen even more so. Income-tax is low, and, rising to a maximum marginal rate of merely 13%, falls hardly more heavily on promotion or overtime than on present or basic earnings. Indeed owing to the low personal allowances it hits the poor rather hard.[1] Similarly indirect taxes are no heavier on luxuries than on necessities. The earnings structure—though not, if we include unearned income, the income structure—is much more unequal than elsewhere.[2] Nor are the social services offered indifferently to all. The high pensions and the sanatoria are for the strong, the hard-working and the loyal. Underneath there are no everlasting arms to sustain the inefficient, the idle or the a-political. Normal pensions are pitifully low. In the 'forties and early 'fifties war-wounded veterans commonly begged in the streets, and there is no catchall Poor Law or National Assistance Board for those who inevitably fall through the meshes of the regular social services, however well designed.

(l) Vested interests of all kinds get very short shrift, whether they be of localities or old-established enterprises in their special products, or of producers in their methods of organization and work, or of any group or individuals in its status or income. With the large-scale aspects of this phenomenon we deal below in Sec. 3. But it has also important consequences for individuals, consequences indeed so important that for the man in the street, uninterested in intellectual freedom, they are perhaps the essential difference between life in a Communist and in a non-Communist society. The *quality of daily economic life* is quite different.

For the citizen's object is to protect himself, and the authorities' object is to winkle him out again, as one extracts a lobster from a crack in the rock. *Their* weapons are mutual supervision, 'criticism and self-criticism' meetings, frequent personal transfers and frequent external audits by numerous independent bodies (the Ministry or Sovnarkhoz, the Ministry of Finance, the banks, the Party, the

---

[1] But it will shortly (1961) be abolished.

[2] Until the late 'fifties, when the earnings structure was again equalized. It is my general impression that it was always pretty equal in other Communist countries.

security police, the Ministry—now Committee—of State Control, *ad hoc* commissions, etc., etc.). *His* weapons are nepotism and mutual insurance (*krugovaya poruka*), which blunt the system of cross-checks and mutual supervision; illicit influence and black marketeering (*blat'*), whereby he induces the planners to reduce their targets to reasonable dimensions, or customers to turn a blind eye; and straight falsification of the books (*tufta*). If he is a worker, not an accountant or manager, he faces the same problems: his norm takes the place of the enterprise plan, and the staff of the enterprise that of the various external bodies, and the weapons in his hand are the same.

(m) Rationalization, specialization and standardization can all be easily enforced, since the parochialisms and vested interests of severally owned and severally managed concerns are not there to obstruct them. This is a short and easy point to make, but the economic advantage it connotes is immense. A good example is that U.S.S.R. was the first country to mass produce machine tools.[1]

(n) Investment has been hitherto concentrated on industry, the sector of increasing returns, rather than on agriculture (decreasing returns) or domestic construction (constant returns). So long as we stick to the base-year weights industry is the line of least resistance, the field of the easy statistical triumph. We have already discussed in Ch. 12 the relevance of this for measurement theory, and the sense in which such an investment pattern increases growth at all. We see also in Sec. 6. below how much truth there is in the accusation that agriculture has been starved of capital.

(o) Then there is the plan itself. We have seen that the state is not troubled with delicate adjustments of quantity, quality and timing. Its planning has a much simpler end in view: to order the producer to produce more than he did last time. *Soviet planning is chiefly a system whereby each individual and organization is permanently under a quasi-legal obligation to increase output.* The object of planning is simply more and cheaper and better, never mind of what. This quasi-legal obligation is clearly more effective than the stimulus of profit. For it is sometimes profitable to restrict, and leisure is often more attractive anyway. Soviet planning is a sort of nationalized standard costing: a continuous comparison by a ruthless police state of actual performance with standard set. It is as if every cost accountant were as powerful and demanding as the Lord himself, in the parable of the talents.

[1] Melman, *New York Times*, Oct. 26, 1959, p. 1. But cf. Florinsky, ibid. Nov. 26, 1959, p. 28.

The matter deserves an excursus. Prof. Holland Hunter[1] calls this state of affairs 'tautness' or 'tension'; we may also call it 'planner's excess demand' as opposed to monetary excess demand, discussed below. Just as the latter can be counter-productive if too great, so can 'tension'. Notoriously in a free economy mild excess demand establishes investment confidence, raises profits, encourages research, etc.; possibly even in the long run establishes union confidence to the point that restrictive practices are relaxed. But 'excessive excess demand' diminishes competition too far, induces complacency, and gives rise to crippling bottlenecks. So also does great tension give rise to crippling bottlenecks and hugely increase administrative expenses, as procurement agencies send despatchers, chasers, reminders, etc., after each other. Thus every increase in tension diminishes plan fulfilment, but beyond a certain point it ceases to raise, even depresses, output. The target goes on rising, but the achievement (which was always smaller) actually falls. In Poland, says Prof. Hunter, all this is recognized, but the whole subject is taboo in U.S.S.R.[2]

Mr. Herbert Levine[3] points out that the very way in which the planners adjust their material balances, heightens tension. The balance of material X shows it to be in short supply; no simultaneous equations are, of course, used to see what would be the total effect of increasing the supply of X and the consequential effects on Y, Z etc., of increasing the inputs into the X industry. On the contrary the tendency is to demand that the X industry 'mobilize its inner reserves', i.e. heighten its output/input ratio. A few 'iterative' steps may be undertaken: say as far as determining what major inputs into X itself must go up—but no serious and complete estimate is made of the total effect, and so 'tension' increases directly, if not in X then in its immediate suppliers.

Note that 'tension' is a product of command planning, whether in physical or monetary terms. Merely regulative planning (cf. Ch. 1), making this or that more profitable, would not have this effect. 'Tension', again, is not caused by high rates of investment or any other growth-promoting factor; but by specific planning habits

---

[1] In *Economic Development and Cultural Change*, Chicago, July 1961. Cf. also A. G. Frank in *Human Organization*, Vol. 17, no. 4.

[2] Compare, however, the brief reference in A. N. Yefimov, *Perestroika Upravlenia Promyshlennostyui Stroitel'stvom v S.S.S.R.*, Moscow 1957, p. 107; and the report of the December 1956 Plenum of the Central Committee, *Pravda*, Dec. 25, 1956.

[3] Source as in Ch. 9, Sec. 1, p. 166.

and a specific political psychology. There could quite easily be central planning and rapid growth without it.

'Tension' can also be very simply produced by large plan over-fulfilment bonuses. With or without a taut plan, the manager will certainly make everything taut if his livelihood depends on it, and over-fulfilment is held to be a virtue and rewarded. This reward is of course independent of anybody's success in actually marketing the extra output. Note in this connexion that a loose plan is rather inflationary in the usual monetary sense, since over-fulfilment will be easier and bonuses higher; and tension is defla-tionary in so far as it lowers money bonuses. So managers have every interest in high bonuses for over-fulfilment coupled with low tension; and one may well imagine the degree of social discipline, fanaticism or terror required to produce tension in face of such a steady pressure. The lowering of tension is a characteristic policy of right-wing Communists.

(p) *Inflation* has long existed but is not an important stimulus to growth. In a free economy where production is for money profit excess demand is undoubtedly a chief cause of growth, so long as the consequent rise in prices does not get so far out of hand as to cause hoarding of materials or a breakdown of foreign trade.

But outside retail distribution and agriculture Soviet money is a mere accounting device, and for excess demand we must substitute the urge for plan over-fulfilment. Nevertheless excess demand does play its part: in making it easier to plan the production of food and manufactured consumption goods, and in reducing the efficacy of consumers' sovereignty with its obstructive effect shown above. Note that the price reductions since 1948, being purely administra-tive and in no way due to competition or falling purchasing power, are entirely compatible with continued excess demand; so that in a planned economy inflation may accompany *falling* prices.

The principal protagonist of excess demand in U.S.S.R. seems to have been A. I. Mikoyan.[1] As the man chiefly responsible for trade he would naturally recognize its stimulating effect, since it is on the trade organs that rests the burden of selling the shoddy qualities

---

[1] Cf. *Pravda*, February 18, 1956; but there are many similar passages in the speeches of Mikoyan and his subordinates, reaching right back into Stalin's lifetime. When I was in Poland in summer 1956 the desirability of excess demand was known as 'the Mikoyan doctrine'. The doctrine is strongly attacked by Chernyak and Stanislavsky in, of all places, *Partiinaya Zhizn'* (Party Life) 12/1956. Evidently it was at this time being debated on a very high level, perhaps in connexion with the annual retail price reductions. These undoubtedly caused grave inconvenience through excess demand. The grossest case was that of potatoes in 1954. Since 1954 there have been no annual price reductions.

and arbitrary quantities that the production plan provides. It is only in extreme cases—e.g. the television factory above—that lack of consumer demand actually results in short-time working; but it hits the trade organs daily.

(q) Then *when there is a balance of payments crisis, a command economy is not compelled to correct it by measures which diminish the rate of growth*, since foreign trade is a state monopoly. Again inflation at home—of which as we have seen there is plenty—obviously need have no untoward foreign effect; the crisis will normally arise through incorrect physical planning, e.g. a failure to allocate sufficient materials to exporting enterprises, or an incorrect prediction of the terms of trade obtainable. Just as in any other economy, the balance of payments crisis means that the nation is living beyond its means; it must either consume less or invest less or both. But there is in this case no technical reason why the whole burden should not be thrown on the consumer: i.e. why domestic investment should not be kept precisely at its previous height and more savings be simply forced out of the population. This is not, of course, to deny that the unavailability on foreign markets of particular goods may impose an input/output type of restraint on particular kinds of investment.

In a market economy on the other hand the solution to a balance of payments crisis is much more complex, since we can now no longer assume Say's law, and we must further reckon with monetary policy. First, the solution of the command economy *can* be adopted: reduce consumption by fiscal means. True, the means are slightly different: in a market economy we raise taxes, in a Communist command economy we can either do that or get the trade unions 'voluntarily' to raise the labour norms. We may speak, then, of a substitution of wage policy for fiscal policy under Communism, both having broadly the same effect. But this difference is trivial beside the indirect effect in a market economy of a fall in consumption upon investment. We may start with the will to repair our international position solely by cutting consumption, but we end up with an induced fall in investment, which no mere monetary policy can correct. One of the principal advantages of a command economy is that it can, of course, command the volume of investment.

But, secondly, it is commoner in a market economy to use monetary policy. This directly cuts at investment, since it is not to consumers that banks make advances. And here again the command economy, at least in its Communist version, comes off better. For monetary policy is very little used, and when it is it must, in the absence of a perfect open market for securities, consist in highly 'qualitative' banking controls. Space has precluded us from saying anything about Soviet-type banking in this book. It is enough here to know that the bank's principal role is to lend short, not long. Long-term capital comes from the budget, and is a matter for fiscal policy. Monetary policy controls only the current operations of existing enterprises. A cut in consumption *could* be brought about simply by cutting short credit to the producers of consumption goods. This would, if not backed up by fiscal or wage policy, of course generate further excess demand. But it would also lower imports, according to the import component in consumption goods. Clearly the very structure of Soviet-type banking impels it to precisely that kind of qualitative control best suited to curing a balance of payments deficit without touching investment.

(r) Naturally *the bank has no independence*: it does what the planners tell it to do. And this, too, if one may speak as a psychologist, makes for growth. Continuous responsibility for the money supply brings with it the banker's notorious *déformation professionnelle*: a fondness for deflation, liquidity and restricted growth. During the NEP, when the Gosbank had some influence, it proved itself no exception to this rule. Recent history, the world over, shows that the influence of bankers[1] is inversely correlated with economic growth.

(s) In a more general way *the existence of an authority able to control the rate of growth* raises the rate of growth. In a market economy, how would a citizen proceed, who wished to promote his country's economic progress? If he saved more he would probably be caught by the paradox of thrift, and succeed only in depressing investment (and, *ex post*, the saving of others). If he saved less, thus promoting the national income and investment, he personally would not share in the capital gains brought about by growth. In a command economy *ex ante* investment invariably exceeds *ex ante* saving (unless the authorities are out of their senses), so that the paradox of thrift is inoperative. By saving more the private citizen adds to his own accumulation and at the same time eases the authorities' task. Thus with an adequate central authority the paradox of thrift disappears.

---

[1] Strictly, of central bankers, and of large and 'responsible' commercial bankers. In the remoter past of today's great capitalist nations the pre-managerial unit bank was of quite another colour, and so is 'native' banking in Africa today.

Nor is this the only advantage of a central authority. For the accidents of history are constantly creating obstacles of all kinds to growth: depressed areas, bad harvests, physical bottlenecks, bad social practices, etc., etc. The market corrects these but slowly, while authority, if motivated to do so, does it quickly.

3. Now let us see if we can explain all this away. Have the developed and underdeveloped countries of the free world perhaps nothing to learn from this achievement? Can comfort of some kind be given to social democrats, *laissez faire* capitalists, Ghandiites, or indeed quite simply to democrats?

To start with, perhaps the whole trick could have been performed in a democracy? This is obviously false. Points (h), (i), (j), (l) and (o) clearly demand not just any legally empowered authority but precisely a political dictatorship. Think, for instance, of the protests that MTS workers would have made in a parliamentary democracy when their enterprises were liquidated (1958), and they themselves changed into inferior beings—mere kolkhozniki. Assuredly they would have had their own protection league, a fighting fund, some lobbyists in Moscow, some pocket M.P.s. They would have bought full-page advertisements in *Pravda*, and staged a demonstration in the Red Square. Above all, they would have struck. The liquidation of the MTS was a major social upheaval, and it would have taken a decade of serious in-fighting in a parliamentary democracy. Or when in the early 'thirties central Asian agriculture was made to abandon its traditional food-crops for cotton; here too was major upheaval, that could not easily have been brought about in a free society. Examples could be multiplied in other fields: e.g. the sudden and silent liquidation of urban co-operative shops in 1948. These decisions were not necessarily good: indeed it was precisely Stalin's folly to create the MTS in the first place. The point is that it *is* good to be able to enforce large and unpopular decisions, if economic growth is your sole end.

Some, especially those who wish to deny any superiority in Soviet institutions and seek solely a technical economic explanation, like to attribute all the increased growth to the greater volume of investment. It would be difficult actually to prove them wrong: one cause out of many alleged ones may be overwhelmingly the most important, indeed some of the others may have been mis-interpreted and have in fact a negative effect. And undeniably the simple overall volume of investment is very important.

Owing to the recent researches of Prof. A. Bergson[1] it is possible to give some kind of an estimate of this importance. It is exceedingly difficult to say for how much growth investment in particular is responsible, for that means to measure its marginal productivity, and plunges us into all the uncertainties of the Cobb-Douglas function. But one can compute the mere quantitative increase in labour, land and capital inputs taken together, and leave a '*residual*': the difference between the growth of the input index thus defined and the growth of the output index.

How reliable a measure is this residual of technical progress? It depends on what other things are left in it. Possible extraneous elements are:

(i) changes in hours of work may not have been counted in the labour input series. Bergson has, of course, not made this error. But it is still worth mentioning in view of the enormous and irregular fluctuations of Communist work-hours. For instance in China in 1958 they nearly doubled!

(ii) the stock of education is part of the national capital, and should count in the capital input series. Bergson consciously, but unfortunately, omits it. Its inclusion would lower the rate of growth of the Soviet capital stock and raise that of the U.S.[2]

(iii) we may well wish to refuse the name of technical progress to the transfer of the Malthusian surplus in agriculture to some urban occupation. For clearly the technique in that urban occupation may be as old as the hills, but there will still be an addition to output. Yet an input index will register equally the useless hours put in on the farm and the useful hours that take their place. For this item I make no correction; it is in any case negligible after the war.

---

[1] RAND Paper P-2148 of Nov. 29, 1960.

[2] T. W. Schulz, in his Ch. 3 of the 60*th Yearbook of the National Society for the Study of Education* (Chicago 1961), defines the stock of educational capital as the replacement cost of the years of formal education received by the labour force. This cost includes a very large item for subsistence while being educated. Thus defined, U.S. educational capital moved from 22% of other capital in 1900 to 42% in 1957. The definition is controversial, but clearly on any other definition educational would have still grown faster than other capital. In U.S.S.R. on the other hand a rough calculation shows that it fell behind. Thus the numbers of middle- and higher-educated people respectively in civilian work were ('000): 288 and 233 in Jan. 1928, 1492 and 908 in Jan. 1941, 2949 and 2184 in July 1955, 4781 and 3236 in Dec. 1959 (N. de Witt, *Education and Professional Employment in the U.S.S.R.*, National Science Foundation, 1961, p. 781). Giving higher education a double weight, we find that the pre-war rate of growth is 11·4%, but we should surely reduce this to 10% for the striking fall in quality that then took place. The post-war rate is 8·7%. The less well educated part of the labour force grew, of course, at a far lower rate: indeed between 1939 and 1959 it actually shrank (*Vestnik Statistiki*, 12/1960). Consequently the total stock of educational capital grew at less than 10% p.a. But other (fixed) capital grew at about 11% in both periods (Bergson, op. cit., p. 28).

These seem to be the main qualifications to the use of the 'residual' as a measure of technical progress. Bergson puts the residual as follows (% p.a.):

(a)	U.S.S.R.	1928–40, weights of 1937	0·1—0·5
(b)	„	„ „ weights of 1937 for inputs and given-year weights for outputs	4·9—5·3
(c)	„	1950–58, either of above weighting systems .	2·9—4·3
(d)	U.S.A.	various weights 1869/78—1899/1908 . .	1·5
(e)	„	„ „ 1899/1908—1929 . .	1·8
(f)	„	„ „ 1929–48	2·1
(g)	„	„ „ 1948–57	1·8

Only between (a) and (b) does the choice of weights really matter. (a) uses Paasche for output in the crucial years 1928–37, (b) Laspeyres. On the extreme differences that these two weighting systems can produce, see Ch. 12, Sec. 11. It is tempting to try to explain either result separately, wise to refrain from comment. The geometric mean of (a) and (b) is 2·5, but this again is a dangerous figure. It is more to our purpose to note that the 'residual' is higher in (c) than in (d), (e), (f) or (g). Moreover, when we look back to our major qualifications to the validity of the concept, we find that (i) is fully allowed for, (ii) serves but to widen the gap, and (iii) is irrelevant. Therefore the Soviet 'residual' exceeds the American, even in technologically comparable periods, and greater investment cannot alone explain the superior Soviet rate of growth.[1]

But the investment effort is very great. E.g. in 1937 net investment was c. 24% of net national income at ruble prices without indirect taxes and subsidies, and it seems to have been about that percentage in other peace-time years.[2] Only Norway and Australia[3] rival that, but if we include Soviet defence expenditures, running at 8–11%, we get a much higher general rate of *saving*.

Certainly this high general rate of saving is a most important element in the superiority of Soviet growth. Yet alas it is of its nature totalitarian to some extent, and it is important to see exactly why. It is not so much that a population might not democratically be brought to vote for a high investment policy, though there are difficulties there too. It is that at one time or another every citizen who so voted would nevertheless be tempted to tax evasion. The taxes would be extremely high, of course, and would necessarily hit the poorest and the most disaffected citizens along

[1] The matter is further alluded to in Ch. 20, Sec. 7.
[2] A. Bergson, *The Real National Income of Soviet Russia*, Harvard, 1961, pp. 144–5, 149.
[3] With rather larger *gross* percentages (C. Clark, *Growthmanship*, London 1962, p. 47).

with the rest. Extremely draconian measures would be required to maintain tax discipline, without which resources would be diverted into consumption. Thus in U.S.S.R. it is forbidden to criticize, forbidden even to state, the general level of the turnover tax, or indeed to criticize the general level of the budget or of investment, even in the technical press; and the police have of course unlimited powers of search for bootleg materials. It is an interesting question, into which we cannot enter here, whether a non-Communist and merely authoritarian régime could maintain a Communist rate of saving by such purely economic-police methods without being sucked into the vortex of general totalitarianism, with a single party, a single ideology and all the rest of it. Personally I am optimistic, but I am bound to admit it has never been tried.

Clearly, then, totalitarianism correctly applied is a stimulus to growth. Even if we wish to deny that Communist economic policy or institutions are better in any more sophisticated way, and attribute all the growth superiority to a greater capacity to save, that is itself an institutional advantage. We should need to change our institutions to save that much.

4. But perhaps they had unusual advantages of a clearly irrelevant sort? For Communist countries generally there have been at least two: technical immaturity, and surplus population.

The advantages for growth of technical immaturity are obvious and great. But many economies were technically immature in 1928, and only one grew so fast. Or again in 1815 the U.S., French and Belgian economies, and in 1870 the Swedish and Japanese economies, were in the same happy plight: they were technically immature and could imitate others. None of them grew so fast. Moreover, today S.E. Asian and Latin American economies are technically as immature as the Chinese and S.E. European. This consolation is therefore quite worthless.

The same arguments rule surplus population utterly out of court. That country is most efficient that actually puts its surplus to work. Moreover, it is incorrect to deny that France or Britain ever had this advantage. For until 1919 Britain included Ireland, and in this context it still does. Britain and Ireland remain one labour market, and there has never been any restriction on Irish immigration, nor much popular resistance to it. It is entirely fair to point out that Britain was much slower than U.S.S.R. in putting 'her' surplus population to work. Similarly France has not begun to exhaust the Algerian labour reserves, though since 1945, 'L'Algérie c'est la France'.

The last of the arguments from adventitious factors concerns U.S.S.R. alone: the relative bounty of nature in that country. Natural endowments are very difficult to measure. The best authority[1] doubts whether U.S.S.R. is so very well endowed, especially in comparison with U.S.A.; Stalinist boosting must be discounted. But in any case it is criminally parochial to stick always to the U.S.-Soviet comparison: what of, say, China and Argentina? Poland and France?

In any case to the arguments from adventitious advantage must be in fairness opposed those from adventitious disadvantage. Stalin's Great Purge (1937–8), which reduced the economy to stagnation, was clearly a product of his own personality: if the Communist political system offers no defence against such a personality, also Stalins are exceedingly rare. If collectivization always incites the peasants to slaughter their livestock, the slaughter has never been so catastrophic as in the Soviet case: which was another product of Stalin's personality. Or take foreign policy. It is no fault of the Communist economic set-up that its magnificent power to generate savings is so commonly wasted on defence. The huge defence burdens of these countries, successfully borne in addition to rapid growth, speak volumes for their efficiency. Nor do they receive foreign aid on any scale.[2] On the contrary, the foreign aid rendered by E. Germany, amounting at the peak of reparations to a fantastic 23% of GNP at market prices, is plainly the first consideration in comparing that country's performance with its western neighbour's. Since the reparations ceased, Ulbricht has presided over a more dynamic economy than Adenauer.[3]

5. Or perhaps instead of explaining Communist growth away we can deny it? One way is to point to the irrationality of Communist prices. With this we have dealt at length in Ch. 12. Drawing upon those results we can say that irrationality convicts normal procedures of uncertainty, not exaggeration; that there are always foreign prices as a last resort; that Soviet-type retail

[1] D. B. Shimkin, *Minerals, A Key to Soviet Power*, Harvard 1953, Ch. 9, esp. p. 342.

[2] The only exception is U.S.S.R., 1945–50, when German and other reparations were about 2% of the GNP at market prices (Bergson, op. cit., pp. 48, 100). But 1950 is during the post-war reconstruction period, so that growth during that year is not normally included as evidence of Soviet efficiency.

[3] W. Stolper, *The Structure of the East German Economy*, Harvard, 1960; P. Wiles, *Social Research*, Autumn 1961.

prices (in allocation model 4) are fairly rational weights for the irrational outputs provided; *and that there are many periods in which the rationality of Communist outputs is increasing, so that normal procedures understate it.* The bare assertion, 'prices are irrational, therefore growth is exaggerated', is unworthy of a scholar.

Then there is a more empirical and *ad hoc* way of denying the *Soviet* rate of growth. Since it has application only to U.S.S.R. it cannot be, as it so often is, taken to deny extraordinary growth under Communism as such, even if it was correct. This is to choose dates which span some major war or other catastrophe unconnected with the efficiency of the economy. Such are the accidents of history that growth rates as low as 3% p.a. can be achieved between carefully chosen dates. Of such a procedure it can only be said that it is self-evidently dishonest. Two justifications can, it is true, be urged: that after a very destructive war there comes a period of easy and therefore rapid reconstruction; moreover, the 'advantage' of immaturity is prolonged by the absence of technical progress during the war. The first point is easily met, and in all serious comparisons known to the author has been met, simply by choosing as a base date after the war a year sufficiently removed from it in time. As to the second, it is entirely correct that the maturity of the United States economy increased in the period 1940–50 while that of the Soviet economy did not. So we are simply thrown back upon the comparison of Soviet performance with American in periods of similar maturity—a point already dealt with, and one which yields no consolation.

6. Finally Communist economic growth is not due to a special pattern of investment, but only to a great volume of it. The pattern of Communist investment is on the contrary in many ways irrational and growth-retarding. This we show in general in discussing investment criteria (Ch. 16). But it is also in particular not true that agriculture, the sector of diminishing returns, has been starved of capital for the sake of easy statistical victories elsewhere.

This common fallacy also deserves an excursus. The statistical yearbooks show that on the contrary inputs of capital and artificial fertilizers into agriculture increased by leaps and bounds. Moreover, both the official figures and Kaplan's calculations put investment in agriculture at 18–20% of all investment under Stalin,[1]

[1] N. Kaplan in (ed.) A. Bergson, *Soviet Economic Growth*, pp. 52–8; *N.Kh.* 1956, p. 158; *Dostizhenia za 40 Let*, p. 208.

during the whole period of his rule. That this is not an utterl\
generous allotment may be best seen from the Canadian example.
Canada was also an industrializing country with a large agriculture
in 1926–55. Of all countries she most resembles U.S.S.R. in natural
resources and climate, though of course her agriculture has always
been more capital-intensive and never remotely suffered from over-
population. It will be seen that Stalin allotted a constant proportion
of a rapidly growing investment volume to agriculture, whereas
in Canada it has received a declining proportion of a slowly growing
volume.

		% in agriculture	
	Civilian employed labour force	Gross invest- ment (excl. houses)	Gross domestic product
Canada 1926–30	33	16	23
Canada 1951–55	17	15	14
U.S.S.R. 1937	55	21	30

Sources: Royal Commission on Canada's Economic Prospects, *Output, Labour and Capital in the Canadian Economy*, pp. 310, 409, 424; Kaplan, op. cit.; A. Bergson, *Soviet National Income and Product in 1937*, Columbia U.P. 1953, p. 98. *Narodnoe Khozyaistvo* 1956, p. 187 (deducting 1% for forestry). Even excluding forestry and houses, the Soviet concept is probably broader.

It was not of capital but of consumption that Stalin starved his
peasantry. One of the main aims of the kolkhoz was to ensure a
large ploughback out of peasant incomes.

7. Since this book was begun, however, there has been a new
development this side of the Iron Curtain, which may if it persists
and spreads destroy the whole thesis that command economies are
best for growth. United Nations statistics show the following
recent percentage rates per annum for the most rapidly growing
non-Soviet-type economies:

Yugoslavia   1952/3—1958/9 (real GNP per head of population) 8·0
Japan   1952–9   („   „   „   „   ) 7·0
W. Germany   1951–9   („   „   „   „   ) 6·0
Greece   1951–8   („   „   „   working age) 6·0
Spain   1950–7   („   „   „   „   ) 5·2
Italy   1951–8   („   „   „   population) 5·0

These are longish periods and highly respectable rates. As this
goes to print questions are left unanswered. Is it an accident that
the market economy which retains Communist social discipline

tops the list, thus showing itself a world-beater?[1] Are these rates really maintainable in the way that Soviet-type rates clearly are? *What* precise traits of policy or accidents of circumstance distinguish these countries from their more stagnant neighbours? Can they be imitated?

Thus the facts of Soviet-type growth remain indisputable, and impossible to explain away. But the exact explanation of them is still highly disputable. Furthermore, our reasoning has been only historical: in the longest of long runs this growth may come to exceed Western growth only in so far as research is superior, as we try to show in Ch. 20. Moreover Communism has yet to solve the twin problems of Malthusian population and agricultural incentives. In China this failure has led (1962) to hunger and to stagnation even in industry. It may yet be a most serious brake upon Soviet growth, too.

---

[1] The U.N. repeats the official Yugoslav figures, but those given here are from Vinski, *Ekonomski Pregled*, Zagreb, 11–12/1959. His real national income series is according to the Western concept, in 1953 prices. His estimate will shortly come out in the National Income and Wealth Series. In qualification of the Yugoslav success we must note that 2% of the GNP is foreign aid, and that the harvest in the base-year was extremely bad. Moreover this growth has not been sustained beyond 1960.

CHAPTER 14

A AND B, OR HEAVY AND LIGHT INDUSTRY[1]

1. WHY do the Communists operate, both in statistics and in actual planning, with the categories that entitle this chapter? The categories are unknown in any strict sense in Western economics, and appear to offer only difficulties. Our investigation will show them to be indeed very crude, and to owe their origin exclusively to ideology. Nevertheless they are not absolutely useless, and their elucidation throws light in many dark places.

In the *Dictionary and Handbook of Social-Economic Statistics*, 1944, A and B are defined as follows:[2]

Means of production and objects[3] of consumption. The whole global social product is divided into means of production and objects of consumption. This analysis of the product of each branch of the national economy is determined by the actual use of the product and in general depends on its material utility [Material-'noi-potrebitel'-skoi prirody]. To the means of production belong such commodities and articles as enter into the sphere of productive consumption.[4] Thus semi-fabricates, for example yarn and sugar, destined to be worked up into other objects of consumption, should be counted among the means of production.

To the objects of consumption belong commodities and products that serve the ends of the unproductive consumption of the population and of unproductive establishments.

The means of production are commonly designated with the letter A, the objects of consumption with the letter B.

The separation of gross industrial production into 'A' and 'B' is achieved in the practice of economic statistics by various means. Since the establishment of the actual utilization of production is often difficult in the absence of the necessary data, the separation of production into 'A' and 'B' is done approximately, on the basis of the predominant category into which one or another product falls. For example, all refined sugar belongs to 'B' irrespective of the fact that a part of it went into the production of confectionery. Or kerosene, for example, belongs entirely to 'A' even though part of it was used by the population for lighting and cooking.

---

[1] An early version of this chapter appeared in *Ost-Europa (Wirtschaft)*, Cologne, December 1958: 'Einführung in die Frage des Verhältnisses von A. zu B.' Other Western literature on this topic is very scanty: N. Kaplan in (ed.) A. Bergson, *Soviet Economic Growth* (Evanston, 1953); M. Dobb, *Soviet Studies*, July 1955; A. Gabor, *Soviet Studies*, Oct. 1955; P. Mahalanobis, *Sankhya*, Sept. 1953; E. Domar, *Essays in the Theory of Economic Growth*, New York, 1957, Ch. 9.

[2] *Slovar'-Spravochnik po Sotsial'no-Economicheskoi Statistike*, Gospolitizdat 1944, pp. 38–9.

[3] Marx says 'means' of consumption—P.J.D.W.

[4] The book has distinguished in its previous paragraph productive consumption, private consumption and accumulation.

There is also in use a still less exact method of dividing production into 'A' and 'B', by assigning the gross production of whole enterprises and even trusts entirely to one or other group in accordance with the predominant category into which its production falls.

Marx uses the same distinction, only he applies it to the whole economy. For A he has 'Department I', for B, 'Department II'.[1] These appear today only in theoretical Communist writing. We shall for the present confine ourselves to the currently used, operational distinction of A and B in industry.

Now this distinction is extremely awkward for all practical and theoretical purposes, as it is by no means equivalent to that between investment (J) and consumption (C).[2] In order to make this clear we must divide the economy into several categories for which particular goods will be taken as typical. First there are 'machine tools' (M), which stand for capital goods that produce other capital goods, including themselves. And this is important: the goods that produce capital goods that produce capital goods are quite normal capital good-producing capital goods! i.e. a machine tool that makes machine tools is much the same as one that makes looms, and we have the good fortune to be able to avoid an infinite regress of concepts.

Second come looms (L), i.e. capital goods that produce consumer goods. Now while in engineering the distinction is reasonably clear cut, as few machines can be turned to making 'cloth' as well as 'looms' and 'machine tools', in the rest of the economy there is no hard line. Thus a generating station or coal-mine can provide power for the production either of cloth or of looms or of machine tools; and a railway can provide transport for any of these uses. Similarly a potato can either be eaten (like cloth, as it were), or go into seed stock on a farm (like a loom) or go into seed stock at an agricultural research station (like a machine tool). But if first and second order capital cannot be operatively distinguished, the concepts are of obvious theoretical utility and may be given symbols in growth models.

Third is steel (S), which stands for the materials that make M and L. Fourth is thread (T), i.e. the materials, still at a very early stage, that make our last category—dresses (D), i.e. the consumer goods themselves. Then in a general way $J = M + L$, while $A = M + L + S + T$.

---

[1] *Das Kapital*, Vol. II, Part 3.
[2] We use the symbol J in order to avoid confusion with Marx' I, in this chapter only.

T

2. First, a comparatively trivial point. The distinction between S and T or D is entirely by the end-use to which it is put, and not by the natural substance itself. Steel for bicycles is T, and a steel-mill producing steel for bicycles is L. Thread for industrial belting is S, and the spindles that spin it are M. So if for convenience Soviet statisticians call all steel A, then an increase in A might not be an increase in J, as all the extra steel might go into bicycles. But if this point presents great difficulties for the practical statistician it presents none for the theoretician.

3. Next, and worse, we note that the dividing line between T and D is utterly arbitrary. Thus steel for bicycles is T and actual finished bicycles are D. But what of steel tubes for bicycles? Perhaps they should be T, while steel tubes made up into bicycle frames and ready for assembly should, perhaps, be D. Doubtless in practice, as our opening quotation indicates, once the raw materials enter the enterprise or trust that will produce the finished bicycle all further work on them is D, while up to that stage they are T; in which case the dividing line depends on the degree of vertical integration that happens to obtain. But the T/D dividing line only bothers those who wish to operate with A and B (it is also the A/B dividing line). Those who operate with J and C face no such problem.

4. Now why insist so much on J and C? The answer is that there is a real economic difference between M and L on the one hand and D on the other: namely, that in order to have the former the community must *save*. The production of D requires no saving, or to be precise, only enough working capital to set the process going. It is the failure of the A/B distinction to correspond at all to the saving/consumption distinction that principally condemns it. The exact translation of the one set of terms into the other is not, moreover, a simple matter, since the A/B categories take no account of stocks. We must write, it seems:

$$J = M + L + S_u + S_s + T_s + D_s$$
$$C = T_u + D_u$$

where J, M and L are taken gross, i.e. without regard to capital retirement; and s means net movements in stocks, u what is actually used up.

5. But even so our translation troubles are not at an end. For to give any serious consideration at all to T_u is to risk *double counting*, as the whole value of its output (stockpiling excluded) is already

reckoned in D. And similarly the whole value of S_u is already reckoned in M + L. We must therefore confine ourselves to net value added in each category: but why not simply abolish S_u and T_u altogether, and take the gross values of the rest?

This double counting merits a further excursus. Reverting to Marx's own I and II, which cover the whole economy in the same way as A and B cover industry alone, we may compare them with investment and consumption as follows. Together, the latter constitute the normal Western GNP, including capital replacement. I + II is the net national income if we add only certain parts of them. Marx, it will be recalled, subdivides I into $I_c + I_v + I_m$, where c is the replacement cost of the constant capital used up in I, v the 'replacement cost of the variable capital' (i.e. the wages) and m the surplus value that the variable capital produces. The net national income is thus $I_v + I_m + II_v + II_m$: the wages and ownership incomes produced in both departments. $I_c + II_c$, the replacement of machinery *and raw materials* in both departments, are excluded by Marx as double counting. I.e. in our own expansion of his phraseology, he excludes both the replacement of fixed assets and T_u and S_u.

However, the typical Communist tendency to think in gross, not net, terms does come out at this point, inasmuch as there is a name for the meaningless total c + v + m: whereas v + m is called the national income, c + v + m is called the 'social product' (obshchestvenniy produkt), or 'cost of production'. The 'social product' involves very much more double counting than the GNP, and this way of thinking has surely contributed to the Communist complacency with gross output indices that involve even still more double counting. Even such deviant thinkers as the Yugoslavs still compute the 'social product' and publish it in their statistical yearbook. It is equivalent to the sum of all the rows in a Western input/output table, whereas the national income corresponds to the sum of only those rows representing the ultimate factors of production.

6. Summing up so far, we have found that the distinction between T and D is purely arbitrary, that S and T are superfluous categories, double counted unless we are careful to take net value added at each stage, and that saving finds no counterpart in any of these categories in their unadjusted Marxian condition.[1] A and B

---

[1] But a change in the A/B ratio is almost bound to lead to a change in the same direction of the J/C ratio, as T is a constant function of B unless input/output ratios change in B.

are thus not as useful concepts as investment and consumption. They are clumsy and appear only to have been brought into use because of their ideological sanctity: they derive directly from Marx's *Kapital*, Vol. 2, Part 3. This Part is in detail an incomprehensible (at least to the present writer) and repetitive muddle,[1] but its general drift is clear enough. A static and an expanding model of an economy are set out ('simple reproduction' and 'expanded reproduction'), and analysed in terms of departments I and II as here defined. The passage became the *locus classicus* on how to expand an economy even under socialism, and has restricted the development of Marxist thought ever since.

Now why does Marx work in terms of I and II, not investment and consumption? Because of his theory of value: I produces the goods that satisfy the demands of 'constant' capital in both departments, while II's output satisfies the demands created by 'variable' capital in both departments. 'Constant' capital, it will be recalled, is more than 'fixed': it is that used to buy machinery *and fuel and raw materials*—all the 'dead' things that cannot create surplus value; while 'variable' capital is less than 'circulating', being that used to buy living labour, the sole source of surplus value. Consequently the distinction between 'constant' and 'variable' always seemed to Marx so much more important than that between 'fixed' and 'circulating' that he apparently never even considered an analysis in these latter terms; though the distinction between the demands created by these two sorts of capital is almost identical to that between investment and consumption.[2]

7. Nor would the charm, such as it is, of Marx's analysis have been reduced by such a change. In a static economy, we read, departments I and II produce as follows:

$$I_c + I_v + I_m = I$$
$$II_c + II_v + II_m = II$$

where $I + II$ is the 'social product', and $I_v + I_m + II_v + II_m$ is the net national income, as explained above. Now Marx's great service to economics at this point is to show that I also $= I_c + II_c$, and II also $= I_v + I_m + II_v + II_m$; so that $I_v + I_m = IIc$. In other words I_c is the product of department I used up by that department

---

[1] Posthumously compiled by Engels from several manuscripts, none of which Marx had deemed ready for publication.

[2] Not entirely so, because circulating capital may be used to accumulate stocks in any enterprise. In particular, any increase in the output of fixed capital necessitates an accumulation of circulating capital by the enterprises engaged on that output.

and $II_v + II_m$ the same in II; so that where there is no net investment $I_v + I_m = II_c$. This means that the wages, rent, profit and interest in I are all spent to buy all the consumer goods remaining unbought by the factors of production in II, and the depreciation quotas and current material production costs recovered by sales in II are all spent to buy all the producers' goods remaining unbought by the enterprises in I. Our next task, then, is to examine the truth and importance of this proposition.

It is true beyond any question, since it is clearly a simple accounting identity. Note that all these magnitudes must be taken *ex post*. E.g. II is the revenue from the sale of goods that turn out to have been consumed in a given period, and $I_v + I_m + II_v + II_m$ is the expenditure that was made upon them in that same period; so that the two are necessarily equal. But Marx does not know the *ex ante/ex post* distinction, and like other Marxists—or for that matter like Keynes himself—ties himself into knots for the lack of it.

Now all this is translatable into Western terms. We might have written instead:

$$J_r + J_c = J$$
$$C_r + C_c = C$$

where $J + C$ is the gross national product, J and C are production for investment and consumption and r and c expenditure on capital replacement and consumption. Then clearly as before $J_r + C_r = J$ and $J_c + C_c = C$, so that J_c, or the expenditure on consumption of revenues earned in the investment sector $= C_r$, or the expenditure on investment of revenues earned in the consumption sector.

The same relations can also be shown in terms of an input/output matrix:

Expenditures on	Investment goods	Outputs of Consumption goods	Total
Investment . . .	J_r	J_c	J
Consumption . . .	C_r	C_c	C
Total . . .	J	C	GNP

Here J and C are treated as if they were industries in a normal matrix. Reading diagonally down from top left to bottom right we find as usual the amount of the product of each 'industry' which it itself consumes.

Moreover, analysis in terms of J and C with net investment does just as well as analysis in terms of I and II with 'expanded reproduction'. Let subscript a stand in what follows for saving (which Marx called accumulation); since we are dealing in *ex post* terms it will also stand for net investment. Then:

$$J_r + J_c + J_a = J \qquad \text{(or the revenue from the sale of invest-}$$

(or the revenue from the sale of investment goods is spent for replacement, consumption, and saving)

$$C_r + C_c + C_a = C$$

But also:

$$J = J_r + C_r + J_a + C_a$$
$$C = C_c + J_c;$$

Therefore $J_c = C_r + C_a$.

And the same goes for I and II, if we create parts of I_m and II_m called I_m' and II_m', which the capitalists do not consume but accumulate.

Thus Marx's point can be translated into more convenient language without loss, and as a tautology cannot avoid being true (so long as we stick to *ex post* concepts). The awkward A/B distinction is not, then, necessary for this purpose at all. Indeed the matter is even simpler and more general: any sector of the economy, however defined (e.g. investment, agriculture or the north-eastern region) will consume some of its own product and sell the rest. If there are no changes in liquidity preference, it will buy as much as it sells.

8. To say this is not necessarily to depreciate Marx's discovery: it *might* be true that the application of this universal tautology to I and II, or to J and C, was particularly fertile. That is, the fact that the same result can be obtained with J and C as with I and II is merely interesting. What we really want to know is, does equation $I_v + I_m = II_c$, or $J_c = C_r$, really matter? Does it help planning or analysis? I think not. Certainly it is striking that although correct and not unknown in the West the equation is hardly used by anybody, and in particular not by national income statisticians.[1] One reason is probably that if *ex ante* $J_c + C_c > C$ it is indifferent to the planner whether abstinence is forced on J_c or on C_c; so long as *someone* who wants to buy consumer goods does a little more

---

[1] I can find no mention of it, for instance, in the following textbooks: Carl Shoup, *National Income Analysis* (Cambridge, Mass. 1947); J. R. Hicks, *The Social Framework* (Oxford 1942); E. Schneider, *Einführung in die Wirtschaftstheorie* (Tübingen, 1947).

saving or pays a few more taxes it matters little whether he is a steel-roller or a baker. In other words $J_c = C_r + C_a$ is not *the* condition of equilibrium, monetary or physical, in any economy; it is merely the corollary of other, more important, conditions. *Ex post* it is simply the passive logical consequence of the other equations; it is as usual the *ex ante* analysis that matters, and here any sensible planner would operate on $J_c + C_c = C$, or, which is to say the same thing, $J_a + C_a + J_r + C_r = J$.

It is true that Marx's equation can be used to show the deflationary consequences of under-investment, but this was not his purpose. Investment, especially in a planned economy, is not peculiarly dependent on or facilitated by the abstinence of those to whom it gives work. In an unplanned economy it will be, to the degree that steel-rollers have lower wages than bakers: this will encourage the substitution of baking machinery for bakers. But even here other influences on the volume of investment are paramount, and a planned economy can normally neglect this point. This being so, I am unable to find any practical use for Marx's equation, and not surprised that the Gosplan[1] and all Western economists neglect it. The equation is simply a curiosum.

9. It is illuminating that neither Malenkov nor Khrushchev in their controversy about the rates of growth of A and B thought of investment and consumption. The relation between A and investment is, as we have seen, very loose. Indeed it is even looser than we have hitherto supposed, since A and B refer to industry alone. Keeping back the growth of A, Malenkov could for instance have expanded domestic construction. But in fact the investment funds that he withdrew from A were not invested elsewhere: he simply let them be consumed, so that the 'volume of capital works' in 1954 was only 4% greater than in 1953—a far lower rate of growth than under Stalin or Khrushchev. But this was not held against him. Serious as the deviation from Communist economic policy appears to us, who stand outside the system, it did not figure as an accusation. The accusation was that he wanted to make B grow faster than A, if only for a period. The share of investment in the whole economy is indeed published, but has no place in the most operative and

---

[1] Such at any rate is the complaint of Academician Strumilin: 'The Balance of the National Economy as a Weapon of Socialist Planning', *Voprosy Ekonomiki*, 11/1954. I can also find no reference to Marx' theorem in Krasnolobov, *Planirovanie i Uchet Narodnogo Dokhoda*, Moscow 1940. This is a Marxist national income textbook.

important documents, such as the speeches of Party bosses, the yearly reports of Gosplan, or the captured 1941 Plan.

10. This is not the end of confusion. For not only are A and B regularly equated by Soviet and Western writers with investment and consumption, they are also regularly equated with heavy and light industry, so that in the Soviet mind three perfectly distinct concepts are normally interchangeable: the production of the means of production = investment = the output of heavy industry. Now heavy industry is not an operative category in Soviet statistics; it finds no place in the Dictionary quoted above. It is much the same fuzzy concept as in British parlance: the output of 'important', 'basic', even of just physically heavy, producers' goods. Nails and transistors are no part of anyone's definition of heavy industry, though they both fall in A—and may or may not, of course, fall in investment. Thus heavy industry is a restricted part of A. Further, Soviet authors lay just as much stress on S and T as on M and L; and many T goods are 'heavier' than S goods. Compare artificial fertilizers with nails, sulphuric acid with plaster board.

So much for 'heavy'; now why 'industry'? In Marx, and also in good logic, I and II, which cover the other sectors of the economy as well, are the basic categories. Thus seed potatoes are both I and investment, and so is the growth of a livestock herd or the use of a railway to transport machinery or seed potatoes; so indeed is technical education, though the neglect of this point is also a Western mistake. Moreover, by Marxist definitions the growing of grain, which must of course subsequently be milled and baked, is I: only the baking and possibly the milling are II (and incidentally also B, since baking and milling are industry, not agriculture). Indeed most of agriculture is I.

Soviet economists, then, whether they use the words A and B or heavy and light industry, or accumulation and consumption, are thinking about that part of the Soviet economy *common* to 'A', 'heavy industry' and even perhaps 'accumulation'. Electricity, steel, machinery of all sorts, heavy chemicals:[1] how much priority shall these and their like receive? All else is kept back: nails, bicycles, agriculture including seed potatoes, transport, distribution and domestic building. We therefore need another name for the favoured sector, devoid of any misleading associations. Let us

[1] Strictly heavy chemicals are not an investment good; i.e. they are T not S, since their predominant end-uses are in agriculture and textiles. It is symptomatic of the vagueness of Soviet thinking that they are nevertheless included without question.

call it the *kernel*. For some purposes the technical education associated with 'kernel' production must be included in the kernel; for
it is equally favoured. And the same applies to the construction
activity that the 'kernel' requires. This also needs to be said, for
construction is not industry, and therefore not A; so that we run
the danger of demanding steel and steel-mills, but not the factories
that house steel-mills.

So if the 'kernel' as defined is to be expanded more rapidly than
everything else then certain ancillary activities not included in it
by definition must expand equally rapidly. Or more broadly,
investment must be so directed as to enable the kernel to expand.
*The doctrine that A must grow faster than B is largely a demand for a
certain investment pattern*, as indeed are most economic policies. But
it is also—and this is more surprising—a demand for a certain investment *volume*, as we try to show in the next chapter.

These confusions are beautifully illustrated by the *Political
Economy* handbook:[1]

> In this way, for expanded socialist reproduction, accompanied by rapid technical
> progress, such a growth of production is characteristic as shows a quicker rise in
> the branches producing means of production (Department I) than in the branches
> producing objects of consumption (Department II). All the same in socialist
> society there is continuous absolute growth of the production of objects of
> consumption, which finds its expression in the uninterrupted rise of the output
> of agriculture, food industry and light industry, in the spread of housebuilding
> in town and country, in the development of Soviet trade.

Note the total confusion between A/B and I/II, the ridiculous
categorization of agriculture as II, and the failure to show how
investment is related to I.

In China on the other hand, it is fully recognized that the heavy/-
light distinction is not the same as the A/B distinction. Messrs. Li
Hui-hung *et al.* produced an excellent cross-classification in the
statistical journal.[2]

Having made many of the points made in the preceding sections
they say:

> Heavy industry means modern industry that provides a material basis for the
> technical transformation of the national economy in the process of industrializa-
> tion and for the modernization of national defence. It means the following
> branches of modern industry:
>   1. Production of the means of production;

---

[1] *Politicheskaya Ekonomia*, Gospolitizdat 1954, p. 546.
[2] *Tung Chi Kung Tso*, September 29, 1957 (=ECMM 113).

2. Production of motive power and fuels;

3. Production of raw materials required for producing 'labour materials' (explained as meaning the materials for (1), and the materials required to create 'labour conditions': rails, metal structures, mine ventilating equipment, draining equipment, cement, etc., required for railways, factories and warehouses);

4. Defence industry.

All these, it is pointed out, are A, except for defence which is neither A nor B. But a lot of A (e.g. milling, spinning) is light. A particular advantage of this classification is that no product has to be split according to end-use, as it must for A and B. 'Heavy' as defined grew faster than 'A' in 1952–55; and no wonder, since it is unencumbered with such things as flour and yarn, which can only grow as fast as B.

There can be no doubt that Messrs. Li Hui-hung et al. have adequately defined the sector to which Communists really wish to give priority. Their 'heavy' means our 'kernel'.

11. So far all has been confusion and ideological doctrinairism. Yet admitting the purely ideological origins of the concepts, how could they still be used today if they had not proved to be useful? Communists are very scrupulous to preserve Marxian tradition, but they are more than willing to shove it into the background or explain it away when inconvenient. This is clearly not the case with A and B. Why not?

The first point is that the whole Communist ethos is or has been to plan in physical, not monetary, terms. 'Investment' is a monetary concept: you encourage it with low interest rates or high taxes on distributed profits. 'The production of the means of production' is a physical concept: A or I is the list of physical outputs designated as such. If a physical planner wants to encourage investment he must order the output of investment goods. And this is, above all, true of A, not I; for it is chiefly in industry that the 'means of production' differ from the 'objects of consumption' by their physical nature, or according to an industrial census classification. Seed potatoes are potatoes, and passenger trains move over the same rails as freight trains; but steel is not saucepans. Hence as a purely administrative device the A/B distinction is not useless.

Indeed we may, quasi-humorously, say that the A/B distinction is useful because A is an end in itself. We here introduce the notion of the 'ideological consumption of semi-fabricates'. Steel happens, in the minds of Communists, to be more beautiful and desirable than saucepans or even guns. This is how their minds work: the tradition has very deep roots. 'Steel was a final good to Stalin, and bread an intermediate one.'[1] Consumption, in Communist economic thinking, is a 'leak', a kind of destruction. It is useful, to be sure, for preventing a worker, especially a worker in A, from dying of cold or hunger; but the be-all and end-all is reproduction, preferably expanded reproduction. Consumer's sovereignty is bourgeois liberalism; producer's sovereignty is the proper proletarian state of affairs. And indeed the Central Committee does find it easier to say what shall be produced than what shall be consumed.[2]

12. Again, if the economy is to grow perhaps it is precisely 'A' that must expand most rapidly? This is of course to pose the one really substantive question in this chapter: was Malenkov or Khrushchev *technically* right when they fell out in late 1954 over the relative rates of growth of A and B? Must A, or I, or M, or 'heavy industry', or 'the kernel' or any other vaguely similar sector of the economy, increase more rapidly than the rest of the economy if the whole is to grow at all? Several points can be made.

(i) where *acceleration* of growth is required this primary sector (however defined) must plainly increase faster than the rest simply because it must increase first. Similarly where deceleration is permitted it must increase slower. But the interesting case is constant growth.

(ii) if all input/output ratios, including especially the capital/-income ratio, are constant, all sectors of the economy however defined must increase at the same rate if growth is constant.

(iii) but there are diminishing returns to labour, capital and industrial inputs in agriculture. Moreover, this is not only a static proposition. Even when we permit time to pass and technique to progress it remains true of agriculture. For the supply of land is fixed, so growth in this field demands that other inputs be continually replacing land, and the input/output ratio is for ever moving against them. But these other inputs come largely from the 'kernel', since agriculture produces few of its own capital goods. Therefore agricultural growth demands and has received a greater growth of its inputs from the primary sector, however defined.[3]

[1] The point was put thus epigrammatically by Prof. Bergson, who however doubts if it is true, even of Stalin.

[2] Cf. Ch. 10, Sec. 15.

[3] And this remains true even if most of agriculture is I, and the primary sector is defined as I. For *some* agriculture remains II, while *all* its inputs are I. The above argument applies only to normal times; in the famine of 1932 it was precisely seed, an agricultural input, that agriculture needed, Stalin having requisitioned the seed grain for the army. Cf. W. Duranty, *U.S.S.R.* (U.S.A. 1944), Chs. 16, 17.

(iv) alternatively it may be decided to leave agriculture in the lurch, confining its growth to what is possible with a fixed input of industrial goods. Then services and industrial consumer goods must bear the brunt of expansion, and they must draw their raw materials *increasingly* from non-agricultural sources. This means again that the primary sector, however defined, must expand more rapidly than they.

(v) but the secular trend of input/output ratios, taking technical progress into account, is quite the other way: less and less raw material and fuel are used per unit of output. Unless the capital/-output ratio is an exception to this general rule, this is Malenkov's trump card: the primary sector, however defined, is becoming less and less necessary.

13. But what, sixthly, of the capital/output ratio in particular? It deserves a section to itself. There is certainly nothing at all in the belief that technical progress *necessarily* requires, or even is identical with, a higher ratio. It is even doubtful whether handloom-weaving had a lower capital/output ratio than powerloom-weaving.[1] Both technical progress and growth are entirely possible—at a very low rate—simply through the spending of depreciation allowances on ever improved machinery: and this would lower the capital/output ratio. The determination of the secular trend in this ratio is entirely a matter of the statistical evidence. Summarizing this, we see that in U.S.A. from 1900 to 1938 the ratio was stable, with minor fluctuations in either direction, at $3 \cdot 5$; but that then fell to about $2 \cdot 8$, where it is again stable.[2] The British figure has fluctuated around $3 \cdot 1$ since 1870, showing no trend.[3]

Now on the one hand both these series, as Mr. Maywald points out, relate national capital to *annual* national income, but since the hours of work per annum have diminished the ratio of capital to *hourly* national income must have diminished relatively to the former ratio. Thus even the British figures prove a diminution in the capital/output ratio owing to technical progress,[4] were it not that none of this takes education into account. The data given in

---

[1] Observers were doubtless confused because the capital/labour ratio increased; but even that is in no way logically necessary for technical progress. It is also irrelevant here.

[2] R. W. Goldsmith in *Income and Wealth, Series II*, Cambridge, U.K. 1952, Table V.

[3] K. Maywald, *Economic History Review*, 1956–57, pp. 94, 102.

[4] Unless consumers' tastes have by chance switched from goods with high ratios to goods with low ones, each ratio remaining the same over time. The British figures also omit consumers' durables from capital.

Ch. 13, Sec. 3, enable us to make this correction. The U.S. capital/-output ratio still declines, but very slightly: from 4·3 in 1900 to 4·0 in 1957. The Soviet ratio rises less rapidly than might otherwise be thought, and in the otherwise delicately balanced U.K. case[1] education is surely decisive in making us suppose the ratio is increasing, rather than stable.

(vii) the view that capital/output ratios necessarily increase with technical progress is very deeply embedded in the Marxist tradition. It can be found in Ricardo;[2] it is carried forward into Marx, who practically defines technical progress as an increase in the 'organic composition of capital,' c/v; it survives the marginalist revolution to be reaffirmed by Böhm-Bawerk with his 'increasing round aboutness' of methods of production.[3] It was also reaffirmed by Lenin.[4] It was entirely refuted by Marshall in a footnote,[5] but some fallacies are very tough. Let us then simply assert: technical progress means making things more cheaply, and if an innovation presented itself which saved capital, or both capital and labour, while maintaining output, that innovation would be technical progress. Moreover, as the statistical sources just quoted show, capital-saving innovations are perfectly possible. Only in fact capital-using ones are commoner, so that the *average* capital/output ratio rises.

But before we apply the above reasoning to A and B we must also consider the capital/labour ratio. In pure logic, *any* change in this ratio can accompany *any* change in the other, and no particular change in either ratio is necessary for technical progress, which is defined as a rise in the ratio between all outputs and all inputs. Thus the substitution of capital for labour can only be said *normally to accompany* technical progress. It is of course entirely compatible with a rising capital/output ratio. I.e. most innovations are labour-saving and somewhat capital-using. But progress is logically conceivable that substitutes labour for capital, while reducing the ratio of both together to output.

Now to say that Marx's c/v increases with technical progress is very similar to saying capital is substituted for labour: for a

[1] Wiles, *Oxford Institute of Statistics Bulletin*, August 1956.
[2] *Principles of Political Economy and Taxation*, Ch. 31.
[3] *Kapital und Kapitalzins*, 4th ed., 1931. For a modern repetition of this confusion, cf. A. I. Pashkov, *Ekonomicheski Zakon Preimushchestvennogo Rosta Proizvodstva Sredstv Proizvodstva*, Moscow 1958, p. 135.
[4] In *Note on the So-called Question of Markets*, 1898-9, Soch. 1935, vol. 2.
[5] *Principles of Economics*, 8th ed., p. 583.

is the capital employed in producers' durables and raw materials together, and thus has a far lower rate of turnover than v, the capital employed in labour; so any increase in c increases the proportion of capital cost to wage cost in unit output. Therefore since progress *does* normally substitute capital for labour it *does* normally alter the 'organic composition of capital' in the direction claimed by Marx; without however necessarily raising the capital/-output ratio, as we have seen.

14. Naturally it is no argument that A, or the primary sector however defined, has in fact grown more rapidly than B in all Communist countries. This may merely explain the *rapidity* of overall growth; it does nothing to prove that without a faster rate for A than for B there would have been no growth. The Malenkov party was of course opting for a lower rate of overall growth, and cannot have seriously pretended otherwise. Whether its contention was correct that *some* growth could be sustained with A and B increasing at the same rate would seem to depend on the balance of many factors that Soviet economists have hardly begun to consider. Without more research than the present writer is capable of, nothing can be proved.

One approach to the question is, however, of great interest: has A grown faster than B over time in capitalist countries? A very interesting question, since it tells us whether A's faster growth is a natural law or an act of policy. W. G. Hoffmann in his *Growth of Industrial Economies*,[1] seeks to prove that all over the (non-Communist) world 'capital-goods industry' grows more rapidly than 'consumer-goods industry'. Its section on definitions provides a plentiful crop of coincidences with what has been said above. Thus (pp. 10-14):

(i) Building is omitted from consideration ('not an industry in the modern sense'). This omission is of course fair if industry only is to be considered; and it is very reminiscent of the Soviet concepts to do so.

(ii) Woodworking is omitted as too difficult to allocate—yet at one time nearly all capital goods were made of wood, and the relatively slow growth of woodworking is a highly important offset to the author's thesis.

(iii) Engineering and metallurgy are allocated wholly to 'capital' goods. This sets up another important bias in the author's favour, since in recent decades metallic consumer goods, many of them with moving parts, have grown from almost zero to very large quantities. It is thus certain that since, say, 1850, the

[1] Manchester University Press 1959; a translation by W. H. Chaloner and W. O. Henderson of an expanded version of *Stadien und Typen der Industrialisierung*, Kiel 1931.

output of metallic consumer goods has grown much faster than that of metallic capital goods. One may comment that while the Slovar'-Spravochnik, as quoted in our Sec. 1, holds it inexact to lump together the output of 'whole enterprises and even trusts' under A or B, according to the predominant end-use, Prof. Hoffmann lumps together whole industries.

(iv) Chemicals are allocated to 'capital goods' on the amazing ground that a 'fairly high proportion of the final output of the chemical industry was probably sold to other industrial firms and consequently the industry must be regarded primarily as a capital-goods industry.' Thus chemicals, which certainly come under the Soviet A, are said *therefore*, to be capital goods—a mistake that no competent Soviet statistician would make. In fact chemicals are, in the terminology of this chapter, partly S and partly T—indeed almost wholly T. In other words chemical goods are in fact consumption goods, and have been wrongly allocated.

The main error in this book seems to be to suppose that a normal census classification of industries corresponds with even reasonable approximation to a classification according to end-use, such as A/B, or 'capital'/'consumption'. Secondarily it seems to have been forgotten that the predominant end-use of a census classification shifts over time.

Whether Prof. Hoffmann's main thesis was true or false, then, could only be settled to a detailed reworking of his statistics, which was not slave to the fallacy that census classification determines end-use. There are, happily, a few such reworkings. Thus the Soviet statistical compiler I. Ya. Ioffe has made estimates as follows (%):

U.S.S.R.[1]							U.S.A.		Ger.		U.K.		France
'913	'28	'32	'36	'37	'40	'55	'29[1,2] '55[2]		'29[1,2] '55[2]		'29[1,2] '55[2]		'26[1]
42·9	46·4	55·7	60·8	59·1	—	—	54·5	60·0	55·9	66·0	54·9	58·9	41·0
57·1	53·6	44·3	39·2	40·9	—	—	45·5	40·0	44·1	34·0	46·0	42·0	59·0

U.S.S.R., a later estimate[2]						
33·3	39·5	—	—	—	61·2	70·6
66·7	60·5	—	—	—	38·8	29·4

Now Mr. Ioffe may possibly be biased: he *must* show such results, and he does not explain his working. It would take us far afield to check his figures, but at least the West German Yearbook splits up industry very conveniently; here are the figures as reckoned (i) by wage and salary bills, (ii) by gross output (%):

---

[1] *S.S.S.R. i Kapitalisticheskie Strany*, Moscow 1939, p. 37.
[2] *Strany Sotsialisma i Kapitalisma v Tsifrakh*, Moscow 1957, p. 49. Note that he repeats his earlier estimates for 'capitalist' countries, but quotes the current revised official estimates for U.S.S.R.

| | 1950 | | 1958 | |
	(i)[1]	(ii)[3]	(i)[2]	(ii)[3]
A (mining, 'general materials', capital goods)	70·0	62·1	62·7	66·0
B (consumer goods, food processing)	30·0	37·9	37·3	34·0

And here are the data for U.S.A. as estimated by Mr. Herbert Levine[4]:

	1928	1940
A	60·8	58·1
B	39·2	41·9

With two out of three Western estimates going the wrong way, doubt as to the Hoffmann/Ioffe thesis is very much in order.

It is not of course necessary that in every short period even in a Communist country A should grow faster than B, and Communists are usually careful to say this. So far as known to me, the complete list of such periods since 1928 is: 1937 in U.S.S.R., the second half of 1953 in U.S.S.R., the first Albanian Five-year Plan, Poland in 1950, various periods of about a year in 1953–54 in all the satellite countries, Bulgaria in 1955.[5] These were in almost all cases periods of economic and political relaxation. They prove, of course, nothing about a long period of more rapid growth in B, with all *ceteris* duly *paribus*.

Yugoslavia has abandoned the doctrine that A should grow faster than B, in both word and deed. From 1947 to 1953 inclusive she 'obeyed the law'; since then B has outstripped A as often as not.[6] But economic thought is still carefully conducted in terms of I and II.

---

[1] *Statistisches Jahrbuch der Deutschen Bundesrepublik*, 1952, pp. 187, 599.

[2] *Jahrbuch*, 1959, p. 174.

[3] *Deutsches Institut für Wirtschaftsforschung*, Berlin, *Wochenbericht*, Mar. 11, 1960.

[4] *Journal of Political Economy*, August 1958. Mr. Levine worked from W. Leontief's *Structure of the American Economy* (New York 1951).

[5] N. Spulber, *The Economics of Communist Eastern Europe* (Wiley 1957), p. 377; D.D.R.: *Statistisches Jahrbuch* 1957, p. 280; A. I. Pashkov, op. cit., Ch. 5. Note that the Chinese record is unblemished!

[6] *Statistički Godišnjak*, 1960, p. 150, taking 'Tools' and 'Materials' as A, 'Consumer Goods' as B.

CHAPTER 15

FIRST AND SECOND ORDER INVESTMENT

1. WESTERN economics is only at the beginning of its study of these concepts, and what is said in this and the preceding chapter will before long seem crude: a stumbling attempt to begin in the middle of things, a crass neglect of obviously more basic and more general propositions (as yet, alas, unrevealed to the author at this writing).

This chapter applies the concepts of the last to the widely held doctrine that investment in steel and machinery is somehow more growth-promoting than investment elsewhere. It tries to show that this is a fallacy.

There are two versions of the argument. The first—which I am unwilling to attribute to any particular person but feel to be generally 'in the air'—may be christened the '*détour*'. Grant, says this argument, a constant volume of investment: invest it most heavily in Dept. A or I, and then while you are undoubtedly sacrificing consumption in the short run you will emerge at the end with more consumption when you finally switch back into B or II.

In order properly to discuss this we must ourselves make a 'détour', and return to our concepts M and L of the previous chapter. We saw there many objections to the M/L distinction, but when all is said and done it is still possible to have an investment policy that leans more or less towards the increase of future investment as opposed to future consumption. In any case, as this is a purely theoretical discussion we shall neglect all practical difficulties of definition and assume that the distinction is clear enough to warrant symbolical handling.

2. Let L be first and M second order capital, and l first and m second order gross investment. Let $a = m + l$ be total gross investment, $A = M + L$ be total national capital. Let α be the rate of annual increase of gross investment, and let α have been constant for at least p years, where p is the average length of life of a capital asset. The role of p is very important: all capital is assumed to be of the 'one-hoss shay' type, functioning perfectly until it collapses. Then an adequate measure of national capital

at any time is simply the sum of the last p years' gross investment, a most useful simplification which does little violence to the facts:

$$A_n = a_{n-p} + a_{n-p+1} \cdots + a_{n-1} = a_{n-p}\left(\frac{a^p - 1}{a - 1}\right);$$

from which it follows that A as well as a is increasing at the rate a.

Let b be consumption and $c = a + b$ be the GNP. Let c/A be written ϕ (N.B. this is the reciprocal of the ratio normally spoken of). Then

$$\phi M_n = m_n + l_n = a_n = a_{n-p} \, a^p.$$

And the proportion of gross investment to GNP is

$$\frac{a_n}{c_n} = \frac{a_{n-p} a^p}{\phi a_{n-p} \dfrac{a^p - 1}{a - 1}} = \frac{a^p(a - 1)}{\phi(a^p - 1)},$$

which is a constant, so that both consumption and investment are also increasing at the rate a. It follows that the proportion of first to second order capital is

$$\frac{L_n}{M_n} = \frac{\phi L_n}{\phi M_n} = \frac{b}{a} = \frac{c - a}{a} = \phi \, \frac{a^p - 1}{a^p(a - 1)} - 1.$$

Now this, too, is a constant. So since A is increasing at the rate a, L and M are also increasing at that rate. So

$$\frac{L_n}{M_n} = \frac{l_n}{m_n} = \frac{b}{a},$$

and everything in the economy is increasing at the rate a. The introduction of the L/M distinction has not disturbed this result in any way. In order to keep up a steady growth of a in everything else, both departments must themselves do so, expanding *pari passu* with each other and with the economy.

Other assumptions made in this chapter, so far as I can detect them, are:

    (i) all machines, L or M, are fully employed at all times;
    (ii) there is no technical progress, only capital accumulation;
    (iii) there are constant returns;
    (iv) demand is neglected: whatever can be produced is produced, and is bought;
    (v) ϕ and p are the same throughout the economy;

(vi) only capital (abstinence) is scarce and has any cost. Labour and land are in free and plentiful domestic supply, but capital can also be imported, in which case it still has a cost. Domestic capital has an opportunity cost, foreign capital costs securities, and both are measured in money;

(vii) it is sometimes necessary also to import machinery, against either borrowed capital or consumer goods;

(viii) all outputs are valued at market prices. Indeed they have to be, since in view of (vi) there are often hardly any costs at all: e.g. once a stock of L exists consumption goods cost almost nothing. But there are of course opportunity costs. In consequence the values of such sectors of the economy as a, b, c, l and m will vary if their physical volumes in relation to each other vary. Thus if m supplies more machines than l can use, its output will meet inelastic demand and its value will fall. In such a case ϕ M will, by definition, fall and ϕ will not any longer be the same in all sectors.

3. Thus equipped we may consider the 'détour', or temporary switch of resources from l to m. Obviously it makes possible a temporarily greater growth in M and indeed in A, at the expense of L and thus of b. But if we then re-establish b, and therefore L, we must switch resources back; will we have gained anything at the end of it all? Mathematically the simplest case to follow through seems to be the superimposition on a constant and steady growth of a once-for-all switch in a certain year. Thus let the economy increase during the year o, as in all previous years, at the rate a. Then we have:

Year	L	M	l	m	a	b
o	aL_{-1}	aM_{-1}	al_{-1}	am_{-1}	aa_{-1}	ab_{-1}

But in year 1 resources to the value k are switched from l to m:

1	aL	aM	$al-k$	$am+k$	aa	ab

Note that the consumer has noticed nothing yet. His consumption, $ab = \phi aL$, still grows at the previous rate. We are not necessarily dealing with an economy in which there is consumer's sovereignty in respect of investment.

The consumer only notices a change in year 2. In this year also the growth of m is continued as if k had never been added, and resources in M to the value of k are switched to the production of L goods. This of course is what is meant by a 'détour', and this decision as to m and l determines the ultimate result:

$$
\begin{array}{llllll}
2 & a^2L-k & a^2M+k\ a^2l+\phi k & a^2m & a^2a+\phi k & a^2b-\phi k \\
3 & a^3L-k+\phi k & a^3M+k\ a^3l+\phi k & a^3m & a^3a+\phi k & a^3b-\phi k+\phi^2k \\
4 & a^4L-k+2\phi k & a^4M+k\ a^4l+\phi k & a^4m & a^4a+\phi k & a^4b-\phi k+2\phi^2k,
\end{array}
$$

and so on until in $p+2$ the extra value k in the l column falls away, and so does the $-k$ in the b column.

We can now see what are the deviations from normal growth of b, l and m:

year	1	2	3	4	....	p+1	p+2	p+3	......	2p+1	2p+
m	+k	0	0	0		0	0	0		0	0
l	$-k$	$+\phi k$	$+\phi k$	$+\phi k$		$+\phi k$	0	0		0	0
b	0	$-\phi k$	$-\phi k$	$-\phi k$		$-\phi k$	$+p\phi^2k$	$+(p-1)\phi^2k$		$+\phi^2k$	0
			$+\phi^2k$	$+2\phi^2k$		$+(p-1)\phi^2k$					

Not one of these terms contains a, and it is instantly evident that it does not matter at present whether the economy is growing, stagnant or declining. The sum of the b row gives the total gain or loss in consumption from the single switch of resources k in year l. The sum is $p\phi k\ (p\phi-1)$. This considerable increase in consumption has been *made technically possible* by a shift of investment from the first to the second order. But that shift is not the only requisite: there has also had to be more investment *in toto*. This extra investment is the sum of all the deviations in rows l and m, which we can see to be $p\phi k$. We have discussed above the origin and meaning of these extra resources; in this particular case they must have been borrowed abroad. Thus at the cost of $p\phi k$ we have got out $p\phi k\ (p\phi-1)$; in other words a unit of capital thus redirected into and out of second order investment has, neglecting time preference, the rate of profitability $p\phi-1$.

4. What is this rate $p\phi-1$? Invest any sum Q. Then over its life, if fed adequately with co-operating factors, it will produce $Qp\phi$ of goods or services. Subtracting its own cost, this is $Qp\phi-Q$, giving the 'rate of gross return' $p\phi-1$. The word 'gross' in this phrase means that we price the co-operating factors at zero, a matter to which we shall come back. We must then conclude that $p\phi-1$ is the general 'rate of gross return', defined by the premises of the system; that all capital has this rate.

It follows that the ultimate return on capital is not stepped up in any way by the 'détour'. Balanced growth would have had the same result. Indeed if we include time preference it would have had a better result: since although it is true that for an extra overall investment ϕk in year 2 a ϕ^2k duly appears in consumption in year 3, there is also in years 2 to p $+$ 1 a negative item in consumption. Since these are the early years they must receive a heavier weight.

But more important than the failure of the 'détour' to enhance profitability is its failure to enhance growth. By year 2p $+$ 2 we are right back on the original growth path.

5. Perhaps things would be different if the switch of k were made every year? In this case a dynamic equilibrium is reached in year p $+$ 2. In this year the total stock of M is pk greater than under 'normal growth'—a maximum state reached already in p $+$ 1. As all this extra stock is being used, *ex hypothesi*, to increase l not m, the excess of l over its expected level under normal growth is pϕk—k. The —k is there of course because we are now continually paying out k from l to m. This excess in turn has now been going on for p years, so that the excess of L over the expected level is at its maximum of ϕp²k—pk. Consequently b is ϕ^2p²k—ϕpk bigger than it would have been under normal growth. This is of course pϕk (pϕ—1), or the same as the net gain in b over time from a single switch of k from l to m. In other words the continuous switch brings no more benefit than the single switch, i.e. no benefit.

6. Next take a once-for-all switch of k from b to m, not l to m; reverting as before to normal growth of m in the next year. We may write the deviations from normal as follows:

ar	1	2	3	4	......	p+1	p+2	p+3	......	2p+1	2p+2
n	+k	0	0	0		0	0	0		0	0
	0	+ϕk	+ϕk	+ϕk		+ϕk	0	0		0	0
	—k	0	+ϕ^2k	+2ϕ^2k		+(p—1)ϕ^2k	+pϕ^2k	+(p—1)ϕ^2k		+ϕ^2k	0

This time the sum of the b row is k(pϕ $+$ 1) (pϕ—1). As before we have a function of the productivity of capital; and as before if the switch of k from b to m is made every year a maximum excess of b over its level under normal growth is arrived at in year p $+$ 2; and as before this excess is pϕ^2k.

This time, too, the extra investment required altogether is greater than the initial increase in m. It is k (pϕ $+$ 1). So the 'rate of gross return' on capital redirected in *this* manner is also pϕ—1.

7. It will be found in most economic thinking before the concept of second order investment was introduced, that the whole of gross investment is treated as if it were of the first order. Consequently what holds in such literature for a switch from b to a holds now for a switch from b to l, leaving m unmolested: the net gain of b for a switch of k is k (pϕ—1), or the usual 'rate of gross return'.

Note that in neither (6) nor (7) is provision made inside the system for the physical capacity to produce more M; since the addition to m is superimposed on normal growth, and all M is already fully employed, the new finance must go to waste unless it is used to import M. It follows that the —k in year 1, row b of (6) and (7) is an export of consumer goods in exchange for machine tools. In (3) and (5) this is not so, since a switch of k from l to m merely releases M capacity from the production of 'looms' for the reproduction of itself.

8. Finally let us examine the case where the initial change does not come from a shift of 'resources' in the system, but via an influx of resources, as in any case all the consequential changes have in the previous examples. In other words the k put into m in year 1 is also imported, and there is no —k in b or l. Then inspection of the previous example shows that the sum of the gains in b is $p^2\phi^2k$, and the sum of investments is $(p\phi + 1)k$, giving a rate of gross return $p^2\phi^2/p\phi + 1$, which is slightly greater than the previous rates. But it is *not* greater because we have begun with m and followed through; quite the contrary, had we taken a much simpler course and invested straightway the imported k into l the rate of gross return would have been higher still, namely $p\phi$.

These rates are greater simply because the borrowed capital is not repaid to the foreign lender within the sequence shown. When it is repaid there are equal and opposite losses.

9. We must also evaluate the effects of reverse shifts, from higher to lower order investment, or into consumption. Inspection of the series set out above shows that we need only reverse all the signs.

10. We have then proved, on very stringent and peculiar assumptions, that the 'détour' does nothing to change the productivity of capital if time preference be omitted, and that it is worse than useless if it be included. Before relaxing these assumptions—which is merely a tedious job of tidying up—it is important to see what we have not proved. We have not shown that the 'détour' is unnecessary or undesirable. On the contrary in the world as a whole, or in a country for good reasons autarkic, it is technically unavoidable, if L is not to be made directly by hand; otherwise no economy can make a start. We are not attacking all investment in M: we have only shown that above the technically necessary minimum it does nothing to enhance growth, or the profitability of investment or the ultimate level of production achieved. It does not pay to fiddle with the direction of investment. The volume of investment

is what counts, and there is no clever Communist way of getting round the necessity to increase it. But there is a necessary minimum of M, which is in the long run that required for 'balanced growth'. For any rate of growth a, and given ϕ and p, there can in the long run only be one ratio $\dfrac{L}{M}$, as shown in Sec. 2. And the higher is a the smaller this ratio must be. a, $\dfrac{L}{M}$ and $\dfrac{b}{a}$ are all interlocked, so that any one of them determines all the others.

11. With this caution let us relax the assumptions of Sec. 2 (v), which impose a single p and a single ϕ on the economy. This is simply a heroic way of making the marginal gross productivity of capital equal everywhere; and so long as it is equal the fact that we are indifferent between the 'détour' and balanced growth merely means that they are equally profitable: it confirms the profitability criterion for investment choice. Let us turn back to Sec. 3, and see if inequality would alter matters. Suppose, then, a shortening of p and a *proportionate* heightening of ϕ, in m but not in l; call the new parameters q and ψ and keep them constant over time. Then since $p\phi-1 = q\psi-1$ the profitability criterion is still indifferent between the 'détour' and balanced growth. Then the extra investment is still equal to $p\phi k$, only over a shorter period, and the extra consumption is still equal to $p\phi k (p\phi-1)$; so nothing has changed.

But this only holds if basic propositions of Sec. 2 still hold. If b, l and L still increase at the rate a, since nothing has changed in their parameters, will m and M still do so? The proof that they will is as follows.

If $b_n = ab_{n-1}$ etc., $L_n = aL_{n-1}$ etc. Now $L_n = l_{n-p} \dfrac{a^p-1}{a-1}$, so $l_n = al_{n-1}$ etc. Define a part of M called M', which is responsible for producing l (i.e. $\psi M' = l$). Then $M'_n = aM'_{n-1}$ etc., and $M'_n = m'_{n-q} \dfrac{a^q-1}{a-1}$. Let the part of M that produces m' be M''. Then clearly it too increases at the rate a, and so *ad infinitum*. Therefore so long as q and ψ are constant it does not matter what values they have, nor whether $q\psi = p\phi$: m and M will increase at the same rate as everything else.

Consequently, if b, l and L increase at a constant rate, m and M must do so at the same rate, even if $q\psi \neq p\phi$. But the profitability criterion indicates otherwise, since the 'rates of gross return' now differ. It follows that if $q\psi \neq p\phi$, but balanced growth is still desired, it pays to export machine tools or looms and import cloth; and vice versa. To the case of an autarkic economy with $q\psi \neq p\phi$ we return in Sec. 12.

Turning to assumption (vi), let the co-operating factors have some cost in m but not in l. Suppose for instance that in m the current cost of production is j per annum. Then in order to produce pϕk in l we must invest $k + pj$ in m. In the example in Sec. 3 the total investment required to produce the sum of the amounts in b rises to $p(\phi k + j)$; but the same would be true in the case of balanced growth, since then too the operating cost in m would be j. So the omission of co-operating factors did not prejudice the comparison. It is thus evident that our two main simplifying assumptions, however drastic, do not affect the argument: the 'détour' is only good for growth when it is also profitable.

12. What if the country is autarkic? i.e. let us withdraw assumption (vii). Now Marxist theory tacitly assumed that all capital goods produced in a country are also installed in it. It needed the Polish thaw of 1956 to bring this issue into the open: détour or no détour, why should any one country produce all its own m goods, or at any rate maintain an even trade balance in m goods separately? What even Stalin did not demand of Albania, perhaps did not hold for Poland either? And in fact it does not hold for U.S.S.R., which always has been and remains a net importer of machinery!

The profitability criterion is, as we have seen, adequate to deal with this problem too. If, for instance, the marginal productivity of capital was so high in m that one was tempted to invest more in it than required for balanced growth, this would nevertheless be the right thing to do. The surplus of m products ('looms' or 'machine tools') would be exported in exchange for 'cloth'. This is precisely what many advanced economies do. Or, vice versa, one could export l products to buy m products, thus achieving a *volume of installation of capital goods greater than the volume of their output.*

But an autarkic economy could never instal more capital goods than it produced, and would therefore have to have an m/l output ratio at least as great as that required by the 'balanced growth' pattern. It could still make the 'détour' if it wished, i.e. adopt a higher m/l ratio for a time. Only if it did so, remembering assumption (viii) in Sec. 2, the price of 'machine tools' would fall, and that of 'looms' and 'cloth' rise. For it is precisely our assumption that there is international trade which keeps these prices stable, and therefore keeps ψ and ϕ stable. In an autarkic country the 'détour' would lower ψ, bringing back $q\psi$ to the level of $p\phi$ and making the path of balanced growth the most profitable one again.

It follows that the 'balanced growth' pattern of production, as opposed to installation, is by no means likely to be the most profitable, except possibly in an autarkic country. But even there we may expect the relative profitability of m and l to vary from time to time, so that the 'profitability of growth' also varies. Thus an autarkic economy is in a worse position to maintain balanced growth all the time, provided that a trading economy can avoid other kinds of international disturbance. For when m is profitable it will want to increase its capital stock faster than its consumption, and vice versa; and installation must vary directly with output.

13. This brings us to our last, miscellaneous, observations on the 'détour'. First, it does of course increase capital stock more rapidly than consumption—but not more rapidly than income, so long as p and ϕ are constant. Second, we have so far assumed constant returns and no technical progress, or only such changes as are neutral to the system. If they differ between branches then of course $p\phi$ will vary in relation to $q\psi$, and so will the costs of the co-operating factors. At given historical moments such things might be very important. Thus in 1928 in U.S.S.R. there were plainly benefits to be reaped from both increasing returns and technical progress in m, so that a 'détour' was desirable, *in the production pattern but not necessarily in the rate of installation*. In a word, m might be an infant industry, but if it were so this would tell us nothing about the desirable growth of M, unless there happened to be autarky both before and after the change in the volume of m. In the Soviet case there was not such autarky, and the importation of machinery fell off during the second (not the first) FYP.

In general terms the supposition that the 'détour' is a good thing *per se* is merely the old Böhm-Bawerkian fallacy of 'roundaboutness' dressed up in Communist terms and on a macro-economic scale. There is nothing specially desirable in 'roundabout' methods of production, and Marshall's refutation of this view, referred to in the previous chapter, is as valid for Lenin and Stalin as ever it was for Marx and Böhm-Bawerk.

14. So much for the 'détour'. Next, the 'solipsistic enclave'. That is, a switch from consumption or first order investment into second order investment need not ultimately yield a return in

increased consumption at all. It could simply raise the growth of second order investment for ever: machine tools producing more and more machine tools which produce yet more machine tools. In this way it is possible for m to grow at a greater rate than b or l indefinitely.

This is what distinguishes the 'enclave' from the 'détour'. In the switches of resources discussed above the ultimate advantage is concentrated, of set policy, in b. Indeed if the switch is into l, not m, policy has no choice: it is a technical necessity for looms to produce cloth, so that a switch into l can only be for the ultimate advantage of consumption. But a machine tool can be very happily occupied without producing a loom, so that a switch into m can chase its own tail for ever. *Mutatis mutandis* the same applies to seed potatoes and breeder reactors.

Imagine, then, a little investment enclave set up in the economy, condemned to indefinite and solipsistic expansion, but continuously fed from outside. In the first year output is k, and we end with a stock of k. So in the second year output is $k + \phi k$, in the third $k + 2\phi k + \phi^2 k$. The rate of growth is thus ϕ until the need for replacement sets in. Thereafter it falls and may well also fluctuate. But it tends to a limit, which, I am assured,[1] lies between ϕ and $\frac{p}{p+1} \phi$. Where p is small it will be observed that this lower limit may be a long way from ϕ; i.e. without specific arithmetical calculations we are not told very much.

This might have some practical relevance to the 'tooling up' period of a rearmament drive, or to the Soviet first FYP; but it also points an important theoretical moral. This is that our investment enclave must in all circumstances grow quicker than the rest of the economy; for the growth of that too depends, by our assumptions, on investment alone, and yet much of the effect of investment outside the enclave is 'wasted' on consumption. So whatever the relation between p and ϕ, however much it depresses the rate of growth of the enclave, it will keep the outside rate of growth lower still.

Now we have seen hitherto that no mere reshuffling of resources between consumption and first and second order investment can

---

[1] By my colleague Mr. M. M. Crum.

increase the rate of growth for long if the ultimate aim is consumption: for the profitability of investment is not enhanced by such reshuffles. There must be extra investment for extra growth. But this new kind of reshuffle—of first into second order investment for the sake of second order investment—is different. It does raise the rate of growth. But the reason is not that the profitability of capital has been enhanced by some reshuffle between orders of investment. This is no more possible than before. It is simply that the 'leak' into consumption has been stopped. For the 'solipsistic enclave' is not autarkic. Very much the contrary: it keeps pulling in savings from outside, it entails a much higher rate of investment in the economy as a whole. And this, alone, is why growth has increased.

15. We have seen that in industry b, l and m goods differ physically as well as by end-use. Hence if we were autarkic and in year 1 we used all our machine tools to make looms we should not in year 2 be *able* to invest much, we should have to choose between cloth (i.e. consumption) and unemployment. But if we had made machine tools in year 1 we should in year 2 have to choose between investment and unemployment. And vice versa: if we had wanted to invest (or consume) in year 2 we should have made machine tools (or looms) in year 1. The Communist stress on A over B is merely the technical, input/output, reflection of the Communist determination to invest.

Thus if the 'détour' does not ultimately increase growth at all, the 'solipsistic enclave' does, but *only* because it is technologically identical with an overall increase in investment. If in an autarkic economy vast funds are regularly set aside *and successfully spent* on investment there must be a vast m industry, for ever reproducing itself: for if it ever produced anything else, such as looms, there would come a time when the vast funds could no longer be successfully spent on investment. *The physical relationships discussed in this chapter entail certain financial relationships, and vice versa.* Outside industry, where end-use is not physically determined, things are more flexible but the essence is the same: *a huge investment programme in a market economy is (if it is autarkic) by definition a decision to expand A at the expense of B.* Detailed physical planning will not achieve more, nor looser planning by monetary allocations less.

This can be put in another way: *there is no such thing in general as a 'growth-inducing commodity'.* Neither 'machine tools' nor 'looms' nor 'steel' are in all, or perhaps even in most, circumstances more growth-inducing than 'thread' or 'dresses'. For, first, the export of these latter categories might well be the cheapest way of acquiring the first three; and this is where we must distinguish between production and installation or consumption. But, secondly and more radically, if the 'looms' are already there 'thread' is the most growth-inducing commodity: and vice versa, only if the 'thread' is already there are 'looms' (or possibly 'machine tools' to make them with) the most growth-inducing. If everything is equally scarce balanced growth is best. In general, bottleneck commodities are the most growth-inducing: a theorem which re-establishes profit as the principal criterion.

What is true, however, is that a rapidly growing economy, even one in which the rate of growth has been arbitrarily raised by central planning, renders profitable (or growth-inducing) a quite different product-mix from a stagnant economy.[1]

16. This type of analysis also throws light on the current (1961) difficulties of Khrushchev, in trying to reduce the 'growth gap' between A and B. Defeated in his main effort to get equal growth written into the plan, he settled for a mere reduction of the growth gap and switched the proportions of l and m within A. Now if we merely plan in terms of A or even I we have left long-run growth indeterminate. For A and I cover a multitude of sins, and it is open to a Communist leader to pay mere lip-service to the ideology, by making looms instead of machine-tools. If he makes enough looms he will for a few years keep A growing faster than B, but eventually he places the economy in the technical necessity of producing cloth instead of either looms or machine tools, so that A decelerates. A permanent preponderance in the growth of A requires the same to be true of m.

It would thus appear that in promising more l and less m within a constant A Khrushchev[2] is either contradicting himself or subtly evading the party line, which demands that the 'growth-gap' continue.

---

[1] This chapter was written before reading Evsey Domar's 'A Soviet Model of Growth' (Ch. 9 in his *Essays in the Theory of Economic Growth*, New York 1957). There are very many coincidences and, I think, no disagreement. Domar's principal variable, y, is A/M in my terms, and he is concerned only with its influence on consumption. His case of y = 1 resembles my 'solipsistic enclave' which, however, he does not work out. He does not investigate my 'détour', since his y is constant. But he does obtain a whole series of extremely interesting correlations of y with the rate of growth of consumption (p. 248). In so doing he starts simply from a point of time and a stock of L and M, and not, as I have done in order to ease the mathematics, from a position of balanced growth. Nor does he end up in such a position, though he does usually approach it. Like me, he has to assume that capital is the only scarce factor.

[2] *Pravda*, Oct. 20, 1961. For the previous controversy cf. Dolberg and Wiles, *Ost-Europa* 1962.

CHAPTER 16

CAPITAL-INTENSITY AND GROWTH

1. IT is often argued, especially by economists who dislike the price mechanism,[1] that profit is a wrong criterion for investment if economic growth is to be maximized out of a given volume of investment; and in particular that one must choose more capital-intensive schemes than the market would make profitable. This chapter sets out to prove the contrary. It is mainly an attack on the various schools of thought that may compendiously be called 'capital-maximizers'. It is *not* an attack on such ancient truths as the 'infant industry' argument.

Clearly no one wishes to deny that growth is enhanced by a greater volume of investment than the market would render profitable. And clearly it is an immense advantage of government intervention that it can achieve that greater volume. But is any stricter planning required, or can the allocation between sectors and between techniques, of the funds thus forcibly gathered, be safely left to the market?

In discussing this question all the normal static qualifications are assumed, which equate private with social profit in simple welfare economics: there is no factory smoke, income is distributed with equal 'justice' before and after any given change, etc., etc. I have already defended in Ch. 5 the acceptance of the assumptions of static welfare economics, not at all because they are logically necessary for us to proceed but because they are broadly true, especially when the objections to them are quantified. Next we state the proposition that *the more net profit there is the more surplus there is for re-investment.* Or to put it another way, it is clearly the most profitable investment which, at the time and in the very short run, will most increase the national income; and this makes the most saving possible. Therefore rapid growth demands the most profitable

---

[1] E.g. N. Kaplan in (ed.) A. Bergson, *Soviet Economic Growth*, Evanston 1953, pp. 83-4; K. Kurihara, *The Keynesian Theory of Economic Development*, New York 1957, p. 59; W. Galenson and H. Leibenstein, *Quarterly Journal of Economics*, Aug. 1955; P. A. Baran, *The Political Economy of Growth*, Monthly Review Press, 1957, pp. 286-8. Further literature on this subject: Holzman, *El Trimestre Económico*, Mexico, Oct./Dec. 1958; R. Nurkse, *Malayan Economic Review*, Oct. 1957; Bator, Eckstein, Sen: *Quarterly Journal of Economics*, 1957; Kahn, ibid. 1951.

investment of a volume of savings which has itself been raised beyond that which would be provided in a free market.

This view is so naïf as to seem, in mid-twentieth century, a sophisticated paradox or wilful perversion. Yet it rests, in my mind, not only on its own obvious rightness and simplicity but also on the falsity of nearly all opposing views. The first two of these— the 'détour' and the 'solipsistic enclave'—have been discussed at length and dismissed in the previous chapter.

2. It is, thirdly, a common argument, on a very low level of sophistication, that capital-intensity as such is a good thing: not for any of the clever reasons advanced in this and the previous chapter but simply because it is technically more 'progressive', it represents a 'higher' level of technology.

This of course is rubbish. Technical progress means making things cheaper, and includes the use of *less* capital per unit of output, as we have already demonstrated at length. Any manual technique might be more 'progressive' than any mechanized technique, as the cost comparison might happen to fall out in a given case. In Marxism, however, such a thing can find no place, as the 'organic composition of capital' must increase for there to be technical progress.[1]

It is undoubted that under Communism the cost of industrialization has been increased and its onset retarded by insistence on capital-intensity. Both the dogma and the practice[2] demonstrate this. Yet in underdeveloped countries capital is always scarce, and the faster they develop the scarcer it is. Surely, then, *some* practical realization has been shown of this? It has indeed: we may give a few instances.

The first is Stalin's forced labour camps. These were indeed starved of capital, and relied on brute manual labour. Roads, rail-tracks, aerodromes, coal-mining, forestry: very much current output and still more construction was thus secretly performed by labour-intensive techniques. The second is the export of timber and food during the first Soviet FYP. Labour, some of it forced and some of it not, was hastily mobilized and thrown into the Northern timber belt, to use very primitive methods. And Russia's traditional food exports were stepped up (while the people starved).

[1] Ch. 14, Sec. 13.
[2] Soviet agriculture employs large tractors where small ones would do: N. Jasny, *The Socialised Agriculture of U.S.S.R.* (Stanford 1949), pp. 460–4. Very capital-intensive forms of electricity generation are preferred: J. P. Hardt in ed. G. Grossman, *Value and Plan*, California, 1960.

Thus foreign machinery was acquired by the use of labour-intensive techniques.

The third and more important exception is China since 1957. In a country far more primitive and far shorter of capital than the Soviet Union ever was, it has been officially recognized that it is foolish to maximize capital-intensity—a real doctrinal breakthrough. That there should be vast public-works projects involving only manual labour is hardly surprising, and merely repeats in public what Stalin did in secret.[1] But that steel, the *sanctum sanctorum* of Communist industrialization, should be produced in millions of little primitive blast-furnaces is indeed a slap in the face for the theology of capital-intensity.

The first Chinese mention of capital-saving known to me was in Jan. 1955.[2] The doctrine attained final respectability in connexion with the draft plan for 1957.[3] The draft was a very right-wing document, intimately connected with the revival of free markets and free production for unimportant commodities,[4] and the general predominance of Chou En-lai and Chen Yün. Admitting that there was great 'tension' in 1956, the above-quoted leader says that in 1957 *and* 1958 investment will be below the level of 1956. Here indeed is a bitter pill for a Communist government. No doubt it was largely because Soviet loans had ceased in 1955, and already in 1956 the Chinese balance of payments was in surplus: i.e. owing to debt service China was investing abroad.[5]

But there is worse than that in the draft: 'Central and local development,' says the leader, 'should be co-ordinated. Judging from the state of fulfilment of the first FYP, the investment made in local enterprises has exceeded the target considerably. Viewed from the angle of investment proportions, it appears that they should be further slashed. But we should cut them as little as possible, since local authorities have to take care of different lines of construction. For instance, some undertakings, particularly the construction of new industrial cities and the production of materials (?),[6] have to be carried out with the aid of local government: small

---

[1] Nor always in secret. For the Baltic-Black Sea canal was dug by forced labour, in the first halcyon days of that institution, under conditions of much publicity: A. M. Gorki *et al.*, *Baltiisko-Belomorski Kanal* (Moscow 1934).

[2] Report of Huang Ching, chairman of State Technological Commission, quoted in *Far Eastern Economic Review*, no. 173.

[3] E.g. leader in *Ch'i Hua Ching Chi*, Apr. 9, 1957 (=ECMM 90).

[4] Cf. Ch. 9, Sec. 7.

[5] Scott, *Soviet Studies*, Oct. 1958.

[6] Presumably building-materials—P.J.D.W.

kilns turning out coal, iron foundries operating in a primitive way and chemical fertilizer production have to be set up by the local authorities to lessen the strains imposed on the supplies to state enterprises. In particular a large part of local investment has a great bearing on agricultural production, such as that in water conservancy. In the use of capital resources we should concentrate our fiscal strength on the urgently required enterprises, and distribute funds rationally.' Projects which need a long construction period and freeze assets over years before coming into bearing must not be begun; they must even be interrupted if only just begun.

All this adds up to a complete reversal of Stalinist investment policy, and as so far stated it would naturally form part of any right-wing Communist interlude. Nagy, Gomulka, Bukharin, even Lenin could have written every word of it. Of much greater interest was that the Left (sc. Liu Shao-chih) swung round to this position too, and built capital-saving, labour-intensive technique deep into the Great Leap Forward of May 1958. In this month right-wing policies were abandoned in many fields, and a fantastic all-out drive for Full Communism in ten years begun.[1] But the primitive blast-furnaces and the intensive mobilization of manual labour remained, indeed were greatly heightened. Capital-saving is no longer in China the preserve of comparatively rational and liberal Communists.[2]

3. Logically, but not psychologically, separate is the choice of the size of the enterprise. Large enterprises can of course always be under-capitalized (e.g. the Chinese People's Communes), and it is at least possible for small ones to have very high capital ratios. However, it will be found that 'capital-maximizers' nearly always favour a larger scale of enterprise than the most profitable, even omitting the increasing returns argument in the next section. There is something 'socialist' and 'progressive' about mere size, even if unaccompanied by lower costs. Gigantomania as such, then, reinforces the view that large capital expenditures are a good thing, even where smaller ones will do.

Soviet gigantomania, and its fluctuating history, are very well

---

[1] Cf. Ch. 17, Sec. 4.

[2] It is particularly interesting that a Soviet statistician agreed with the new Chinese view shortly after the issue was raised: 'The Questions of Result and Economy in Capital Investments', notes on a speech by Soviet statistical expert Comrade Semikievkin, *Tung Chi Kung Tso*, Aug. 14, 1957 (=ECMM 100, pp. 38–9).

known.[1] But the purest examples of this attitude are Chinese, where small enterprises are amalgamated in left-wing periods, and were disaggregated in the intervening swing to the right, already referred to, without technical change. Both agricultural and craftsmen's co-operatives were at that time disaggregated.[2] The initial unitary People's Commune of 1958 represents in this matter a very extreme leftward swing. But now the agricultural co-ops have reappeared as subordinate units within the Commune, enjoying great operational independence.

4. This leads us to the argument from the *earlier enjoyment of increasing returns*.[3] A large and not a small factory is set up at once, in view of future expansion. Either it at once begins mass production or it stands partially idle. In any case it makes a loss, until the economy has grown enough to accommodate it; and this is somehow a good thing.

First note that the more rapid the rate of growth the less loss is caused by 'building ahead of use'; and since undoubtedly it is a pity not to be able to exploit increasing returns this is a strong argument for rapid growth. But is it an argument for building ahead of use? It seems on the whole that the free market will of itself induce just the right degree of 'early enjoyment of increasing returns'. Thus suppose a choice between two factory sizes A (small) and B (large); that there is no technical progress (except that labour can become more skilled), and no other plant size than A or B. Then first take the case where A can always be converted into B without extra cost; i.e. either (i) the cost of physically converting A into B = the green-field site cost of B minus the value of A in the books at the time, or (ii) A can always be sold for its full book value at historical cost. Then obviously there is no point at all in building ahead of use: we can always get the plant-size we want when we want it, and production at a loss before that time is simple waste.

Other cases are more complicated, and for reasons of space we must over-simplify. Let the current production cost with factory A be X_1, X_2, etc., for the output required in each year, and let it for that same output be Y_1, Y_2 etc., with factory B. Each plant lasts 10 years, and we use straight line depreciation. The rate of interest (i) is charged on the whole sum borrowed, and this sum is

[1] The best description is in Leon Smolinski's *The Size of the Soviet Enterprise*, Harvard doctoral dissertation, 1961. Smolinski omits, however, agriculture. For this see Jasny, op. cit.

[2] Chou En-lai, op. cit.

[3] Cf. Streeten, *Oxford Economic Papers*, June 1959.

X

redeemable at will. S is the scrap value of A in any year, and there is no futurity discount. Then the same output stream might be produced, *inter alia*, by these two ways:

Year	Path I		Path II	
	Depreciation and interest	*Current cost*	*Depreciation and interest*	*Current cost*
I	(install A)		(install B)	
	$A(i + \frac{I}{IO})$	X_1	$B(i + \frac{I}{IO})$	Y_1
5	,,	X_5	,,	Y_5
6	(Install B, write off the whole of A and redeem the corresponding debt)			
	$B(i + \frac{I}{IO})$	Y_6	,,	Y_6
10	,,	Y_{10}	,,	Y_{10}

Total cost to year 10:
capital $A + \frac{1}{2}iA + \frac{1}{2}B(1+i) - S_6$ $B(1+i)$
current $X_1 + \ldots X_5 + Y_6 + \ldots Y_{10}$ $Y_1 + \ldots Y_{10}$

Now if output is growing the whole time the 'early enjoyment of increasing returns' might mean that while $X_{1 \ldots 3} < Y_{1 \ldots 3}$, $X_{4, 5} > Y_{4, 5}$. Grant, then, some slight economy in current costs for path II, what of capital costs? Suppose the scrap value = the value in the books, i.e. $S_6 = \frac{1}{2}A$. In this case the capital costs of Path I are lower than those of Path II by no small sum: $\frac{1}{2}(B-A)(1+i)$. It seems entirely plausible that this might exceed the saving on current costs. Moreover, if the scrap value has been, as is highly probable, over-stated, it is also likely that current cost advantages of Path II have been over-stated. Suppose that Y did not fall below X until year 7; it would then certainly pay to run A until that year, indeed probably until it collapsed in year 10.

Furthermore the rate of depreciation is itself a function of time. This is a dynamic concept, in the sense that in year 1 the labour force may be unskilled, both in constructing and in operating factories. Much better, then, to let it learn by ruining a small factory, and postpone a large one until it is immediately necessary. In terms of our table, Path II might be unable to carry B beyond year 5; and it would be only from year 6 that either plant *could* last 10 years. In this case Path II would be obviously inferior to Path I. This is very likely in a backward country.

There is thus no *a priori* case for a forced 'earlier enjoyment of increasing returns'; it is simply a matter of calculation in the circumstances. *Moreover there is no divergence between private and social profit, since all the above elements enter into private cost and calculation.* A private entrepreneur might of course have a shorter time-horizon than is rational, or he might have to bear risks that a central planner would not. But those are old truths, with a much more general application than to this argument.

I conclude that the argument for building ahead of use, in order the earlier to enjoy increasing returns, rests in its usual form upon an elementary mistake: its proponents omit the scrap value, in whatever use, of the old plant. When this possibility is taken into account it cannot be sustained that private profit is misleading. Communists of course build ahead of use on a grand scale, though not only with the motive of earlier enjoying increasing returns. And we have not in this section discussed any other motive.

'Building ahead of use' is almost the same as 'infant industry'. In the former case the large enterprise or even industry[1] is actually created, and then subsidized either to produce at high cost below full capacity or to use its full capacity and make more than can be sold. 'Infant industry' stems from the same basic situation: there are increasing returns but we do not yet want the full output. In this case however a small enterprise or industry is set up, suitable for the size the market, and is expected to grow. In other words conversion costs and scrap values are, by implication, correctly treated. Were there no divergence between the interests of one nation and another 'infant industry' would be an entirely unremarkable phenomenon, and no argument against *laissez faire*. But in the face of foreign competition it is of course an argument for tariffs.

5. Then there is the maximization of the 'reinvestible surplus', i.e. of net profit plus replacement.[2] Capital-intensive techniques are to be preferred because they require more replacement, which means more funds each year for the purchase of capital assets.

The idea that replacement as such is a good thing is very strange

---

[1] A whole industry enjoys increasing returns, even if its enterprises do not, if the enterprises supplying factors to it enjoy increasing returns.
[2] Galenson and Leibenstein, op. cit.

indeed. Why is it better to be for ever replacing machinery than, for instance, raw materials? If one maximized raw material costs instead, one could have a simply splendid annual turnover of the capital invested in *them*; perhaps that too would be a good thing? Why not, indeed, maximize all costs? At first blush all such ideas appear wrong-headed, and at tenth blush the impression remains.

Messrs. Galenson and Leibenstein's central thesis has been described by me, polemically, as the maximization of replacement. The crucial passage, in which they pass from the criticism of simple profit to the advocacy of their new criterion, is surprisingly short. I reproduce it *in toto*, but interspersed with my comments (their italics):

> Apart from the human factors, it is the capital/labour ratio that determines output *per capita*. From this point of view the criterion to be adopted is the one that ultimately leads to the maximum capital/labour ratio.

—we have already condemned (Ch. 11) the *maximization* of growth as a literally murderous economic policy, stinting present consumption to below subsistence level for all but workers and children. Similarly the capital/labour ratio can only be maximized by maximizing investment—net investment, to be precise. And here again once it is admitted that capital has a cost in current abstinence it is elementary that its amount must not be maximized—

> The amount of capital per worker that is created in the long run depends on two broad factors: (1) the amount of investment year by year stemming from the product of the initial investment;

—but it is not clear why money should stem from any particular 'initial' investment: it might equally stem from a mere current rearrangement of resources, or from the more efficient exploitation of the sectors (e.g. the peasantry) that have *not* used any initial capital—

> and (2) the increase in the size of the labour force. We must therefore take into account the initial investment plus the sum of all subsequent reinvestments divided by the size of the labour force at the end of the stipulated time horizon.

—reinvestments of gross or of net profit? If, as is made clear, of gross profit, and therefore including replacement, we must object that the stock of capital, which it is desired to increase, depends on *net* investment and this stems from *net* profit. Moreover not *all* increases in the stock are good. Some cause painful abstinence, some are technically unnecessary.

If the reader still does not believe that replacement has been forgotten, let him look at the careful algebraical exposition on p. 357 of the article cited. There is no symbol for or mention of replacement, and I, or gross investment, is flatly stated to $= c \triangle N$, where c is the cost of a machine, and N the number of machines. In other words replacement is tacitly put at zero, and the maximand thus happens to be formally identical with profit. But since depreciation is not in fact zero the criterion is very precisely a demand that net profit plus replacement be maximized. The very word 'replacement' appears first and only on their p. 362.

Strictly, replacement is a function of two things: capital-intensity and low asset durability. A high rate of replacement could as well be obtained by buying short-lived fixed assets as by substituting fixed assets for labour. This point is not always made by capital-maximizers: naturally so, for low asset durability is at the opposite psychological pole from high capital-intensity. Indeed at this juncture Messrs. Galenson and Leibenstein make a most curious volte-face, and demand very durable assets, thus rendering more difficult that high rate of replacement they require. Wanting high replacement and durable assets, they are logically bound to want very great capital-intensity indeed. In this context they use the results of Domar[1] as follows (p. 362):

If the capital stock is to be maintained intact, then eventually replacements must be made. But even after the advantage of the early no replacement period has passed, there is still an advantage in a capital stock that is on the average longer-lived than shorter-lived under conditions of growth. This is because the longer the average life of the capital, the smaller is the proportion of gross investment needed for replacement,[2] and therefore the larger is gross investment less replacement cost period after period.

So much, then, for the fact that the authors here go against their earlier desire for large replacement: in demanding great durability they are now demanding small replacement. The basic point is that they share a tendency very common in the recent, more sophisticated Western literature: to think replacement away, and deal only in gross investment at all times. In the more naïve economics of Communism this is happily not the case, and here we must give them best. But to our authors gross investment is their basic concept, net investment a residual. They have now switched from their

[1] *Economic Journal*, March 1953.
[2] This is because the economy is growing—P.J.D.W

earlier maximization of gross investment, and admit that there is an advantage in high net investment. But how tortuously! Gross investment is still basically the maximand, and net investment is to be increased, not by anything so simple as a greater abstinence effort, but by lowering depreciation. Yet in truth it is as arbitrary to insist on high durability as on low: here too net profit is the proper criterion. And the way to attain high net investment is to have it, not arbitrarily to maximize some irrelevant magnitude and then arbitrarily to minimize the deductions from it. Thus the way to raise net investment might in some circumstances be to raise both gross investment and replacement, but the former more rapidly; and in others it might be lower them both, but the former more slowly.

In sum, it is a tautology that the capital stock depends on net investment. Those who want a large stock should want large net investment. It does not matter what the gross figure is, nor what replacement is. Only the difference matters.

Another offender along these lines is, in his otherwise admirable chapter on 'Capital Formation and Allocation', Mr. Norman Kaplan (op. cit.), who lays completely disproportionate stress on the fact that the U.S.S.R. does not devote an exceptional proportion of its *gross* national product to *gross* investment. I.e. if we include capital depreciation and exclude armaments the Soviet investment effort is not in overall volume very great; nor in consequence is its saving effort, since saving = investment. But, one must reply, capital replacement is no part of income. It is true that replacement is a very small part of the Soviet GNP, since in a rapidly growing economy there is always proportionately little old capital equipment in existence to replace. And it follows indeed from this circumstance that even if—nay precisely because—current net investment is a very great part of the national income, gross investment is only a moderate part of the GNP. But this fact has nothing to do with the measurement of the Soviet saving and investment effort, since it is not saving that finances replacement.

In general it would be as sensible to include the replacement of raw cotton stocks in the national income as the replacement of spindles. Income excludes costs, and replacement is a cost. The Gross National Product is a bastard concept having scarcely any justification except statistical necessity. However often it is used by statisticians who shirk the complexities of measuring depreciation or replacement, it remains for almost all purposes an inferior tool of analysis to the Net National Product.

6. In opposition to the doctrine of Messrs. Galenson and Leibenstein, there is, paradoxically, something to be said for low durability. This is that it means a high rate of obsolescence. For it can justly be said of certain economies that they have an irrational fear of obsolescence. But this certainly does not apply where capital is scarce. It is in a mature, stagnant economy like the British that the rate of obsolescence should be raised, but raised to a level that it can easily afford. An underdeveloped country should keep its scarce capital for priority objects, and not hesitate to rub along with obsolete capital if it will still function.

Curiously enough the Soviet authorities behaved very rationally in this matter, refusing to recognize obsolescence at all until 1956, i.e. until about the time capital had ceased to be really scarce. When capital widening, i.e. the employment in industry for the first time of the surplus rural population, ceases to be possible, new investment can only have two ends: new products or the improvement of old techniques. This latter end raises fairly and squarely the question of obsolescence. Strictly speaking, however, it was ideology and not economic rationality that kept obsolescence out of Soviet accountancy so long, and the post-Stalin thaw, not capital superfluity, that finally introduced it.[1] Nevertheless we may be sure that had the need for an obsolescence concept been really acute it would have been introduced under Stalin.

A more rigorous analysis is presented in Sec. 8.

7. Then there is the argument from the *costs of urbanization*. Take a country that is bringing in surplus rural labour to newly founded industry. Of two projects promising an equal output over an equal period of time, we are asked to choose the most capital-intensive, since it employs least labour and thus incurs least capital cost in housing, street-building, etc.[2]

A fantastic argument in the mouth of a capital-maximizer! We must choose the apparently more capital-intensive because it is really the less capital-intensive, and capital is short! Starting with a general bias in favour of spending capital, they so far forget themselves as to recommend ways of saving it! The explanation can only be sought in psychology: your capital-maximizer has his romantic vision of modern factories, and he wants somehow to

---

[1] Cf. R. W. Campbell, *The Soviet Power* (Houghton 1960), pp. 104-6.
[2] Galenson and Leibenstein, op. cit.; Baran, op. cit.

persuade us to spend our capital on such projects. If they appear to be capital-intensive he will present any sophisticated argument that makes heavy expenditure of the scarcest factor seem good. If on reflection they appear to be capital-extensive he switches, within the confines of the same book or article, to a plain man's approach, and recommends them because they save capital. His real motivation is not to save or to spend capital, but to instal bright, new, costly equipment in extensive palaces of industry. This is the vision of Communist and non-Communist capital-maximizers alike.

Eloquent indignation must, alas, be based on rigorous analysis. To this we now turn. First note that the urbanization capital itself produces an income. It is of course a dull, invisible service income; it is not some splendid material product like sulphuric acid or toothpaste or locomotives, it is only shelter, warmth, shop-gazing, a stroll in the park. For Marxists this is simple: services do not count anyway. For non-Marxist capital-maximixers the omission is a little more surprising.

Even in the case of a rural surplus, moving from a place where it is already sheltered and warmed after a fashion, this point remains. For in the ordinary case[1] the new urban services are superior to the old rural ones; and in all cases the remaining rural population benefits by having more house-room per head—a social profit that cannot be left out of account.

Suppose, then, that we want an additional output of X over a fixed period, consisting partly in some rather capital-intensive factory production, e.g. of 'aluminium', and partly of the urban services rendered to its labour force (defined above as net extra services); and that 'we', the state, have to find all the capital. The X costs:

capital: $F + U$, where F is factory capital and U urbanization capital;

labour: $M + S$, where M is the manufacturing labour force, S the service labour force in the new town.

Alternatively we could obtain X from a capital-extensive enterprise such as 'wood', where the factory costs would be

capital: fF,
labour: mM,

---

[1] Britain of the 1830s and U.S.S.R. of the 1930s are obvious exceptions.

where $m > 1 > f$. Or 'wood' and 'aluminium' could be two different ways of making the same product. A complication now arises about the urbanization costs, since the larger number of factory workers of course require more U, and this U of course requires an increase in S: but this greater S in turn requires more U, and so on. Assume a constant requirement of U per worker, $\dfrac{U}{M+S}$, and a constant labour/capital ratio S/U. Then the infinite series thus generated boils down to:

$$capital = fF + mU$$
$$labour = mM + mS$$

Note that with 'aluminium' the factory product is a larger part of X than with 'wood', since the output of urban services shrinks by the factor m. Those who hold urban services not to be output will of course infer that 'aluminium' is preferable to 'wood', but with such there is no arguing.

Now for the effective capital ratio in 'wood' to be greater,

$$\frac{F + U}{X} \text{ must} < \frac{fF + mU}{X} \text{ , or } \frac{F}{U} < \frac{m-1}{1-f}.$$

Is this likely? Unfortunately no data from an underdeveloped or Communist country are reliable enough, but U.S. figures are at least illustrative. According to my own very rough calculation F/U is about 40%. In a poor country, where machines remain expensive but there is an altogether lower standard of urban amenity, the ratio might be much higher: so put even so high a ratio as 1·0. Then even quite moderate and probable values for m and f make 'wood' the more capital-intensive of the two projects. E.g. if $m = 2$, $f = \frac{2}{3}$ it still needs much more capital than 'aluminium'.

But however the magnitudes work out the main point is that this is a simple profit-maximization theorem like any other: we are asked not to forget the costs of urbanization, but to choose the cheapest projects with them in mind. It would carry us too far afield to pursue this subject to death, so let it be briefly stated that the price-mechanism does not normally by any means fully reflect these costs, and that it surely should be made to. Relax, then, the assumption that the state bears all the urbanization costs. In most countries, *including Communist ones*, townward migrants pay for at least some of these costs out of their incomes, and willingly. They even build their own houses: the rash of peripheral, privately owned huts and holes in the ground is a universal phenomenon in growing towns.[1] But where there is a rural surplus the new factory generates the incomes *and the savings* of the migrants. No pre-existing capital funds, no already given capacity for abstinence, is used up by the migrants' own investment in their own town, unless (a) the town is subsidized or (b) the municipality, or the migrants themselves, borrow from the state. Were (a) and (b) both zero the argument from the capital-intensity of urbanization would collapse altogether, and the state would simply face the choice between the factory costs of 'aluminium' and those of 'wood'.

Or again suppose there was no rural surplus, so that the factory generates little if any new income, and the migrants' saving capacity already existed and is diverted into the building of the new town. Then if at least the costs were always borne fully out of the wages of M,[2] they would influence the entrepreneur's or planner's decision, and this section need again never have been written. But central government grants to local authorities regularly lower the private marginal cost of urbanization all over the world. And the local authority itself, and the public utilities, very seldom charge the immigrant the full marginal cost of new streets, new drains and new electricity connexions. Quite likely too the new houses are subsidized; if by the factory, all is well: but if by any other body, further distortion arises.

Interesting and important as it is, however, the argument from the costs of urbanization brings no comfort at all to a 'capital-maximizer'. It merely indicates one of the forgotten capital costs that must be minimized.

In this connexion we have again occasion to praise Chinese policy. China is to my knowledge the first country to have conceived *industrialization without urbanization*.[3] One of the many advantages of the People's Communes is that under such a strong and all-inclusive local authority small industry can be brought to the village. Of course it has to be small: a really large plant might admittedly not bulk large in a People's Commune of 40,000

---

[1] In the 1930s the town of Karaganda consisted of almost nothing else but private *zemlyanki*—half huts, half holes in the ground. When the population came to exceed a certain size all the zemlyanki were nationalized! This information is from Mr. S. V. Utechin of the London School of Economics, who was there.

[2] Except of course the social costs directly attributable to production: smoke, commercial traffic congestion, etc. These should be borne by the new factory directly.

[3] Gandhi only wanted non-industrialization without urbanization. But there have been some anticipations of this policy in Japan, and they were even recommended to Stalin. Cf. I. Kan, *Planovoe Khozyaistvo*, 8/1928.

inhabitants, but it would certainly bulk large in a particular village, and the laying together or extension of villages incurs the costs of urbanization. Note that the important thing is not that the enterprises should be capital-extensive, but that they should be small; though doubtless, as we have seen, the two things go hand in hand.

In U.S.S.R. on the other hand the policy has always been *urbanization on the cheap*. Stalin never questioned that there should be new towns, and he regularly presented them as one of his great achievements. But he did keep their costs down, by reducing urban living-space per head and providing very few urban services and scarcely any amenities. This policy caused much misery; after the temporary failure of the food supply in 1932–33 it was undoubtedly the main blow that Stalin directed against his subjects' standard of living.

Cheap urbanization raised its ugly head in another context in Soviet history: Khrushchev's agro-gorod campaign of 1950–51. For this we have no space. Enough here to say that when the villages were to be laid together the proposal seems to have been to put the peasants' simple wooden huts on skis and slide them over the snow. Thus prior to the building of proper new houses, the agro-gorod would arise very cheaply indeed: it would require little transport equipment since snow is a free gift of nature; little construction material since the houses would be moved, not built *de novo*; and little labour cost since peasant labour is also a free service when there is snow on the ground. And of course the proper new houses themselves were to be built by kolkhoz building brigades, whose labour would at least cost the state nothing. This fantastic proposition—which is of course a technical absurdity—seems to have made in all seriousness.[1]

The capital-maximizer undoubtedly likes towns. Gleaming cities of the future, with many-storied buildings and ramps and through-ways and over-passes and chromium-plated pubs, are all part of his psychological syndrome. Thus Khrushchev is for ever insisting on two-storey buildings in the countryside: they are somehow on a higher ideological plane than one-storey buildings.

---

[1] All of this appeared in Khrushchev's speeches at the time. Cf. B. Nicolaevsky, *Ost-Probleme*, 1951, pp. 390 sqq., 645 sqq.; Khrushchev, *Moskovskaya Pravda*, early 1951, *passim*; Khrushchev, *Pravda*, March 4, 1951. The only doubtful point is how the peasants were to live in the agro-gorod while the new houses were going up. Khrushchev was quite silent on this, and the only evidence known to me for the huts-on-skis proposal is a cartoon in *Krokodil*, Jan. 21, 1951. It is just possible that the high-level opposition that eventually overwhelmed Khrushchev prompted this cartoon in a satirical spirit. But the wording and the drawing are far from satirical, and it is better to take it as evidence that the proposal was at that moment seriously entertained.

And Stalin's 'tall buildings' and his Moscow Metro show the same hankering; cheap urbanization was but a temporary expedient for him. The prejudice of the Western architectural world against suburbia is another excellent instance of capital-maximization at its deadly work. We must not beautify suburbia, say by suppressing the advertisements and changing the lamp-posts; we must destroy it and build upwards instead. Not Bauhaus but Hochbauhaus: from the *machine à habiter* to the *fabrique à vivre*—and all regardless of its greater cost[1] and inferior amenity.

8. Our next two arguments are of a different kind. It is possible, after all, to err the other way, and insist on using less capital than would seem profitable. The first of these may be called the argument from *craft employment protection*. Thus in India there is vast unemployment and a large manual textile industry. Should not then capital be forcibly diverted into, say, steel and be forbidden to set up a mechanized textile industry even if it is more profitable than steel? Or would this also be wrong, and is private profit a better guide here too?

It seems on the contrary that this argument is right, *if there is no growth in the demand for textiles*. Since there is unemployment the marginal social opportunity cost of labour is, in general, zero, and certainly zero in steel. But new mechanized investment in textiles would put craftsmen out of work and reduce output, since it is directly competitive under our assumptions. Therefore labour has in this particular case an opportunity cost. Yet private profit in textiles could quite easily be as high as in steel; for the existence of competitive production might well be quite irrelevant. If you can undersell your competitors you are as likely to be profitable as if you are a monopolist. Social and private profit would only coincide if textile factories had, and steel factories had not, to pay wages. This is both the static and also, as so often, the dynamic position; as before, we have reason to condemn the easy sophistication that assumes without due thought a difference between the two. For what maximizes the national income here and now maximizes (subject to the qualifications of Sec. 12) its investible surplus.

If however there was room for more textile output textiles and

---

[1] In Southern England in 1955, £2.5 a square foot as opposed to £1.6 a square foot for a two-storey house: Osborn, *Lloyds Bank Review*, April 1955. Furthermore a moment's calculation will show that the loss to agriculture of land for low-density suburbs is quite negligible, in any country.

steel would be in the same boat. The social cost of labour to both would be nil, the same high cost of capital should be charged to both, and both should settle their techniques accordingly. True, there might be some discontinuities in the spectrum of alternative techniques, which in the unavailability of precisely the right alternatives indicated very manual techniques in textiles and very mechanized techniques in steel. But that would be chance, and chance might equally well indicate the opposite.

There is an equally well-known case, slightly different: the choice between sheep and grain in the enclosure movement of sixteenth-century England. Land is in many ways similar to capital, and the choice lay between a land-intensive product that created unemployment and a labour-intensive one that was unprofitable. In making the social cost comparison labour should have been entered as a free good in the case of grain alone. It can similarly be argued that in nineteenth-century U.K. the building of mechanical textile factories should have been limited, since it tended to throw the handloom-weavers out of work, and they were mostly Irish, i.e. they came from a part of the kingdom where there was a surplus population.

Fundamentally 'craft employment protection' is like the obsolescence of capital. It is wrong to invest so as to render plant obsolete while there are other, perhaps less profitable, openings for capital. To be precise, let there be three projects. X is an existing project, Y is a new one competitive with it, Z a new but non-competing project. Then Y is a preferable method of production to X, and should be invested in, only if the average[1] total cost of Y does not exceed the average current cost of X, where 'current' means total minus the service of past debt. For then the new project will from now on save resources overall. The repudiation of past debt under such circumstances is an accepted feature of capitalism, but it may have—under capitalism—bad redistributive effects. E.g. what about capital of the handloom-weavers? This consideration gives X a further advantage over Y. But Z, the project that does not compete with X in output but does compete with Y for funds, requires only to be profitable taking total costs into account. So Z will nearly always beat Y.

Virtually the same example copes also with craft employment protection. For in the Indian textile case not only are the hand

---

[1] Average, not marginal, because whole projects are being compared. Cf. Wiles, *Price, Cost and Output*, 2nd ed., Oxford 1961, p. 299.

looms rendered obsolete but the labour workless. Then, reverting to X and Y, and *mutatis mutandis*, Y is only now preferable if its average total cost does not exceed whatever X costs may remain after both debt service and wages have been deducted. A possible case might be where X's raw material is expensive and deficitary, while the value X adds is small. But in general the case for Z is now greater than ever.

We have been careful to call this argument the argument from craft employment protection. *It does not necessarily demand a bias against capital-intensity since there is no evidence that the capital/output ratio is lower in crafts than in mechanized industry.* Certainly the capital/labour ratio is lower: but then so is the output/labour ratio. Crafts are simply less efficient than mechanized operations, and it is to their capital as well as their labour that protection should be extended. But certainly the argument does operate against 'modernity', until labour is fully employed. In other words it cuts across all the things that capital-maximizers really stand for, and at no point is it more clear how absurd it is to wish to increase *any* cost of production.

Communists are of course violently opposed to craft employment protection. Stalin's first FYP saw the virtual end of Russian crafts. Even though the peasant's long winter remained free under collectivization he ceased to get the raw materials he needed. The decline of small-scale industry in that period was a very considerable offset indeed to the claimed increases of large-scale industrial production.[1] Such occupations are opposed not only because they are labour/intensive, but even more because they are ideologically unsound. The craftsman is necessarily small and unorganized. He naturally works, either alone and directly for the market, which is 'capitalism', or in groups and subject to very decentralized planning—and that is merely co-operation. The failure to preserve crafts and traditional skills is one of the principal economic wastes of Communism. Thus, for instance, it is impossible to replace a wooden cart-wheel in rural U.S.S.R.

The Yugoslavs, the Poles and to some extent the Chinese, have all improved on the Soviet model here. The first two nations, since 1950 and 1956 respectively, have simply given more market freedom and more generous allowances of raw materials to craftsmen. This is quite straightforward right-wing Communism.

[1] Cf. Adam Kaufman, *Small-Scale Industry in the Soviet Union*, National Bureau of Economic Research, July 1959.

After early disasters the Chinese in 1956 took the same course, as already described (Ch. 9). But they then swung round (early 1958) into an idiosyncratic position much like that adopted on capital-intensity (Sec. 2). In the name of using up all resources, especially resources of surplus labour, they have now compulsory socialized craftsmanship.

Craft employment protection is not the same as maximum labour absorption. This would be positively to invest in X, since it is the most labour-intensive method of production. It would of course be a 'waste' of capital, in the sense that national income would grow less rapidly than if Z were chosen. But employment would grow more rapidly, and our values might be such that we would prefer that. Certainly 'labour-maximization' is a much more plausible end than 'capital-maximization', and a much more serious rival to the income-maximization which we have assumed as an end. As means to the third end, however, neither of the first two is satisfactory at all.

9. Perhaps however we should, taking a dynamic view of what is socially profitable, choose new techniques and projects from the point of view, what is most educative? What will most influence the workers on the project, and the surrounding population who see it, to accept modern technology? This may be called the argument from 'technical demonstration effect'. Which way does it cut?

On one side is the 'Moscow Metro' case. With its marble underground halls, so very much bigger than those of Western systems, it played the role of a medieval cathedral: it was the 'stone book' of the illiterate masses. Yet Moscow's streets are broad and its buildings low: even today there are few traffic blocks and in the 1930s private cars hardly existed. A few 'buses and trams would have been infinitely cheaper. The thing was an advertisement, but just possibly a worthwhile one. Certainly few advertisements have been more capital-intensive.

On the other side is the 'Afghan scythes' case. The peasants always used sickles for harvesting, until foreign aid came along. A Communist adviser would have brought in tractors, and upset the whole system of tenure and way of life. So, logically, should any Western 'capital-maximizer'. The tractors would of course have largely broken down; they would have diverted scarce capital from other—and better—uses; they might well—as in U.S.S.R. during collectivization—have induced a spasm of peasant Luddism. The adviser came from the West, however, and he substituted scythes for sickles.[1] At almost no cost productivity rose steeply, and the peasants were thereby painlessly introduced to the whole idea of economic progress. Changes in land tenure, social structure and religious attitudes could follow: they had been softened up. Scarce Afghan capital was saved for better uses.

On a pure economic reckoning it is of course crystal clear that 'Afghan scythes' is right and 'Moscow Metro' is wrong. On a sociological reckoning it is much more difficult to generalize. The urban population of Moscow, already quite used to modernity and technical change, may well have been inspired by the marmoreal vulgarities of Komsomolskaya station, or at least by the whole network as a technical achievement. Or, with greater economic insight, it may well have been stirred to passionate resentment by the waste. But we must at least allow for the appeal of such things to people without much economic insight. And in any case they differ altogether from Afghan peasants with still less economic insight, to whom existing techniques are an organic part of a whole traditional way of life.

The writer is in principle hostile to 'technical demonstrations' of an uneconomic kind. The best demonstrations are those that are demonstrably useful, i.e. make a profit. But there may be a case for a few follies.

10. Then let us remember that if the investment is to be for growth we must choose projects where the extra income will not be consumed; and be prepared to sacrifice profits if, extra consumption being smaller, accumulation is nevertheless greater. Call it the argument from *accumulative efficiency*. In a trivial way this might be a matter of investing, say, in regions or industries where the marginal propensity to save is greatest. Mostly the choice lies between institutions however. One certainly must diverge from pure profitability to favour *types* of enterprise with the highest voluntary propensity to save or, perhaps more important, the best record as taxpayers (high propensity to pay tax). Had Messrs. Galenson and Leibenstein meant only this with their 'marginal reinvestment quotient'—and they undoubtedly had it in mind along with replacement costs—there would have been no quarrel with them.

What types of enterprise, then, observe better tax discipline or save more of their profits? Certainly the division is not into more

---

[1] Although I believe it to be factual I have been unable to check this story. Let it stand as a useful parable.

nd less capital-intensive: that is absurd.[1] Rather is it sociological, nd too complicated to bear generalization. Thus in an advanced Western country one might say that the preferred type of enterprise was a large public company—a nationalized board is usually under such close and foolish public scrutiny that it cannot charge high enough prices to make any profits or pay any taxes. In a backward non-Communist country tax evasion is the main problem, and the preferred type of enterprise will perhaps be one run by foreign white capitalists frightened of expropriation. They at least will keep adequate accounts, and have no relatives in the Inland Revenue. But if the country has not yet won its independence the local administration will be better able to tax native capitalists. Public utilities are a special case, since they are large bodies trading directly with the public, whose pricing policy is necessarily arbitrary;[2] hence they will find extreme difficulty in ever raising their prices. In the special case of an underdeveloped country, subject of course to xenophobia and anxious to expropriate the foreign devil, it is disastrous that the public utility should be foreign-owned: its rates will always be kept below the break-even level. Better, in contrast to what we have found above, that the owner should be a native nationalized board.

It will readily be seen how dangerous these generalizations are. When we turn to Communism we are on somewhat firmer ground, since here there is no 'institutional *laissez faire*' (Ch. 1). On the contrary, institutions have been designed partly with accumulative efficiency in mind. The obvious case is the collective farm, which in 1929–58 served mainly the purpose of a 'grain pump': a way of getting the cheap compulsory deliveries collected. But from the beginning the duty of saving so much of its income (officially, 'transfers to the indivisible fund') has also been imposed on the kolkhoz. Thus central fiat can determine peasant saving: a thing impossible if the peasants were all working individually. Of course individual peasants will save much more in a non-Communist country, where the spectre of the kolkhoz is banished, even than under Lenin's NEP or in Gomulka's Poland, but it is still certain that they will never save as much as a kolkhoz.

[1] Capital-intensity raises gross, not net profits, and we are only interested in the saving of net profits. The argumentation in Bator, op. cit., pp. 104–5, would therefore seem to be unnecessary.

[2] Cf. Wiles, op. cit., p. 156, on 'prices in the public eye'.

Y

Since all Communist industry is nationalized there are no institutional variations in accumulative efficiency. But in any case, even in a capitalist country, these propositions are an argument not for *investing in* a particular kind of institutional set-up but for *having* it. Whether or not more funds are directed to kolkhozy, limited companies or what not, there will be more investment simply if such organizations are created by fiat.

11. It is often believed that to accelerate growth we must invest in manufacturing industry not agriculture or services, or 'secondary' not primary or tertiary production, whatever profitability may indicate. There are many objections to this doctrine, which is believed in by Communists above all.

(a) Industry is not necessarily the first or principal sector of the economy in which there is technical progress. Thus in eighteenth-century Britain the agricultural revolution preceded the industrial: enclosures and new crop rotations long pre-dated the majority of manufacturing innovations. Again in underdeveloped countries it has normally been agriculture that first adopted foreign techniques and admitted foreign capital. Nevertheless in a very general way technical progress is indeed more rapid in industry.[1] Indeed we may speak in the ordinary case of the 'specialization trap': an underdeveloped country will specialize on the best Ricardian grounds in agriculture to find decades later that continuous and rapid progress has been denied to it.

(b) Industry is not of course the source of capital for itself or for the other branches of the economy. Quite the contrary, it normally absorbs capital from the primary and tertiary sectors. Thus in eighteenth-century Britain capital came from the increasing rents of agricultural landlords, from the capital profits of the owners of urban sites and from foreign trade; and industry was the bottomless pit into which this capital was poured. In Communist countries again the avowed intention is to extract capital from agriculture and invest it in industry.[2]

(c) Industry is not 'the sector where productivity is highest'. That is a meaningless phrase, since between sectors the measurement

---

[1] It is the growth of output per directly employed worker that sometimes grows faster in agriculture. When we take into account inputs of capital and industrial raw materials, agriculture shows slower progress than industry.

[2] Though Bukharin and Dzerzhinsky demanded during the NEP that industry find its own capital by reducing its costs, or even take it from state trade, the costs of which were also grossly inflated. A self-financing industrial expansion is of course a right-wing Communist conception.

of productivity depends largely on the prices of products. Indeed if the labour market is perfect, marginal productivity will be equal in every sector; so that to say that productivity is higher in the output of steel than in the output of carrots can only mean that a worker of 'equal' skill obtains more in steel. Otherwise it is difficult to see what the phrase can mean, except perhaps that steelmaking techniques are less backward, compared with what they might be, than carrot-growing techniques. Now this might well be true in a backward country where most workers are engaged in agriculture. For when secondary and tertiary industry are set up they step instantly into the more advanced technique, while agriculture, the sector of illiteracy, tradition and stagnation, must be slowly and painfully reformed. But even here there are exceptions: Australia and New Zealand—virgin countries occupied all at once by technically advanced populations—have tended to show an agriculture more nearly approaching the limits of technical modernity than local industry. The point is conclusively demonstrated by the protection granted to industry in Australasia; perhaps the only case of an industry more heavily protected than an agriculture.

(d) Capital invested in industry is thought to be somehow 'more productive' than that invested elsewhere, especially in service trades. Thus the economy will grow more rapidly if we set up textile factories than if we build houses. This doctrine of 'productive' and 'unproductive' investment, distinguished this time not as between first and second order investments, but as between industry and services, appears to be without any substance whatever. A house is entirely as productive as a loom; the one of shelter, convenience and warmth, the other of personal decoration—and warmth. True, in the one case the capital asset directly produces the final service, so that its services are not sold separately to the consumer, but he must purchase or hire the asset itself; while in the other the product of the capital asset is materially separable from it and must be separately sold. But this is merely an interesting and irrelevant technical distinction. It is not too much to say that this doctrine rests, however confusedly, on the fallacy that only material goods are productive and services really have no value.

Needless to say the distinction between first and second order investment has only coincidental similarity to that between industrial and service investment. As we saw in Ch. 15, Sec. 10, technical education is a second order service investment, and a very important one too; expressed as a capital sum it is probably of a greater order of magnitude than the value of industrial capital. It may indeed well be that the capital/output ratio is different in industry and in services; but we have already seen that this ratio is not an investment criterion. Nevertheless as the example of the Soviet policy of cheap urbanization (Sec. 7) demonstrates, the Communists above all others believe in a distinction of this kind—and so have caused much unnecessary privation by over-investment in textiles relatively to housing.

A house, then, is like a loom except that the capital/output ratio for shelter is greater than for clothes, and the labour/output ratio less. Growth depends primarily on the volume of second order investment, and scarcely at all on how first order investment is allocated. With a given volume of the former, the same rate of growth will result whether we use the rest of our capital to make shelter with houses or clothes with looms. Of course if capital is short it will be more profitable to make clothes, if labour is short, shelter. But even a permanent misallocation towards, say, shelter will not matter very much: for although growth is lost in the first year of the misallocation thereafter the output of both houses and looms expands just as fast as if there had been no misallocation.[1]

(e) The final argument in favour of industry is that a country should concentrate on the sector of increasing returns and avoid that of constant returns (services) and of decreasing returns (agriculture). The fallacy of this argument can be shown if we revert to the measurement problem described in Ch. 12, Sec. 13. We observed there that where base-year prices (assuming that they correspond to relative scarcities in that year) are used to weight given-year outputs, the presence of increasing returns will make for a higher index of output than with the use of given-year prices. For the easy statistical triumph a combination of base-year prices and investment in the sector of increasing returns is unbeatable. But any régime, even a Communist one, wants to make a good show in the shops or on the battlefield, not only in the statistical yearbook; and whereas given- and base-year prices are equally valid in inter-temporal statistical comparisons there is obviously no case at all for base-year prices as investment criteria in the given year. When it comes to growth of the national income here and now we must

---

[1] There are also complicated questions, which we here leave on one side, of the capital ratios in the particular second order capital goods industries that make houses and looms respectively: e.g. are brick-works more capital-intensive than machine tools?

of course think in terms of this year's prices (provided always that they correspond to this year's scarcity conditions). So if it is more profitable to invest in sectors of decreasing and constant return this should be done, since as we have seen profitability is the criterion of choice between particular investment projects that maximizes growth.

This argument has of course been presented in terms of constant techniques. It is safest, at the risk of insulting the reader, to recall that when economists speak of increasing, decreasing, etc. returns, they refer to constant techniques, unless they have lost their heads. If the sector of increasing returns happens also to be that of greatest technical progress that is coincidental. There is a strong argument for concentrating in the sector of greatest technical progress, and this has been presented in Sec. 11(a). But even the attractions of greater technical progress must at some point yield to the sheer scarcity of technically stagnant products. If all underdeveloped countries concentrate on industry the terms of trade will move so sharply in favour of agriculture that even Britain's hill farms will become a worthwhile proposition; and our economy will grow most rapidly by expanding them.

In general there is no essential difference between one branch of an economy and another. All have their utility, measured by prices, and this is one of the great triumphs of Menger, Jevons and Wicksteed. We cannot agree with Quesnay that agriculture is somehow more basic than the rest, nor with Ricardo and Marx that agriculture and industry are both somehow more basic, nor yet again with inchoate modern feelings that industry alone is.[1] Of all the arguments for forcing industry in particular, only that from the 'specialization trap' will stand up.

12. Will not the refusal to favour capital-intensive investment lead to low labour productivity?[2] The answer is certainly not. On the contrary, if capital is diverted unto capital-intensive projects it is taken away from other projects and the productivity of labour in these latter is lowered. Since social profit is not being maximized the overall productivity of labour is actually less under such a system. Again it is not in any simple sense true that 'high labour productivity makes possible high levels of living'.[3] For the other two factors of production, land and capital, are also under the

---

[1] Cf. Bauer and Yamey, *Economic Journal*, Dec. 1951, March 1954.
[2] Galenson and Leibenstein, op. cit., p. 350.   [3] *Ibidem.*

control of human beings, whether private individuals or the state, and the production that accrues to them is also enjoyed by human beings. It is therefore the high productivity of all factors of production that makes for high levels of living. One might just as well maximize the productivity of capital or land as of labour, and divert the artificially heightened interest and rent to general social needs, instead of taxing for this purpose the high wages produced—for a few—by capital-intensive projects.

Again in a given period of time we are certainly not called upon to 'maximize the amount of capital per worker', simply because— it is a truism but truisms are often forgotten—this demands too great a sacrifice of consumption on the part of the present generation.

13. The last argument for a capital-intensity greater than that induced by the market is that from 'machine-paced' techniques.

If a modern technique is built round a moving belt, a standard rhythmical sequence of operations or the service of a more or less self-operating machine, then the capital partly determines the efficiency of the labour. Backward and uneducated labour is thereby raised to a high level at one blow. But if the technique is 'operator-paced'—individually operated machines, repair work, etc.—the labourer has no such incentive. Nor has he much if dilution is possible in the machine-paced case: fewer looms per man, fewer parts to screw on per moving belt attendant.

This qualification notwithstanding, machine-paced techniques do raise labour efficiency, and this must be taken into account when choosing between projects. There is at present no reason to suppose that machine-paced techniques use more capital than operator-paced ones: consider, for instance, that cogging mills and railways are both operator-paced. But automation is constantly reducing the number of operator-paced techniques, while being very capital-intensive; so that in the future capital-intensive projects will have the added attraction of reducing the inefficiency of labour. But there is no reason to mistrust private calculations of this effect. *Sheer profitability* may drive investors to choose labour-saving techniques which happen also to be capital-using. There neither is now, nor would be then, any good reason against accepting the market rate of profit as the criterion.[1]

14. So for all our general scepticism about Robbinsian economics, this and the preceding chapters point a general moral of some

[1] Taken, with a few modifications, from A. O. Hirschman, *The Strategy of Economic Development*, Yale 1958, pp. 145–152.

importance: *growth criteria are of identical type with welfare criteria.*
A better 'static' allocation of resources is merely one way of making
the economy grow, and an investment that 'dynamizes' the economy
can only be justified by 'static' comparisons of the situation with
and without that investment. If some 'static' project shows more
profit, it should be preferred. The ancient classical 'static' economics
provides us with precisely the tools we require for judging 'dynamic'
situations: the rate of interest and the concepts of external economy,
time preference and the disutility of abstinence. When we 'choose
between choice and growth' we choose between men, institutions,
degrees of standardization, amounts of risk, probabilities of waste,
rates of abstinence, atmospheres, time scales. We emphatically
do not choose between an old and a new set of principles.

For there is no new set of principles. 'Dynamic' means 'having a
smaller *ceteris paribus* clause than static', or if you will, it simply
means 'complicated'. 'Static' is just a special case of 'dynamic'. If
technical progress is not pursued resources are incorrectly allocated.
If on the other hand we invest so much in it we cannot pay for our
breakfast, resources are again incorrectly allocated. To maximize
growth is, literally, to starve the present generation, as Stalin did
in 1932 and 1946. That is a 'misallocation'.

To fix our ideas let us compare three projects. One is a straightforward private investment in an extra cotton-mill (the country
already has some). The second is a smoke abatement scheme,
involving smoke cleansers in factory chimneys, several new coke
ovens, the conversion of many furnaces to oil, and an inspectorate;
this requires legislation and some public subsidy. The third is a
new Institute of Technology, all on public money. The achievement of the old 'static' welfare economics was correctly to show
that the second might be as profitable as the first: either raises
welfare, *pro tanto* either causes growth. The achievement of the
new 'dynamic' economics is to draw attention to the immense
possibilities of the third—and incorrectly to imply that it cannot
be judged in the same way as the other two. But this is not so.
Judging it is merely a more complicated exercise in the same
principles, with a longer time scale and greater external economies.
And it is just possible to waste money on institutes of technology
as on looms and spindles.[1]

[1] Cf. Imre Nagy, *On Communism*, Praeger 1957, p. 225.

15. However, the mention of education brings us to one specifically Communist investment policy which is a definite advantage:
they try to use all their educated people, and to educate only for use.
Both items are rather startling by Western standards. The first
means principally that most women enter non-home employment,
and stay in it after marriage. It also means intermittent official
hunts for trained people doing unskilled work, and their redirection
when found. The second means considerably less attention to the
liberal arts, and the direction of students into particular subjects in
accordance with planned projections of the labour market; rather
than following the tastes of donors or parents, and the vested interests
of teachers, or even the inclinations of students themselves. In any
society, education is obviously a kind of investment, and it is
tragic that it should ever have been classified as consumption by the
fathers of national income accounting in the first place. The
expenditure that has been made on educating the active and
potentially active labour force is part of the national capital. To say
these things is not of course to say that housewives should never
receive higher education, or that the liberal arts should be abolished.
It is not to make any policy recommendations at all, but simply to
classify things under their correct economic names, and to draw
inferences for economic growth.

It is difficult to over-estimate the importance of this. First, take
sheer magnitudes. The private return (i.e. the present value of the
extra before-tax income earned over an average working life,
divided by the full cost of education and of foregone earnings) on a
college education in U.S.A. is about 9% p.a. for white urban
males.[1] At replacement cost, and again taking account of foregone
earnings, the investment represented by the education of all adults
of working age in U.S.A. was about 42% of the national tangible
capital in 1957.[2] Naturally, if we take into account the low direct
use to which American women put their education, a higher
proportion of tangible than of intellectual capital is actually
employed.

Education is not chicken-feed, then. Major improvements in
its productive use mean more productive use of large segments of
the national capital. Suppose, for instance, that all graduate women

---

[1] Becker, *American Economic Review*, May 1960. The estimate is too low because college is
pleasant, i.e. it is also present consumption. Nepotism pulls the other way: many white
urban males are guaranteed a job anyway, and college is just another privilege of their station.
[2] T. Schulz, Chapter 3 in the 60*th Yearbook of the National Society for the Study of Education*,
Chicago 1961, Table 14.

were to work, under present American conditions. Higher education is 27% of the stock of all education at present in the labour force by value, but *graduates'* education is a higher percentage: 40.[1] One-third of the higher educated at present in the labour force, or 4 million, are women, so they represent 13% of the stock of intellectual capital in use. Their 'unemployed' sisters of working age are about 3 million, so they would represent an addition of 10% to the educational stock, or of 3% to the total stock of capital.[2] Note, however, the important qualification 'higher' education: it is by no means obvious that it is in any sense economical to put a less educated woman, who is a mother of small children, to any sort of work outside the home. If her mother—that key Russian figure the *babushka*—takes care of the children we must deduct what babushka might else have earned outside. If she puts them in a crèche we must deduct the costs of the crèche. And these are just the sort of 'service' costs a Marxist will ignore.

But having agreed that this is indeed a Communist secret weapon consider *why* it is: *they use market principles in shaping education, and we do not!* Whether the demand for labour is planned, as in a command economy, or free, as under capitalism, it is still possible to adapt education to it; and this is simple profit maximization on the part of pupil or parent. Needless to say, Communist adaptation is very imperfect, the most notorious fault being an over-production of engineers for purely managerial jobs. But it is still surely more perfect than the West, with its classical languages (which tend to absorb the best brains), its liberal arts colleges and its anti-technical snobbery. Let me repeat, we judge the adaptation here in purely economic terms.

If this chapter is correct, then, one striking conclusion emerges: Communism has no secret weapon, no way of allocating capital that enhances growth, unless it be the ruthless application of market criteria to education. Quite the contrary, Communist allocation policy is irrational and therefore a brake on growth, and all the more tribute must be paid to the other factors enumerated in Chapter 13: a conclusion comforting to orthodox welfare economists but disturbing to parliamentary democrats.

[1] 18% of the labour force had higher education, so *ex hypothesi* $\frac{18}{100}(100-27)\% = 13\%$ must be reckoned to it as its share of lower education.

[2] Sources: Schulz, op. cit., Tables 11 and 14; *Statistical Yearbook of U.S.A.* 1960, Tables 136, 139, 262.

PART IV

ESCHATOLOGY

Introductory Observations

Fitzgerald: 'The very rich are different from us.'

Hemingway: 'Yes, they have more money.'

The chapters of this Part are dedicated to showing that Hemingway's reply was Philistine and imperceptive, indeed positively un-Hegelian. Certain differences in quantity make for differences in quality too, and the progress towards 'affluence' is one of these. Moreover, the concepts of the Affluent Society entertained in Western economics are trivial and superficial[1] compared with the grand sweep of their Marxist rivals. Beside science fiction must stand economics fiction—indeed they are two sides of one coin; and it is into such fiction that we now take our plunge.

We begin with an exposé of Communist thinking on this topic. As with 'distribution', the treatment is more exhaustive than elsewhere because there is no other introductory source to which the student can be referred.

---

[1] This is very far from saying that Prof. J. K. Galbraith's book of that title is trivial or superficial. On the contrary it is an immense leap forward from commonplace Western ideas. But the paucity even of this work indicates how far behind Marxism we are at this point.

CHAPTER 17

FULL COMMUNISM, THE PRINCIPLES[1]

1. *Definitions.* There has always been much talk among Communists about the remoter social, political and economic future; indeed doctrine on this point forms part of the official theology. Eighty years ago Marx laid down in the *Critique of the Gotha Programme* that after the proletarian revolution there is a transitional stage in which the remnants of hostile classes must be 'liquidated' (this is the 'dictatorship of the proletariat') and in which productivity is still so low and social attitudes still so backward that citizens can only be paid in accordance with the work they have done ('from each according to his capacity, to each according to his labour'). There must therefore be set up a proletarian state to administer the distribution of the scarce goods and the suppression of the undesirable classes. Later as productivity increases and the older habits and people die out we achieve a classless[2] society in which there is no scarcity of anything anyone wants and no need for any state. The state 'withers away'; i.e. the organs for keeping order, army, police, law, etc., become atrophied; the distribution formula becomes 'from each according to his capacity and to each according to his need'; mankind has leaped from the realm of necessity to the realm of freedom; Full Communism, Utopia, Heaven on Earth, has arrived.

'Necessity', be it noted, means economic constraints, and freedom means the full development of the personality: intellectual emancipation, leisure and a high standard of living. Marx himself had ever an ambiguous attitude towards freedom of thought and political opposition, and indeed towards simple tolerance of one's neighbour's eccentricities. In principle he approved of them but gave them very little thought, and had not the slightest idea what a menace he was to them. In practice he trampled on them whenever they got in

---

[1] A shortened version of this chapter appeared in *Ost-Europa* (Stuttgart), 1959.

[2] Marxists define a class not by any of the sophisticated sociological categories that free scientists use but simply by the kind of ownership it exercises or does not exercise over the means of production. It is therefore irrelevant that in U.S.S.R. as much as anywhere else in the world society is divided into the rich, clean, proud, pompous, self-righteous, powerful, privileged and educated on the one hand and the poor, dirty, ignorant and down-trodden on the other: the Soviet Union is a classless society because all these people together exercise the same formal ownership rights over the means of production.

his way. Temperamentally opposed, like any German professor, to other people's exercise of freedom, he asserted nevertheless that the revolution would enhance this sort of freedom too, since it would give it a proper, classless economic basis. Above all, whatever his prevarications on the subject, the promised 'withering away of the state' must lead, and was meant by him to lead, to actual anarchy. From which it might superficially be supposed that the individual would be quite free even on a rational definition of freedom, let alone a Marxist one. But this is not so, for Marx could not conceive anarchy without the prior unanimity of a perfectly rational citizenry. Freedom never meant for him freedom to choose or to disagree or to do as one pleases: it meant to see what is necessary and inevitable, and to want to do it. *Per contra* to be unfree was not to be in prison, or subjected to a tyrannical government, or anything simple like that; it was not to realize necessity, and find oneself performing the inevitable as before, but forced and unwillingly.

Full Communism has always possessed in Communist doctrine (other than Titoist) much the same status as Utopia, or the City of God in a religion; with this essential difference, that it can and must be built by human effort within the foreseeable future—Communism is nothing if not a doctrine of permanent revolution. So the more time elapses after the seizure of power the more urgent the duty becomes, until today, when the question of the nature of Full Communism has become *the* question for Communist parties, involving as it does both the exact ultimate structure of society and (in 1958) the present seat of the spiritual leadership of the movement. It is in particular quite untrue to say that the question is purely ideological, or not practical; for it touches long-term social aims, day-to-day economic policy and intra-bloc diplomacy at a hundred points.

Full Communism was supposed by Marx and Engels to have the following economic characteristics, in rough order of importance:

(i) distribution of income according to need, no longer according to labour performed;

(ii) no social classes any more; which for a Marxist is as much as to say that all property in the means of production is owned in the same way, to wit nationalized (but personal property remains private);

(iii) the state withers away, as coercion is no longer required—see (ii);

(iv) very high productivity, so that there is plenty for all. This also reduces social conflict, and makes (i) possible;

(v) high socialist consciousness: work becomes the first necessity of life, and people work without incentives—see (i);

(vi) more equal, but not absolutely equal, pay and living conditions;

(vii) no money;

(viii) a command economy;

(ix) the economy is managed by a 'free and equal association of producers', whatever that means;

(x) the differences between occupations disappear, so that there is no social distinction between town and country;

(xi) each person does about as much physical as intellectual labour, and is practised in many jobs: there is thus little specialization of persons, and above all no manual/intellectual distinction, although of course particular jobs remain specialized;

(xii) the system, as Stalin was the first to show, is worldwide, for obviously (iii) is incompatible with the survival of hostile capitalist states.[1]

---

[1] Sources:

   (i) Marx, *Critique of the Gotha Programme* (p. 21); Marx, *Die Deutsche Ideologie* (MEGA 1/5, p. 526).

   (ii) Marx and Engels, *Communist Manifesto* (MEGA 1/6, p. 539).

   (iii) Engels, *Anti-Dühring*, III/2; Marx, Conspectus of Bakunin's 'Government and Anarchy' (*Sochineniya*, 3rd ed., vol. XV, pp. 188–193). The same thought is given more exact meaning in the *Communist Manifesto* (MEGA 1/6, p. 546): 'Public power loses it political character'. This is almost exactly repeated in Engels, 'On Authority', 1874 (*Soch*. XV, p. 136); Engels, Letter to Bebel, March 18–28, 1875 (*Soch*. XV, p. 292).

   (iv) *Die Deutsche Ideologie* (MEGA 1/5, p. 64); *Critique of the Gotha Programme* (p. 21).

   (v) *Critique of the Gotha Programme* (p. 21).

   (vi) Engels, Letter to Bebel, March 18–28, 1875 (*Soch*. XV, p. 292). Cf. Stepanyan, *Komsomolskaya Pravda*, Oct. 16, 1951.

   (vii) Marx, *Die Heilige Familie* (MEGA 1/3, p. 224); Marx, *Das Kapital* (Vol. II, XVI/3, XVIII/2).

   (viii) See Ch. 18.

   (ix) See Ch. 18.

   (x) *Communist Manifesto* (MEGA 1/6, p. 545); *Anti-Dühring*, III/3.

   (xi) *Die Deutsche Ideologie* (MEGA 1/5, p. 22); ditto, p. 373.

   (xii) Stalin, *Report of Central Committee to 16th Party Congress*, June 27, 1930.

   There is a valuable collection of these quotations in Ralf Dahrendorf's *Marx in Perspektive* (Dietz, 1952), pp. 167–182. Although his collection is not complete, especially on the practical side, I am heavily in his debt; also in that of Mr. Wolfgang Leonhard. Lenin's views on Full Communism may best be pursued by using the *Sochineniya*, 3rd ed., in association with the *Spravochnik k II i III Izdaniyam Sochinenii Lenina* (Partizdat, 1935): see the headings 'Gosudarstvo Proletarskoye: Yego Otmiranie', 'Trud Sotsialisticheskiy i Kommunisticheskiy', 'Elektrifikatsia v R.S.F.S.R.', 'Kommunism: Yego Fazy'.

The state between the proletarian revolution and Full Communism is known as 'socialism'.[1] Hence 'socialist camp', 'socialist countries', etc. Socialism is pretty well whatever the current state of affairs is, in any country which has nationalized its industry, collectivized its farms and liquidated its bourgeoisie. There is no space here for the questions of 'People's Democracy' and 'Our Own Road to Socialism'.

2. Within this list of items there are two major polarities. First, (ii), (vi), (vii) and (viii) are incompatible with (iii) and (ix), for you cannot nationalize all property without a state, nor can there be a command economy without a state, or 'free associations (plural) of producers' without a free market and money. This may be referred to as the *Tito-Stalin polarity*. Stalin postponed (iii) indefinitely, pointing to the crude fact of (xii); and simply dropped (ix) out of the canon. (ix) is an obscure, almost apocryphal, article of dogma,[2] and this presented him with no difficulty. But (iii) is notorious, elementary and crucial; it gave Stalin much difficulty, and it was an absolutely regular part of all deviation from Stalinism to complain that even under 'socialism' there should be some faint beginnings of (iii), not an obvious retrogression from the capitalist position.

Stalin's successors have handled this better. The revived workers' production conferences in factories are at least a façade, a moderately adequate propaganda retort to Tito's fully fledged workers' councils. Of course, being under control of the centralized trade unions, they are eminently compatible with a command economy and thus at bottom quite bogus. Moreover the true, and very non-Titoist, meaning of (iii) has been brought out: what Marx *meant* by the state was solely its coercive political organs; the apparatus of a command economy is not, or need not in an advanced state of society be, the state, but a 'social organization'. And this indeed is precisely what Marx and Engels did say, many times over and very

[1] 'Full Communism' is my own phrase, used here to avoid confusing the Western reader. It has cropped up in Soviet writers, but mostly they just say Communism. The words 'Socialism' and 'Communism' were not used in these senses by Marx, Engels, or (usually) Lenin. All three used 'dictatorship of the proletariat' for the transitional phase immediately after the Revolution, and for the beginnings of 'Socialism'; for developed 'Socialism' and for 'Full Communism' alike they said 'Socialism' or 'Communism' more or less indifferently. But the two words, used to express this latter distinction, occur at least as early as 1919 (Buhkarin and Preobrazhensky, *ABC of Communism*, Sec. 121); indeed there is a foretaste of this usage in Lenin's *State and Revolution* (1917).

[2] The plural 'associations' so essential to Titoism, is an invention. Marx uses the singular.

clearly. Engels perhaps put it best when he said we shall pass from the governance of persons to the administration of things.[1]

Nay more, it is also exactly what Lenin said:[2]

> There is no doubt that the further the conquests of the October Revolution move on, the deeper the changes go that it began, the more firmly founded are the conquests of the Socialist Revolution, and the more socialist construction is consolidated, the greater and the higher will be the role of the councils of the national economy, which alone of all governmental agencies will retain a firm place, which will be the more firm the nearer we are to the establishment of the socialist order and the less use we have for purely administrative apparatus, an apparatus the nature of which is only to give orders. That apparatus is doomed, after the resistance of the exploiters is finally broken, after the workers begin to organize socialist production—that apparatus of administration in the genuine narrow sense of the word, the apparatus of the old government is doomed to die, but apparatus of the type of the Supreme Council of the National Economy is marked out for growth; it will develop and strengthen itself, taking upon itself all the most important activity of organized society.

That is, in Lenin's time, and especially under 'War Communism' (see below), the idea was very much alive that, in preparation for Full Communism, the economic and social administration should be carried on by organs parallel to, but not essentially part of, the state. The state is the coercive organs only. This is largely the origin of that most embarrassing provision in the 1919 Party Programme (Point 5), that 'the trade unions ought in the end actually to concentrate in their hands all the administration of the entire national economy'. And the idea is revived in Khrushchev's Sovnarkhozy. The Sovnarkhoz, as we see in Ch. 2, revives a Leninist organ of economic administration under its same name, which being literally translated is 'Council of the National Economy'. True, Lenin's Sovnarkhozy were the lineal descendants of local trades councils, and—at least in their origins—expressed very directly the purpose of Point 5 in the 1919 Party Programme; while Khrushchev's Sovnarkhozy are mere late-born creatures of state and party. But the intention is undoubtedly present, with Khrushchev as with Lenin, to build up these organs into an independent parallel administrative system, and the claim has been expressly made that

---

[1] *Anti-Dühring*, 111/2, *sub fin.* Nearly all the other sources for item (iii), quoted above, make the same point.

[2] Speech at the first session of the Council of the National Economy, May 26, 1918 (*Sochinenia*, 3rd ed., vol. XXIII, p. 36).

the Sovnarkhozy are a step towards the withering away of the state.[1]

However seriously we take this particular claim, it is certainly the Soviet intention to develop the various 'social organizations' and hand over to them the administration of society and the economy: the union of sportsmen, the union of Soviet writers, the trade unions, the workers' production conferences, the Komsomol, etc. In contrast to socialism, Full Communism is to be characterized by self-administration: the 'broad masses' will run themselves. From a non-Communist point of view this is of course all hypocrisy, since these new organs must and will have exactly the same bureaucratic nature as the old: new 'social organization' is old 'state' writ large. But at least legally and theoretically this is not so, as they have no coercive power, and one must not underestimate the long-run liberalizing effect of the change in doctrinal status.

On the question of 'social organizations', incidentally, the Yugoslavs are in full agreement; they also understand the withering away of the state to mean 'self-administration by the broad masses'. Only they do not need to excuse the continuation of central planning by the pretence that Sovnarkhozy are 'social organizations'. Yet here again we must ask whether the Yugoslavs are strictly orthodox. For what did Engels mean by that 'free and equal association of producers' who should take over society? Did he necessarily mean workers' councils? Why not, as in U.S.S.R., the union of sportsmen, the trade unions, etc.? In its context, as Ch. 18 shows, the 'free and equal association of producers' is *one*, not many, associations. And that is no accident, for there is no suggestion in the vast corpus of Marx' and Engels' writings that authority should be subdivided under fully developed socialism. But that is just what the Yugoslav type of 'social organization' does; while the Soviet type merely specializes an authority still exercised from the centre.

It follows that Tito's rejection of (vi), (vii) and (viii) in the name of (iii) and (ix) is less orthodox. (ix), after all, is very disputable (see Ch. 18), and what is really meant by (iii) is best explained on the above lines. Nevertheless, it was on this more whole-hogging interpretation of (iii) that Titoism based itself; and this

[1] By Ostrovityanov, *Voprosy Ekonomiki*, 9/1958. Naturally this claim should be taken with several pinches of salt: it was not made in the great crisis of the introduction of the Sovnarkhozy in early 1957, but only when the Chinese started their competitive version of Full Communism. And the Sovnarkhozy do not by themselves imply any decentralization at all, as we show in Chs 2, 7, 8.

has had a curious consequence. For if in Yugoslavia in 1948 you believe that the state must begin to wither away here and now you naturally cannot begin with the army or the security police: you need those against Stalin and your own compatriots. But you must make a show of some kind, so you begin with the economic bureaucracy. So it is precisely and only the economic organs of the Yugoslav state that have withered away, and Titoists are now compelled to assert that economic organs are necessarily part of any state: otherwise the whole basis of their movement crumbles.

A Titoist would reply that he was a much better Marxist than the foregoing implies. For, first, we must give some Marxist interpretation of that great and undeniable fact, the manifest corruption of Stalin and his system. In so doing it is surely orthodox to revert for an explanation to the complaints of Zinoviev at the 14th Party Congress in 1925: the centralized planning bureaucracy was merely another form of 'state capitalism'.[1] True enough, one may reply, that Stalin's planning bureaucracy is part of the state— did he not abolish the Sovnarkhozy and subject the economy to regular ministries? But that surely implies that planning must be 'socialized' or de-statified, not abolished.

Another Titoist argument is that a detailed command economy *alienates* the worker from his work. Alienation is a fluid and obscure but basic Marxist concept.[2] The root of it is that man is only perfect when he directly enjoys his own product and controls his own environment. While any fair-minded man will agree that the worker is as much 'alienated' by a central planner as by the blind operation of a market he cannot control, this is not Marxism. For that creed, with its pathetic Rousseauian belief in direct democracy and the general will, undoubtedly holds that there is a social mechanism laid up in heaven which can centralize without alienating.

Thirdly, one might argue—though this is not an actual Titoist argument, to my knowledge—that the 'relations of production' are the basis of all society, and the state is mere superstructure: whatever else may or may not be Marxism, that certainly is. With a command economy as a basis you get one sort of superstructure (a Stalinist or authoritarian); with a free market another (a 'democratic' one—

[1] See Ch. 1, Sec. 2.
[2] Cf. Daniel Bell, *Journal of Philosophy*, Nov. 1959; Robert M. Tucker, *Philosophy and Myth in Karl Marx*, Cambridge, England, 1962.

Z

for of course Titoists believe themselves to be democratic). Therefore if the state is to wither away there must first be a change in the 'relations of production', to wit, from Stalinism to Titoism.

It may well be unprofitable to pursue this argument, for we are now at the frontiers of what these divergent groups of Marxists have actually said to each other; and it is dangerous for a sceptic to extrapolate. But my own reading of Marxism is that technology *univocally determines* the 'relations of production'; so that the *choice* between command economy and free market has no business to exist. Moreover, the guilty party is the free market: technical progress is held to centralize things more and more, so that railways and electricity grids put paid to the 'anarchy of production'. In setting up free market socialism in industry (in backward agriculture it would have been tolerable) Tito torpedoed the philosophical foundations of Marxism, by demonstrating that technology does *not* univocally determine the 'relations of production', and that there *is* a choice. The point is obvious enough, even before the Yugoslav model was set up, from any period of economic history, but it is deeply disturbing to a Marxist.

What Marx *really* meant or *would have* said (!) is that just as hand-mills generate slavery, water-mills feudalism, steam-mills capitalism, and, finally, electric mills generate socialism,[1] so within socialism further technical progress generates at one and the same time higher and higher productivity and more and more centralization; and Full Communism is related to this as superstructure to basis. Therefore under Full Communism there will be a perfectly centralized economy in which, there being no classes, there need be no coercive organs. Further, the rise in productivity brings with it ever greater 'socialist consciousness' and so we may dispense with money (see Sec. 5 below). This, then, is the true Marxist view: however many contrary references a scholar may dig up, another scholar could cap them with favourable references three to one. But this is pretty exactly the modern Soviet view. Therefore again Titoism is unorthodox. Of course the facts are too.

3. Before we come to our second polarity, we must go a little further into the nature of *property under Full Communism* (item ii). Communism being an unregenerately Victorian creed, the notion of property in it retains all that pristine importance that it has lost in the West. Concepts such as the Managerial Revolution and the

---

[1] On the automatic centralization of society by technical progress, cf. Ch. 20, sec. 3.

divorce of ownership from control, which tend to devalue property, are extremely unpopular among Marxists.[1] Property for them is no mere random bundle of rights, attenuated by law, custom, etc., but the Badge of the Ruling Class, bringing with it possession, control and all. Property is a Relation of Production, and therefore the basis on which all else rests.

The question here, then, is what is the nature of proletarian property? Just how does the victorious proletariat own the means of production? The answer until Tito came along was of course by centralized state ownership, an ownership which, as we saw in Ch. 1, is so centralized that it is not even exercised through independent public corporations but through civil servants, subordinate to ministers who sit in the cabinet. Titoism flatly substitutes co-operative for state property as the highest form, a manœuvre which seems to those who are out of sympathy with the Marxist metaphysics merely the linguistic counterpart of substituting (ix) for (viii). And the matter might have rested there, with the Yugoslavs insisting on a formulation that put *their* industrial set-up nearer Full Communism, and the Russians on one that did the same for theirs. But there was the condition of agricultural property to consider also. Now since Titoism is essentially a doctrine of 'socialism', and there is, as we shall see, no developed Yugoslav view of Full Communism, Titoists are not unduly worried that since 1953 (when collectivization was declared voluntary) their agriculture shows only the primitive peasant form of private property. It is indeed nothing for a Communist Party to boast about, but it certainly does not affect the standpoint that *co-operative* property is better than *state*. Indeed quite the contrary: for Yugoslav agriculture is still scheduled for ultimate co-operativization. In U.S.S.R. on the other hand there was a difficulty: if state property is best kolkhozy must be nationalized.

The proposal to nationalize kolkhozy has a long history. To my knowledge it was never proposed directly to nationalize pre-collectivization peasant property: indeed in East Germany, Poland and Hungary (and of course in U.S.S.R.) large capitalist farms suitable for direct conversion into state farms have actually been broken up among private peasants, with the ultimate intention of collectivizing them. The only exception proves the rule: Cuba in

[1] The only serious Marxist approach to these concepts known to me is that of Mr. C. Wright Mills, in his *White Collar*, pp. 101–2. His line is that they designate only a transfer of power among sub-groups of the capitalist class.

1960. Fidel Castro, a very unorthodox Marxist, did directly nation-alize peasant property into his *granjas del pueblo*, which are sovkhozy. In U.S.S.R. in 1932, that is to say after the 'success' of collectiviza-tion, a few proposals were seriously made to change kolkhozy into sovkhozy, a policy later known as 'sovkhozizatsia'. But they were condemned as premature.[1]

Yet there can be no question that under Stalin kolkhozy were due to be nationalized one day. This intention was never expressed in so many words, but it was rigidly entailed by many authoritative and transparent periphrases. Thus Stalin:

> It is necessary, in the second place, by means of gradual transitions carried out to the advantage of the collective farms, and hence of all society, to raise collec-tive-farm property to the level of public property, and, also by means of gradual transitions, to replace commodity circulation by a system of products-exchange, under which the central government, or some other social-economic centre, might control the whole product of social production in the interests of society.[2]

Stepanyan puts the same point dialectically:

> Only if we strengthen and develop the Kolkhozy as much as we can, if we recognize and profit by all the advantages of the Kolkhoz order, are we in a position to create the necessary basis for the gradual lifting of co-operative Kolkhoz property to the level of national property.[3]

The 1950 conference on Full Communism, referred to in Ch. 18, Sec. 1, concurred, though the veil of periphrasis was particularly thick—doubtless because Stalin had not yet spoken.[4] Indeed Stalin himself was on balance exceedingly cautious, and his sole practical proposal was to nationalize *trade* between kolkhozy and the state, i.e. presumably to assimilate the zakupka to the zagotovka.

When Stalin died the proponents of 'sovkhozizatsia' had a few initial successes, in the strengthening of the planning and audit power of the MTS over kolkhozy, the actual sovkhozizatsia of certain kolkhozy, and the colonization of the virgin lands mainly by new sovkhozy. But as early as 1953 Stalin's proposal to nationalize trade between the kolkhoz and the state was publicly rejected,[5] and in 1958 the reverse occurred: the zagotovka was abolished, being assimilated to the zakupka. Still more important, in 1958 the main issue was decided against 'sovkhozizatsia': the MTS were abolished

---

[1] Compare the references in V. Gsovsky, *Soviet Civil Law*, Ann Arbor 1948, Vol. I, p. 708.
[2] *Economic Problems of Socialism in U.S.S.R.*, 1952, 'Concerning Yaroshenko'.
[3] *Voprosy Filosofii*, 1/1954. Compare also *Voprosy Ekonomiki*, 10/1950, p. 99.
[4] *Voprosy Ekonomiki*, 10/1950.   [5] Makarova, *Pravda*, 29 May, 1953.

and 'we shall take the kolkhozy with us into Full Communism'. So the nature of property under Full Communism had to be re-defined. As this is written, it is orthodox to say that both state and co-operative property will develop into 'general national property' —a phrase clearly intended to take the sting out of changes that must remain tantamount to the nationalization of the kolkhozy. It has not yet been revealed what—if any—changes will be made in industry, etc., to convert 'state' into 'general national' property. Thus for reasons entirely un-Yugoslav,[1] Khrushchev also has demoted 'state' property from first place.

Nevertheless many, indeed very many, kolkhozy have been turned into sovkhozy under Khrushchev, for various reasons: because they were hopelessly inefficient, because they were very extensive and had little labour, or in order to specialize them in suburban horticulture. Khrushchev is certainly not dogmatic on this point.[2] Moreover he has declared the 'indivisible funds' (i.e. the collective property other than land) of the remaining kolkhozy to 'belong to the whole people'. The phrase is largely meaningless but has at least two practical consequences: kolkhozniki get no com-pensation when their collective property is sovkhozized, and kolkhoz managements can be ordered to perform such state tasks as school-building out of their own money.

It is important to remember, however, that in so doing Khrush-chev has by no means sanctified the present type of co-operative property. Thus essentially a kolkhoz, 'democratically' owning and managing an independent bundle of means of production, resembles a Yugoslav factory with workers' control. Whatever 'general national property' may mean, it certainly does not mean that. And the rejection of such a view led official spokesmen to reject also, even before it was ever formulated, the late 1958 Chinese claim that Communes are a step towards Full Communism. For no matter how many of the classical items of Full Communism are realized within a Commune—e.g. (i), (ii), (v), (vi), (vii), (x), (xi)— the Commune remains an individual group differing in productivity and income levels from other Communes, and less than perfectly subject to national central planning. Full Communism is, if not world wide, certainly at least nation wide. Thus:

---

[1] 'General-social' (opšte-društveni) is a normal Yugoslav word for property in the socialist sector of that country, since workers' control was introduced.

[2] Ballard, *Problems of Communism*, July 1961.

... does this mean that the kolkhozy will come to Communism in the form of agricultural artels or will they grow over into Communes, enterprises also based or group property, but which apply the Communist principle [item (i)—P.J.D.W.]? Evidently such a Commune is an unlikely phenomenon under social-ism, for the economic conditions at this stage differ from the economic conditions under Communism precisely in that they are not ripe as yet for the application of the Communist principle of distribution. And under Communism a Commune, as a collection of owners of group property, is obviously senseless. The Commune proved to be unviable at the dawn of the kolkhoz system. It is also unsuitable during the period of transition from Socialism to Communism.[1]

In conclusion on the Tito-Stalin polarity, Titoism really has no developed doctrine of Full Communism. For instance there is nothing about it in the 1958 Party Programme.[2] The Yugoslav secession occurred before Full Communism became a serious issue; and despite all its insistence on item (iii) the Titoist complaint is essentially that the state should begin to wither away under 'socialism'. Titoism is a doctrine of 'socialism' only—which will make it seem irrelevantly old-fashioned to other Communists before long.

4. The second great polarity within our list of twelve items may be called the *Khrushchev-Mao polarity*. This one differs in being, as Marxists say, non-antagonistic. For items (iv) and (v) do not contradict each other; it is simply that the more there is of the one the less there need be of the other in order to achieve the immense change in human attitudes implied by items (i) and (vi). Men can either be psychologically reconditioned so as to go on working when items (i) and (vi) obtain, or they can be made so productive that it does not matter if their will to work slackens. Again as consumers, if there is to be no money (item vii), men must be either (a) rationed, (b) psychologically conditioned not to want much, or (c) supplied very liberally indeed. In the period of the great Chinese 'take-over bid', (May–December 1958) when in the first hectic months of the People's Communes China set up her own model of Full Communism, Mao was offering (v), (a), (b). In December 1958 he withdrew this claim, and at the 21st Party Congress (January 1959) Khrushchev successfully insisted that (iv), (c) is correct.

[1] I. Glotov, *Kommunist*, April 1958. Much the same in N. Strumilin, *Literaturnaya Gazeta*, March 25, 1958. As late as 1946 the contrary view was orthodox: kolkhozy would indeed become Communes under Full Communism (A. Lapin in *O Pyatiletnem Plane Vosstanovleniyasi Razvitiya Naradnoyo Khozyaistva S.S.S.R.* 1946–50, Highest Party School at the Central Committee, Moscow 1946). This is a repetition of Stalin's views at the 17th Party Congress (*Questions of Leninism*, 1953 ed., pp. 633, 666).

[2] Mr. Wolfgang Leonhard tells me there is nothing about it in the official textbook *Historic Materialism*, by Ilija Kosanović (Sarajevo 1958).

Communism is science fiction translated into practical politics, and this issue can only be discussed by the imaginative. Imagine, then, a scale of various brands of Full Communism. At one end stands a society more fantastically wealthy than Aldous Huxley's *Brave New World*.[1] A rich American's standard of living is available to all citizens. Their capacity for food, clothing, education and entertainment is limited by their biological nature, so all of these things are issued free: they just go into the shops and take what they want, without payment. A basic house, garden and vehicle (? a helicopter) are also free. Only such exotic and still expensive articles as space-travel, large country mansions and *objets d'art* are scarce; and these must be paid for with money or rationed. The sybaritic citizenry do as little work as they please—just an hour or two a day, to lighten the tedium of leisure. Productivity is so high that this suffices.

Now turning to the middle of the scale, we see a prosperous lower middle-class society like William Morris' *Word From Nowhere*. Serious, modest, honest and sweet-natured, the citizens' marginal propensity to consume falls to zero when each has his clay pipe and can take a boat up the Thames. These things are, as before, free and in unlimited supply. As conscientious craftsmen the citizenry put in a 30-hour week,[2] and this, not consumption, is their chief joy in life. Not only space-travel but Cadillacs, Grand Marnier and black nylon must be paid for.[3]

Thirdly, at the other extreme of the scale, stands no science fiction, but something well known to 500 million people. There are no houses but communal barracks. Man and wife meet only to sleep, children and grandparents sleep elsewhere in their appointed dormitories. Work extends to the physiological limit, except for a modicum of guided collective leisure for the young, who have a slight surplus of energy in the evening. Indistinguishable clothes

---

[1] In *Brave New World*, however, incomes are extremely unequal, and the whole vision is darkened by the author's conviction of original sin: society's main task to drug and hypnotise people into stupefied contentment. A much more optimistic and egalitarian vision of a high-productivity Full Communism, containing many valuable practical insights, is Edward Bellamy's *Looking Backward*. As this book came out in 1888 and sold more than a million copies straight away, it must have contributed something to Marxist lore. Bellamy himself was not, on the whole, a Marxist, however.

[2] On the work week compare Ch. 3, Sec. 3.

[3] Or, in Khrushchev's words (*Pravda*, Jan. 28, 1959): 'Certainly when we speak of the satisfaction of men's needs we do not mean their whims and their demands for luxury articles, but the healthy needs of a culturally developed person.' The 30-hour week is from Stalin (*Economic Problems of Socialism in U.S.S.R.*); evidently he had much the same standard of living as Khrushchev in mind.

are issued from the store as required, all meals are taken in the canteen. What comforts are not provided free by the collective are unthinkable. This too is Full Communism: it is the Chinese People's Commune, 1958 model. Or rather, to be fair, it is not *quite* Full Communism, which will only be officially declared when productivity has risen a bit. But if old peasants in their simplicity or lower party cadres in a hurry say it is Full Communism they are not rebuked.

In this latter model the worker is of course dragooned; without force and brain-washing it will not work at all. In the intermediate model he is persuaded and educated. This is precisely Khrushchev's model, based on a higher standard of living than the average in U.S.A. today, but fairly plainly not very much higher. The first model requires no economic discipline or restraint of any kind. Yet either the first or the second may properly be called Full Communism; the canonical works are silent as to what exactly is meant.[1]

However, the third, 'Maoist', version can certainly not be called good Marxism, as condition (iv) is an indisputable part of the canon. Now if the Yugoslav system is obviously more rational, liberal and efficient, that does not of course make it more orthodox. But in this case orthodoxy and reason go together. As we see in Ch. 20, the Marxist dogma that the technical economic base, the relations of production, determines the social superstructure is obviously wrong in numberless important instances; but it is only common sense here, since plainly very few human beings will work without direct reward at subsistence level.

In any case for Marx, higher social consciousness (condition (v)) goes hand in hand with higher productivity (condition (iv)). Indeed (v) is precisely part of the superstructure resting on (iv) as a base. So Full Communism of a kind without plenty is indeed thinkable,

---

[1] Compare the vagueness of Bukharin and Preobrazhensky (loc. cit.): 'Communist society will know nothing of money. Every worker will produce goods for the general welfare. He will not receive any certificate to the effect that he has delivered the product to society; he will receive no money, that is to say. In like manner he will pay no money to society when he receives *whatever he requires* from the common store' (my italics). Lenin is equally vague: 'Then there will be no need for society to make an exact calculation of the quantity of products to be distributed to each of its members; each will take freely "according to his needs". From the bourgeois point of view it is easy . . . to sneer at the Socialists for promising everyone the right to receive from society, without any control over the labour of the individual citizen, any quantity of truffles, automobiles, pianos, etc. . . . The great Socialists, in foreseeing its arrival, presupposed both a productivity of labour unlike the present and a person *unlike the present* man in the street, who, like the seminary students in Pomyalovsky's story, is capable of damaging the stores of social wealth 'just for fun', and of demanding the impossible' (*State and Revolution*, 4).

and with the evident superiority of Chinese over Soviet thought-control it is particularly likely to be attractive in China. But it is scarcely a practical possibility: even Chinese Communists cannot flout human nature to that extent. And it is certainly bad Marxism.

The Khrushchev-Mao polarity has been met before: under War Communism (1918–21). It is commonly held that the total central planning, abolition of money and egalitarian payment of incomes in kind during this period were due to the objective necessities of war; that War Communism was just a war economy.[1] Nothing, as we saw in Ch. 2, could be further from the truth. On the contrary, 'War Communism' was called at the time simply 'Communism', was confirmed as the peacetime model of the economy, and was a conscious and serious effort to establish what we are here calling Full Communism, without any transitional phase. *Eo ipso* it was, again in our own terminology, Maoist, not Khrushchevian. It obviously could not wait for the growth of productivity, so had to rely heavily on what was then termed 'revolutionary pathos'. And this was indeed, apart from the phase of Mao's take-over bid, the high point in Communist history of demands made upon people's altruism. There was, for instance, voluntary unpaid Saturday work (subbotniki) on a highly organized nation-wide scale, all very reminiscent of the People's Communes in their early phase. On both occasions, too, there was very naturally little talk of the withering away of the state.

5. Both under the People's Communes, 1958 model, and under War Communism there was a serious attempt to *abolish money*. It is of the essence of this version of Full Communism that money dies away early, not late, i.e. before productivity has risen. In 'Aldous Huxley Full Communism' money might indeed possibly disappear without rationing or direction of labour being necessary (see Ch. 20), but that all three could be dispensed with in 'Khrushchev/William Morris Full Communism' is already impossible. Far too many articles of ordinary use would be in short supply for it, nor would everyone work 30 hours a week without either some monetary incentive or a direct administrative order. The abolition of money becomes more totalitarian the more premature it is; this is the principal reason why 'Mao' Full Communism is so absolutely intolerable and contrary to human nature: indeed it is

[1] The myth is perpetuated, for instance, by Khrushchev: *Pravda*, Jan. 29, 1959.

the most totalitarian of all systems of society hitherto attempted.[1] For under this system force is substituted for ordinary economic motives at a stage where the latter are still very strong indeed.

In elementary Western textbooks money has two general functions: to be a medium of exchange and to be a store of value. The latter function clearly falls away even under 'socialism', since large money hoards in the hands of people or enterprises frustrate the central planners and lead to speculation. But how about money as a medium of exchange? The concept is for our purposes too all-embracing, and we must split it into money as:

(a) an accounting device;
(b) a distributor of incomes among people;
(c) an allocator of scarce resources among competing uses.

The Marxist tradition recognizes (b) alone. Money is something to do with wages and surplus value; its abolition means equal pay *in natura*, and therefore raises problems of the will to work. With all this side we have dealt briefly above, and we return to it more fully in Ch. 19.

(a) and (c) are purely afterthoughts in Marxism, imposed upon the rigid canon by the practical necessities of life after the revolution. In the 'Mao' version they remain totally unimportant, with the result that the People's Communes in 1958 had indeed no proper conception of economic behaviour and wasted their efforts on steel-making (thus depriving the modern works at Anshan of scrap, and overloading the railways) to the detriment of harvesting (so that there had to be rationing in major towns). Moreover, the larger the economic unit the more important is its *internal* scale of priorities: its allocation of the scarce resources it disposes of between its own competing ends. If this problem is acute for a kolkhoz and more acute for an amalgamated one, it is overwhelming for so monstrous a unit as a People's Commune with 40,000 people in it. Shall we build a new cow-shed or drain the fields? Shall we cultivate the potatoes or cement the tractor-yard? To these

---

[1] In the nineteenth century anti-socialists used to pretend that Mao Full Communism was the only kind of socialism. This made excellent propaganda. E.g. Bismarck: 'Now in a prison, there is at least an overseer to check the work; he is a respectable official on whom one can rely. But who will be the overseers in the general socialist prison? They will be the orators, who through their eloquence win to themselves the great mass, the majority of votes. There will be no appeal against them, they will be the most pitiless tyrants ever known. I believe no one will want to live in such conditions.'—Speech in Parliament, September 17, 1878. Bismarck only failed to add that the 'orators' would all belong to one tightly knit party, recruiting itself by co-optation. In general his picture is surely just, as far as Babeuf and Buonarroti went.

extremely important questions the initial moneyless set-up of the People's Communes provided no answer at all. Yet obviously only an extremely affluent Society can afford to neglect these problems.[1]

The modern Soviet attitude to money is clearly correct: just as the state must be strengthened in order that it may wither away[2] so also the role of money must be strengthened in order that it may be liquidated. The reason is the same in both cases: Full Communism requires many changes, which can only be brought about by great effort, and such ancient bourgeois tools are necessary. Only through inequality of incomes, strict accountancy and a rational allocation of resources can the economy achieve the required growth. So while Chinese agriculture was being withdrawn from the market and subjected to arbitrary *in natura* decisions the Soviet kolkhoz was being 'monetized' both within and without. The prices for agricultural products were unified, the MTS liquidated, new concepts of the real cost of kolkhoz labour evaluated for planning purposes,[3] regular monthly advances of pay introduced in order to assimilate the labour-day dividend to an industrial wage, and distributions of this dividend in kind diminished in order to enhance money payments. Yet it was precisely the *in natura* elements of the kolkhoz economy that the Chinese seized on and developed: what in U.S.S.R. are recognized as survivals from the barter of primitive peasants, having nothing in common with the abolition of money under Full Communism, were made in China the basis of Full Communism.

There was in this, by Marxist standards, a profound inconsistency, for *it meant that agriculture would reach Full Communism before industry*: the developed sector of the Chinese economy continued to use money (and continued, indeed, to earn unequal incomes) while the undeveloped sector had moved 'on' to 'higher' things. This was, doubtless, a hark-back by Mao to his old feeling that the peasants are, 'objectively', a more revolutionary class. But even the proponents of War Communism (as all orthodox Marxists, as indeed all men of common sense) would disagree. For all its 'Maoist'

---

[1] Cf. Ch. 20.   [2] Stalin: see Sec. 7 below.

[3] Generally speaking, the real cost of kolkhoz labour is some standard, nation-wide wage, even if it is never actually paid. Obviously the labour day, which varies from kolkhoz to kolkhoz, is of no use to planners (but it will do as an opportunity cost for intra-kolkhoz economic choices).

tendencies, War Communism did at least put the proletariat in front of the peasantry.[1]

Money is of course absolutely necessary for the Yugoslav system. We have seen that Titoists have no doctrine of Full Communism, but even an anarcho-syndicalist state that was genuinely without administrative compulsions (no nonsense here about 'social organizations' which are simply the MVD under another name), would require a very high 'Aldous Huxley' level of productivity. On this, however, there is a special kind of Yugoslav wishful thinking. It is that the 'socialist consciousness of the masses' (i.e. *inter alia* their will to work without direct return) is in fact very high, and can shortly be made much higher by a painless process of mere education. Only Stalinist bureaucracy holds it back, the mere introduction of the free market released spontaneous creative forces. This exaggerated faith in automatic socialism was very much a part of the original Titoist reforms in 1950, though it is of course weaker today.

6. Could there be a free market Full Communism without money? We try to show in Ch. 20 that there could not, that no level of wealth could dispense with both money and rationing.

But does Marx really mean to have no money? In one place he speaks as if there would be ration cards instead:

In the case of Socialized production money-capital is eliminated. Society distributes labour-power and means of production to the different branches of industry. The producers may eventually receive paper cheques, by means of which they withdraw from the social supply of means of consumption a share corresponding to their labour-time. These cheques are not money. They do not circulate.[2]

If this is all, and if the passage really refers to Full Communism, not 'Socialism', we are almost entitled to call moneylessness a mere play on words: the receipt for work done *is* money.

But there is one big difference: the receipts 'do not circulate'. I.e. the enterprise which hands over goods against them cannot use them in any way, but must destroy them or possibly deliver them to some central authority for re-use. If the enterprise could buy raw materials or labour with them they would 'circulate', and

---

[1] In a sense the 'Maoist' group within the Chinese leadership recognized the force of this objection, when they tried to introduce urban People's Communes. But the absurdity of the concept was patent, and it is said that it was primarily on this issue that they lost their majority. Cf. the Central Committee resolution of December 1958 (*Peking Review*, December 23, 1958).

[2] *Capital*, II. 18. 2.

be 100% money. This indeed we may take as the definition of the difference between ration cards and money.

An administrative allocation without ration card, say, of an apartment to a family by a letter from a housing committee, is indistinguishable from rationing. Thus when the new Soviet Draft Party Programme promises free housing in twenty years' time[1] it must mean that there will still be administrative allocation. But when it promises free urban transport it must mean genuinely free supply.

So a system of rationing, whether openly by cards or implicitly by administrative allocation, is quite different from genuinely free supply. But it is also different from normal monetary arrangements, and is a step from them on the road to genuinely free supply. It is not a necessary step: thus the U.S.S.R. intends to omit it in the case of urban transport. But it is clearly often a useful one, since it makes it possible to break the link between production and consumption, and go over to universal 'distribution according to need' even while some objects are still scarce.

It will be noted that Marx's passage leaves rationing under Full Communism impeccably orthodox.

The abolition of money of course reduces rationality and increases waste and bureaucracy. Communism has always been theoretically opposed to these latter, and the new Programme also has a whole section on rationality. How can this circle be squared? The old, genuinely Marxist, idea was that when an economy is very advanced somehow this problem would solve itself.[2] But that is absurd. The right answer is, evidently, only by perfect computation. Prices which are only parameters in electrical relays are, ideologically speaking, unprices. If only they remain, money is abolished. This, then, is a further very strong argument for perfect computation.[3]

---

[1] *Pravda*, July 30, 1951.
[2] E.g. Kidrič, *Komunist*, Belgrade, November 1950.
[3] There is as yet no Soviet source for it, as far as I know.

CHAPTER 18

FULL COMMUNISM, ITS HISTORY AND FURTHER DETAILS

1. WE may now attempt a history of ideas about Full Communism to date. It occupies the whole of Sec. 1. In it we shall spend most time on those, less important, events not already analysed.

In the nineteenth century many 'Utopian' socialists put forward ideas of an ultimate state of society akin to Full Communism: Fourier's Phalansteries, Owen's Parallelograms of Paupers, New Harmony, etc., etc. What is more—and here Marx sharply disagreed—they went straight ahead and put them into practice. This was to anticipate the inevitable march of history, and in particular to build an advanced social superstructure on a primitive economic basis that would not carry it. Marx was therefore not surprised that they all failed. Incidentally the kind of Full Communism usually aimed at resembled very closely a 1958 People's Commune, with genuine democracy thrown in! We may, then, share Marx' lack of surprise.

For all their condemnation of Utopian socialism Marx and Engels were far from silent about Full Communism, attributing to it no less than the eleven characteristics enumerated in Ch. 17, Sec. 1. There is no truth in the common statement that Marx and Engels left no blueprint for socialism; it was merely rather less detailed than that of other socialists, and took account of the necessary time-span.

Lenin also had a sense of timing,[1] but in the civil war his attention was diverted and other, hastier, hands plunged directly into a type of Full Communism already described. This too was 'Utopian', and led to the setback of the NEP—Lenin's own work. At the introduction of the NEP the actual words 'Socialism' and 'Communism' (which latter we have here called Full Communism) were distinguished, and the previous period re-named 'War Communism'.

[1] In 1920 he predicted Full Communism by 1930 or 1940 (*Soch.*, 3rd ed., XXV/397).

According to the new phraseology the NEP was not even 'socialism', except only in the nationalized sector; it was 'state capitalism' in the reprivatized factories and foreign concessions;[1] and 'Peasant Economy' in agriculture. The Proletarian Revolution had occurred in a very backward country, and could not build 'socialism' until it received help from the victorious proletariat of an advanced country, to wit Germany. But the German revolution never came off, so Stalin promised 'Socialism in One Country', and won power on that slogan.

Meanwhile, however, there were certain direct attempts at Full Communism, of an entirely voluntary character. These were the so-called 'Communes' (Kommuny). They were mainly entirely self-supporting agricultural communities in which everything was held in common, including the less intimate personal belongings. Now it is by no means certain that collectivism in such delicate matters is any part of Full Communism (see Sec. 6), and the whole movement was plainly a continuation of nineteenth-century Utopianism. As such it was far too advanced for Stalin, who also mistrusted its spontaneity, its independence of the Party, and its appeal to the free-thinking intelligentsia. By 1933 all Kommuny were destroyed, mainly as a result of the collectivization campaign, which was as hostile to more as to less socialistic forms than the kolkhoz.[2]

Stalin was thus the 'socialism' expert. As such he took power, as such his opponents always hesitated to overthrow him, and as such he will go down into history. We must be very brief with his contributions to Socialism here, as they only concern us in so far as they affect Full Communism. Already Lenin had put an end to the notion that there could under socialism be a democracy of many proletarian parties, as there had been of bourgeois parties under the 'dictatorship of the bourgeoisie'. This put paid to freedom, at any rate under 'socialism'. Stalin also made two important alterations. First, since the revolution evidently does not happen everywhere at once we must build 'socialism in one country', and face 'capitalist encirclement'. Therefore an army against foreign aggression and a police force against foreign spies are

---

[1] This is Lenin's use of the words State Capitalism: *Sochinenia*, 3rd ed., XXII/513–16, XXV/305–7, 322–29. He meant simply capitalism controlled by the workers' state; or indeed by any state, since the German war economy was also State Capitalism. The Titoists, and Zinoviev at the 14th Party Congress, refer to the 'deformed' socialist economy of Stalin as State Capitalism. Cf. Ch. 1, Sec. 2.

[2] Cf. Ch. 1, Sec. 4.

necessary, and the state cannot wither away during the building of 'socialism'. Secondly equality forms no part of 'socialism'.

In 1935 and 1936 Stalin and Molotov declared that socialism had been fully victorious,[1] but from then on Stalin's course towards Full Communism is consistently that of *sauter pour mieux reculer*. Prof. Pashukanis, perhaps the chief legal theorist of the time, predicted in 1937 that the state would seriously begin withering away in that year.[2] Later that year he himself withered away. At the 18th Party Congress in 1939 it was only asserted that 'socialism' was 'practically' built in U.S.S.R.; nevertheless the 'transition to Communism' was still on.

Early after the war Full Communism was again near, but later it again receded. In September 1947, at the first Cominform meeting, Malenkov spoke of the preparations for the 19th Party Congress, which 'was to adopt a 15-year plan of transition from socialism to Communism. After he had completed his report Malenkov observed that the Soviet Union was drawing in detail upon the Utopian Socialists.'[3] Alas, we know no more about this fascinating incident. But that the Utopian Socialists were being read with attention is indeed an important fact.

In 1948 Ts. A. Stepanyan, who has subsequently become one of the most authoritative philosophers of Full Communism, published a contribution[4] on the 'Conditions and Roads of the Transition from socialism to Communism'. He said, 'It follows that the generation which was 15 to 20 years old in 1920 will live in the Communist society.' I.e. 1960 was then the tentative date, as also with Malenkov.

By 1950 things had again quietened down. In June of that year a conference of economists[5] was held in Moscow on Full Communism. It agreed that the state must still wither away, whatever monstrous proportions it had meantime reached. While it plays a decisive role in the development of the economy under socialism,

---

[1] B. Meissner, *Europa-Archiv*, 1959.

[2] J. Hazard, *American Quarterly on the Soviet Union*, April 1938, pp. 11–12.

[3] V. Dedijer, *Tito Speaks* (Weidenfeld and Nicholson 1953), p. 305. Dedijer adds on his own account: 'But there is undoubtedly great ideological confusion in the Soviet Union. There are many questions that cannot be answered. They speak about the transition to Communism when they are faced by a maze of unsolved questions. The peasant problem, for example, remains a bad headache, as does the question of nationalities.' This is a typical Yugoslav reaction to talk about Full Communism, as we have seen.

[4] In *O Sovetskom Sotsialichestom Obshchestve*, ed. F. Konstantinova, M. Kammari and G. Glezerman (Gospolitizdat 1948).

[5] Reported in *Voprosy Ekonomiki* 10/1950 (=*Current Digest of Soviet Press*, February 24, 1951). I quote the page references in the latter.

under Communism 'from the point of view of internal tasks it exhausts itself and will not be needed'.[1] What this might mean for central economic planning does not emerge from the published account. However, the state is still needed, 'only for the purpose of defence against military attack and intrigues by foreign enemies, while capitalist encirclement still exists'.[2] This phrase at any rate has definite meaning: there must still be an army and a secret police. Further, the transition to Communism is gradual, not sharp. Like all good Hegelian changes it is of course revolutionary; it begins as a mere quantitative change, but goes so far that it becomes a qualitative change; it is dialectical and embodies an interpenetration of opposites. Like all good Marxist changes it is caused by a change in the underlying 'relations of production', which renders obsolete the old superstructure of social relationships and brings new ones to birth in the womb of the old. But in opposition to all changes hitherto known it is gradual and non-violent: it proceeds by general social agreement and without class struggle. The two remaining classes, workers and peasantry, quietly merge into one. This all simply means that the Kremlin will remain in power for ever.[3]

The 1950 conference was divided on the all-important question, what is free distribution of goods? Some held that individual goods could be distributed in kind (say bread or tram journeys) while the rest were still paid for; others that all goods must become free together. The latter pointed out that medical treatment had been free from the Revolution, and no one had yet regarded this as a harbinger of Communism: indeed it was not, since such treatment was still distributed according to production not need.[4] Thus in the published version the essential question, does free distribution mean a limited ration given out gratis or an unlimited quantity available to the first comer, was skirted but not faced.

Summing up on Stalin, his personal contributions to the theory of Full Communism, and the ones he permitted others to make, were as follows:

(a) he postponed it to the Greek Kalends. Theoretically this was not on the grounds of 'capitalist encirclement', since he said the state

---

[1] Conference, p. 4.

[2] Conference, p. 3. This was exactly Stalin's view of the state under Full Communism (*Voprosy Leninizma*, 11th ed., p. 606).

[3] Conference, p. 1. Cf. footnote to (d) below.

[4] E.g. Stakhanovites go to better sanatoria. In general to distribute things free, but still under some administrative restraint, entails no more equality than if money were demanded; and this was more characteristic of the privilege-ridden social services run by Stalin than of Western social services. But Stalin's successors are about as egalitarian as we.

might continue into Full Communism if there were still capitalist encirclement; but in fact Full Communism is so inseparably bound up with item (iii) that this was the reason for his lukewarm attitude to the whole subject. His lack of interest is demonstrated by a curious little fact. It was the practice to celebrate the anniversaries of trivial speeches he had made, and every 9th of February it fell to the lot of propagandists to find headlines for the celebration of his electoral speech of February 9, 1946. This had been on the long-term economic future of U.S.S.R., and did not contain a single reference to Full Communism. Nevertheless the same anniversary headlines did:

'Great Programme for Building Communism in U.S.S.R.'
    —For a Lasting Peace, For a People's Democracy, Feb. 9, 1951;
'The Majestic Programme of Communist Construction'
    —Pravda, Feb. 9, 1952.

I.e. the cupboard was so bare that the propagandists had to scrape the bottom of the barrel; all Stalin's direct references to Full Communism had hitherto been extremely negative, so they had to dress up something irrelevant.

Similarly his 'Economic Problems' puts off all serious change to a far future, after a very great rise in productivity; it does not so much as mention item (iii), and indeed hardly deals with Full Communism itself directly.

(b) insistence on productivity. As we have seen, he himself seems to have felt that his own practical production plans were his greatest contribution to Full Communism. In consonance with this the press came out in 1951 with references to Full Communism chiefly condemning the insistence on consumer abundance to which the contemplation of it so naturally leads. To the incorrect 'consumer standpoint' was opposed the correct 'producer standpoint'—that the main thing about Full Communism was very high productivity and a willingness to work without direct reward.[1]

(c) he especially disliked item (iii)—never was a man more enamoured of coercive power, or more attracted to policies requiring it. So he said on this subject:

We are for the withering away of the state. But at the same time we stand for a strengthening of the proletarian dictatorship, which constitutes the most powerful, the mightiest of all governing powers that have ever existed. The

[1] E.g. Ostrovityanov, Pravda, June 27, 1951; Stepanyan, Komsomolskaya Pravda, October 16, 1951. Cf. cartoon in Krokodil, Nov. 10, 1952.

highest development of governmental power for the purpose of preparing the conditions *for* the withering away of governmental power, this is the Marxian formula. Is this 'contradictory'? Yes it is. But this contradiction is life and it reflects completely the Marxian dialectic.[1]

(d) he was anxious to emphasize that there would be no sharp break between 'socialism' and Full Communism. Dialectics and contradictions were fine things, but they must not rock the boat, and above all there would be no discontinuity in the exercise of political power, nothing that could conceivably be called a political revolution. All this is best set out by B. Kedrov,[2] who was, however, developing Stalin's own ideas, expressed briefly in his *On Marxism In Linguistics*. Stalin says here that after the proletarian revolution all further revolution will come from on top: quite contrary to pre-proletarian times, it is the continuing proletarian government, and no spontaneous mass movement, that sees the thing through. This is the 'active role of the superstructure'.[3]

(e) he wanted to nationalize kolkhozy. True, he opposed immediate 'sovkhozizatsia' in 1932 (see Ch. 17, Sec. 3); but some kind of sovkhozizatsia was his ultimate aim. This comes out, as we have seen, discreetly in his *Economic Problems of Socialism in U.S.S.R.*; where nevertheless he takes an exceedingly gradualist attitude to Full Communism in general and to this in particular, so that the only measure he actually proposes for the near future is the nationalization of *trade* between kolkhozy and the state.

(f) Stakhanovism is the beginning of the New Soviet Man, who works for the love of it and thus fulfils item (v) of Full Communism. Distribution according to needs means levelling people *up* towards a Stakhanovite standard of living.[4]

It seems that even these 'contributions' to the lore of Full Communism were wrung from Stalin by ideological necessity; the doctrine of Marxism has its own logical momentum, which the most arbitrary Marxian autocrat can hardly resist. The 19th Party Congress (Oct. 1952) had almost nothing about Full Communism. Evidently the old man had had serious second thoughts about its

---

[1] Report of Central Committee to 16th Party Congress, June 27, 1930. Cf. Glezerman, *Isvestia*, October 12, 1951, for an emphatic restatement.

[2] On Forms of Leaps in the Development of Nature and Society, *Bol'shevik*, August 1951.

[3] *Pravda*, June 20, 1950. The 'Active Role of the Superstructure', an idea very attractive to lawyers, was further developed by N. D. Kazantsev in *Sovetskoe Gosudarstvo i Pravo*, September 1950. Kazantsev specifically mentioned the 'active role' as a factor in the transition to Full Communism, which Stalin had as usual not mentioned. On the whole doctrinal contribution of Stalin's linguistic letters cf. the *Pravda* leader of October 5, 1950.

[4] Speech, Nov. 17, 1935 (*Problems of Leninism*, 1945 ed., p. 527).

timing: the Party 'has assured the building of the socialist society', and 'the chief tasks of the CPSU are now to build the Communist society through the gradual transition from Socialism to Communism'[1]—a more cautious statement than in 1939, thirteen years before.

After Stalin's death the course of events is reasonably clear from the preceding chapter. So we may end by pointing out the *essential orthodoxy of the Soviet line on Full Communism*. War Communism deviated in coming too soon, and Stalin's socialism deviated in not preparing the way at all, but rather heading in the opposite direction. But Lenin and Khrushchev went down the straight and narrow path, following the unforced meaning of the majority of the relevant quotations, unlike Mao or Tito. Indeed the pursuit of Full Communism shows most clearly the extent to which Communists are governed by their sacred texts. It is more than seeking doctrinal justification for what they want or are forced to do; that also happens, especially in the short run, but Stalin, and indeed also Mao and Tito, have led us to overstress this sort of cynicism. After all, the abolition of money, the equalization of wages, or—to take a different field—the collectivization of the peasantry are very difficult and disagreeable feats. No one is forced to perform them; no one in his right mind would want to perform them. Yet they have been achieved and/or are again under active discussion. The reason is of course that the Communist leaders are not in their right mind; they are in Marx' mind. Nor, for all that, is Marx' blueprint so absurdly unpractical—otherwise how could Khrushchev have come so far along the way? Indeed its ultimate practicability is so important a question as to deserve two chapters to itself.

2. Does Full Communism mean a command economy or anarchosyndicalism? Just what are the sacred texts relevant to the 'Tito-Stalin polarity' of the previous chapter?

It is not really to be doubted that Marx and Engels wanted (i.e. predicted: it is the same for a determinist) a command economy; though the *dicta* are *obiter* and we may be sure they had no clear picture of it. As the matter is of great importance I set out all the passages known to me which seem to support it:

---

[1] Revised Statutes, I/1: *Pravda*, October 14, 1952. In Malenkov's report to the 19th Congress there is a short passage at the end on Full Communism. It is very gradualist and simply repeats Stalin's Economic Problems.

... whereas in communist society, where no one has an exclusive sphere of employment but can train himself in any branch he wants, society regulates general production and precisely thereby makes it possible for me to do this today and that tomorrow, in the morning to hunt, in the afternoon to fish, in the evening to tend livestock, after dinner to be a literary critic, just as I please; without ever being huntsman, fisher, herdsman or critic.

—Marx, Die Deutsche Ideologie (MEGA I/5, p. 22).

Or how comes it that trade, which is after all nothing more than the exchange of the products of various individuals and countries, rules the whole world through the relation of demand and supply[1] ... whereas with the removal of the basis, private property, with the communist regulation of production and the consequential abolition of the alienation which is the relationship of men to their own product, the power of the relation of supply to demand falls to nothing and men take into their own hands again exchange, production and the manner of their mutual relations?

—ibid., pp. 24–5.

Let us for a change imagine a union of free men, who work with communal means of production and consciously give out their many individual labour forces as a single social labour force. All the conditions of Robinson [Crusoe]'s work repeat themselves here, only socially instead of individually. ... The social planned regulation [of labour time] controls the right proportion of the various work functions to the various needs. ... The *religious reflection* of the real world can only disappear at all when the relations of men's practical workaday life show continuously and obviously rational connexions to each other and to nature. The form of the social life process, i.e. of the material production process, only strips away its mystical veil when as the product of socialized men it stands under their conscious, planned control.

—Marx, Das Kapital I, i/4.

Accountancy as a check and synoptic *aide-mémoire* of the process, becomes more necessary the higher the process goes up the historical ladder of social stages and loses a purely individual character; more necessary, then, in capitalist production than in the scattered production of artisans and peasants, and more necessary in socialized production than in capitalist. But the costs of accountancy are reduced with the concentration of production, and the more it turns into social accountancy.

—ibid. II, vi/1(2).

The realm of freedom begins in fact only where work, which is required by need and external expediencies, ends; so in the nature of things it lies beyond the sphere of actual material production. As the wild man must struggle with Nature to satisfy his needs, to keep alive and to reproduce himself, so must the civilized man, and he must do so in all social forms and all possible modes of production. With his development this realm of natural necessity increases, because his needs do; but at the same time the productive forces which satisfy them increase.

[1] [Zufuhr.]

Freedom in this field can only mean that the socialized man, the associated producers, rationally regulate this exchange of materials with Nature, bring it under
their common control, instead of being dominated by it as by a blind force;
and effect it with the least usage of energy and under the conditions most worthy
of and adequate to their human nature. But this always remains a realm of
necessity. Beyond it begins that development of human forces which is an end in
itself, the true realm of freedom, which however can only flourish upon the realm
of necessity as its basis. The shortening of the labour day is the fundamental
condition.

—ibid. III, xlviii.

The determination of value remains predominant after the abolition of the
capitalist mode of production, but with the retention of social production, in
the sense that the regulation of labour time and the distribution of work among the
various production groups, and lastly the accountancy of all this, becomes more
important than ever.

—ibid. III, xlix.

The whole of Engels' Anti-Dühring (a key work for nearly every
aspect of Marxism) is devoted, of course, to upsetting the doctrines
of Eugen Dühring. But these are that socialism should be organized
in the form of independent communes: a doctrine that is first cousin
to anarcho-syndicalism. Compare especially:

The seizure of the means of production by society puts an end to commodity
production, and therewith to the domination of the product over the producer.
Anarchy in social production is replaced by conscious organization on a planned
basis.

—Engels, Anti-Dühring, III/2.

The national centralization of the means of production will become the natural
base for a society which will consist of an association of free and equal producers,
acting consciously according to a general and rational plan. This is the end to which
the great economic development of the nineteenth century leads.

—Marx, Sochinenia first edn., XIII, pp. 341–2.

The anarcho-syndicalist passages on the other side are very thin.
They mostly arise from Marx' need to sanctify ex post facto the Paris
Commune, which followed if anything the doctrines of his enemy
Proudhon, correctly described in modern Soviet textbooks as a
'petty-bourgeois anarchist'. Marx' Civil War in France takes in
part the line of denying Proudhon's influence and in part that of
quoting the numerous Proudhonist actions of the Commune
with what appears to be approval, but when looked at closely
is seen to be a very qualified approval, not extending to principles
at all. The most directly relevant passage is:

The great social measure of the (Paris) Commune was its own working existence. Its special measures could but betoken the tendency of a government of the people by the people. . . . Another measure of this class was the surrender, to associations of workmen, under reserve of compensation, of all closed workshops and factories, no matter whether the respective capitalists had absconded or preferred to strike work.

—Marx, *The Civil War in France*, 1871, III.

The Paris Commune kept, and rightly so in Marx' opinion, capitalists in charge where they co-operated; it was at war and it had very many petty bourgeois adherents. It represented therefore the 'dictatorship of the proletariat', not 'socialism';[1] and it would be a gross misinterpretation of the above to suggest that Marx was approving of such a measure in fully developed socialism (what we have here called Full Communism).

Here follow three very similar quotations from Engels, of which the same may be said:

On the 16th April the Commune ordered a statistical survey of all the factories brought to a standstill by their employers, and the working out of plans for the reactivation of these factories through the workers hitherto employed in them, who were to be united into co-operative societies; and for the organization of these societies into a great union.

—Engels, Introduction to *The Civil War in France*, 1871, III.

By far the most important decree of the Commune ordered an organization of large industry and even handicrafts, which was not only to rest on the association of workers in each factory but to combine all these societies into a great union; in short an organization which, as Marx said quite rightly in his *Civil War, must in the end have resulted in Communism.*

—ibid. (my italics).

It stands to the highest honour of the Commune that in all their economic regulations it was not some principle or other that provided the dynamic, but simple practical need. Therefore these regulations—the confiscation of stopped factories and their transferral to associations of workmen—were not at all in the spirit of Proudhon but rather in that of German scientific socialism.[2]

—Engels, *On The Housing Problem* (1872), iii/1.

But already in 1874 Engels was attacking libertarian socialism again:

Let us suppose that the social revolution has toppled the capitalists. . . . Let us suppose, looking wholly from the viewpoint of the anti-authoritarians, that land and equipment have become the collective property of the workers using it. Does authority vanish or only change its form? Let us look.

[1] Cf. footnote 1, p. 334.
[2] (This was Marx' and Engels' name for Marxism—P.J.D.W.)

Take, for example, cotton-spinning. . . . The workers must above all agree on hours of work, and once these have been decided they are obligatory for all without exception. . . . And however they decided these questions, whether by an elected person who lays down the work of each branch, or, *where that is possible*,[1] by a majority of votes, the will of each must in any case be subordinate, and that means that questions will be resolved in an authoritarian manner. The automatic mechanism of a big factory shows itself to be more despotic than the small capitalists for whom workers work. At least, in so far as hours of work are concerned one might write on the gates of these factories: *Lasciate ogni autonomia, voi che entrate!*

(other examples: a railway, a ship at sea)

. . . Besides, we have seen that the material conditions of production and exchange lead inevitably to the development of large-scale industry and large-scale agriculture and tend to an ever greater development of the sphere of this authority. . . . Authority and autonomy are relative things, and the sphere of their application changes with the various phases of social development. If the autonomists only wanted to say that the social organization of the future will allow authority within the boundaries inevitably laid down by the conditions of production, then one might agree with them.

— Engels, *On Authority*, 1874 (*Sochinenia*, 3rd ed., xv, pp. 135–6).

Nor is there any comfort in Engels' later writings. Thus this might seem a promising passage:

The society that organizes production anew on the basis of a free and equal association of producers, transfers the whole state machine to where it then belongs: into the museum of antiquities, along with the spinning-wheel and the bronze axe.

— Engels, *The Origin of Family, Property and State* (1884), IX.

But what is this association and how is it defined? The fact that it is in the singular is itself highly suspicious. And since the *dictum* is but *obiter* we must clearly refer back to the earlier literature if we want more detail. But that literature is, as we have seen, depressingly centralistic. The last quotation commonly urged is as follows:[2]

Complete self-administration in Province, County and Parish, through officials chosen by universal suffrage. Abolition of all local and provincial authorities appointed by the state.

— Engels, *Criticism of the Social Democratic Draft Programme of 1891.*

But this, undoubtedly Proudhonist as it is, refers to the immediate demands of the proletariat under capitalism.

The classic Yugoslav position on all this is given by Tito himself,

---

[1] My italics.

[2] I owe most of these quotations to Mr. Wolfgang Leonhard.

in his speech to the Skupština on the introduction of the workers' councils.[1] None of his quotations from Marx even approximates to a defence of workers' councils or decentralization. He appears to deduce them both directly from the doctrine of the withering away of the state; in which context he does not see any distinction between the planning bureaucracy (clearly a 'social organization', as we have seen!) and the state proper. He also takes as a serious ideological pronouncement the cry 'the factories to the workers'; whereas this is either pure anarchism or a tactical piece of agitation on the part of Bolsheviks anxious to gain power—as Soviet history very clearly shows.[2]

Thus there seems to be no single passage that, unforced and in its proper context, lends any colour at all to anarcho-syndicalist or free market socialism, in the whole enormous corpus of Marx' and Engels' writings.

In all this literature there are really three separate issues:

(a) the survival of the coercive organs of the state for a period after the revolution;

(b) free market versus a command economy under socialism and communism;

(c) the internal structure of the enterprise under socialism and communism.

On (a) and (b) Marx and Engels were absolutely firm: there must be coercion for a limited period and there must be central planning for ever (whatever 'central planning' might mean). The free market is the same as the 'anarchy of capitalist production', and that is a very bad thing. On (c) they never really said anything much: even the quotation from *On Authority* leaves the door open to workers' councils.

It must be remembered whom they were arguing against: Bakunin, who held the *destruction* of the state (not its withering away) to be the essential and indeed only task of the revolution, as it was the (bourgeois) state that caused capitalism, not vice versa; who 'objectively' wanted a free market but never raised the issue seriously; and who talked as if modern industry should be rather abolished than subjected to workers' control. But throughout the main argument was about (a), and all the other *dicta* are *obiter*.

One might suppose that Marx' and Engels' views on freedom

[1] *Komunist*, Belgrade, July–Sept. 1950.
[2] Some Titoists also quote Lenin's tactical flirtation with workers' control in 1917 as if it had been seriously meant.

were relevant at this point. The subject is of great length and well documented. I must simply confine myself to saying that nearly always they used Hegel's definition of freedom, and by democracy meant 'totalitarian democracy'.[1] I.e. they were absolutely confused about freedom, and somehow failed to find room in it for disagreement; they could only conceive the freedom of people who were unanimous and rational. Since this is a view an anarcho-syndicalist might well share, it throws no light on the problem posed in this section.

Marx' view on democracy under socialism (and, doubtless, still more under Full Communism) does however contribute to our understanding. Democracy is of course quite separate from freedom, and either may exist without the other. An anarcho-syndicalist may well take the Hegelian view of freedom, but he is bound to support democracy. Now Marx' opinion is exceedingly hard to discover. That he denied the possibility of democracy under capitalism is no more significant of his authoritarian belief than that he never officially or publicly discussed democracy under socialism. However, this passage can be culled from his private papers. It is a comment on Bakunin; we quote Bakunin's text and Marx' interpolations.

> This dilemma in the theory of the Marxists is easily solved. By the people's administration they understand the administration of the people by a small number of representatives, chosen by the people (*Asine!*—interpolates Marx—demagogic rubbish, political phrase-mongering! Elections are a political form already known in the tiniest Russian commune and the artel. The character of elections does not depend on these verbal categories, but on the economic bases, on the economic relations of the electors among themselves, and from the moment when these functions have ceased to be political, (1) there are no further governmental functions, (2) the distribution of public functions is a business question, giving rise to no sort of domination, (3) these elections have now no political character).
>
> —Marx, Conspectus of Bakunin's 'Government and Anarchy' (*Sochinenia*, 3rd ed. xv, p. 191).

Thus whether or not there should be democracy is 'a business question, giving rise to no sort of domination'. Elections appear to be optional. And in all his years Marx only wrote this one short inconclusive passage on the subject. Therefore again he was not a democrat. Nor, of course, was Lenin.

6. But mere economics pales into insignificance when we

---

[1] Cf. J. L. Talmon's classic of that name (London, 1952).

contemplate the full grandeur of the question of Man under Full Communism. Crime and education we have not space to deal with. Religion must obviously be abolished. What of a thing more important than any of these, the *family*?

The neglect of the family in Western economics is amazing and lamentable. For it is of course among its many attributes, an enterprise. The family, especially the very poor family, used to be a great producer for sale, and it has not ceased to produce with the Industrial Revolution. It has simply switched to what used to characterize only very rich families, the processing of semi-finished articles for its own consumption. For as we have seen (Ch. 12, Sec. 26) only a buttered slice of bread, on the plate before the eater, is a final good. Moreover, with the increase in consumer durables this kind of production is growing rapidly. It uses up enormous quantities of vital national resources. So do the care and education of children. Only very recently, with the growth of the economics of underdeveloped countries and the first stirrings of economic interest in education and hedonic price indices, has even the ground-work existed for an economics of the family. So even if little is added to that ground-work here, the structure and functions of the family have a proper place, indeed pride of place, in any fairly comprehensive work of economics.

That Marx and Engels wanted (i.e. predicted, for, to repeat, this is the same for a determinist) to abolish the family is undoubted, though it is absolutely unclear exactly what their constructive proposal was:

The positive removal of private property, as the appropriation of human life, is then the positive removal of all alienation, that is the return of the human being from religion, family, state, etc., into his human, i.e. his social, existence.
—Marx, *Nationalökonomie und Philosophie* (Paris MSS., *MEGA* I, 3, p. 115).

Abolition of the family! Even the most radical flare up at this infamous proposal of the Comminists.

On what foundation is the present family, the bourgeois family, based? On capital, on private gain. In its completely developed form this family exists only among the bourgeoisie. But this state of things finds its complement in the practical absence of the family among the proletarians, and in public prostitution.

The bourgeois family will vanish as a matter of course when its complement vanishes, and both will vanish with the vanishing of capital.

Do you charge us with wanting to stop the exploitation of children by their parents? To this crime we plead guilty.
—Marx and Engels, *Communist Manifesto*.

There seem to have been two separate motives here: the humanistic insistence of the young[1] Marx on the full development of the individual, which he thought family life constricted; and the sexual Bohemianism of Engels, who found fidelity dull and never married. These motives combine well, and issued on the one hand in the free-love doctrine and practice of Mrs. Kollontai after the Revolution, and on the other in Lenin's legal and economic emancipation of women (Lenin was against free love but he did have a mistress; he also had no children, though it is not known whether because it would have hindered his revolutionary life or because he and his wife could not).

During War Communism, then, there was a serious effort to abolish the family, with the aim of emancipating women legally, sexually and economically. The economic aim concerned not the state as employer, but the woman as employee: she was not conscripted for others' good but offered a job for her own good.

Stalin conscripted women's labour for the good of the state, and thus in his own way contributed to the break-up of the family; also by putting husbands in concentration camps and making everybody spy on everybody. But this was in a way accidental: his main policy was, here as elsewhere, to put a brake on the previous futurism and settle down to a long period of 'socialism', which must be taken seriously. Thus we have no utterance of his on the ultimate future of the family, and while he drove women out to work he also put a stop to all sexual bohemianism, made divorce and abortion difficult, and slowed down the construction of crèches. The flood of delinquent orphans left by the civil war (bezprizornie) left him in no doubt that the family was an excellent stop-gap.

Indeed the care of children is the principal omission from Communist doctrines of the family before Stalin. Marx, Engels and even Lenin were so obsessed with the emancipation of women that they 'emancipated' the children too. It was not enough appreciated how expensive crèches are; though he expanded their number, Stalin could not provide anything like enough crèches for Soviet children, and the majority were, even at his death, cared for by the family or by private arrangement.

---

[1] If the old Marx was an economic determinist and a protagonist of the dictatorship of the proletariat, the young Marx was a left-Hegelian humanist. On the embarrassment that the Paris MSS., quoted above, have caused in U.S.S.R., cf. Goldhagen, *Soviet Survey*, April-June 1959.

With Mao it was otherwise. He also wanted economic productivity, and saw in woman-power, 'freed' from the kitchen, an addition to the labour force; and the false Marxist definition of income, which excludes services and allows only material products, helped him to do so. To abolish the family, then, is to conscript more labour; but for Mao it also meant to nationalize personal property: since the restaurant replaces the private kitchen, and the crèches the nursery. The 1958 People's Commune was directly and openly[1] to be a substitute for the family. Men and women were to—often did—cohabit by night only, and neither enjoy leisure nor of course work in the family unit. Children and grandparents were to—often did—sleep elsewhere. Children's lives were spent in crèches. A big popular complaint was that wives had no time to mend their families' clothes. Meals, needless to say, were in common. And at the same moment Khrushchev was promising the Russian housewife every sort of individualized consumer's durable! Is it any wonder whose version of Full Communism won? Note, too, yet another parallel between War Communism and Maoism.

Yet did Khrushchev mean anything permanent with his gas-cookers? One may well doubt it. There has always been something ideologically inferior about personal property, and Khrushchev has also promised more collective living as part of Full Communism:

Already there are developing more and more the communist forms of work and of organizing production, and such social forms for the satisfaction of citizens' needs as communal feeding, boarding-schools, kindergartens and crèches. In our society many traits of communism can be felt and seen, which will develop and perfect themselves.[2]

Thus the threat that Engels, by practice and precept, posed to sexual 'morality' has been decisively rejected—this is one thing on which Lenin, Stalin, Tito, Khrushchev, Mao, Gomulka, and all

[1] There was never any official confirmation, but the lower cadres were permitted to be very frank in the press: out of very many instances I single out Jen Min Jih Pao, Dec. 16, 1958.

[2] *Pravda*, Jan. 28, 1959. The same was already asserted by 'a number of speakers' at the June 1950 conference on Full Communism (see Sec. 1 above): 'the development of public dining and other public facilities and the extension of the network of kindergartens and crèches are already gradually narrowing the sphere of individual housekeeping in urban areas. All this leads to increasing the relative importance of public property and of the public economy, and obliterates the social boundaries between people' (p. 7). There is an even more full-blooded attack on the family under Full Communism in Strumilin, *Novy Mir*, July 1960. S. G. Strumilin is an honoured, orthodox and independent authority on economics generally and Full Communism in particular.

are agreed. But this by no means saves the family under Full Communism, since Marx' and Engels' guarantee of personal property in the *Communist Manifesto* (item ii) has been thrust into the background, and with it the family's new economic basis is threatened. For as we saw, deprived since the Industrial Revolution of a role in production for the market, the family has built up a new role as processor of semi-finished goods for its own use. The Communists want to take this also from it. The reasons for this new and more serious threat are twofold: the state's need for female labour and its resentment of natural ties and traditions. Man under Full Communism is to be 'free' in that he is an atomized, traditionless unit; to pervert Leibnitz, a transparent monad, open to the influence of society at every pore. The Communists have no longer the typically young-Hegelian aim of freely developing the personalities of husbands and wives by liberating them from each other: they want to capture the labour of the women in the factories and the minds of the children in the boarding-schools.

CHAPTER 19

FREE SUPPLY AND INDEFINITE ECONOMIC GROWTH[1]

1. THE previous chapters posed, and we now try to answer, the question, will the free supply of goods and services to unrationed consumers ever be possible? On any ordinary assumption about the wants of consumers and the willingness of workers to work this presupposes a level of productivity so much greater than that in any country of the world today that we may properly speak of indefinite economic growth. The correct word is 'indefinite' and not infinite, for there will always be a finite number of consumers and producers and each of them must consume and produce a finite quantity. The unphilosophical need merely note that infinity is not a number, while here it is of numbers, however large, of consumers, producers, goods and services that we are speaking.

In venturing into *terra incognita* the writer is conscious that he may lose his way. Sticking at trifles he may easily miss important points; deprived of a map he may take very roundabout routes. But the general question must at some time be answered and therefore somebody must begin. Even if the question cannot in fact be answered, the problems raised by asking it are interesting and important.

We divide our discussion quite simply and crudely into two main parts: demand and supply. We shall postpone all practical problems of the transition to Ch. 20. Beginning then with the latter, can supply per head expand indefinitely? An elementary question shapes our answer: what is the availability of land, labour and technique? We shall deal first with capital and technique, together. Obviously merely extensive investment must come to an end when all idle land and labour is put to use.[2] Imitation of

---

[1] The non-Communist literature on this is very meagre. Compare, however: E. Bellamy, *Looking Backward*, New York, 1898; Engelbourg in Columbia University *Forum*, Fall 1960; J. Schmookler, *A Critique of Patent statistics and a Review of the Literature* (Minneapolis 1960, unpublished); F. P. Ramsey, *Economic Journal*, 1928 (I might comment that this celebrated article assumes far too much that we need, in fact, to prove; it is not very useful); M. Bronfenbrenner, *American Journal of Economics and Sociology*, 1961; J. M. Keynes, 'The Economic Possibilities for our Grandchildren', in *Essays in Persuasion*, London, 1951; J. Ise, 'Consumer Values' in his *The American Way* (Kansas 1955); Center for the Study of Democratic Institutions (Santa Barbara, Calif.), *Bulletin*, Jan. 1962; Gerard Piel, *Consumers of Abundance*, and Donald N. Michael, *Cybernation* (same Center, 1961). A shortened version of this chapter appeared in *Ost Europa* (Stuttgart) 1961. Cf. also Zauberman and Wiles in ed. L. Schapiro, *The USSR and the Future*, N.Y. 1962.

[2] Ramsey (op. cit.) seems to assume the opposite, without explaining why.

others' techniques is clearly irrelevant here. The answer to our question depends mainly on the overall progress of technique among mankind. *In what immediately follows we exclude new types of consumer good.*

One trivial exception to this must be noted before we pass on. With a sufficient rate of gross investment and no technical progress consumers' durables could be indefinitely accumulated. Provided that there were no co-operating factors required to make them function, and that their marginal utility never sank to zero despite the indefinite shift of proportions in their favour, such consumer durables could, merely by being piled up, increase consumer satisfaction indefinitely at the cost of a constant share of a constant national income. But what could such durables be? Only ash-trays and china dogs even appear to need no co-operating factors; but even that is not true. An indefinite number of ash-trays or china dogs requires an indefinite number of dusters. Without them their marginal utility would quickly and certainly become negative. Even with them the outlook for their marginal utility is rather bleak. So capital alone will certainly not do the trick.

2. Turning then to technical progress, first is the number of possible inventions infinite? I.e. is the number of new, economically useful propositions about the nature of matter infinite? In order to discuss this question we must first define for statistical purposes a 'unit invention'. E.g. can we say that a way of making fire counts two to the Otto Cycle's one, or relativity is fifty times the thermionic valve? Presumably these things should be given some kind of money value, but this would in practice be impossible. Yet even though the 'standard unit of invention' is extremely arbitrary not much precision is required of it in the present context. For if the apparent number of inventions were to be infinite while the sum in standard units was finite it would be necessary for some standard units to contain an infinite apparent number—a most unlikely thing. Nay more, there would have to be a historical trend: the number of apparent units per standard unit must be increasing, i.e. inventions must be becoming less and less basic or important; of which there is no sign.

Questions about the number of inventions, then, are of an implicitly statistical character, and the concept of a 'standard unit' invention is not so utterly absurd as to render the questions *ipso facto* absurd.

Could it then be shown that an infinite number of inventions is not logically possible? That granted a few empirically known propositions about the nature of matter it involves a contradiction? For instance there are only 92 natural elements, and only a finite portion of the universe is or can ever be visible. So if the volume of matter we can study is finite, and the varieties of it are finite, the number of different generalizations we can make about it is finite.[1] But this obviously does not follow: elements have isotopes, and we have no assurance against the discovery of further important sub-classifications of the natural elements, or indeed of entirely new basic classifications that dispense with atomic weight as a factor. Again, to say that only a finite portion of the universe is *visible* is not to say that only that portion is *accessible*—we have no assurance that radically different means of perception will not be discovered and harnessed for scientific use, such as telepathy.

3. Thus there can be no doubt that infinite technical progress is a logical possibility. It seems impossible, however, to decide whether it is a practical one. The fundamental reason for our difficulty here is very simple: extrapolation and induction depend on some 'law of the uniformity of nature'—or at least of the uniformity of what is studied. But technical progress arises from studying different things in different ways, and it is only in the vaguest possible way that one can speak of the uniformity of science. Yet without such a postulate how can generalizations about science be made—such as that past rates of technical progress can or cannot be maintained?

Nevertheless this is or should be one of the most important questions in all economics, and even a little ground-clearing would be valuable. We have, it seems, to choose between at least three metaphors. Is progress like a fire in an infinite prairie on a windless day? The fire spreads out in an ever-widening ring, and at every moment the ratio of the immediately burnable to the at present burning is constant. Or is it like—how shall we put it?—an infinite crossword in which every word has an infinitely long clue, defining it in terms of all the other words? In this case the more we have solved the easier it is to solve the remainder. Or is it like the field of

---

[1] Prof. F. Hoyle fell a victim to this fallacy when he asserted that the astronomer in 100 years' time must have the same basic view of the universe as himself. For the universe expands at ever increasing speed towards the 'horizon', at which its retreat from us is at a speed equal to that of light. Consequently, beyond this finite horizon nothing is or ever will be visible, and since our largest telescopes nearly reach it already we already know most of what there is to know (*The Nature of the Universe*, Blackwell 1960, 2nd ed., p. 98). This leaves utterly out of account other means of knowledge than light.

gravity of a star? This is of infinite extent but at great distances exceedingly faint (i.e. discovery proceeds more and more slowly).

Any one of these metaphors may apply if possible discoveries are infinite in number. If the number is finite the 'field' of possible facts might still be one of these three kinds, with discovery proceeding at a constant, increasing or diminishing rate to a finite limit. Since we cannot reason here from the known to the unknown it seems impossible to tell whether the field is finite or infinite, or which of the three metaphors best describes it.

Yet if past experience is here no basis of proof it may perhaps illuminate. Some believe that invention has hitherto proceeded and will proceed at an accelerating rate;[1] indeed this was until recently the common assumption. Schmookler (op. cit.) believes the opposite, and presents *inter alia* this more or less *a priori* argument:

> That changes in techniques could increase in frequency indefinitely, moreover, is a logical absurdity. Acceleration of this sort would require that each decade, each year, each month, and finally each minute, workers would have to learn new techniques of production. Ultimately, they would have to spend all their time learning and everybody would starve to death. It would mean presumably that the lifetimes of buildings would finally be reduced to an infinitesimal fraction of a second, so that men would have neither a place to live nor a place to work. There are, in short, limits imposed on the frequency of technical change by the needs of survival.

To discuss this properly we must make several distinctions:

(i) the increase in sheer knowledge;

(ii) inventions, i.e. the increase in economically applic*able* knowledge;

(iii) technical change, i.e. the applic*ation* of inventions;

(iv) technical improvement, i.e. the increase in the 'residual' of Ch. 13, Sec. 3;

(v) patents.

(iv) differs from (iii) in that we need not and do not apply all inventions. Provided that (i) and (ii) accelerate there is no need for (iii) to do so; yet by due selection (iv) may also accelerate. I.e. the improvement factor between those inventions we actually apply might steadily increase. So Schmookler's almost *a priori* argument falls to the ground.

---

[1] E.g. Ogburn and Nimkoff, *Handbook of Sociology*, London 1947, pp. 525, 539.

His more empirical argument however remains: the number of patents taken out is certainly not accelerating, whereas during the nineteenth century it did. Indeed the generally accepted 'accelerationist' view also rests on counting patents, but only up to the 1930s. But their number is nothing like an adequate measure of the number of inventions, since (a) patent law keeps changing, (b) entrepreneurs find it less and less worth while to patent things, and (c) government and university research expand. For all these three reasons (well set out by Schmookler himself, incidentally) the number of patents falls increasingly short of the number of inventions. The number is thus useless, and in the absence of direct statistics for inventions we cannot say anything about their rate of growth.

More important is the constancy of the 'residual'. It is a matter of simple fact that output indices have outstripped input indices in U.S.A. always by about the same percentage.[1] Technical improvement, then, in the only country for which it has been measured over a long period has in fact been constant.

4. We have decided, then, that there certainly *can be* an infinite number of more useful things to discover; let us assume there *are*. Then what of the future course of the *costs of discovery*?

There is some slight reason for pessimism here, i.e. for preferring our 'field of gravity' metaphor. Up to the nineteenth century discovery was very cheap indeed. The will to invent, the will to fiddle with things, was principally lacking; for those who had it, nature was their oyster. They did not need much formal education, indeed too much of what then passed for formal education would have been a hindrance. Many of their discoveries were pretty obvious—a thing unlikely now. The costs of research weighed, no doubt, heavily upon these eccentric individuals: the poor inventor, sacrificing happiness, comfort and life itself to his *idée fixe*, was a stock figure. But in the national scale such costs were quite trivial. Today research, quite apart from technical education, takes about 2% of the U.S., British and Soviet national incomes.[2] Here is exponential growth indeed, very possibly at a greater rate than that of discovery.

---

[1] Ch. 13, Sec. 3.

[2] U.K.: £450 million in 1959 (Williams, *Times Review of Industry*, March 1960), and £300 million in 1955–56 (DSIR, *Estimates of Resources Devoted to Scientific and Engineering Research and Development in British Manufacturing Industry*, 1955). U.S.A.: $10·3 billion in 1957 (Department of Commerce, *Historical Statistics of the U.S.*, 1961, p. 614). U.S.S.R.: R.23·9 md. in 1958, R.28·2 md. in 1959 (*Zasedania Verkhovnogo Sovieta*, Dec. 1958, Oct. 1959).

May there not be *diminishing returns to research?*—a sort of Malthusian pressure of researchers and laboratories on facts, not indeed on all undiscovered facts but on those immediately available from the standpoint of existing knowledge. Such a view is particularly plausible when we reflect that as research expands stupider and stupider people, with ever more lengthy, intensive and specialized educations, must be employed. For a time the improvements of communication and co-ordination, at present making such rapid strides, may offset these costs by reducing duplicated effort. But that is a once-for-all process.[1] Moreover every new specialized course must include most of the basic knowledge of the previous course from which it hived off.

Let us be optimistic and suppose that the metaphor of the infinite crossword puzzle is correct. Then these people will have an ever-expanding number of facts to go on, and if there really is an infinite number of useful facts to discover they will be ever better and better placed to 'enfilade' the undiscovered from various points of vantage in the territory already mapped. But this does not tell us *exactly how easy* the new facts will be to discover—perhaps the Setter of the Crossword Puzzle made one bit specially easy for us?

Indeed it is almost certain that the new knowledge will be more complicated than the old. The clues in the crossword puzzle that historically were solved first were in fact almost all of them easier to explain than those solved more recently. True, great simplifying concepts (heliocentric astronomy, atomic weights) do come along to reduce incomprehensible multiplicity to order, so that the progress of science is indeed punctuated by great leaps into simplicity. But there is progression in these simplifying concepts too: they become more difficult! Compare the special theory of relativity with Newton's theory of gravity. And not only that: they do not altogether supersede each other—a scientist must learn more and more of them.

So even the most optimistic metaphor for the nature of scientific knowledge gives little hope as to costs. It is plausible to hold that returns to research are diminishing and will continue to do so. But even if this is true it does not exclude infinite technical progress. For clearly old inventions release resources, and a rise in the cost of research may easily be financed out of these resources and leave something to spare. Now this is certain to be the case, since over

[1] Cf. Ffrangcon Roberts, *The Cost of Health*, London, 1952, Chs. 4–8. This chapter owes a great deal to Mr. Roberts' book, too much neglected by economists.

time *the resources released by any one invention are infinite*. The proof of this is simple. Keeping still to our exclusion of new consumer goods, an invention is by definition a new technique that cheapens the production of old consumer goods, however indirectly. This new knowledge once discovered has indeed to be perpetuated, and that has costs: the costs of teaching and library space.[1] We know too little about these, and they may possibly be much greater than they seem. But at first blush one is inclined to dismiss as negligible the cost of teaching to people the use of a given invention, even if it bears *pro rata* its part of the whole cost of general education. So there is little to set against the cost economy, and since the invention is never lost the economy continues *ad infinitum*. It is therefore only necessary for the cost of the next invention to be finite, and the previous one will take care of it in time.

This is not to say that every particular piece of past research has actually been worth while. Naturally money invested in improving the horseshoe[2] in, say, 1905 was wasted. But the very fact that it was wasted means that something better came along, that was able eventually to pay for all money spent on itself *and* on horseshoe improvement. Research would be conducted more cheaply with more foreknowledge, so that more individual projects were profitable. But the whole is profitable even as things are.

It may seem unnecessary to introduce a rate of futurity discount into the above argument, for the costs of the second invention can be spread out over time, just as are the benefits of the first. Indefinite technical progress is therefore possible without a reduction in present living standards. But would we willingly undertake it? Here is where the futurity discount is important. If the annual value of the economy is E, and the rate of discount r, the present value of the sum to infinity is no longer infinity but $\frac{E}{r}$, and the cost of the invention should, it appears, be less than this. However abstract and non-operational such a concept may appear, it is in fact eminently practical. It is irrelevant that no one knows E, not even the cost, when he embarks on the research; we should—and do—choose between research projects on the basis of the best information we

[1] Short of a major war scientific knowledge can never now be lost: printing and technical education make this impossible. In the past, in a Dark Age between civilizations, this could happen on a grand scale.

[2] J. Schmookler, *Address to American Association for the Advancement of Science*, Dec. 26, 1960.

have, and however vague it is it does take that form. But where such a simple-minded calculation really is misleading is in neglecting the further discoveries likely to flow from the one under consideration. Basic research has $E = 0$, but it is not less worth while for that.[1]

In fact the future often seems very remote to private individuals, and it is not enough that an investment, such as a research project, will pay for itself over an indefinite period of years. It must be a short and definite period of years, or the private entrepreneur will not put up the money. This is simply the usual futurity discount. It is one of the main distinctions between a centrally planned and an individualistic economy that the state may well not feel such a discount. Note that I say 'may'—some public authorities discount the future very sharply, and 'distinction'—it is not from all points of view an advantage.

Clearly then if the discount be operative it is not enough that research projects pay their way eventually: they must do so rather quickly. And we cannot prove that this must always be the case. Even without a futurity discount the time required to finance the next invention without lowering the present standard of living might become longer and longer, as the cost of invention went up. I.e. the growth-curve of invention, plotted against time would turn out not to be exponential over its whole length, but after a few centuries it would turn over, so that the whole was shaped thus: $\int$ or even thus $\frown$. And if we add in the futurity discount, as in a free market system we must, the research game may actually come to seem not worth the candle. An 'exhaustion of research opportunities' is at least logically possible, however remote it may appear from us today. But such an exhaustion would have to be total: so long as humanity conducted *any* research with success, so that even one invention was made in a century, there would be indefinite economic growth.

5. So much for capital and technique. With land we may be much more brief. Clearly if there were resource depletion or Malthusian pressure research would become profitable again. This consideration reveals to us that we have been speaking hitherto of 'net' research, destined to improve, not merely to maintain,

---

[1] Even here, however, research is and should be directed with a view to its 'profitability' or 'productivity'. Of basic research projects those are preferred, *ceteris paribus*, that seem likely to give rise to most new basic or applied research, i.e. to the greatest profit in terms of intellectual interest or sheer money. Note that basic research corresponds to the M and applied research to the L of Ch. 15.

man's position *vis-à-vis* nature. Production per head being our
objective, we need of course to avoid Malthusian pressure. While
emigration to other suitable planets will doubtless be possible it is
not without its costs, and there can be no doubt that contraceptives
are a cheaper way of keeping 'land' in good supply. Yet hitherto
in human history Malthus has lost his battle with technical progress,
however careless humanity has been. So it is difficult to persuade
ourselves that 'land' in general will ever be a bottleneck. As to
'land' in particular, however, certain amenities and perhaps certain
minerals will surely be bottlenecks for ever. To this we return
in Sec. 7.

The supply of labour is best dealt with along with demand,
since both depend on the kind of human being we assume.

To sum the most probable of these alternatives is largely a matter
of guesswork, and therefore doubtless of temperament. The writer
feels that the 'exhaustion of research opportunities', if possible at all,
is so extremely distant that indefinite economic growth may indeed
be spoken of, even in a market economy in which the futurity
discount operates; especially since research is an end in itself, and
would be conducted by very many in a highly affluent society
regardless of gain.

6. Turning now to demand, how may we classify the types of
consumer for our purpose—which is to analyse the possibilities of
free supply?

(a) The consumer may on principle want very little: such are
ascetics: hermits, monks, simple lifers like Thoreau or people disgusted with the vulgarity of materialism rather than with materialism itself—beatniks. A similar type, not yet instantiated, is
presented in G. B. Shaw's *Back to Methuselah*: the highly sophisticated
intellectual of advancing age who has tasted every pleasure and
finally finds only higher mathematics really satisfying. Clearly
with such consumers nothing very much need be produced; but
would they produce it free of charge? It would lead us unnecessarily afield to answer this question at length. Enough to see that it
depends on the attitude to work and society of the particular kind
of ascetic. Certain monastic orders might well, indeed have,
operate a system of free supply, whereas a mendicant friar depends,
by definition, on a differently organized sector of the economy
from which he can beg. The same applies to beatniks and tramps.
Free supply uncovered by production is of course beggary.
However, a society of monks or beatniks is unlikely to come about,

so we must reluctantly return from this interesting footpath to the highway.

(b) *'Primitive idlers.'* Such are Tahitians and, possibly, British miners before the nationalization of coal. Owing to their cultural isolation or their limited social horizon primitive idlers never want very much. If, *per impossibile*, techniques could advance considerably while not broadening these horizons they too would clearly be able freely to produce all they want. In this case, however, we cannot assume that the advance of technique or even the lapse of time is compatible with the present state of mind of the consumer. The primitive idler is rapidly disappearing from the face of the earth, and it is precisely technical progress that helps him to his grave. In contrast to him, the beatnik is a man of principle.

(c) *The rationed consumer.* Obviously the effective demand of the rationed is limited and—were it not that the Communists are most seriously considering such a consumer—it would seem to be cheating to bring in rationing at all.[1] For ration cards are a kind of money, and it is in a sense trivial to suggest that we can abolish money by introducing rations. Nevertheless the point remains that after considerable technical progress it is at least probable that the rationed consumer would be willing to do enough work for nothing to produce everything that he is permitted to consume. The Chinese system, in the first year of the People's Communes, of 'free but limited supply' is merely a cardless rationing. Instead of getting a card he can take to a shop the consumer receives the right to eat in such-and-such a mess-hall, the right to sleep in a named lodging, etc., etc.

(d) *The 'educated' consumer*: this is the most common and serious Communist proposal. The education referred to is pressure from the Party, and general propaganda to keep down the demands of the consumer to what is 'reasonable'. Instead of keeping up with the Joneses the educated consumer keeps down with the Ivanovs. Such people should also be willing to do sufficient work freely and for nothing to produce what they want to consume if technical progress continues for a sufficient time. This is the new Communist labour morale, in which work becomes a psychological necessity and a matter of honour; it is no longer performed against direct payment.

(e) *The 'rational' consumer*: this is the normal, ideal Western man

[1] Cf. Ch. 17, Sec. 6.

of the textbooks and the indifference curves. He requires a very great deal but not an indefinite amount. He will after all require leisure *from* consumption, he will retain a certain delight in simple things. There will be biological limitations on his capacity to consume: not only food but clothes (he has not time to be for ever changing his clothes), travel (he gets tired of seeing new places) and shelter (he does not want a house too big to walk over). He has, too, a 'leisure ceiling'. Beyond a certain point he is bored and feels socially useless, if he does not work. If this type can satisfy himself without using money we shall call it 'genuinely free supply'.

(f) Then there are various people, unorthodox but in a sense still rational, whose demands are virtually unlimited. If the consumer wishes to be a collector of reproducible objects of any kind, e.g. ICBMs to put in his garden, the economy is likely to be over-strained unless he has to pay. Similarly if he wishes to keep up with or ahead of the Joneses, and is prepared to put himself to some inconvenience in order to consume more than they, there is no upper limit to his demands. But one may question whether in an exceedingly affluent society such inclinations could persist. If the Joneses with whom one is keeping up are themselves actually experiencing physical inconvenience in demonstrating their wealth it is silly to imitate them. It is, again, silly to collect ICBMs if anybody can do it.

(g) The plain cussed: this type of consumer simply wishes to beat the bank, to demonstrate that free supply is impossible in a highly affluent society by deliberately demanding the impossible. Other forms of waste are tolerable, but this is plain delinquency. Since political anarchy—*pace* Marx—is impossible even under extreme affluence there will still exist a government, which will inevitably pass legislation against such behaviour (cf. p. 344).

7. Now so long as there are no new final goods unlimited free supply is surely quite possible for type (e) as far as demand goes. This follows from the very first principles of Western economics: each good and service is subject to the law of diminishing marginal utility, therefore any finite number of goods and services is also so subject. However simple this may seem, it is not illegitimate aggregation. The 'insatiability of human wants', which appears in this context in many textbooks, is precisely what we now call in question: it could not possibly be true unless there were an infinite number of goods and services, i.e. indefinite product innovation.[1]

---

[1] This point is of respectable antiquity. Cf. W. S. Jevons, *Political Economy* (1882), p. 17.

On the labour supply side type (e) presents more difficulty. It is not that he will fail to work, say, twenty hours a week without compulsion; our trouble is whether he will do the unpleasant jobs. Reasons are given for supposing that he will not in Ch. 20, Sec. 9. But our concern here is not with the state of society under Extreme Affluence; it is not with the social but with the technical possibility of free supply. And technically it would of course be easy to extract the due inputs of labour.

So far we have assumed no new products. Yet in fact there will always be new products, indeed increasingly so. Some will make no difference to the above argument, but some will be *technically* new, i.e. require some skill or material that is at present scarce. Thus suppose that at a given time trips to the moon are commonplace routine, and there has been enough investment in this industry over a century or so to satisfy all demands, so that the service is available free of charge. Trips to the spiral nebula in Andromeda are still technically impossible, so the question of a price for them does not arise. But there are still adventurous and inquisitive people who would like a trip to the corona of the sun, and this is *marginally technically possible*, at a cost of 10% of the national income. Then such services must still have a price on them, and this means that all services must.[1] And in fact very many such demands will arise, many of them very reasonable. Thus Our Boys On The Moon will need entertainment, and it may seem desirable to transport the Metropolitan Opera or a Giorgione exhibition or the Folies Bergère to them in the slack summer season. This will of course overload the economy. Or to take less extreme examples it may be marginally technically possible to make men immortal, or to carry them from London Airport to Piccadilly in thirty minutes. Reasonable or not, such demands are hard for any society to outlaw.

The 'marginally technically possible' enters in another way. The economy would be equally overloaded if consumers were permitted to buy not only products but techniques: atomic tin-openers, where hand-cranked ones will do; Harris tweed, where the machine product will do; telepathic entertainment, where television will do.

It would therefore appear that the genuinely free supply of the reasonable consumer will never be possible, under whatever ownership or allocation model.

---

[1] Except for the almost impossible case that all the factors thus rendered scarce are specific to such services alone.

The nearest to genuinely unforced free supply that we can expect is that while no factor of production is paid and all commonplace goods and services are free, some things are openly rationed. Such things would be the marginally technically possible, the ir-reproducible (e.g. Old Masters), and various amenities subject to Malthusian pressure (with a rich and numerous population access to nearly all beauty-spots would have to be rationed).

Just below this height there would have to be a mild but com-pulsory labour service. Lower again, there could be wages and most of the economic phenomena we now know, but free supply of goods with a low elasticity of demand; such goods would have to be subsidized.

8. Since this was written Mr. Khrushchev's plans for the first phase of transition to Full Communism have been published.[1] They fit very precisely the above description of the lowest stage. There is no mention of abolishing wages, quite the contrary, and certain goods only will be free: urban transport as suggested, water, heating, gas, housing, education and medicine. Now urban trans-port and water both have a low price-elasticity of demand. Con-sequently it should be possible to distribute them free of charge, in the quantity that people happen to require, without rationing—what we have called genuinely free supply. Naturally the demand for them will change: inelastic is not stable demand, for tastes and incomes change irrespective of prices. But such changes can be discovered and followed in the production plan; the price is not necessary to discover demand.

One small trouble, however, there will be. It is that to make urban transport free is to discriminate against countrymen, who do not use it. This is obviously a mere transitional problem, of a kind any change must bring: the countryman will eventually catch up.

Housing is quite different, since the price elasticity of demand for it is very high, even when there is already a great deal of it. Thus it is absolutely certain that it will be administratively allocated. One may ask, then, why it was included at all. First, it is very easy to ration. People buy or hire houses at very long intervals, so the number of transactions to administer is extremely small. Moreover, a house is a large and visible object, so regulations are difficult to evade. And anyway they already exist. Rents are far below market equilibrium as it is in U.S.S.R., so the reduction of the price to

---

[1] *Pravda*, July 30, 1961. The best Western source on transitional problems is Knirsch, *Ost-Europa*, 1961. It contains also many Soviet references.

zero causes no new practical difficulty. But more important than the ease of administration is the weight of tradition: there can hardly be a socialist in the world who accepts that rents should rise to a level equilibrating supply with demand. From Gaitskell to Mao Tse-tung, every socialist wants a rent subsidy, and feels that housing is a priority candidate for the social service approach over almost all other goods and services. To the writer, this left-wing consensus seems to rest on emotional and fallacious reasoning: there is nothing special about a house. But that is a large subject into which we cannot enter here: it is enough to note that the consensus and the tradition are there.

Gas and heating have also high price-elasticities, so it is difficult to see why they have been chosen either. We must simply accept the reason given: they count as ancillary to housing, and so have become infected with the tradition surrounding the latter. They present the further problem of being used as industrial inputs as well. If industry continues to be planned as it is now, mainly in physical terms, it should not be too difficult to supply it with gas free of charge. For the physical plan is *ex definitione* a rationing scheme. But it is also quite possible to keep prices in one market while simultaneously abolishing them in the other.

Thus free gas for consumers is Full Communism, but the same in industry is a blow at Khozraschet. The passage on planning, with its strong emphasis on rationality, rational prices and specifically Khozraschet, makes it virtually certain that industrial gas will still have a price. It is thus implicit in the Draft Programme that industrial transfer prices will survive retail prices.

Finally, free education and medicine are a simple extension of what already exists, and not only in Communist countries. An unsentimental and economically sophisticated enquirer, e.g. a member of the 'Chicago School', would ask whether education and medicine are in fact good candidates for liberation from the market. Their price-elasticities of demand are high, and there is a strong tendency, evident wherever they are free, to waste them or use them in irrational proportions and dosages. From this controversy we must also refrain. It is enough that the weight of tradition is here overwhelming.

In sum, precisely those things that are first socialized in capitalist countries will now be first communized in socialist countries! There is no rhyme or reason behind it: tradition, not economic thinking, has dictated the choice.

CHAPTER 20

FULL CAPITALISM?[1]

'Better a cycle of Europe than fifty years of Cathay'
—With apologies to Alfred, Lord Tennyson.

1. IN Chs. 17 and 18 we spoke of Full Communism as a problem in Communist theory and practice. That is not all: it is an almost equal problem for a non-Communist economy or country. For one thing, if any Communist country, after reorganization and further economic growth, declares itself to have reached Full Communism this may present major propaganda problems in the Cold War. How, for instance, will things look for Polish and Yugoslav Communists, with their insistence on liberalism and gradualism, if Full Communism finally arrives in U.S.S.R.? Unless they have a clear doctrinal line on such things as, say, the abolition of money their doubts and deviations will surely seem petty and irrelevant, even in their own eyes, compared with the sweeping grandeur of this event. They, and the issues upon which they take their stand, will be *out-dated*—one of the worst accusations a Marxist can suffer.

It is equally important for non-Communist countries to have a view of where they are going: an image of the far future to oppose to Full Communism, or even conceivably a peaceful road to the same state of affairs. For while the far future as a whole cannot be foreseen in an open society—in a closed one, naturally, it can—at least certain tendencies and probabilities can be spotted, and encouraged or discouraged according to taste. Moreover, a view, however vague, on this subject, gives us that vital sense of direction we at the moment so wholly lack: it functions, indeed, as the ill-starred American Statement of National Purpose[2] was supposed to function. I am myself insufficiently anti-American to find the whole idea of a Statement of National Purpose ridiculous. Plainly Party Programmes and other basic Communist documents are just such statements, and so too was the idea of the City of God in the Middle

---

[1] A previous version of this chapter appeared in *Survey*, London 1961. My thanks are also due to Prof. Bronfenbrenner for many corrections.
[2] *New York Times*, Sept. 18, 1960: it was drawn up by a committee of Wise Men appointed by President Eisenhower.

THE POLITICAL ECONOMY OF COMMUNISM

Ages, or the original Islamic programme of world conquest and mass conversion. Tacit agreement on how society ought to be now is not enough: we need fairly explicit agreement on what it ought to become. Indeed, such agreement may well be easier to obtain.

This chapter, then, is an impertinent attempt to supply the economic side only of a non-Communist Statement of National Purpose. It is obviously deficient on the sociological and political sides, and no attempt is made to remedy this. It is also of its nature deficient on the side of foreign aid to backward countries, but then so are most doctrines of Full Communism. The mere fact that most of the world is extremely poor is no excuse for not thinking about the special problems of the rich.[1]

2. Now we have seen that only the 'Aldous Huxley' type of Full Communism is compatible with political freedom, though of course it does not entail it, unless we accept the false Marxian definition of freedom. Moreover, there is neither economic nor social attraction in any other kind of Full Communism. So for our present purposes only 'Aldous Huxley' is relevant, and what we have to consider here is whether there can be other forms of Extreme Affluence than Full Communism, just as there are different forms of Socialism. We answer by asking three more questions:

(i) is indefinite economic growth likely? For clearly only so can this type of Full Communism or any form of Extreme Affluence be achieved.
(ii) can any type of organization achieve it, or only some?
(iii) what are the *natural* economic and social consequences of Extreme Affluence in a democratic, capitalist society? Could they be described as Full Communism?

It is my thesis that 'Capitalism' will in fact autonomously grow over into something rather more desirable than Full Communism, without any intervening nonsense of 'Socialism', 'Proletarian Revolution' etc., if only it is left in peace.

3. The merely technological side, question (i), was answered, so far as it can be, in the previous chapter. That leaves, however,

---

[1] Note, however, that when the Communists promise that all Communist countries will reach Full Communism at about the same time (Khrushchev, *Pravda*, Jan. 28, 1959; cf. Yowev, *Munich Bulletin*, Jan. 1960) they are implicitly promising astronomical quantities of aid to the poorer ones among them. But in practice one sees very little indeed of such aid. Indeed the Soviet Communists have tacitly withdrawn this promise: Satyukov, *Pravda*, 27 Oct., 1961; Titarenko, *Politicheskoye Samoobrazovanie*, March 1962.

(ii) the institutional side. If indefinite economic growth is possible at all, is it possible through the market, and with our present capitalist organization and political democracy?

That it should be possible without a command economy but through the market, if only by means of a Titoist economic structure, is a valid inference from nearly every page of this book. A command economy has only one *intrinsic* advantage for growth over other models, and that not a decisive one: the incentive of 'planner's tension' described in Ch. 13. We have shown in Chs. 14–16 that it does not make possible a more growth-promoting investment pattern, because the best investment criterion for economic growth is precisely profit. Nor does it increase the volume of investment, since that is a political decision as easily enforced upon the unwilling population by taxation as by a physical plan.

It may be objected that this is a very short-run view: that a market is only possible if decisions are decentralized, and this depends on the size of decision-making unit that technique imposes. But the trend of technical progress is no longer so obviously towards yet more centralization. Marx could always effectively jeer at Proudhon, how would he run a railway? The modern liberal has a retort: how would Marx run a million motor-cars?[1] Indeed if the future is with the personal helicopter we may go still farther, for motor-roads require a large central planning body in their building if not in their use, but the air is there already. Similarly the old medium-wave broadcasting was suited to a few monopolistic transmitters, since its range was long and the possibilities of interference great. But we now have UHF and FM, which make possible a multiplicity of competing stations. Or take yet again the supply of power. When the industrial revolution began it was practically synonymous with the concentration of artisans into a single building where their machines all ran off a single source of power: first water, then steam. Electricity takes us in two directions from the position thus achieved: its own supply is by technical necessity vastly more centralized than that of water or steam, but its use can be almost as decentralized as that of man- or bullock-power. Full many an obsolescent craftsman, or do-it-yourself

---

[1] Throughout the world people of a left-wing complexion are almost invariably hostile to private motor-cars and even to road haulage, in all matters where they conflict with railways. No wonder, for the motor-car came after the railway, and is the principal demonstration that time is not necessarily on their side, or that technical progress is sometimes right-wing.

enthusiast in his basement, depends on the electric grid. Undoubtedly the economy will never be so technically decentralized again as before the industrial revolution, but in which direction is it moving at the moment?

Moreover, even when the size of the decision-making unit does increase the market still has functions to perform, in that large enterprises each produce many products, and must choose between them. The simplicities of textbook economics, which deals with one product per diagram, entirely obscure this basic point. Furthermore, large enterprises produce things for themselves, since they tend to be vertically integrated; they thus need *internal* criteria of choice. Planning could, as we saw in Ch. 10, provide these two kinds of criterion, after various technical developments have taken place. At present it cannot, and even when it can it might not perhaps show such serious advantages over a market as to make us wish to sacrifice our social structure.

4. Technology, therefore, shows some bias against the market mechanism, but not a big one. It certainly does not go far enough to show that indefinite economic growth technically entails collectivism.

It *is*, however, necessary for any economy aiming at Extreme Affluence within measurable time to grow fast. This means at least to maintain full employment and to force the overall volume of investment. Now while this is entirely compatible with a free market in everything else, political freedom is quite certainly a brake here.

In that great right-wing anarchy, the U.S.A., there is serious and successful opposition to even such a trivial strengthening of central power as is needed for perpetual full employment. And a really large increase in investment is more difficult still. That it should be financed by people's voluntary saving is out of the question. So to accommodate it to Western institutions with least damage to them we need, as we saw in Ch. 11, heavy taxation, the accumulation of a large 'above the line' surplus in the budget, and its disposal by a public investment board to public or private capital-users. The really difficult item is the higher taxes, i.e. the increase in the abstinence of the population; and nothing need be added to what was said in Ch. 13, Sec. 3.

5. Then again, Western democracy means letting economic agents do more or less what they like, and therefore tolerating many comfortable abuses, restrictive practices and traditional ways of

carrying on that have little or nothing to do with the volume of abstinence. We listed many of these in Ch. 13, and must now consider how serious they really are. First accept the pessimistic assumption that few of them could be abolished without a dictatorship; then I believe that paradoxically most of our economically inefficient institutions can be tolerated.

For we must distinguish most carefully between institutions that reduce the *level* of productivity ('handicaps'), and those that retard its *rate of growth* ('brakes'). This distinction can best be explained in terms of its most important application, which is to the structure of agriculture. The small farm is obviously less efficient than the large,[1] and the 'institution' of the family farm with capitalistic ownership keeps farms small; nay in many cases it actually diminishes them by parcellation, if younger sons cannot find work off the land and primogeniture is not the rule. But the vast bulk of agricultural improvement is independent of scale, being concerned with the qualities of seeds or the utilization of new, vertically disintegrated, special services (such as artificial insemination). It is incontestable that if we in Britain amalgamated our farms on a large and brutal scale—whether into sovkhozy or into private latifundia makes little difference, of course—we would increase agricultural productivity *once for all*. But the political presuppositions are quite other-worldly, and indeed quite specifically undemocratic: for as we saw in Ch. 1, 'institutional *laissez faire*' is one of the most important of all democratic freedoms, and it is simply arbitrary and immoral to deprive farmers of a way of life which they love and which yet makes them an *adequately* productive food base for a progressive economy. So there is no reason why we should not accept the *handicap* of our farm *structure* provided we remove the *brake* of too little farm *investment*. If we choose to grow from a lower point we will nevertheless get there in the end. Indeed, how big *is* the handicap? How much would farm amalgamation lower agricultural costs? By 10%?—who wants a bloody revolution for the price of four years' growth?

Some institutional inefficiencies, then, are brakes and some are only handicaps, and it is of the utmost importance to know which is which. I have suggested that by a merciful dispensation of providence the ones with deepest social roots are mostly handicaps.

[1] Cf. A. H. Maunder, *Size and Efficiency in Farming*, Institute for Research in Agricultural Economics, Oxford 1952.

2C

Upon the rightness of this generalization nearly everything turns, so we must take a few more examples before leaving the subject of 'brakes versus handicaps'.

Moderate protectionism is a most interesting case, though one strictly irrelevant to the Political Economy of Communism: of a handicap that so far from being a brake is actually an accelerator. Protection is, of course, a handicap in that it reduces the efficiency of the current allocation of resources; but it is also an accelerator for at least two reasons. The first is the 'infant industry' argument, which is too well known to be enlarged upon. The second reason is that free trade is deflationary. Now at least a mild inflation indubitably accelerates growth, so that we have here a very strong contrast between rates of change and absolute levels. 'For instance,' as I have said elsewhere:[1]

an attempt to quantify the advantages of free trade and inflation respectively might run thus in a given case. Suppose that 25% of the gross national product (GNP) benefits from protection, and costs in this sector of the economy average 20% above the costs of potential imports in home currency. If protection were abolished factors would be diverted to exports. Let these have constant costs. Then so far the economy stands to gain by 20% of 25% = 5% of the GNP. But free trade brings with it a need for greater deflation, international liquidity, adaptability to foreign demand, etc. This need is permanent and will reduce employment by say 1%. Let this mean a loss of 0·75% of the GNP (marginal factors being less efficient than the average). Also free trade worsens the terms of trade: let this reduce the GNP by a further 0·25%. Then in a static economy free trade is far better (4% better) than full employment through protection. But the same deflation, liquidity, etc., reduces also the rate of growth of the economy by say 0·5% p.a., since they entail less investment and occasional actual setbacks in current output. Then in eight years, mild inflation shows itself superior to free trade, in the particular country and given all the circumstances.

Thus a 'handicap' is not without incidental influence on the speed of advance, nor doubtless can a 'brake' be altogether dissociated from the absolute position of the starting point. In other words many influences play both parts.

Planner's tension is an important case, as being one of the great specific differences between Soviet-type economies and others. It is clearly a 'negative handicap' not a 'negative brake', or if we will a boost, not an accelerator. It is introduced once and for all, and raises economic efficiency as much as it can in one period. If thereafter it is relaxed, the absolute advantage it confers disappears, and the rate of growth actually diminishes.

[1] In *Europe and the Europeans*, ed. M. Beloff (Chatto & Windus 1957), p. 221.

Perhaps the most interesting case is restrictive practices, including trade unions, cartels and the withholding of new knowledge by patents. These on inspection turn out also to be only handicaps. Invention goes on, technique after new technique is developed; what happens to a country or industry that refuses to adopt them? It simply stagnates, becoming more and more backward, until finally the dam bursts. No restrictive practice lasts for ever, and then one of two things must happen. First, it may go straight for the most advanced technique available. At this point it benefits from all the usual 'advantages of immaturity', and grows faster than those who have kept up all the time; reaching, moreover, the same point in absolute development as they over the same long period. Over the average of all industries such a country will of course suffer a lag, but it is unlikely to increase or diminish. Or secondly the restrictive practices merely impose a permanent lag in techniques, the adoption of every successive innovation being delayed in each industry. This obviously has not even a temporary effect on the rate of growth. Only if, thirdly, the technical lag increases all the time do restrictive practices become a break as well as a handicap. I.e. they must become more and more restrictive for growth to be slowed down.

The principal brake, then, one is tempted to say, is low investment. But not even that is necessarily true, in the longest of long runs.[1] For it is a commonplace that once all employable land and labour are fully equipped with the latest devices that capital can buy, productivity can only grow at the rate of technical progress.

Now this might not require any net investment at all, but merely the employment of depreciation allowances in research and replacement. For it could be the case that research saved so much capital that depreciation allowances were enough for both. Plainly, however, the more humanity invests in research the more rapidly it will progress. But if knowledge is cheaply shared particular nations need not invest much. It follows that given a very generous attitude to trade secrets, and no change in capital/output ratios, everybody could keep up, once they caught up. Greater or less net investment would redound only to the progress of the world, not to the nation that made it.

However technical knowledge is not so easily shared; indeed in the Cold War most discoveries are of military origin and are state

---

[1] I owe this insight to Mr. Walter Eltis (private correspondence).

secrets. And, as we saw in Ch. 14, Sec. 13, the amount of capital employed per unit of output is in fact increasing if we allow for education. Of these two considerations the latter is probably the less important. Thus if the capital/output ratio grows at 1% p.a., and output at 5% p.a., and initially net investment is 15% of the national income, and the assumptions of Ch. 15, Sec. 2 are all accepted, net investment has to be 16% of the national income in 10 years' time. This will not kill anybody.

On the other hand the fact that technical secrets are long kept merely imposes a lag on a country that does no research. If it waits it will get them all: there is no brake here, only a handicap. So too—indeed it is the same point—if a country does not try to modernize all its equipment at any one time. So long as its equipment is on the average always obsolete by the same number of years, it will grow at the same rate as the most modern and strenuous of countries.

The only qualification here is the rate of obsolescence of capital assets. Should this be continually increasing, while our low investor continues to replace assets at his old rate, an ever larger proportion of them will be obsolete at any one time, and his technical lag increases. This remains true even if not all technical progress takes place at the moment of replacement. Thus in truth there is progress simply through training on the job, and machines can be up-dated in the course of maintenance. But so long as replacement is necessary for only some progress, it must keep up with the rate of that progress.[1]

So a free economy and society seem to suffer mainly from handicaps. The superiority of Communist growth is, if this analysis is correct, partly due to a single long-term factor: more abstinence; and partly to many historically circumstanced, once for all factors: the exceptionally rapid removal of all the old handicaps of an underdeveloped economy, without permitting the new ones to arise that characterize an advanced one. Moreover even the superiority of abstinence may not continue for ever to be an advantage.

6. It is, then, clear that different forms of Extreme Affluence are technically possible. To Full Communism will be opposed here two of these possibilities: Affluent Individualism and Affluent Socialism. The former offers of course the more perfect contrast.

---

[1] An uneconomically high rate of obsolescence is entirely possible: it may be better to apply only every other, or every third invention. We have not space to develop this point, and need only note that it does not of course exclude uneconomically low rates.

It is based simply on the notion of increasing wealth, without moral 'improvement', whether inevitable or induced. Money, the market and private ownership of the means of production are entirely retained, and the social services disappear as people become more and more able to support themselves—not quite the same, this, as 'the state withering away'! The ideal is, as under Full Communism, a rich, fully developed individual; only this time there is no bias towards Puritanism and uniformity. And there is one other big difference: the Affluent Individualist works for himself and his family, not for society; his virtues are not self-sacrifice and enthusiasm but responsibility and self-support. He has no more 'socialist consciousness' than twentieth-century John Smith, or that regrettable survival of outmoded capitalist mentality, twentieth-century Ivan Ivanov. This, precisely, is why the market mechanism has to remain.

Affluent Socialism differs from Full Communism mainly in that while the government is not totalitarian, minimal demands are yet made upon the individual for moral 'improvement'. The social services are, however, built up and eventually engulf the market sector: in stark contrast to Affluent Individualism in which the social services are confined at first to the provision of a minimum for all, and eventually wither away. Thus the question of 'socialist consciousness', i.e. of the will to work without private reward, does arise. But Affluent Socialism, being less in a hurry than Full Communism, simply permits the falling will to work to slow up the rate of growth.

7. It may well be asked, why have Affluent Socialism at all? Surely the choice lies between the two extremes, the one quick-growing but totalitarian, the other both preserving political and creating economic freedom.[1] The writer himself can see no advantage in Affluent Socialism, but feels it must be included; first in order to show that there are very many practicable models of Affluence, just as we saw there to be of Socialism; and secondly because many people find individualism as morally repulsive as totalitarianism. Such people should be consoled with the prospect

---

[1] It will be observed that I do not fall into the trap of equating a free market with economic freedom. Economic freedom is a nebulous and troublesome concept. It either means freedom from material anxiety, i.e. great wealth and leisure, or freedom to 'do what I like with my own'. On the former definition it is assured by any form of Extreme Affluence. On the latter it arises from a *combination* of affluence and a free market; only the rich can have it, since only they have any 'my own' to do 'what I like with'.

of a genuine third way, though one cannot help asking why they need it.

Why, after all, is collectivism more moral than individualism? Charity is moral, the succour of the needy; and if there are many needy charity must be collectivized or it will not be big enough. But when there are no needy all this falls to the ground. Collectivism without charity has no visible charms. It is good to work for society if society is helping the poor. But it is rather silly to set up all these centralized pooling arrangements otherwise. It remains, of course, altruistic, but what superiority over individualism has the altruism of one millionaire working for another?

This is an awkward question, more suitable to the theologian or politician than to the economist. One may be pardoned, however, for asking whether sometimes ethical judgments are not unconsciously predicated upon contingent circumstances. Female chastity seemed good before contraceptives: now one begins to wonder. So also economic altruism—we do not here speak of altruism in other respects—may possibly be found to rest on the assumption that 'the poor ye have always with you'. Or again, to attribute to central planning some moral superiority over the market—or vice versa—is surely too absurd and eccentric for serious consideration. Of course many people, at both ends of the political spectrum, contrive to feel ethically here. For such the writer has only blank incomprehension: to him these two different ways of allocating resources are morally quite neutral. When— as is surely inevitable—they one day become equally efficient the choice between them will be political: the more decentralized is the more compatible with personal freedom.

Moreover, Affluent Socialism would appear gratuitously to raise the question of the will to work of unpaid men: and thus to impale itself deliberately on the dilemma, economic stagnation or totalitarianism. But the devotees of the non-Communist left are many and respectable; I am myself quite out of sympathy with them, for the reasons sketched above, but they too, it must be admitted, have their Own Way to Extreme Affluence.

Not that Extreme Affluence was ever an ideal of such people, but rather the 'William Morris standard of living' referred to in Ch. 17. What we did not say there was that with it went a whole William Morris culture or society. In his review of Raymond

Williams' *Long Revolution*[1] Mr. Richard Wollheim describes the latter succinctly:

... what, in contrast to the American Dream, the ideal of affluent and assertive individualism, might be called the English Dream: the ideal of the collective, unalienated folk-society, where honest men work together and create together, the ideal of Ruskin and William Morris and Leavis. Born of Nonconformity, it has only too easily shown itself indifferent to the values of nonconformity with a small 'n'.[2]

One might add, indifferent also to the value of mere prosperity as such.

8. What would be the fate of money under Affluent Individualism? To do absolutely without money is, as we have seen, probably incompatible with any system unless rationing is used instead. The 'marginally technically possible' presents an insoluble problem to all systems alike. Leaving it on one side, we find that under this particular system moneylessness has special aspects.

First, as people get richer they become more and more careless about little things. Consider the contemporary American, whether corporate or individual. He expects and gets a large number of *small free things*: free paper napkins, free water in the train, free lavatories, free air in his tyres, a free wipe of his windshield, free matches, free road maps, etc., etc.; above all, free information. And these things are not part of the public sector, like free entry into museums (which he also enjoys, more than a Russian). Nor are they really loss-leaders, advertisers' giveaways. For although they mostly began as such they are now regarded by one and all as a right. Secondly, Americans create a lot of *usable waste*: cars that still go, picnic leavings, cast-off clothing. These things have no money value, yet with sufficient ingenuity and determination a man can live off them: the U.S.A. is a paradise for bums, beatniks *et hoc genus omne*. Then thirdly an American does not count the cost: he uses either the telephone or the mail on no sort of calculation, but as mood and convenience urge. He appears more hospitable, in that he makes his guests free of more facilities in his house—this in addition to the unconnected fact of *being* more hospitable, i.e. giving up more of his time to guests, being more genuinely pleased to have them. Nor is he interested in small economic crime: he hardly picks pockets, in areas where an *unskilled* honest man can get a decent living with no risk. Major economic crime, and

[1] London 1961.   [2] *Spectator*, March 10, 1961.

especially the corruption of government and the police, still interest him; and crimes of violence of course persist—but the pursuit of a modest competence by physical theft has almost died out.

Thus undoubtedly money, and economic calculation generally, will count for less in Affluent Individualism than under ordinary *laissez faire*. Yet all the instances we have mentioned are very small beer, and it is hard to see how any important production could be carried on under *laissez faire* except for money; for what other motivation could voluntary economic activity have?

It might be objected that this holds until the time when labour is provided free of charge; i.e. when productivity is so high that the working week is so short that men's natural abhorrence of continuous leisure drives them to work. At this admittedly almost unthinkable level of productivity a moneyless version of Affluent Individualism becomes possible. People voluntarily produce, without any central planning, as much in total and in particular as people want to consume, although their consumption is not disciplined in any way. All the organization there is is that shops give orders to factories, and the work of people in their work-places is hierarchically organized as at present. I.e. people do not, on the whole, sabotage the system; they not only work without pay but observe labour discipline and commercial commonsense without economic sanctions.

9. A plausible picture but for four points. The first is that people must for some reason rather do the unpleasant jobs than no jobs at all. But this surely cannot be brought about under *laissez faire*. For the jobs they really want to do will still be relatively scarce. These are the jobs that people already at our present standard of living do for nothing, or at least put in overtime at for nothing: e.g. local government, entertainment, the administration of sports, university teaching. Disappointed in their applications here, but still over-burdened with leisure, people must in fact volunteer to become dustmen,[1] or the system breaks down. No doubt technical progress will have much lightened the task of the dustman, but even so it is difficult to imagine labour freely allocating itself among all the required activities. Pleasant jobs would have to be rationed by a central authority, and labour directed to unpleasant ones.

Secondly, there is the problem of the transition to moneylessness.

[1] When in his vision Marx said he would be a huntsman in the morning and a literary critic in the afternoon, he never mentioned collecting the garbage!

If any single firm ceases to demand money for its products it must cease to pay its factors; they will go elsewhere and it will go out of business. Affluent Individualism provides no means whereby moneylessness can take root and spread—in contrast to Affluent Socialism and Full Communism, which can both convert more and more things into social services. The act of abolition would have to be an act of state, affecting everybody at once.

Thirdly, what of capital (i.e. abstinence) and land? It is easy to see that when labour need not be paid saving need not either. Indeed a permanent superfluity of saving is a very near possibility, and Western economics has long been familiar with the zero rate of interest. But 'land', meaning all the gifts of nature, is as we saw in Ch. 19 a quite different matter. It is grossly improbable that these, or many of them, will lose their scarcity until long after labour has. They will therefore continue to command a price.

So while there is psychologically nothing impossible in people saving or even working for nothing they will only do so if enterprises can be induced to supply goods free in the shops. For naturally if money is required for goods people must have money, and will charge it for such labour and abstinence services as they provide. But if 'land' continues to command a price enterprises will continue to need money, and therefore to charge it for their products. There is thus a vicious circle: so long as something somewhere is 'scarce' money will be needed for it, and it is impossible under *laissez faire* to keep money out of nearly all other transactions as well.

Moreover, even supposing that *all* the fundamental factors of production become so plentiful as to be free, there remains the problem of motivating investment. For it is easy enough to see why people would save—they would have no need to consume all their output; and why they would work—they would like it and need it. But why should any manager invest, and expand 'his' enterprise? Deprived of all pecuniary motive, we are thrown back on the will to power, or the mere will to expand business. Power, however, in turn becomes a doubtful motive. For in what sense, in so affluent a society, can the means of production be said any longer to belong to anyone? When our incomes are simply whatever we choose to take out of shops, plainly the means of production are not required to yield an income. Titles to them will then tend to lapse, and the whole concept of property will 'wither away'—including personal property, which will be so easily replaceable it is not worth protecting. This is in itself a highly desirable and easily comprehensible situation, but it leaves the maintenance and further accumulation of capital goods very oddly placed. The writer cannot see how they could be provided for under *laissez faire* without money.

Indeed even the close approach to moneylessness would lead to stagnation. As the rate of profit finally fell towards zero in any line, research and investment would be choked off and diverted elsewhere, until they finally ceased everywhere. Not only the actual transition, but also the final steps towards it, would have to be an act of state. It is, then, perhaps as well that the close approach too can only be made on very special assumptions: a cessation in product innovation, the willingness of people to work for nothing at jobs they do not like, and a plentiful supply of *all* raw materials.

The most, then, that Affluent Individualism can offer us in the way of moneylessness is 'Americanization': a steady increase in the volume of *unimportant* free goods. Coupled with that would go a diminishing legal interest in titles to property, and an increase in common or unclaimed property. But this too would stop very far short of an automatic socialization of private property. Affluent Individualism would need both money and legal titles for ever. The attempt to do without them, even at a very high level of productivity, would lead straight to collectivism. This collectivism would, however, as Ch. 17 shows, be extremely mild since the administrative compulsions would need only to be weak. Moreover, a great deal of inefficiency and waste could be tolerated under Affluent Individualism, so that the central planners who succeeded it would not need to go into great detail either. With rather few central instructions, and those enforced but laxly, the threat to political freedom would be minimal.

10. But do we need these consolations? Why would anybody *want* to switch from Affluent Individualism to Full Communism? Surely on the contrary a bold Western propaganda has very much to offer in the field of Extreme Affluence just because Full Communism can be avoided. Taking some sensible mixture of Affluent Individualism and Affluent Socialism we can say:

(a) distribution according to need is far advanced in Western capitalism, which shows no fewer social services, and very much better ones, than any Communist country. Moreover, the 'social service' approach to distribution according to need is not the only, nor in the writer's opinion the best. The alternative is some form of co-ownership or 'people's capitalism', in which the capital itself—

i.e. the private ownership of the means of production—is 'distributed according to need'. The individual can then fall back on his own capital and decide his own needs. He thus escapes from the probably totalitarian consequences of submission to a central authority that decides what he needs. It need hardly be added, however, that propaganda abroad about 'people's capitalism' must await its rigorous and effective practice at home: not, as in U.S.A. and West Germany, ludicrously precede it.

(b) money will indeed not wither away, but this is in no sense a disadvantage. The prejudice against money is absurd and has no intellectual basis. It is absolutely vital as an alternative to compulsion, in any remotely likely society. In purely economic terms, moreover, the abolition of money leads to waste and irrationality. It does nothing to raise production, rather the contrary, and therefore nothing to raise the standard of living.

(c) many of the items in Full Communism, as enumerated in Ch. 17, Sec. 1, are soulless and humourless, delighting in uniformity for its own sake. In particular the difference between town and country is a delight to all, and the very stuff of life to many. There are, by nature and nurture, urban and rural types, and urban and rural phases in the life of an average man. Extreme Affluence would enable these demands to be met far more fully than at present; as indeed all other demands for differentiation. There is no case for deliberately assimilating the internal structure of the farming enterprise to that of a factory: many people *like* small personal enterprises, the present structure of capitalist farming caters to a genuine human need. It is tyrannical to try to alter both the farm and the farmer. Moreover, the undoubted cost of small-scale family farming in efficiency is offset by the economic cost of compulsory collectivization, the unpopularity of which makes it equally inefficient. The correct way out is the natural, voluntary, American way: the heavily capitalized medium-scale family farm. In a word, Affluent Individualism would preserve the *institutional laissez faire*[1] that Full Communism would destroy. This is an unmixed blessing.

(d) the further collectivization of consumption is a monstrous objective, having no economic necessity and exactly contrary to many tendencies within any Affluent Society. Indeed we may boldly generalize about the present trend of technical progress as follows: it at no point actually favours small-scale operation, since

[1] See Ch. 1, Sec. 3.

small units can always be duplicated and the large-scale management of such combinations is an established technical possibility.[1] But it may quite well operate less sharply against small-scale units at some times than at others, and especially so if there is urgent demand for inventions suitable to small units, so that research is directed that way. Now it so happens that all over the world two small economic units have immense social advantages and traditional prestige: the family and the family farm. Their obstinate survival has created those deeply unMarxian objects, the individual washing-machine and the rotavator. The loss in efficiency compared with the laundry and the large tractor is perceptible but not tragic. And in any case the loss is only a 'handicap' not a 'brake'; technical progress is as likely in these small things as in big ones. In a word, if people like to live that way they can certainly afford it. If they lose a decade or so in their march towards the economic Utopia they at least do not lose sight altogether of other human values, unknown to Full Communism.

(e) not only is there no place for privacy in general under Full Communism, there is no place in particular for the family itself. The grandeur and the horror of this prospect need no elaboration.

(f) it is not only Puritanism and uniformity from which those suffer who live under Communism. The very generalized feeling of constraint and effort makes the whole of economic activity unpleasant. 'Planner's tension' is at present the main item here: it takes enjoyment out of work at all levels, and encourages corruption, the cutting of corners, etc., etc. In future the unpleasantness will arise from the attempts to establish the new Communist labour morale. For naturally one cannot change human nature to the extent of substituting altruism for personal gain without pressure, propaganda and hypocrisy, even neurosis. A man should be happy while he works; and this matters because work is such a large part of his life.

So even if we look into the farthest future more liberal systems of economy, while necessarily less dynamic, can be made dynamic enough given the will, and are on the balance of other considerations vastly superior, because more *human*. Bert Brecht used to say of Capitalism and Communism: if you had enough drug to cure only one person of a fatal disease, and two people lay dying of it,

---

[1] I.e. the L-shaped long-run average cost curve is, in a sense, an *a priori* law. See my *Price, Cost and Output*, 2nd ed., Oxford 1961, p. 220.

an elderly roué and a pregnant prostitute—to whom would you give the drug? It is out of place to be dogmatic, and more than foolish to be complacent—the writer for one has no great confidence that the capitalist will to grow will ever be sufficient. But still, surely Brecht had the roles mixed up.

—These fragments have I shored against my ruins.

INDEX

HARVARD UNIVERSITY

http://lib.harvard.